Threshold of War

Threshold of War

Franklin D. Roosevelt and American Entry into World War II

Waldo Heinrichs

New York   Oxford
OXFORD UNIVERSITY PRESS
1988

Oxford University Press

Oxford New York Toronto
Delhi Bombay Calcutta Madras Karachi
Petaling Jaya Singapore Hong Kong Tokyo
Nairobi Dar es Salaam Cape Town
Melbourne Auckland

and associated companies in
Beirut Berlin Ibadan Nicosia

Published by Oxford University Press, Inc.,
200 Madison Avenue, New York, New York 10016

Oxford is a registered trademark of Oxford University Press

Library of Congress Cataloging-in-Publication Data

Heinrichs, Waldo H.
Threshold of war: Franklin D. Roosevelt and American entry
into World War II / Waldo Heinrichs.
p.   cm.   Bibliography: p.   Includes index.
ISBN 0-19-504424-X
1. World War,   1939–1945—Diplomatic history.   2. World War,   1939–1945—United
States.   3. Roosevelt, Franklin D. (Franklin Delano), 1882–1945.   I. Title.
D753.H38   1988   940.53′2—dc 19   88-5303 CIP

Printed in the United States of America

for Dorothy Borg

Preface

The literature on American entry into World War II is rich and abundant but mostly segmented, concerned with particular topics, regions, or relationships. Histories of the Pearl Harbor attack, for example, form a world in themselves. Yet world politics was not compartmentalized. The cataclysmic changes in the configuration of world power that occurred in 1940-41—the fall of France, Japan's alliance with the Axis, the German attack on the Soviet Union—reverberated between East and West. The configuration of world power was moving from one of interconnected regional crises toward a unitary global balance of forces. The United States always needed to consider the implications elsewhere of a move in any particular direction.

To understand fully American entry into World War II we need a modern synthesis combining the story of deepening participation in the war against Hitler with the related story of the road to Pearl Harbor and placing American policy in its global context. The 1952-53 work of William L. Langer and S. Everett Gleason, *The Challenge to Isolation* and *The Undeclared War*, provides a model in this respect. We need a book of that scope, incorporating modern scholarship, integrating the military side—intelligence and operational capability as well as strategy—with the diplomatic, and attentive to public and congressional opinion.

By striving for comprehensiveness we may also gain a better understanding of the foreign policy of Franklin D. Roosevelt. So little record exists of the thoughts of this most elusive and dissembling of presidents that we must rely on inference and try for better sleuthing. Assessments differ widely, but Roosevelt has impressed me as an active and purposeful maker of foreign policy, the only figure with all the threads in his hands. He also had a keen sensitivity for relations among nations and grasp of great power politics. He took a comprehensive view. Accordingly, the more completely we reassemble the pieces of what we can reasonably assume he knew of world developments, and of what he could do about it and was advised to do, the better we may understand his policies.

Comprehensiveness in these dimensions requires concision in others. The question was how far back from Pearl Harbor could I go in this fashion within the compass of one volume—and the answer was, not far. March 1941 offers a natural starting point. Earlier Roosevelt had been preoccupied with gaining a third term in the election of 1940 and winning the Lend-Lease debate. In foreign policy matters he was at his most opaque. With passage of Lend-Lease he had a mandate to act. Nineteen hundred forty-one was not necessarily more important than 1940, but it offered me more of an international harvest. Also the beginning of spring brought World War II into a new compaigning season with possible outcomes even worse than those of 1940. Increasingly in my research the nine-month period from March to December 1941 took on a character of its own with a separate yarn to tell.

More than anyone else, Dorothy Borg has made it possible for me to reach the point of telling this story and with heartfelt thanks I dedicate this book to her. Her high expectations, rigorous standards, gentle prodding, and constant, warm encouragement and support have brought out the best in me as a historian. The East Asian Institute of Columbia University with its kindred spirits, workshops, and conferences has been a second home for me professionally. Lectures to Carol Gluck's Columbia students have greatly helped me develop the ideas on which this book is based.

My education in Japanese foreign relations and the international history of East Asia began with Akira Iriye, when we were graduate students together at Harvard, and I have been tapping his rich and abundant scholarship ever since. His kindness and help have powerfully assisted me in this project. Of particular benefit was his faculty seminar on the 1931–49 period, sponsored by the Henry Luce Foundation, which started me organizing research and writing and provided me the expert criticism of its members, Warren Cohen, Gary Hess, Sherman Cochran, and Bob Messer. Akira and Gary have given me the additional benefit of their criticism on the completed manuscript.

The writing of this book would have been impossible without the concentrated time and energy permitted by a fellowship from the Woodrow Wilson International Center for Scholars in 1985–86. I wish to thank the directors and staff of the Center, especially Associate Director Samuel Wells, my colleagues there, especially Jon Sumida, and my research assistants Michael Ciriello and Ann Heyer for making that year so enormously beneficial. Professor Arthur Schlesinger, Jr., who has helped me so much along the way, was kind enough to serve as commentator at my Wilson Center symposium.

I wish to thank the Earhart Foundation of Ann Arbor, Michigan, for a fellowship which made it possible to continue writing through the following summer. Travel for research was made possible by a grant from the American Philosophical Society. To Temple University I owe repeated thanks for research support of many kinds since the inception of this project. In my department at Temple I am deeply grateful to Russell Weigley and to the late Shumpei Okamoto, whom we miss so much.

This manuscript has been greatly improved as the result of a careful evaluation by Robert Dallek. I am indebted again to my mentors at Harvard: Ernest May for his early suggestions about the project and Frank Freidel for his examination of the product and his sage advice. More errors than I care to admit were uncovered by the eagle-eyed scrutiny of portions of the manuscript by Jim Field, Charles Neu, and Dick Leopold. Scott Sagan gave me a valuable critique from his perspective in political science. To all these readers as well as Gary Hess and Akira Iriye my deepest thanks.

My research has been facilitated by the knowledge and professional skill of many archivists; their courtesy and efficiency has eased my way through countless boxes and hours. My special thanks to Bill Emerson at the Franklin D. Roosevelt Library for the key suggestions he made; to John Taylor at the National Archives for his unparalleled knowledge of military records; to Dean Allard, director of the U.S. Navy Operational Archives for showing the way to so many valuable naval records and sharing his knowledge as a naval historian; to Milt Gustafson and Sally Marks for the best-run archive I can imagine—the Diplomatic Branch at the National Archives; and the many other archivists who have helped: Richard Von Doenhoff, Howard Wehman, Tim Nenninger, Ed Reese, Bill Heimdahl, Fred Pernell, Richard Boylan, Richard Gould, Robert Parks, Martha Crawley, Bernard ("Cav") Cavalcante, and Elaine Everly.

At one stage or another in this project historians and experts of various kinds have kindly given of their time and knowledge. My thanks to David Reynolds, Daniel Harrington, Charles Maechling, Vice Admiral (Ret.) Edwin B. Hooper, Bob Love, Hugh Gallagher, "Sandy" Cochran, and W. A. B. Douglas and Marc Milner of the Directorate of History, National Defense Headquarters, Ottawa. My thanks also to Timothy J. Heinrichs for an expert editing of the manuscript. I have been fortunate, even after entering the world of personal computers, to be able to call on the word processing skills of Gloria Basmajian, Anita O'Brien, and Jack Runyon.

Scholarly Resources Inc. has granted permission to publish here excerpts from my article "President Franklin D. Roosevelt's Intervention in the Battle of the Atlantic, 1941, " which originally appeared in *Diplomatic History.*

I have followed the Japanese style of giving Japanese last names first.

My wife, Audrey Stewart Heinrichs, with her own intense professional career to manage, has been a constant source of support. My deepest thanks go to her for her patience, grace, and wise advice.

Shoreham, Vermont   Waldo Heinrichs
August 1987

Contents

Maps

(All maps reproduced from *The New York Times* of 1941 by
permission of The New York Times, Inc.)

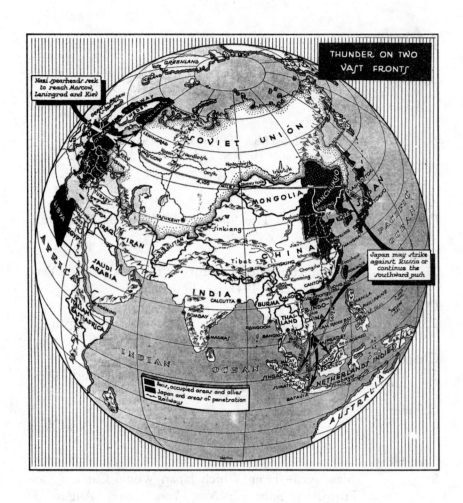

"Thunder on Two Vast Fronts": *New York Times*, July 27, 1941.

Threshold of War

Prologue

Before war pounced on the United States on December 7, 1941, it crept up, stage by stage, over many years. First came the world economic crisis, beginning with the American stock market crash in 1929, undermining confidence in the world order, shaking the foundations of political power in every country, and promoting authoritarian rule. Japan's conquest of Manchuria in 1931 was an isolated case, but aggression and pressure for territorial revisions dominated international politics from the mid-thirties onward, as the sad litany of Ethiopia, China, Austria, and Czechoslovakia attest. Hitler's violation of the Munich agreement over Czechoslovakia and the determination of Britain and France henceforth to resist led to European war in 1939. In 1940 Hitler's conquest of France, siege of Britain, and alliance with Japan shredded America's sense of security. In 1941, European and East Asian conflicts extended and interconnected, the world divided, and war became virtually global. It is with the last climactic stage in 1941 that this book is concerned.

The World War of 1914–18 was supposed to be the war to end all wars. Thirteen million combatants died, one in five, and twenty-two million were wounded, one in three.[1] The great object of the Paris Peace Conference and the diplomacy of the 1920s was to make a repetition unnecessary and impossible. The dominant values of international relations remained those advanced by President Woodrow Wilson: national self-determination, guarantee of territorial integrity, peaceful settlement of disputes, disarmament, freer trade, and collective security under the aegis of the League of Nations. In significant ways these principles remained unfulfilled in the twenties. The peace settlement bore the marks of revenge and national self-aggrandizement; collective security was incomplete without United States membership in the League. Nevertheless, the United States played an active if behind-the-scenes role in diplomacy and dominated the Washington Conference of 1921–22 on arms limitation and Pacific-

East Asian affairs. Universalism and multilateralism, conciliation and consultation, diplomacy not force—the spirit of Locarno, Geneva, and Washington—were the predominant motifs of those years, and it would have been hard to believe in 1929 that the world was already half the years to another war.

The world economic crisis of the 1930s shriveled internationalism. A chain of failures and errors occurred in systems already weakened by war: declining commodity prices, exchange difficulties, foreign trade shrinkage, debt default, collapse of investment values, bank closings, factory shutdowns, and devastating unemployment. Britain was unable to continue as stabilizer of the international system and no successor appeared. Economic disorder led to political instability. Governments were less concerned with harmonizing relations with other nations than with staying in power. Nations turned inward and autarky prevailed.

Most of the noteworthy events of the early and mid-thirties involved repudiation of internationalism. The failure of the London Economic Conference of 1933 marked the end of currency stabilization and the very idea of a managed world economy. At Geneva the exhaustive search for European disarmament died, and at London in 1936 naval limitation expired. League sanctions failed to prevent Italy's conquest of Ethiopia in 1935–36, and the United States Senate rejected even a highly conditional membership in the World Court. Regional security pacts fared no better. The Locarno pact dissolved with Hitler's occupation of the Rhineland in 1936, while the Brussels Conference of 1937 marked the demise of the Nine-Power Treaty designed to protect China. One by one the symbols of postwar accord and the Wilsonian New Diplomacy collapsed.

In the wake of economic and political chaos arose two regimes seeking hegemony and prepared to use force, in Germany and Japan. Adolf Hitler, coming to power in 1933, planned step-by-step the conquest of Europe, the sequence and timing depending on circumstances. Furthermore, as Gerhard Weinberg contends, Hitler's Nazi system depended on ever more space and resources. This insatiable expansionist appetite would ultimately have led along the paths of Hitler's early visions to an attempt at world domination. Certainly the laying of keels of 56,000-ton battleships in 1939 suggests wider ambitions than Europe. Nazi persecution of the Jews and ruthless suppression of democracy and dissent aroused revulsion and fear abroad, but in the first years of his regime Hitler avoided confrontation while he concentrated on rearmament and consolidation of power. Historians now see the Nazi state as far from monolithic,

rather as a congeries of bureaucratic and private empires, but the ultimate and absolute authority in all great questions was the Fuehrer's
and his alone.[2]

Though German and Italian interests in Austria and the Balkans
clashed, the two nations had powerful ideological affinities and saw
common adversaries in France and Britain. Benito Mussolini and the
Fascists, who came to power in 1922, were moved by illusions of
Roman glory and empire, but until the mid-thirties Il Duce acted
with caution in foreign affairs. Germany's benevolent neutrality
toward Italy's conquest of Ethiopia eased the path to accommodation, and in late 1936 the two dictators inaugurated the partnership
known as the Axis. Both assisted General Francisco Franco in the
Spanish Civil War between 1936 and 1939, and Italy bowed to Hitler's annexation of Austria in 1938. Now Germany was on the march.

Japan had led the way. On September 18, 1931, a bomb ripped out
thirty-one inches of track in the South Manchurian Railroad just
north of Mukden. It had been set by the Japanese army to serve as a
pretext for the takeover of Manchuria, which was then accomplished.
The League of Nations condemned the aggression, and Japan withdrew from the League. In the next several years Japan extended its
sway beyond Manchuria (renamed Manchukuo) into Inner Mongolia and North China.

The sources of Japanese expansionism were deep and complex. Of
immediate importance was the rise of Chinese nationalism in the
1920s and the threat this posed to Japan's interests, especially its
imperial holdings in Manchuria and its visions for the future of those
rich northern provinces of China. Behind that concern lay fear of
the Soviet Union, then turning to development of the resources and
defenses of Siberia and the Pacific maritime provinces. The world
depression affected Japan especially severely because of its dependence on foreign trade. Japan's exports fell by one-half from 1929 to
1931, driving down incomes and employment and destroying faith
in Western political and economic systems. The military became a
determining influence in Japanese politics and foreign policy, leading
Japan down the path toward imperial self-sufficiency and hegemony
in East Asia.

While Germany's imperial vision was singular, that of Hitler,
Japan's was pluralistic. The Japanese army anticipated war with the
Soviet Union sooner or later, but the navy considered the United
States its chief hypothetical enemy. The army looked northward, the
navy southward toward the rich resources—particularly oil—of
Southeast Asia. The more Japan challenged the existing order in East

Asia—represented by the Washington treaty system of 1922—the more it estranged itself from the Western powers with interests in the region and the greater its affinity for the revisionist powers of Europe—Germany and Italy. In 1936, Germany and Japan signed a limited pact directed at the Soviet Union, to which Italy adhered the following year.

Japan was not looking for war in China in 1937, but its arrogant pretensions and progressive intrusions from the north so roused the Chinese, both Nationalists and Communists, that the government of Chiang Kai-shek perforce determined to resist. A clash between Chinese and Japanese troops at Marco Polo Bridge, south of Peking, produced an uncontrolled escalation of conflict and full-scale war. Chiang and the Nationalists (Kuomintang) retreated westward into the mountains at Chungking. As the Japanese army swept up the great cities of eastern China it destroyed or jeopardized all of Western enterprise, business and missionary, and the treaty system on which it was based. Its bombing and massacre of civilians hardened anti-Japanese sentiment in America.

By 1938 the United States faced a very different and dangerous world. Japan seemed well on the way to East Asian dominance. Hitler, having gobbled up Austria, prepared for the next victim, Czecho-slovakia. The democracies lacked the will and capability to stop the aggressors.

Three attitudes dominated American world policy in the mid-thirties: isolationism, preoccupation with internal affairs, and complacency. American practice had been to stand aloof from Europe's quarrels. The exception had been the World War and Wilson's crusade for permanent peace. Historical accounts in the thirties, blaming the victors as well as the vanquished for World War I, the apparent injustices of the peace settlement, and the rising clouds of another war, confirmed Americans in their traditional belief and passionate determination to stay out of the next conflict. In 1934–36 an investigation led by Senator Gerald Nye into war profiteering by munitions-makers and bankers propelled legislation through Congress to prohibit the transactions with belligerents which seemed to have brought the United States into war in 1917. By 1938 the United States was strongly committed to isolationism. However deep American sympathy for China and its future, for example, little disposition existed to assist it and provoke Japan.

What did seem critical to the American people was the devastating economic depression of the early thirties, followed by slow recovery and a sharp recession in 1937. President Franklin Delano Roosevelt, elected on a platform of recovery and reform, spent his energies and influence on enacting the New Deal, raising prices, and putting people back to work. Reformers were often isolationist, recognizing that preparedness and intervention abroad strengthened existing elites and precluded social spending. Radical change wrought by the New Deal plunged the country into heated political conflict, absorbing American public awareness. Roosevelt's efforts of 1937-38 to perpetuate the New Deal by enlarging the Supreme Court and purging conservative Democrats failed, leaving him a weakened, presumably lame-duck president. Politics was central to American concerns; Ethiopia, Austria, and Manchuria were at the margins.[3]

Finally, it was very hard for Americans to conceive of Hitler or the Japanese as posing a direct threat to the United States. True, the German army was outstripping any single potential foe, but the French army ensconced in the Maginot Line with its allies and putative allies—Britain, Poland, Czechoslovakia—far outnumbered the Wehrmacht. Italy's alignment with Germany was by no means definitive, and a German-Soviet pact hard to imagine. Above all, between the United States and Germany stood, as always, the British navy. Too many steps would have to succeed, too many questions be answered in a certain way, to envision a physical threat to the United States from Germany.

The threat of Japan seemed confined to East Asia. Prolonged conflict in China seemed more and more likely. Powerful Soviet forces lay to the north, the bulk of the American fleet—including twelve battleships and four aircraft carriers—operated in the Pacific, and while British Commonwealth, French, and Dutch naval forces in East Asia were negligible, the great base at Singapore provided a port of reentry for European naval power. Above all it seemed unlikely that Japan, so lacking in war resources, would dare challenge the United States, from which it imported 80 percent of its oil products, 90 percent of its gasoline, 74 percent of its scrap iron, and 60 percent of its machine tools.[4]

Franklin Roosevelt, who entirely lacked an isolationist mentality, worried about the drift of world affairs, but not to the point of sacrificing his domestic objectives. He supported in spirit League sanctions against Italy by calling for a moral embargo against export of oil to Italy, and he repeatedly spoke for peace, disarmament, and international mediation of disputes. He encouraged Britain's and France's efforts to limit and prevent European conflict. At no time, however, did he offer guarantees or alliances to deter aggressors. Quite apart from the difficulty of imagining public support for such a move, it was by no means clear how American power might be brought to bear and how welcome it might be to Europeans in the era of appeasement. Thus American policy toward the rising threat in Europe had a nebulous, indecisive quality. It did nothing to slow Hitler.

East Asian policy was not quite the same. The United States never condoned Japanese aggression. It regularly protested Japan's treaty violations and injury to American interests and rights in China. However, it always sought to avoid provoking Japan. In these respects American East Asian policy was as cautious and passive as its European counterpart. But it had more active implications. Recognition of the Soviet Union in 1934 suggested the possibility of a North Pacific alignment against Japan. Throughout the thirties Roosevelt built up the United States Navy, first to treaty strength and afterwards well beyond it. He kept open the possibility of retaining a naval base in the Philippines after independence, and in naval treaty negotiations rejected an increase in Japanese strength relative to the British and American navies. Secret British-American naval conversations at London in January 1938 led to agreement that in case of a Japanese threat the American fleet would move to Pearl Harbor and a British fleet to Singapore. In the background of American restraint toward Japan lay a disposition to use power that was absent from policy toward Europe.

The Munich agreement of September 30, 1938, conceding to Hitler strategic portions of Czechoslovakia, brought about a basic shift in American foreign policy. Vast relief that war had been averted was followed by a deepening realization that Hitler's ambitions made war inevitable sooner or later—indeed sooner, for the following March he took the rest of Czechoslovakia. Munich spurred American rearmament, especially in warplanes. Roosevelt sought an increase in aircraft production capacity not only for defense but also to help build up British and French air power and deter Germany. Further to convince Hitler he would have to reckon ultimately with American economic might, the president sought revision of the neutrality laws, including repeal of the arms embargo. So strong was isolationist sentiment in Congress, however, that he failed, so the United States remained a helpless onlooker when Hitler, after reaching an accommodation with the Soviet Union in August 1939, attacked Poland on September 1. Great Britain and France stood by Poland, and once again Europe went to war.

Coincidentally American policy toward Japan stiffened. In November 1938, Prime Minister Konoe Fumimaro of Japan, encouraged by Hitler's challenge to the status quo, issued a statement pro-claiming a "New Order in East Asia" under Japan's leadership, directly contradicting America's traditional Open Door policy for China and dismissing the Washington treaty system. The United States protested and, more significantly, provided its first direct assistance to China, small as it was, a credit for twenty-five million dollars. In July 1939 the United States gave the required six months' notice for terminating its commercial treaty with Japan, opening the way for its most rigorous form of pressure, the trade embargo.

Seven shadowy months of "phony war" passed from the conquest of Poland to the next German venture, the invasion of Denmark and Norway on April 9, 1940. The administration finally succeeded in repealing the arms embargo; now Britain and France had access to American arms production but would have to take title in American ports and ship the goods themselves. Almost all American inter-course with the belligerents—shipping, travel, loans—remained pro-hibited. Appeasement was discredited, but American interest in peacemaking persisted. To keep Italy out of the war if possible and to delay if not prevent the coming fury, Under Secretary of State Sumner Welles journeyed to Rome, Berlin, Paris, and London with-out result. At Tokyo the American ambassador, Joseph C. Grew, gin-gerly investigated the possibility of easing tensions over China in return for extension of the trade treaty, but Washington preferred to hold the threat of trade restriction over Japan, and the treaty duly expired.

Blitzkrieg began in the west on May 10, 1940, and by the end of June the Low Countries were overrun, France was defeated, Italy was at war at the side of Germany, and Britain was a lonely outpost of democracy at the edge of a virtually totalitarian continent. By the end of the summer, air battles raged over southern England, and invasion was expected any day. Taking advantage of the collapse of Western power, Japan moved southward. It applied pressure on the successor regime in France, that of Marshall Philippe Pétain at Vichy, to permit the stationing of Japanese troops in northern Indochina, further encircling free China; on the British to close the Burma supply route to China; and on the Dutch East Indies for huge supplies of oil. In September, Japan joined the Axis.

Almost overnight the "free security" enjoyed by the United States since the Napoleonic Wars disappeared.[5] The Atlantic was no longer a friendly ocean: Hitler controlled the far shore. The French navy was neutralized, while the British were struggling desperately to keep open sea lanes to the Western Hemisphere and the empire. A very real possibility existed that the Americas would find themselves an island in a world dominated by the Axis.

President Roosevelt's immediate response was an exponential increase in American armament. In the balance of 1940 the United States Navy ordered nine new battleships, compared with eight ordered in the years 1937–40, eleven aircraft carriers, three battle cruisers, and eight heavy cruisers, compared with none of these types in the earlier period, as well as thirty-one light cruisers and 181 destroyers.[6] The president set an annual production target of 50,000 airplanes; Congress raised the authorized strength of the army from 280,000 to 1,200,000 and more when feasible. The problem was no longer money but time and capacity. Congress enacted required military service, and the president called the National Guard into federal service and tightened defense ties with Latin America and Canada.

Defense of the Americas did not mean writing off Britain. On the contrary the survival of the beleaguered island seemed even more vital as the threat of Hitler to American security grew and his ultimate defeat became more important. As Britain battled on and the summer passed without invasion, American assistance seemed more realistic as well. The British desperately needed destroyers for defense against an invasion fleet and German submarines, the U-boat, so in September, Roosevelt agreed to provide fifty of World War I vintage. In return the United States received leases to certain British bases in the Western Hemisphere. The most valuable of these, in Newfoundland, Bermuda, and Trinidad, would provide Atlantic outposts for American naval and air power. Prime Minister Winston Churchill also gave public assurance that the Royal Navy would never be scuttled or surrendered.

Toward Japan the United States showed ever increasing firmness. To guard against Tokyo's taking advantage of Western vulnerability, Roosevelt moved the Pacific Fleet, which had been based on the West Coast, to Pearl Harbor, where it would lie on the flank of any Japanese advance southward. Pressure rose for more forceful measures. In July heavy Japanese orders for American iron and steel scrap, which according to administration statistics supplied 40 percent of Japanese iron production, and for aviation gasoline led the president to begin applying economic pressure.[7] Under a new law permitting restriction of the export of defense materials, he placed curbs on high-octane gas and high-grade scrap. In September, after Japan's move into Indochina, he turned the screw again, banning the export of all scrap, and each month thereafter a new list of restricted materials appeared. But he stopped short of an oil embargo, fearing the Japanese would attack

to seize the Dutch supply. The president and Secretary of State Cordell Hull, recognizing the greater and more immediate threat posed
by Germany, were determined so far as possible to avoid provoking
Japan.

The destroyers-for-bases agreement was a matter of dire necessity
at a time when Roosevelt feared that any departure from traditional
policy might defeat his bid for an unprecedented third term as president. The 1940 election had a numbing effect on policy. Under
attack as a warmonger and would-be dictator, Roosevelt stressed the
theme of defense and in his speeches dealt most deviously with the
implications of aid to Britain and the strategic imperatives the nation
faced. As it was, his margin of victory over the Republican contender
Wendell Willkie was substantial, twenty-seven million to twenty-two
million votes, but not the overwhelming triumph of 1936.

Aid to Britain, postponed by election politics, became a matter of
urgency thereafter: Britain was running low on funds to pay for
American arms. Ruminating on the problem during a post-election
cruise in the Caribbean, Roosevelt hit on the brilliant notion of lend-
ing American goods to Britain, thereby circumventing instead of
assaulting neutrality laws, loans, and the American horror of repeating 1917. Lend-Lease would give Britain assured access to the American arsenal while enhancing American production capability. In
January 1941, on the wings of powerful messages to the people and
Congress, he asked for appropriate legislation, and behind the scenes
he carefully guided presentation of the administration's case.

The Lend-Lease debate in Congress was the last great fight of the
isolationists. Senators Burton K. Wheeler, Arthur H. Vandenberg,
Hiram Johnson, Robert M. LaFollette, Jr., Bennett Champ Clark,
their allies in the House of Representatives, and their spokesmen outside, in particular Charles Lindbergh, were on the defensive, themselves increasingly isolated. Public sentiment as measured in polls was
overwhelmingly against a declaration of war, to be sure, but a growing majority favored aid to Britain short of war even at the risk of
war. The isolationist aggregation of Republicans, Roosevelt haters,
New Deal activists, midwest Progressives, and spokesmen of an earlier, simpler, safer America no longer represented the mainstream.
On March 11, 1941, the Lend-Lease bill, skillfully amended to
enlarge the majorities but safeguard the intent, passed the Senate by
a vote of 60 to 31 and the House by 317 to 71.

From May 10, 1940, until March 11, 1941, during these ten months
of unprecedented peril for the United States, the American people
struggled through their presidential election and Lend-Lease debate

to achieve a new foreign policy consensus. Aid to Britain was a new departure, establishing as it did a deep-set congruence of interest, though not an alliance, with one of the European belligerents. Roosevelt achieved a powerful mandate in his election and the Lend-Lease law. Nevertheless traditional forces of aloofness and separateness could not be dismissed, so it was impossible to say how far down the road that risked war the American people were prepared to go, or how far they could be led.

Meanwhile the world did not wait merely upon American consensus. Japan needed time to gain security in the north by some sort of accommodation with the Soviet Union before it could pursue the southward advance. Europe waited for spring, and, as the first months of 1941 passed, speculation intensified as to which way the German war machine would turn. Germany and Japan were reaching the limits of regional expansion. Any further aggression would have global reverberations. The Soviet Union, the United States, and Japan, though by no means neutral, had yet to cast their lots. The tendency as the sun arched northward was toward a global alignment of forces, and the question was what sort of balance might be struck, tipped which way, with what result.

Chapter 1

March 1941
The Aura of German Power

On March 1, 1941, leading elements of the German Twelfth Army crossed the Danube from Rumania to Bulgaria on pontoon bridges. Soon, under a warming, drying sun, German infantry, armored, mountain, and anti-aircraft troops were streaming south through Bulgaria toward the passes of the Rhodope Mountains, the Greek frontier, and the Mediterranean. Hitler, as the *New York Times* said, was "on the march again." Trains from Istanbul to Belgrade experienced delays of up to a full day; even the crack Simplon Express was running hours behind schedule.[1] The Nazi buildup to seventeen divisions for Operation MARITA, the conquest of Greece, had begun. The 1941 campaigning season was under way.

Hitler's foremost objective in 1941 was to crush the Soviet Union. That had always been his underlying purpose, an ambition deriving more from fundamental ideological preconceptions than from strategic realities. Subjugation of Russia would go far to fulfill the central aims and values of the Nazi state. The Fuehrer considered absolute control of the resources of the Soviet Union, particularly the oil of the Caucasus and the grain of the Ukraine, essential to the sustenance of a Nazi Europe. His intent to attack at the first opportunity in 1941 hardened when the Soviets disclosed ambitions in eastern Europe and the Balkans late in 1940. On December 21, 1940, Hitler issued his directive for the Russian campaign, known now by its code name, BARBAROSSA, after Frederick Barbarossa, the twelfth-century German empire-builder.[2]

By March the eastward movement of troops was under way. The German General Staff was gathering the largest military force ever concentrated on a single front: 75 percent of its army, or 3.3 million men in 142 divisions. This vast array would form three groups of armies on a front of one thousand miles, from the Baltic to the Black

German-controlled Territory in the Balkans: *New York Times*, March 2, 1941.

Sea, each with a powerful spearpoint of Panzer and motorized divisions, the largest group aimed at Moscow. In fact two kinds of army were involved, the fast or *schnell* forces and the marching infantry, using 625,000 horses for transport. Berlin estimated that most of the Red Army was stationed forward, near the frontiers. It aimed to drive armored wedges through Soviet lines, then encircle and crush the enemy within roughly 300 miles of the border, in easy reach of the German supply system. Hitler and his generals were determined to avoid getting lost in Russian space and bogging down in a war of attrition. The final objective, a line from the Caspian to the White Sea, would place the heart of Russia in terms of food, resources, and production in the Nazi grip. The attack was planned for mid-May or as soon thereafter as the roads dried.

In contrast to the plan against the Soviet Union, Hitler's aims in the Balkans were distinctly limited. He wanted to secure the north coast of the Aegean and, if necessary, the Greek mainland to protect the right flank of BARBAROSSA. Ulterior objectives in the Mediterranean would have to wait. The Luftwaffe until redeployed to the east and the German navy would heavily attack Britain and its supply lifelines, but invasion of Britain would also have to wait for completion of the Russian campaign.

Washington, suffering from heavy March snows, bitter cold, and "howling" winds, heard these rumblings of coming blitzkrieg in the Balkans with the deepest foreboding. The European situation, wrote Assistant Secretary of State Adolf A. Berle, Jr., was "thick and ... getting infinitely thicker by the minute." The lightning campaigns of 1939 and 1940 had created such an aura of frightening power and efficiency surrounding the German war machine that the coming "eruption of violence" in the Balkans seemed only a prelude to further stunning conquests. "Practically everyone in Europe seems to think he is next on Hitler's list," Berle observed. Americans sensed a great historical juncture with vast forces gearing for "hideous" struggle and events unrolling too "horrible" to watch. Secretary of War Henry L. Stimson warned a select group of correspondents that the United States was "in great world-wide peril."[3]

Franklin Delano Roosevelt had just turned sixty. Entering his third term, he was the longest-serving president in American history. His hair was thinning and turning white, and the burdens of the 1940 election and constant world crisis were leaving their mark. More than usual in the spring of 1941 he was ill in bed. Yet a fishing trip to Florida or the Caribbean or even a long weekend at Hyde Park seemed to restore his health and spirits. Roosevelt was at a peak of skill and experience while retaining his buoyancy and strength.

On March 8, 1941, the Senate passed Lend-Lease by vote of 60 to 31. Three days later the House of Representatives concurred, and the bill went to the White House for signature. The "great debate" was over, and the American people had chosen by decisive margins to intervene in the war at least to the point of supplying aid to Britain. Throughout the two-month Lend-Lease debate and indeed back through the presidential campaign in the latter part of 1940, Roosevelt had been severely circumscribed by politics in dealing with burgeoning threats abroad. He had to gain a mandate for his leadership and his party's and in Lend-Lease secure the foundation of British resistance and American rearmament before risking new military or diplomatic initiatives. Now at last he had some elbow room.

He could not move too fast or too far, however. The nation was not ready for war as a matter of choice. Public opinion, as Roosevelt probably saw it, was touchy. It was moving in the right direction, passing the marker buoy of aid to Britain even at the risk of war. But a declaration of war was not even in sight. Decisive executive action might slow or shift it. Isolationism as it weakened became more bitter and vindictive. It would revive with attacks on Roosevelt as warmonger and dictator. The result would be division and disunity when national consolidation was essential. He must avoid being the issue. He needed to dispel complacency, but opinion could not be forced: it must flow from the facts of international life themselves, from the very real menaces. It required education, subtle reinforcement, nurturing—in short, time.

Time was desperately needed to retool for war as well. The economy was still only in the first stages of transformation. War orders were reviving it. Consumer demand was rising; cars were selling. Profitable at last, business resisted conversion. As profits and the cost of living rose so did labor's demand for its share. The spring of 1941 was a time of labor strife. Violence occurred at the Ford River Rouge plant, Bethlehem Steel, and International Harvester, and in Harlan County, Kentucky. By April the strike at Allis-Chalmers, a key machinery manufacturer, was entering its third month. For major constituencies of the Democratic party, the New Deal was at stake as the Roosevelt administration moved from reform to rearmament, from partisanship to consensus, and as Republicans began filtering back into Washington to supervise war production. Changes in the American economy produced division enough for the president.

The establishment of a war economy had its own dynamics, as Roosevelt knew from World War I. The theoretical sequence was simple enough: first allocation of resources, then building plant and obtaining machine tools and manpower, and finally switching on the assembly line. Setting up priorities and sequences for the economy as a whole was a different matter. First one needed timber, girders, cement, riggers, masons, and skilled machinists. Bringing together the components of new factories at the right time and place was itself impossible in 1941; delay was inevitable. The steel industry was reaching full capacity. Plant construction, ship hulls, and tank production would have to vie with each other for a limited output until steel could build new plants itself. Keeping the completely different aircraft-engine and air-frame industries in tandem so that one did not wait upon the other was another headache, to say nothing of propellers, generators, ammunition, and radios. Manpower problems were always acute. Should industry and the armed services maintain existing units—factories, warships, infantry divisions—because of their present efficiency or withdraw cadres of skilled personnel to form new units, thereby multiplying size?

These immediate questions raised larger ones. At what point in time was this national effort aiming? Should the nation ready itself for war immediately, sacrificing time-consuming armaments like battleships, or for the longer pull? What kind of war would be waged with what arms and what enemies? Defending the Western Hemisphere or invading Europe? Germany alone or the Axis? America alone or with allies, and which allies? These questions were impossible to answer in any satisfactory way in the spring of 1941.[4]

Roosevelt went about these problems with his distinctive decision-making style. Never given to formal bureaucratic ways, he dealt with officials in terms of competence and function rather than hierarchical position, as well as the relative importance of a particular policy domain and his interest in it. Thus, as usual, his involvement varied widely across the policy spectrum.

His closest involvement was in regulating, as commander in chief, the strength, dispositions, and rules of engagement of the United States Atlantic Fleet. Of course naval affairs had always aroused Roosevelt's keenest interest. Over the mantelpiece in the Oval Study hung a painting of the four-stack destroyer *Dyer* on which he had traveled to Europe as assistant secretary of the navy in World War I. This was the same type of destroyer exchanged for bases with the British in 1940, the same that still in March 1941 composed most of the destroyer force of the Atlantic Fleet. According to the flag lieu-

tenant to Admiral Harold Stark, chief of naval operations, the president would phone frequently to say, "Betty [Stark's nickname from
Naval Academy days], I want this done right away," and then rattle
off a list of five or six assignments. The White House maintained a
direct wire to the navy's Ship Movements Division to keep track of
vessels on neutrality patrol in 1939–40. The president rarely saw Secretary of the Navy Frank Knox alone. He not only dealt directly with
Admiral Stark, his vice-chief of operations, and his war plans director, but also individually with the dour and driving commander-in-
chief of the Atlantic Fleet, Admiral Ernest J. King. Not just a passion
for seafaring encouraged his intervention in Atlantic problems, but
U-boats and the risk of war as well.[5]

In dealing with the army, Roosevelt developed a different method.
He usually did not see the uniformed head of the army, General
George C. Marshall, except in company with Stimson and others. He
meant no disrespect, for the good judgment and forthrightness of
this austere soldier were winning admiration in the administration
and Congress. More likely, Roosevelt was operating the way Stimson
preferred, through the secretary of war rather than around him. Stimson the president did see alone, and not just on army and war production business. The secretary of war, age seventy-three, had served
in the cabinets of Presidents William Howard Taft and Herbert Hoover. As secretary of state during the Manchurian crisis he had tried
his best to mobilize public opinion and Anglo-American resistance
to Japanese expansion. Now, assuming the role of senior statesman
and high policy adviser to the president, he lost no opportunity of
vigorously urging intervention in the European war.

The two men were a study in contrasting styles of national security
management. To Stimson, who believed in orderly, hierarchical pat-
terns, Roosevelt's informal, ad hoc practices were a constant source
of despair. "It literally is government on the jump," he complained.
The one had the rational, analytical, argumentative mind of a successful trial lawyer, the other the well-guarded intuitive faculties of a
consummate politician. Stimson at first found conversation with the
president "like chasing a vagrant beam of sunshine around a vacant
room." The orderly secretary was ardent for action, the improvising
president persistently wary and cautious. However, they shared the
same patrician background, the same vision of an orderly, peaceful
world so powerfully articulated by Woodrow Wilson, and the same
respect for the reality of national power and the art of its use. Somewhat reluctantly Stimson came to admire certain qualities of mind in
his chief, the "wonderful memory," for example, and the "penetrative

shrewdness." As confidence if not easy agreement built between the two, Stimson became one of the very few to get a glimpse of Roose-velt's inner thinking on policy. A long talk on strategy in January provided him an "almost thrilling evening."[6]

The British-American relationship was a decision-making universe in itself. At the heart of it was Harry Hopkins, one of Roosevelt's most zealous and trusted New Deal lieutenants, whose frail health and incisive mind were now totally at the service of the president. During his trip to London the past January, Hopkins had cultivated closer ties between Roosevelt and Prime Minister Winston Churchill, and by March the two were exchanging messages briskly, Churchill usually seeking and Roosevelt occasionally providing. Supplement-ing the principals were the ambassadors, John G. Winant in London providing key reports on the mood and unspoken needs of the Churchill government, and Lord Halifax in Washington sending what the president preferred to convey orally, informally, and out-side American channels. These formed only the tip of the iceberg, however. Anglo-American collaboration was becoming an unprece-dented trans-national enterprise. Hopkins would now expedite Lend-Lease from the White House assisted by his aide Averell Harriman in London. Every agency seemed to require liaison. Dozens of purchas-ing missions, special observers, communications experts, and military delegations crossed the Atlantic both ways. As the historian of the relationship put it, "The cords that bound the two countries were becoming thicker, more tangled and more secure."[7]

In most policy areas Roosevelt preferred not to involve himself personally. American-Soviet relations, for example, were exceedingly cold on account of Nazi-Soviet ties and the Russian war on Finland. Even so, the president and Secretary of State Cordell Hull considered it prudent to keep the way open for improving relations, so Under Secretary of State Sumner Welles had been engaged in a series of fruitless discussions with the Soviet ambassador, Constantin Ou-mansky, since mid-1940. The haughty Welles, a family friend and close adviser of Roosevelt, was the perfect foil for the surly Russian.

Roosevelt stayed aloof from the Chinese too, but for different rea-sons. He gave them every encouragement in their lonely war with the Japanese but very little material aid. Generalissimo Chiang Kai-shek and his agents in Washington pestered officials for more. Secretary of the Treasury Henry Morgenthau and White House adviser Lauchlin Currie represented their views to the president, but the Chinese were rarely allowed to approach the throne themselves.

Relations with Japan most closely approximated the bureaucratic paradigm. Roosevelt was happy to leave the difficult and dangerous problems with Japan in the hands of the secretary of state and his Far Eastern experts. He put his finger in the pie occasionally but he knew that the wily and cautious Hull, the very essence of rectitude in international conduct, would neither provoke nor condone Japan but keep relations in satisfactory suspense. The constraints on Japanese conduct, however, military deterrence and trade restrictions, were not in Hull's hands.

All the threads of policy led ultimately to the White House. By this flexible and eclectic system Roosevelt could oversee or intervene depending on the issue. Only three trusted advisers—Stimson, Hopkins, and Welles—secured both ready access and some appreciation of the president's thinking and outlook. Morgenthau remained a close friend and retained influence on economic and financial questions but drifted out of the mainstream of decision-making as military issues became more prominent. Hull had ready access but little empathy. Frequently now the president called together at the White House the two service secretaries, Knox and Stimson, and the two uniformed heads of the services, Stark and Marshall, as well as Hull and Hopkins. This group, which Stimson called the War Council and which resembled the Defense Committee of the British War Cabinet, was as close as Roosevelt came at this stage to institutionalized decision-making in national security affairs.

In his estimate of German intentions for 1941 President Roosevelt depended on a chaotic supply of intelligence. Alongside American military and diplomatic reports, occasionally brilliant, usually sketchy because of wartime restrictions, and too often mediocre, a mélange of rumor, desultory fact, and limp estimate, were the tantalizing secrets of MAGIC, the closely guarded American process of decrypting Japanese diplomatic messages. However, what was valuable in the intercepts was difficult to isolate from a mass of irrelevant data that strained available reading time. No digest was provided; no copying was permitted. Use of this raw intelligence, as one authority has said, "had to be impressionistic."[8]

In 1941 the United States government had only a meager ability to coordinate and effectively evaluate the rising tide of information from abroad. President Roosevelt was keenly interested in improvement. He authorized a separate agency for intelligence in June 1941, but it needed time to establish itself and contributed little that year. Change came slowly or not at all: both the president and Stimson wished to replace the army's chief of military intelligence, Brigadier General Sherman Miles, but he hung on past Pearl Harbor.[9]

Roosevelt soaked up facts, taking particular interest in reports of German and Japanese war resources and American production figures. A steady flow of letters from friends abroad and American diplomats who knew him personally, such as Lincoln MacVeagh in Athens, William Phillips in Rome, and Joseph Grew in Tokyo, provided mood and context. A special delight must have been one from the former French ambassador in Washington and poet, Paul Claudel, forwarded by Claudel's son. The distinguished old man wrote of the Italian attack on Greece in 1940: "Every evening at the radio we give ourselves the pleasure of listening to the Italian commentators explaining in a sorrowful, encouraging, and consoling voice the daily defeat." The president read MAGIC or heard the gist of it from regular briefings by army and navy intelligence officers, usually in the late afternoon after callers. Probably a great deal of what he learned came from talk with his advisers and from voracious reading of newspapers at breakfast. It may not be far from the truth to say that page one of the *New York Times*, assigning relative weights to stories by position and multi-column headlines, framed his view of the day's foreign affairs.[10]

The most prized American source of intelligence about Hitler's intentions was a German who remained anonymous but who in all probability was Dr. Erwin Respondek, a former civil servant in the finance ministry, Catholic Center party member of the Reichstag, supporter of former Chancellor Heinrich Brüning, professor of economics and consultant to I. G. Farben and other German corporations. This very brave anti-Nazi retained highly placed connections in the Nazi party, the Reichsbank, and the army high command. He was in touch with the former crown prince of Saxony who was now a Catholic monk, who in turn was a friend of General Franz Halder, chief of the German General Staff. Respondek's American contact was Sam E. Woods, commercial attaché of the American embassy in Berlin, a genial southerner with a breezy disregard of diplomatic conventions.[11]

Respondek would reserve side-by-side seats at a movie theater and in the dark slip his reports into Woods' pocket. Woods forwarded these first through the American military attaché in Berlin in January 1941 and then by diplomatic pouch to an administrative official in the Department of State who brought them to the attention of Assistant Secretary of State Breckinridge Long. Brüning, at the time a professor at Harvard, authenticated the source. Examination of the typewriting by the Federal Bureau of Investigation established that the author of these and earlier reports possessed by Brüning was the same person. The Department of State was satisfied that it was not the victim of a "plant."

Respondek's reports dealt with a wide variety of problems facing Germany: raw material stocks, manpower, food, finance, and morale. Those of January 3 and February 19 conveyed information about strategic plans. Both stated that Germany had two objectives in 1941: the invasion of England and the conquest of the Soviet Union. The January report stated that Britain would come first in the spring, followed by the Soviet Union in the summer. The date of the attack on England would depend on the weather and the amount of American arms assistance, especially airplanes, Britain had received. The earlier the invasion, the better Germany's opportunity.

According to Respondek the German high command anticipated a short, decisive campaign against Russia, using "motorized attack divisions" in three main concentrations: one in the north, including Norway, East Prussia, and north Poland, to contain Soviet forces in the Baltic region; a second in the center attacking eastwards through Kiev to Kharkov; and a third, the main thrust, in the south aimed at Odessa and Rostov in the Caucasus. Arrangements would be made for Japanese forces to contain Soviet armies in the Far East. The information was second-hand, simply a stark outline of "massed possibilities" without documentation. It fitted no particular plan under consideration, least of all the final directive for BARBAROSSA of December 18, 1940, with its concentration in the center toward Moscow. The report was a hazy reflection of the uncertainty over priorities and debate over strategy for the Russian campaign preoccupying the General Staff during the latter part of 1940.

The February account placed greater emphasis on the east. Because of Italian defeats in Albania and North Africa and the "increasing offensive power" of Britain, plans were now "variable." The invasion of England remained one of the two objectives, but the report dwelt on the "territorial liquidation of the land war in Europe" which included "the smashing of the Red army" and the military and economic advantages this would provide.

The two reports indicated a distinct and rising possibility of a German attack on Russia but they failed to reveal that Hitler intended to attack the Soviet Union unconditionally and had set aside the invasion of England. Assistant Secretary of State Adolf A. Berle, Jr., who dealt with intelligence matters, reflected the indecisiveness promoted by the reports. Before the first report he thought a German-

Russian deal dividing Turkey the most likely possibility. After its receipt he predicted German operations in the Balkans as a prelude to the "real drive" on Russia. The war would then come to a climax in an "ocean of anarchy and bloodshed." But it was "not clear whether they will attack Russia anyhow, or whether they propose to do so after they have conquered England, as they expect to do."[12]

The Respondek reports provided a prominent but by no means unique indication of German intentions. They came in on a rising tide of European diplomatic speculation about Hitler's plans in the east conveyed through American embassies and legations. The Swedes, with excellent contacts in Berlin, were more definitive about a German attack on Russia than Respondek. At the end of February the Swedish minister in Moscow told American Ambassador Laurence Steinhardt that, if the German submarine campaign failed to subdue England by March or April, Germany would turn on Russia. A month later the same minister provided some excellent information: three German army groups were forming up, on Koenigsberg, Warsaw, and Krakow (the last true for the main weight of Army Group South), and the commander of the Central Group was Field Marshal Feodor von Bock. Hitler would not necessarily attack, however. According to Swedish information, he would first offer Stalin full participation in the Axis alliance of Germany, Italy, and Japan with territorial compensation and would resort to arms only if rebuffed.[13]

The American legation in Bucharest reached the same conclusion by a circuitous and confusing path. With German troops streaming into Rumania for the southern wing of BARBAROSSA as well as the Balkans campaign, Minister Franklin Mott Gunther, a thirty-year foreign service veteran, was in a choice position to predict German moves. He was impressed with the numbers arriving: 1,500 troop trains reserved for January alone, he heard, and a total force of one million or even 1,200,000. "If all this is just for Greece and even Turkey," he advised, "then the Germans are driving tacks with sledgehammers." Yet he was bewildered by contradictory rumors and German deception. At first it seemed an attack on Russia was likely, but whether before or after an invasion of England he could not say. Then the German object seemed to be defense of Rumania against Soviet or British intervention or an attack toward Suez. On March 18 he concluded that war in the east was unlikely because Stalin, "hemmed in" and "overawed," would make almost any concession to perpetuate his rule.[14]

The switching of German forces to, from, and within southeast Europe was highly suggestive of German intentions. On March 27 a military coup overthrew the Yugoslav government, which had just bowed to German pressure and joined the Axis. Furious, Hitler immediately ordered expansion of forthcoming operations against Greece to include Yugoslavia. Two Panzer divisions and the SS Adolf Hitler Division, which had begun moving from blocking positions in Bulgaria toward their starting points for BARBAROSSA in southern Poland, were wheeled around and directed against Yugoslavia. The British detected this shift by the ULTRA process of decrypting German radio messages, and to Churchill it "illuminated the whole Eastern scene like a lightning flash": Yugoslavia was an unexpected departure from the basic plan, which was an attack on the Soviet Union. The American legation in Bulgaria noted and reported a reverse in the "direction of flow of German troops and guns through Sofia" on March 27, but neither it nor Washington sensed the implications.[15]

American military attachés forwarded impressive evidence of the eastward deployment of German forces. The attaché in Switzerland had excellent contacts. He noted the departure of elite units from northern France, the Netherlands, and Belgium and their replacement by older, less experienced troops. In the face of this sort of substitution, Vichy officials were becoming dubious about an invasion of England, according to Ambassador William D. Leahy. From Switzerland also came the report of a "continuous current" of trains heading eastward through Belfort, clearing out German divisions from the departments of occupied France bordering Switzerland. Eighty-five trains crossed the Rhine at Neuf Brisach on March 19-20 alone; 142 passed through Besançon on March 24-25. A Warsaw-to-Berlin passenger counted forty-one trains headed the other way on the night of March 3-4.[16]

Seeing was not necessarily believing. The Germans explained away the evident growth of forces in Poland: that country provided more room for maneuvers and a better food supply. They planted rumors and false information about preparations for invasion of England, such as the movement of poison-gas shells to northwest France, the manufacture of black silk parachutes at Beauvais, and the concentration of 300,000 paratroops and transport gliders.[17] Colonel B. R. Peyton, military attaché in Berlin, noting the rising number of German divisions located opposite Russia, was nevertheless impressed with the "unbelievable pains" the Germans went to in preparing for the invasion of Britain. Furthermore, he had learned that the Red Army had withdrawn from the frontier, making an envelopment like the one achieved by Hannibal in the battle of Cannae more difficult. He concluded, as did the Military Intelligence Division in Washington, that, while an attack on the Soviet Union was possible, it was the last on Hitler's list of objectives. First still was invasion of England.[18]

The difficulty in divining German intentions was not due to lack of experience. The list of American chiefs of mission in and near Europe reads like one from the 1920s: Leland Harrison at Bern, Switzerland, Frederick Sterling at Stockholm, William Phillips at Rome, John Van Antwerp MacMurray at Ankara, Arthur Bliss Lane at Belgrade. Roosevelt, for all his complaints about the flaccidity of the State Department, turned to professional diplomats again and again. Nor was there lack of ability. Assisting the chiefs and providing much of the political reporting were foreign service officers who would go on to become leading lights of American diplomacy after World War II: George Kennan, Jacob Beam, and James Riddleberger in Berlin, Llewelyn Thompson in Moscow, Robert Murphy and H. Freeman Matthews in Vichy, Herschel Johnson in London.[19]

Of course good information was exceedingly scarce in the totalitarian, machiavellian, militarized world of continental Europe in 1941, and so misinformation abounded. Diplomats were thrown in upon each other and usually repeated around the circuit of embassies and posts the same scraps of rumor and fact that came their way, thereby amplifying them. The main problem was intellectual, however. Information pointing to a German attack was hard to believe because Hitler, it seemed, could get what he wanted without war, because it was unwise for him to engage a new enemy before finishing off the British, and because war between Russia and Germany was too good to be true. Hitler had made no mistakes so far. Loy Henderson, an officer in the European Division of the Department of State, provides an example of the problem. The "growing coolness" between Moscow and Berlin was naturally a matter of keen interest in Washington, he said in March; "credible evidence" was available of a German plan to attack the Soviet Union "at an appropriate moment." He warned against wishful thinking, however. He found it difficult to believe the two powers would end their cooperation and go to war.[20]

Foreign estimates were no more definitive. Not all Churchill's colleagues were alive to the possibility of a German attack eastward. British army intelligence, relying on worst case analysis, insisted that invasion of England was first on the German agenda. The Foreign Office was divided, some impressed with the "stream of information" pointing to an attack, others more skeptical. The Swedish information about army groups and commanders seemed proof Germany was "flaunting" an attack to intimidate the Russians into a closer partnership.[21] Japanese diplomats, though Axis partners, were no better informed. MAGIC intercepts documented the growing coolness in Nazi-Soviet relations, but without agreement on the consequences. One observer saw Suez as the German objective, another, Suez and Gibraltar, a third, England, and a fourth believed that military preparations in the east were "aimed resolutely" at meeting any hostility from Russia.[22]

The problem of German intentions in the spring of 1941 was never so simple as deciding whether or not Hitler would attack a certain country but rather which of several directions German aggression would take and in what order the victims would fall. Thus evidence of preparations against Russia could be seen (and German intelligence cultivated the view) as preparations for a southeastwards advance: Greece would be the springboard to Suez.[23] Or word would pass that they were a cover for the invasion of England. But even these three vectors of attack did not comprise the full range of Western fears: signs also pointed to a German thrust southwestwards through the Iberian peninsula to Gibraltar, northwest Africa, and the Atlantic islands, the Azores, Cape Verdes, and Canaries.

American officials were especially sensitive about the possibility of a southwestward thrust toward Africa because Dakar was within aircraft range of Brazil. Hitler wanted Gibraltar and had moved sufficient strength to the Pyrenees to secure it, but General Francisco Franco proved difficult. Imparting sentiments of the deepest loyalty and devotion to the cause of fascism, the ruler of Spain resisted all blandishments to join the Axis and open the road to Gibraltar. He was not convinced Britain would lose; the capture of the western gate to the Mediterranean, he slyly suggested, would not be decisive unless Suez was in the bag as well.[24]

Creating another roadblock for the Axis, Spain coveted France's northwest African colonies, and for Germany to help Franco satisfy these ambitions would certainly have thrown General Maxime Weygand and the Vichy forces he commanded in North Africa into the arms of the British. Most importantly, Spain could obtain food and resources it desperately needed only from Britain and possibly the United States. The vital interests of Spain mandated a subsidized neutrality, and in this policy Franco stubbornly and cleverly persisted. In February the German divisions at the Pyrenees began moving east for BARBAROSSA.

Though Washington learned of the transfer, its anxiety continued. Armed passage through Spain might not be necessary. Germany might leap the strait and neutralize the "Rock" by securing bases from Vichy France in French Morocco. German forces gathering at Tripoli, an army estimate warned, placed Hitler in a position to dictate a North African division of spoils and exact concessions from the French. According to a March 10 report, Luftwaffe ground crews had arrived in Morocco at Tetuan opposite Gibraltar; rumor was that Germany had secured three air bases south of Tangier along the Atlantic coast and that Tangier, Cadiz, the Canary Islands, and Casablanca would become German submarine bases. During March the number of Germans in Casablanca rose to 250, according to one report. "They really are establishing their wings on the Atlantic line in Norway and Dakar," Berle concluded. Past experience with German fifth-column penetration roused fears, inflated facts, and made rumor credible.[25]

In the spring of 1941 the German army possessed almost mythic qualities. Stimson spoke of its "superb efficiency."[26] Given the contradictory and ambivalent intelligence picture, the warming sun brought a host of dangerous possibilities. Lacking precise, authentic sources, ways of theorizing about German intentions, and a central evaluation process, American officials, most likely including the president, wavered in their estimates, bobbing with each ripple of reports from Europe. Confused and uncertain, they were the more inclined to wait and see.

Even more ominous and urgent was the successful German war on British shipping and communications. This campaign, under way since the beginning of the war, widened after the Nazi conquest of Norway, the Low Countries, and France. In the late winter and early spring of 1941 it intensified, pressed by surface vessels and air armadas as well as U-boats, and not just on the high seas but also in the coastal waters and firths of Great Britain, and onto its docks, depots, and railroads. The main object was to cut off the people and factories of Britain from their crucial overseas sources of food and raw materials, to "strangle" them, to starve them into submission.[27]

A new aerial blitz began at the end of February with successive attacks on the coal city of Swansea in Wales. Then the "tour of the ports" began with heavy night incendiary raids on Cardiff, the Bristol area, Plymouth, Portsmouth, Southampton and, of course, London, all "targets the destruction of which will assist or supplement the war at sea," as the Fuehrer's directive put it. Singled out for special attention at London were the Albert and Victoria and King George V docks and the shipping concentrated at Tilbury. Then on the moon-lit nights of March 12, 13, and 14, the Luftwaffe carried out "furious" full-force attacks on Liverpool and Glasgow, especially on the Merseyside and Clydeside docks, warehouses, and shipbuilding yards.[28]

Altogether the Germans delivered twelve major blows in mid-March and continued attacking in a rising crescendo during April to a climax in the greatest raid of the "night blitz"—May 10 on London—after which "charred paper danced in the woods thirty miles from the city." Of sixty-one raids between February 19 and May 12, thirty-nine were against the western ports. A German victory in the Balkans would be bad enough, wrote Joseph Alsop and Robert Kintner in the *Washington Post*, but if they "succeed in closing Glasgow, Liverpool, Bristol, Cardiff, and Swansea, it will be disastrous."[29]

In retrospect the threat posed by the "night blitz" to Britain's war production and physical sustenance seems manageable and transient. The raids averaged only 100 tons of bombs compared with 1,600 during the allied bombing offensive against Germany in 1944-45. Electronic countermeasures and decoy fires deflected bombers from vital targets. In time better management of docks and rail cars speeded deliveries. Food stocks in the year as a whole actually increased.

The outlook from within the escalating blitz, however, was fearsome, especially to foreign observers. Plymouth's city center suffered "almost total destruction"; Southampton was "badly crippled"; Cardiff, the Germans boasted, looked like the "Ypres of 1917"; Portsmouth at night was like a "tomb." Damaged or destroyed besides port facilities were telephone exchanges and rail junctions. Cargoes piled up on the docks as the British rail system tried to adjust to arrival of goods mainly at western rather than eastern ports. A million to a million and a half tons of shipping lay over in British yards awaiting repair. British aircraft production was down one-third. One-fourth fewer imports were arriving than anticipated. Oil stocks were dangerously depleted. Stimson was alarmed at the "low level" of British food consumption.[30]

Morale was sorely tried. The March raids destroyed or damaged all but seven of Clydebank's 12,000 houses. The May 1 attack on Liverpool left 76,000 homeless. In the great raids of that spring the dwellers of Plymouth and Merseyside fled their cities by the tens of thousands, rending the fabric of urban life and community. Even small raids were exhausting. In six days of March Southampton had twenty-four air-raid alarms lasting a total of forty-eight hours, breaking the pattern of work and sleep. The blitz of 1941 was impossible to escape: "Even on the Welsh hills, one saw the searchlights groping over the midlands and heard the throb of the bombers looking for Liverpool ...."[31]

The Luftwaffe also attacked individual ships and convoys as they bunched up near port and laid mines in the Thames, Humber, and Mersey estuaries. Long-range Focke-Wulf "Kondor" bombers shuttled between Bordeaux and Stavanger, Norway, in an arc west of the British Isles, spotting convoys for U-boats and conducting low-level attacks.[32]

More and more U-boats were prowling the North Atlantic. From a dozen or so in October 1940, the number of operational boats rose to thirty in April 1941. U-boat commander Karl Doenitz expected fifty-two by August. British countermeasures in home waters forced the U-boats westward in March 1941 to the vicinity of Iceland and Greenland, where Hitler extended the war zone on March 25. Taking advantage of lengthening daylight for better observation and using new tactics of wolfpack deployment and night attacks on the surface to avoid detection by underwater listening devices, U-boats took a mounting toll.

Early in April, SC 26, a slow convoy from Sydney, Nova Scotia, ran into a wolfpack southwest of Iceland and was badly mauled. The loss of ten ships in this attack was decisive: the British Admiralty hurried construction of Iceland bases, dispatched aircraft and escort groups there and extended convoy protection to the mid-Atlantic. But the longer the coverage the thinner. U-boat sinkings rose from twenty-one in January to forty-one in March.[33]

British escort forces were strained to the utmost by the needs of these and other convoy routes, distant imperial lines of communication, guarding against invasion, and the war in the Mediterranean. The Royal Navy now had fifty former American destroyers of World War I vintage, exchanged for bases in the agreement of September 1940, but their short cruising radius, lack of maneuverability, and material defects due to age limited their usefulness. The blitz delayed repairs. In March over half the escort vessels in the Western Approaches to the British Isles were immobilized for lack of dockyard facilities and labor.[34]

This was also the most active period of the entire war for the big ships of the German navy. In contrast to World War I, Germany had access to the high seas through Norwegian coastal waters and preferred to attack British shipping abroad than to challenge the Royal Navy nearby. Though modest in size, the German navy was modern and well suited to commerce destruction. Its two remaining pocket battleships, the *Lützow* and *Admiral Scheer*, could cruise a great distance, outgun any cruiser, and outrun any but the most modern bat-tleship. Heavier and faster still were the twin battle cruisers *Scharn-horst* and *Gneisenau*. Most powerful of all was the newly completed *Bismarck*, the equal of any battleship afloat, soon to be joined by its sister ship, *Tirpitz*. German admirals sought to pass these heavy ships out into the Atlantic past the Faroes or Iceland for raiding cruises, but simply by riding at anchor in Kiel they tied down much heavier forces of the Royal Navy.

Early 1941 was a time of breakout and good hunting for the Ger-man navy. The *Scheer*, already at large, sank seventeen ships in a cruise to the Indian Ocean. In February the cruiser *Hipper* caught an unprotected convoy east of the Azores and sank seven. In February and March the pair of battle cruisers, prowling the shipping lanes near North America, scored twice. On March 15–16, some 500 miles southeast of Newfoundland, where traffic concentrated to pass around the Grand Banks and escorts departed, they destroyed or cap-tured sixteen ships and left convoys in that part of the Atlantic scat-tering in their wakes. Late in March the *Scheer* and *Hipper* broke back to Norwegian waters through Denmark Strait, between Iceland and Greenland, while the *Gneisenau* and *Scharnhorst* diverted British attention by reaching Brest. Meanwhile raiders in distant oceans dis-guised as merchant vessels sank thirty-eight ships in the first half of 1941. And the great *Bismarck* readied for sea.[35]

In March 1941, Britain was losing ships at the rate of over 500,000 tons a month, and losses were on the rise. U-boats were sinking about half the ships, with naval raiders and aircraft accounting about equally for the rest. This gave an annual rate of more than five mil-lion tons, roughly a quarter of Britain's merchant fleet. New building in shipyards now under blitz would replace at best only 30 percent of the losses. At this rate Britain would import for the year 14 percent less than its required minimum.[36]

The British government was not slow in conveying a sense of the threat to Americans. To begin with, Churchill gave "this new battle" a name. It was now not just a battle on the approaches to the British Isles but the Battle of the Atlantic, on the doorstep of the Americas as well. The prime minister formed a committee with that name to deal more effectively with the many-sided threat, and the name began appearing in American headlines. "The Battle of the Atlantic Is On," proclaimed the *New York Times* on March 11. The *Washington Post* reported that German submarines were now operating on the Amer-ican side of the Atlantic. A U-boat, it was even said, was coming to sink ships off New York harbor. At the end of March, Churchill sent word to Roosevelt of "heavy disastrous losses."[37]

Now the principal concern of the president and his advisers, well bruited in speeches by officials and by the press, was how to ensure that the wealth of war materials becoming available under Lend-Lease arrived safely in Britain. On March 15, at the annual dinner of the White House correspondents, the president delivered a speech described as "one of the most powerful of his career." Roosevelt made it a bipartisan occasion, warmly greeting Wendell Willkie, his Republican opponent of 1940. He sought to move the minds of Americans ahead from the "great debate" over Lend-Lease to the delivery of goods to the battle lines. Upon the will of his countrymen to sacrifice, work harder, and increase the tempo of production depended "the survival of the vital bridge across the ocean—the bridge of ships that carry the arms and the food for those who are fighting the good fight." But "[s]peed, and speed now" must be the watchwords, "now, now, ... NOW."[38]

That same day orders went to the United States Atlantic Fleet, then conducting amphibious exercises in the Caribbean, to return at once to home ports on the East Coast, there to strip ship of inflammables and peacetime conveniences, undergo overhaul, apply camouflage paint, and prepare for active duty. A squadron of destroyers due for transfer to the Pacific was to remain. Except in the Caribbean, neutrality patrols ended. Admiral Stark informed Admiral King that this was in effect an Atlantic war mobilization.[39]

Then on March 19 the president and his most comfortable friends—Robert Jackson, Harold Ickes, "Pa" Watson, Ross McIntyre, and Harry Hopkins—left for Fort Lauderdale and a fishing cruise to the Bahamas, his first vacation in several months. The presidential yacht *Potomac* was escorted by two destroyers. The sea was rough, but Roosevelt "worked at his stamps and fished much more assiduously than any one else," according to Ickes. As the Atlantic Fleet readied, the president soaked up sun and sea air and turned over in his mind how to protect the "bridge of ships."[40]

Chapter 2

April
Balancing Risks

As Roosevelt headed south to relax and ponder, Matsuoka Yōsuke, foreign minister of Japan, journeyed westward across the Soviet Union dreaming of accomplishing a diplomatic coup by his forthcoming negotiations in Moscow and Berlin. He envisioned a four-power entente embracing the Axis powers and the Soviet Union through which Japan could adjust problems in the north and free itself to achieve self-sufficiency in resources in the south and a New Order in East Asia. As his special train traversed the unending white wastes of Siberia, the diminutive, combative diplomat passed the time drinking vodka, telling his staff "how he would make puppets of Hitler and Stalin," writing short poems "full of subtle twists of thought," or simply meditating while sipping tea.[1]

A decade earlier, during the Manchurian crisis, the Japanese could not have imagined their foreign minister settling accounts in Moscow, or seeking Berlin's help in the matter. Neither could they have conceived of their nation's present sweeping confrontation with the British Commonwealth and the United States on top of a never-ending war with China. As Japan expanded, so did its problems. Its feeling of vulnerability intensified; fears of encirclement magnified. As defense needs increased, so did impoverishment in war resources. By 1941 Japan had greatly enlarged the portion of the world it considered vital. The precise nature, boundaries, and means of accomplishment of the "Greater East Asia Co-Prosperity Sphere" were still uncertain, but the military was increasingly taken with the idea of seizing Southeast Asia, especially for its oil, and securing a broad realm of imperial self-sufficiency.

Japan's aggressiveness derived from more than its share of irrationality. Policy was misconceived because the process that formed it was basically incoherent. The problem was not simply that the military

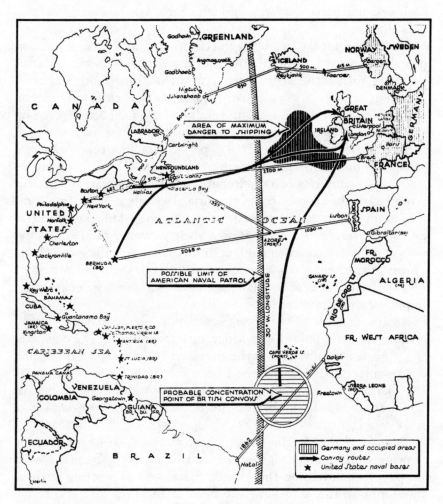

The Battle of the Atlantic: *New York Times*, April 27, 1941.

dominated policy from 1931 onward and civilian restraints were lacking, for officials in the foreign ministry and elsewhere, indeed prime ministers, often shared military preconceptions. Nor was the problem limited to differing strategic objectives and bureaucratic interests of the army and navy, so that policy usually embraced something of both and more than Japan could afford, though this was a central difficulty.

The main fault lay in the way decisions within the bureaucracies percolated upwards rather than flowed downward from some central authority, such as the Meiji oligarchs of the late nineteenth and early twentieth century, with a broad perspective and the capability of establishing priorities and judging ends and means. The influence of subordinates was not necessarily insubordinate. That had existed, it is true, in the army in the 1931–36 period, reaching proportions of conspiracy and mutiny. But discipline had been restored. Nevertheless, subordinates retained the initiative. They precipitated policy by action, as in the cases of the Kwantung, Tientsin, and South China field armies, or, as factions or committees in the middle range of the military bureaucracies, they pressed their views on their superiors, who endeavored to accommodate them. As a result the more chauvinistic, parochial, and activist elements of both the army and navy had undue influence so that Japanese policy was the more belligerent, impulsive, and opportunistic.[2]

Japan's inchoate drive for self-sufficiency interacted with violent changes in world politics and widening opportunities. The debilitating struggle in China turned the attention of the army southward to the resources of Indochina, the Dutch East Indies, and Malaya and the chance these weakly protected colonies presented of sealing off China from outside aid. In this direction of advance both army and navy could agree.

German victory in the west in May and June 1940 presented a glowing opportunity. Matsuoka saw alliance with Germany as a means of immobilizing the United States and preventing it from interfering in the southward advance. He and Prince Konoe Fumimaro, the prime minister, also saw the pact as a means of improving relations with Moscow by way of the Nazi-Soviet ties of 1939, thereby gaining security in the north before prosecuting advance in the south. At the same time, the terms of alliance left Japan considerable flexibility in determining whether it would enter a German-American war.

Matsuoka stopped in Moscow for a day to prepare the ground for negotiations before continuing to Berlin to see what influence Germany might bring to bear. The answer was none. Hitler did not disclose his intent to attack the Soviet Union to his Axis partner, though Matsuoka undoubtedly picked up the rampant diplomatic speculation on this question. The Fuehrer, showing no interest in an improvement in Japanese-Soviet relations, urged a Japanese attack on Singapore. The Japanese army and navy were not yet ready to go that far, so Matsuoka had to decline a commitment. Leaving Berlin empty-handed he returned to Moscow on April 7 to see what could be salvaged in a separate Soviet-Japanese agreement.

Evidence of growing Japanese ambitions in the south was accumulating in London and Washington. Japan was seeking a vastly greater allocation of oil, especially aviation-grade crude and aviation gasoline, from the Dutch East Indies. American Standard-Vacuum Oil Company, a principal producer in the Indies, was keeping the Department of State closely informed. The Dutch and the oil companies fended off Japanese demands with a temporizing agreement in November 1940, but the contracts were soon due for renegotiation.[3]

In February 1941, Japan, with appropriate displays of naval strength in the Gulf of Siam and South China Sea, insisted on mediating border clashes between French Indochina and Thailand, leading to fears of French or Thai compensation in the form of bases opening the way to Burma, the Indian Ocean, and Singapore. Britain sounded the alarm and urged an American warning. A war scare ensued with Australian reinforcements moving to Malaya, the Dutch recalling their shipping, and warnings in the press of an impending Japanese "lightning stroke." The American embassy at Tokyo on its own initiative warned the vice minister of foreign affairs that if Japan threatened British imperial communications it "would have to expect to come into conflict with the United States." Shocked, Ōhashi Chuichi replied: "Do you mean to say that if Japan were to attack Singapore there would be war with the United States?" Eugene Dooman, counselor of the American embassy, replied, "The logic of the situation would inevitably raise that question." American leaders, with MAGIC to go by, correctly doubted that Japan was ready to go as far as base acquisition at the moment, and indeed the crisis subsided.[4]

Only at the moment, however; the menace persisted. MAGIC intercepts revealed that Japanese consular officials at Singapore were ordered to secure evidence of Chinese dissatisfaction with British rule because "our troops are moving southward." Urgent instructions went to consuls in the Dutch East Indies to secure maps of the islands. In an intercepted report of March 24 from the Japanese embassy in Berlin, Reichsmarshall Hermann Goering had strongly urged on Matsuoka a Japanese attack on Singapore, confiding that after the forthcoming invasion of Britain, Germany would crush the Soviet Union.[5] Accordingly Washington looked upon Matsuoka's journey with apprehension, fearing some agreement that would accelerate the southward advance.[6]

Franklin Roosevelt had not really found any answer to Japanese aggression. He was a Europeanist. As a child he had spent time in England, France, and Germany and had been taught German and French. He believed he understood Europeans. Of Asia he had no direct experience. Often he spoke of his family's involvement in the China trade as if seeking authority in ancestry. He could be discerning about China and was positive about its future, but his tone was patronizing and he kept Chinese problems at arm's length. He knew a great deal about the Japanese navy from his experience in World War I, and this inclined him to be distrustful and negative about the nation as a whole.[7] In thinking about Asia he was not immune to the stereotypes and racial bias of his class and society.

Americans, in contrast to the Japanese, operated from a sense of invulnerability, at least until 1940, and resource abundance. Europe was at the center of their world concerns, Asia at the edges. Americans had invested great hopes in China. Its struggle against the Japanese invaders aroused widespread sympathy and deepened hostility toward Japan, yet China's portion of American trade with Asia in the 1930s, which in itself was a minor portion of total foreign trade, was only 13 percent, while trade with Japan was 36 percent and with Southeast Asia 35 percent.[8] The Philippines were due for independence in 1946. Defending them were one weak American-Filipino division, a hundred or so obsolete airplanes, and an Asiatic Fleet of World War I vintage except for one modern cruiser. The United States Pacific Fleet at Hawaii lacked the superiority, training, and auxiliaries to risk an encounter with the Imperial Japanese Navy in the western Pacific.[9]

Preoccupation with the economic depression and weakness at the Asian periphery made for caution and avoidance in dealing with Japan. During the 1930s, non-condonation and non-provocation governed policy.[10] As Japanese expansion widened, the policy of gingerly complaint persisted, but behind it the outline of a blunter conception appeared: the idea that the nations surrounding Japan should cooperate to stop Japanese aggression. Multilateralism had been the dominant mode of nations dealing with the international problems of East Asia, tolerable even to a United States otherwise horrified by foreign entanglements. Secretary of State John Hay's

Open Door notes (1899) seeking to maintain the old treaty system in China and Secretary of State Charles Evans Hughes' leadership of the Washington Conference (1921–22) are cases in point. The idea followed from Wilsonian faith in collective security and the appeal to principle in successive American protests against Japan's unlawful aggressions.

In October 1937, as the fighting in China escalated to full-scale war, the commander of the United States Asiatic Fleet, Admiral Harry E. Yarnell, cast about for a concerted way of dealing with the "international gun man" of East Asia. In a letter which came to President Roosevelt he drew attention to Japan's dependence on external sources of raw materials. The United States, Britain, France, the Netherlands, and the Soviet Union should join in a common front to cut off all trade with Japan, simply attacking Japanese commerce from their distant encircling bases, while China tied down Japanese troops. The result would be "strangulation" of Japan without the cost of huge armies or the risk of Jutland-style naval battles.

This made a "lot of sense" to Roosevelt. It reminded him of the successful American strangulation of Tripoli in the Barbary wars and of an article he had written for *Asia* magazine in 1923. That piece, aimed at bettering relations with Japan, had warned that war between the two nations would result in strategic deadlock and the outcome would be decided by economic strength, "in which the United States had, and has, a vast superiority."[11]

The idea of concerted action and long-range blockade of Japan in the worst extremity was dormant but by no means extinct in Roosevelt's thinking. Under consideration in 1940 were plans for sending a task force consisting of the aircraft carrier *Yorktown* and four heavy cruisers with escorts to the Java Sea to assist the British and Dutch in defending the so-called Malay Barrier (the line of the Malay Peninsula, the Dutch East Indies, and eastward to the Fiji Islands). In October 1940, when Roosevelt was considering various measures against Japan, he toyed with the idea of setting up two lines of patrol vessels to intercept Japanese shipping, in effect a long-range blockade, but was dissuaded by the navy.[12]

However, joint containment of Japan remained only an idea. World concern focused on the German threat in Europe. British naval power concentrated in European waters, leaving the Singapore base vacant. Soviet-American relations, which had never solidified in the thirties, turned abysmal with the Nazi-Soviet Pact of 1939 and the subsequent Soviet attack on Finland. In November 1940, Amer-

ican strategic policy itself turned away from the Pacific to a preoccupation with ensuring the survival of Britain.

Strategic reassessment began among American naval leaders frus-
trated with the immobility of the Pacific Fleet, tied to Pearl Harbor,
too weak for its original mission—a main fleet engagement with the
Japanese in the western Pacific—yet too far away to be of practical
use in the desperate circumstances which the United States faced
across the Atlantic. On November 12, 1940, Admiral Stark and his
staff completed a report for the president setting forth various strategic alternatives for the United States, among which the fourth, or
Plan D (in naval parlance Plan Dog), was the one they recommended.

The vital interest of the United States, according to the so-called
Plan Dog memorandum, lay in defending Britain and the British
Empire, requiring a concentration of effort toward Europe and invasion of the continent to defeat Germany. The memorandum questioned the wisdom of even limited war in the Pacific. The United
States simply did not have the ships to project American naval power
far west of Hawaii and also protect its more vital interests in the
Atlantic. The navy doubted how willing or able the British and
Dutch were to resist Japan or how much better chance of success they
would have with help from a reinforced Asiatic Fleet. Operations in
the western Pacific would divide the fleet and quite likely create their
own dynamic to the detriment of effort against Germany. A strategy
of Europe first meant a strict defensive in the Pacific and avoidance
of war with Japan if possible. The Pacific Fleet must be held close to
Pearl Harbor for possible recall to the Atlantic.[13]

The strategy of Plan Dog gained the support of the army and
implicitly of President Roosevelt, though he never formally endorsed
it. Thus at the end of 1940 a powerful consensus for strategic focus
on Germany developed at the highest levels in the American government. At a meeting of his defense advisers on January 17, 1941,
Roosevelt concluded that the primary objective must be maintenance
of the supply lines to Britain and ordered the navy to prepare for
escort of convoys. That meant standing on the defensive in the
Pacific, keeping the fleet close to Hawaii, sending no Asiatic reinforcement, and permitting the Asiatic Fleet to withdraw from the
Philippines if necessary. The military course for the United States
would have to be very conservative while its military power developed. However, Roosevelt did ask the navy to look into the possibilities of bombing Japanese cities.[14] The new strategic emphasis on
Europe was embodied in the individual and joint plans of the armed
services entitled RAINBOW 5.

The next step was to integrate American and British strategy. From the end of January to the end of March 1941, British army, navy, and air planners secretly met with their American couterparts in Washington. The result was an American-British-Canadian plan (ABC-1), in case the United States entered the war, for protection of Atlantic shipping, defense of Britain, buildup of forces there, and eventual invasion of the Continent.

The area of sharpest disagreement among the planners was cooperative action against a Japanese southward advance. The British strongly urged that the United States Pacific Fleet, or major portions thereof, be sent to Singapore, from which base, they argued, it could far more effectively deter a Japanese advance than at Pearl Harbor. Singapore, they held, was of cardinal importance to the British Empire and its war effort. If Japan could be deterred from seizing the resources of Southeast Asia by defense of the "Malay Barrier," they argued, economic pressure would then be sufficient to keep Japan in check.

The Americans, with their new-found Atlantic orientation, strongly disagreed. United States assistance in the defense of Singapore would be "a strategic error of incalculable magnitude," the army warned. American planners were dubious about the facilities and defenses of Singapore and worried about the risk of provoking war with Japan by sending the fleet to Asian waters. Furthermore, they resisted identifying the United States with European colonialism in Asia by participating in the defense of a British imperial bastion.

As a compromise the two sides agreed that in case of war approximately one-quarter of the Pacific Fleet would transfer to the Atlantic. Thereby an American force of battleships, a carrier, escorts and submarines could base at Gibraltar, releasing a comparable British force for transfer to Singapore. In this curious musical-chairs fashion the British at Singapore and the Americans at Pearl Harbor would provide a show of combined deterrence against Japan.[15]

The wraith of containment persisted. A letter of January 21, 1941, from Roosevelt to Joseph C. Grew, the American ambassador in Japan, emphasized the importance to Britain's defense at home of the resources and lines of communication in Southeast Asia. Yet the president could not say what might be done to protect these imperial interests or when. The letter to Grew from the president was written not by Roosevelt himself but by the State Department's political adviser for Far Eastern affairs, Stanley K. Hornbeck, who had the keenest interest in emphasizing East Asian stakes at a time when the strategic inclination was strongly toward Europe.[16] In the spring of

1941, President Roosevelt and his advisers really had no idea how the yawning chasm of military deficiency in Southeast Asia might be filled.

As Roosevelt rested during his fishing cruise in late March and considered what to do about the German threats to British shipping and communications, he had detailed recommendations from the United States Navy before him. Admiral Stark, chief of naval operations, urged maximum naval assistance to Britain as soon as possible, in effect full-scale entry into the Battle of the Atlantic. The German battle-cruiser attacks on shipping off the Grand Banks were challenging the U.S. Navy in its own front yard, but the devastating losses Britain was suffering on the Atlantic and in the western ports and the approach of the invasion season were matters of deep concern. Stark advised the president to put into effect, with modifications, the ABC-1 war plan which the navy was just then, with the British, shaping into final form. The reinforcement from the Pacific called for in the ABC-1 plan should come immediately so that the Atlantic Fleet could enter the battle as fast as ships became available and ready for action.[17]

Under the stern command of Admiral King, considered just the leader to shake the navy out of its "peacetime psychology," the U.S. Atlantic Fleet was beginning to evolve from a patrol and training force into a hard-bitten, make-do fighting organization.[18] It consisted of three battleships, five heavy cruisers, four light cruisers, two aircraft carriers, and fifty-nine destroyers. The Pacific reinforcement would add three battleships, one carrier, four light cruisers, and eighteen destroyers.

One of the main tasks of the beefed-up fleet would be to protect convoys in the western Atlantic against surface raiders. The battleships transferred from the Pacific, originally assigned to Gibraltar, would now join the existing Atlantic Fleet battleships and two heavy cruisers to provide each convoy with a battleship or pair of heavy cruisers as escort. None of these ships was a match for the *Bismarck* or *Tirpitz*. The *Texas, New York,* and *Arkansas* were built before World War I. Even so, they had heavier guns than Germany's pocket battleships and were comparable to the Royal Navy's Ramillies class of battleships, which they were supposed to replace. The Pacific reinforcements, the battleships *Idaho, New Mexico,* and *Mississippi,* had been extensively modernized with new turbines and gunfire controls and additional armor. More powerful than the German battle cruisers, they were now considered "the most effective fighting units in the battle line." The experience of February and March was that German raiders—even the *Scharnhorst* and *Gneisenau*—backed off in the face of any battleship escort.[19]

Equally important was the escort of convoys in the Western Approaches to the British Isles. Stark, who had been a staff officer to Admiral William Sims in London in World War I, was thoroughly familiar with such destroyer operations. The navy had already established a force of three destroyers squadrons, nine ships to a squadron, for this assignment. Two of these squadrons were composed of ships of limited utility—World War I four-stackers like those provided Britain in the destroyers-for-bases agreement; one boasted newly completed ships. These twenty-seven destroyers, gathering at Newport, Rhode Island, with additional patrol planes and Coast Guard cutters, formed what the navy designated enigmatically as the Support Force. It was to be ready for action by mid-May 1941 after six weeks of intensive antisubmarine warfare training, alterations, and trials. According to plans, it would operate from bases in Northern Ireland and Scotland and eventually from Iceland. Another squadron would join the three in July, and a fifth was promised for later. This would be a substantial reinforcement for the hard-pressed escort groups of the Royal Navy but still, even at maximum strength, amount to less than one-third of the British number.[20]

The remaining elements of the Atlantic Fleet and its Pacific reinforcement were given roving assignments. The two aircraft carriers, the *Wasp*, the navy's newest, and the *Ranger*, the oldest, were to form a striking force based at Bermuda for "catching" German raiders. A third carrier from the Pacific would make it possible to keep two always ready for sea. Four light cruisers from the Pacific, assigned to accompany the carriers, would relieve two heavy cruisers to form a striking force based on Iceland. Finally, four old light cruisers, each with two scout planes, would patrol the gap between Africa and Brazil.

Alongside the navy's proposal, and in fact prompted by it, was a plea from Churchill of March 19. The prime minster was frank to admit Britain's desperate circumstances, both to get help and to draw the United States as far as possible into the war. The onslaughts of the German battle cruisers gave him further opportunity. He carefully pointed out the novelty of attacks "so far to the west of the thirtieth meridian" which passes through the midpoint of Denmark Strait (between Greenland and Iceland) and which the Washington staff conversations were designating as the boundary between British and American command in case of war. Churchill dwelt on the difficulty of supplying convoys with battleship protection and then made a specific request for assistance. Raiders depended on supply ships stationed in little-frequented parts of the ocean such as the Sargasso Sea southeast of Bermuda, which the Royal Navy was unable to patrol for lack of ships. The United States, Churchill advised, could render aid under the banner of neutrality by sending warships with aircraft to "cruise about" in these "almost unknown waters," disclosing and disconcerting these secret rendezvous.[21]

This was all Churchill asked for personally but not all he sought. In January he had explained that the delay in bringing American destroyers already transferred into action had been due to refitting the ships not to lack of crews. Indeed, he said, the Royal Navy could man another thirty by April. The suggestion of another transfer also arose in the Lend-Lease debate as an alternative to American escort of convoys. Influential members of the House and Senate foreign relations committees favored it. So did the public. In a Gallup poll a majority approved turning over to Britain another forty or so destroyers. Congress defeated amendments to prevent it.[22]

On March 16, Ernest Lindley reported in the *Washington Post* that the administration was under "terrific" British pressure for more patrol bombers and destroyers. Bad news about the Atlantic arrived in a steady dirge, Churchill regretting the loss of valuable cargoes produced by American labor. March 27, the day Hitler extended the combat zone to Iceland, Harriman in London suggested sending ten destroyers or Coast Guard cutters. Few doubted that some would be sent. Either the United States would have to join in escort or provide escorts.[23]

The ever-cautious Cordell Hull feared that American participation in the Battle of the Atlantic, or even partial intervention leading to an incident and war with Germany, would raise a critical question for the Japanese of their obligations under the Axis alliance. War with both Japan and Germany must be avoided at all costs. Transfer of destroyers promised to provide the necessary assistance without war. On April 18, Lord Halifax reported that Hull had asked him personally and privately if Britain could find crews for twenty-five to fifty American destroyers.[24]

The United States Navy did not take kindly to this chorus of suggestions on how to use or dispose of it. It had seventy-four old destroyers left and despite their shortcomings was exceedingly reluctant to part with thirty, ten, or any. Rear Admiral Richmond Kelly Turner, director of the War Plans Division—"Terrible Turner" as he was known for his corrosive temperament—argued that every one was needed, eighteen now and nine as soon as possible for the Support Force, thirteen for the Asiatic Fleet, its only destroyers, eight for training sonar operators in tracking submarines, and only twenty-six to patrol the entire Caribbean and Pacific coast from Panama to Alaska. Besides, American crews used them more effectively than British because they understood them better. In case Britain were defeated, he added, or in case the United States entered the war it would need all the ships it could get its hands on for American requirements.[25]

The navy was indeed short of destroyers, old and new. The westward migration of U-boats forced it to provide at least two escorting destroyers for every cruiser, battleship, or carrier at sea. Aside from the Support Force, the Atlantic Fleet had only fourteen modern destroyers. Nine of these were due for major overhaul in May, and four were promised to the Support Force.[26] Two new destroyers were due in May, four more in June, and six later in the year, but "working up" took time—five months, reduced by Admiral King to two. To make up escort for warships he borrowed some of the modern destroyers of the Support Force, disrupting their submarine tracking, anti-aircraft, and depth-charge practice.[27]

That year tension was always severe in the navy between operational responsibilities and orderly expansion. All indicators known to its professional officer corps pointed to the need for more time. New destroyers needed time to overcome design problems, to catch up with scarce communications equipment, to install splinter shields to protect gun crews, to expand depth charge capacity, and to add anti-aircraft guns with compensating weight reductions topside.[28] Manning new ships meant breaking up trained ship companies and diluting the corps of veteran petty officers and skilled technicians. Ships were going to sea undermanned, with green crews. The supply of sonar operators from the fleet school at Key West was wholly inadequate. Destroyer crews needed the skills, supervision, and equipment provided by division and squadron command, especially for gunnery and the complex maneuvers and techniques of antisubmarine warfare and escort operations. Searching vast stretches of ocean for German supply ships seemed a waste of precious time. The navy believed it needed concentration not dispersion.[29]

Rather than dwelling on these deficiencies, Admiral Stark urged battle if not war. Britain's plight was certainly compelling, but the navy's zeal for action was reinforced by bureaucratic imperatives. Had the navy argued against assisting Britain on grounds of unreadiness or dwelt on the need for progressive intervention as contingents became ready, the argument for Lend-Leasing warships would have been hard to resist. Not to make too much of a point, there is some truth in the notion that the navy had to join the battle to save its ships.

On April 1, President Roosevelt returned to Washington from his vacation looking refreshed and tanned, and the next day met with his principal military and foreign policy advisers to consider what major steps might be taken to assist Britain. He had returned from his previous vacation in December with the idea for Lend-Lease. This time he had no new ideas, no tricks. He was in a discursive, reminiscent mood which kept his anxious advisers and their urgent problems at bay.[30]

On the one hand the navy urged intervention, a course strongly pressed by Stimson and Knox. For the hawks it was not only a question of critical, practical assistance for Britain but of providing evidence to occupied Europe and wavering neutrals of American leadership in the cause of freedom and determination ultimately to overcome Hitler and liberate Europe. At the moment the darkness over Europe seemed to be lifting slightly. The British had sunk three Italian cruisers and badly damaged a battleship at the Battle of Cape Mattapan. They had captured Addis Ababa and redeemed Ethiopia, the first victim of fascist aggression. The Greeks fought on against Italy. Britain was sending an army to help defend Greece against the approaching German Goliath. The *Washington Post* caught the excitement with a banner headline: BRITISH MASSING 300,000 MEN IN GREECE. It spoke of tanks "pouring" into Greek ports from a "vast convoy" of British ships. Roosevelt doubted the number of soldiers was as high as 100,000; in fact 62,000 arrived.[31]

Most "thrilling" of all to Stimson was news on March 27 of a coup in Belgrade overthrowing the government of Prince Paul, which had bowed to German pressure and signed up with the Axis two days earlier. With 1.2 million Yugoslavs moving to battle stations against the massing German forces, a Balkan front seemed to be forming. War in the Balkans at the very least would preoccupy and extend the Wehrmacht. Germany, said Britain's Foreign Secretary Anthony Eden, would be "only playing football in her own cabbage patch."[32]

The Yugoslav uprising was the first "great European event" since Lend-Lease, argued Walter Lippmann, evidence that the progressive abandonment of American isolation was changing the world balance of power. Lend-Lease, interventionists contended, made possible Britain's commitments in the Balkans, which in turn encouraged the Yugoslav uprising. According to Assistant Secretary of State A. A. Berle, Jr., some presidential advisers—Morgenthau and Supreme

Court Justice Felix Frankfurter, for example—thought that Britain and the United States were the only two civilized peoples in the world and that "the entire Continent of Europe ought to be written off...." However, Roosevelt, he believed, shared the contrary view that the United States needed all possible European support. Resistance to the Nazis depended on "faith in us, and hope that we will ultimately navigate their liberation." With Yugoslavia wavering, on March 24, Stimson noted in his diary, escort of convoy must come "practically at once." It was essential in the view of Alexander Kirk, a veteran diplomat who had just left the chargéship of the American embassy in Berlin, that Hitler's opponents conduct a display of force to prove to neutrals that "power is not the monopoly of Hitler alone."[33]

Roosevelt could do practically nothing to assist the victims and intended victims of aggression directly. He followed up Anthony Eden's suggestion through Hopkins of encouraging Turkey and Yugoslavia by informing them of American plans for support of Britain on a vast scale. To the government of Prince Paul he promised Lend-Lease if it resisted and warned implicitly that a Yugoslavia tamely submitting to threats would receive less sympathy for its postwar claims than one which fought even though vainly. He had promised the Greeks P-40 fighters but found none available and was not prepared to wrest any from the American army or the British. Older planes were substituted but even these could not be delivered in time. Informed of the further delay, the Greek prime minister remarked bitterly, *"Enfin seuls"* (In the end alone).[34] Illusions swiftly vanished on April 6, when the German army struck at Greece and Yugoslavia.

Disaster widened in the Balkans as Roosevelt searched for an Atlantic solution. In doing so he was certainly aware of the unreadiness of the Atlantic Fleet. In April he met exclusively with admirals at least five times. He knew that no destroyers would be ready for escort duty until mid-May at the earliest, that one of the battleships would be under repair until April 28 and another under overhaul until May 19, and that the *Ranger* required a three-month overhaul and installation of new arresting gear. The Pacific reinforcements, even if ordered immediately, would not arrive until the end of May. The United States had not enough troops for an expeditionary force of any importance, not enough transports to send them in, and not enough warships to protect them. In January 1941 American assembly lines turned out 159 bombers, of which seven went to the Army Air Corps and fifty-two to the navy. The rest went to Britain. They produced 248 fighters of which eight went to the army and twenty-five to the navy. A huge armament program was under way, but the keel of only one aircraft carrier had been laid since 1938.[35]

With such an immediate poverty of resources, how much of a contribution could the United States make by entering the Battle of the Atlantic immediately? Would it justify the probability of ensuing war with Germany and possibly with Japan as well? Would it justify the larger call on limited resources placed by the American armed services in case of war? Would it be wise to place scarce American naval vessels under British command in the United Kingdom when Hitler might yet strike through Spain toward Africa and the Atlantic islands or invade and defeat England before help came?

Roosevelt had solid reasons for shying away from escort of convoy quite apart from the American people's attitude toward a decision probably involving war, but public opinion certainly reinforced caution. Postmaster General Frank Walker and Secretary of Labor Frances Perkins, just back from the West Coast, reported that opinion there was "unsettled"; "lethargy and ignorance prevailed." The latest Gallup poll found that 83 percent of those surveyed would vote to stay out of war. At the same time, when asked whether it was more important to keep out of war or to help England, even at the risk of getting into the war, 67 percent chose to help England and risk war.[36] Opinion was educable, as it had been in the past, but Roosevelt undoubtedly believed that the benefits of intervention now did not justify the risks, domestic and external. As Roosevelt told Stark during a similar dilemma in 1940, "When I don't know how to move I stay put."[37]

Roosevelt did not plunge into the Atlantic war, but neither did he exactly stay put. On April 7 he ordered the battleships, aircraft carrier, cruisers, and destroyers of the Pacific reinforcement transferred to the Atlantic.[38] On April 10 he disclosed further plans to his closest advisers. He wanted an extension of the American defense zone across the Atlantic to include the Azores, some of the Cape Verde Islands, and Greenland (but not Iceland). He arrived at a boundary running well into the eastern part of the North Atlantic at first by picking the line of 25 degrees west longitude, which bisects the distance between northwest Africa and northeast Brazil, as the limit of the Western Hemisphere. As plans developed, Roosevelt dropped a hemispheric definition of the American security zone as too confining, but for the time being he shifted to the twenty-sixth meridian, one degree closer to the United States, excluding the Cape Verdes.[39] This was an historic departure. Before, American security had always depended on British control of the Atlantic. Neutrality patrols kept to the western side of the Atlantic. Now President Roosevelt incorporated the great basin of the North Atlantic in the American sphere.

At this time Roosevelt wanted not control but presence, a constant display of naval power by sweeps, patrols, and cruises of the Atlantic Fleet. Contrary to naval advice, he ordered dispersion and rejected escort. The navy bowed and devised Western Hemisphere Defense Plan One.[40] According to this plan the six battleships of the reinforced fleet, comprising Task Force 1, would individually patrol a set course running east in the latitude of Philadelphia to fifty degrees west longitude (the line of the west coast of Greenland), then northeast toward Iceland to the twenty-sixth meridian and the edge of the war zone declared by Germany and back. They would be like sentries marching toward and away from each other on their appointed path, parallel with the convoy lanes but several hundred miles to the east and south of them.

The aircraft carriers, Task Force 2, would meet Churchill's request for scouring untended waters. Each carrier would reconnoiter a slightly different wedge of ocean east of Bermuda toward the Azores. Task Force 3, the four old cruisers, would sail individually, with escort, from Puerto Rico or Trinidad southeastward toward Africa then back to Brazil and home. Task Force 4, the Support Force, would prepare for "distant service in higher latitudes." The deployment, if not the patrolling assignments, followed the navy's initial recommendation. All naval vessels were to trail the Axis ships they sighted and broadcast their location for British benefit.

Western Hemisphere Defense Plan One also for the first time permitted use of force, though under narrow constraints. American warships were ordered to prevent interference with American flag vessels in the expanded defense zone. Furthermore, in waters close by—the Gulf of St. Lawrence, the Caribbean, Bermuda, and otherwise within twenty-five miles of Western Hemisphere territory—patrols should warn away Axis ships (technically, vessels of nations having no territory in the Western Hemisphere) and attack them if they failed to heed the warning. Use of force extended to the defense of Greenland as well. In a direct challenge to the German combat zone proclaimed in March, the United States concluded an agreement on April 10 with the Danish minister in Washington bringing that entire Danish territory, even the portion east of the twenty-sixth meridian, under American protection.

For the press Roosevelt described the patrols as a reconnaissance in force and likened them to the band of scouts sent out far ahead of a wagon train to find Indians and prevent an ambush.[41] Roosevelt was barely edging into the Battle of the Atlantic. The novelties of Plan One were more symbolic than substantive. Nevertheless, it would establish a regular American naval presence in the central North Atlantic and raise the strategic question for the German naval command of whether to restrict operations or risk a major incident and war with the United States. Furthermore this established presence would endow American action in case of an incident with a defensive character, permitting Japan, if it chose, to avoid invoking its alliance obligations. And Plan One crossed a threshold in use of force.

American assistance was not entirely symbolic. Roosevelt could spare, if not destroyers, Coast Guard cutters. On March 29 he had ordered ten of the sturdy little ships, which were practical for escort duty, into British service. Then he approved a large new shipment of arms including sixty amphibious patrol planes which were exceptionally useful in spotting submarines.[42] In February the Admiralty had asked for repair in an American dockyard of the carrier *Illustrious*, its aircraft elevators damaged in a German dive bombing attack in the Mediterranean. That request was shelved while the Lend-Lease debate was going on. With Lend-Lease in hand the president immediately approved, and when Churchill asked assistance for the battleship *Malaya*, damaged by a torpedo, Roosevelt responded from his cruise that he would be "delighted," offering the Boston, New York, and Philadelphia yards. Upon his return to Washington, with warnings from Britain that the shortage of drydocks was critical, he sent Assistant Secretary of the Navy James V. Forrestal to London, where he and Harriman worked out an extensive, long-term warship repair schedule.[43] Thus American ports became a sanctuary for the Royal Navy.

By various devices Roosevelt also strove to thicken the "bridge of ships." On March 29 he authorized seizure of sixty-five ships of Axis and occupied nations in American ports. Altogether the United States managed to convey to the British about one million tons of Axis shipping and arranged for time charter of other vessels. On April 2 the president approved funds for building 200 more ships for Britain. Repair facilities were extended to the British merchant marine. In the last nine months of 1941, British shipping under repair in American ports averaged 430,000 tons a month.[44] The capture of Massawa in Italian Eritrea on April 8 cleared the Red Sea of

Axis forces and enabled Roosevelt to remove it and the Arabian Sea from the list of combat zones forbidden to American ships. This opening permitted the United States to take over a major share of the supply of British forces in the Middle East. As Harriman suggested, British arms and supplies for that front could now be sent in what otherwise would have been empty bottoms to the United States for transshipment.[45]

The logical corollary of deepening involvement on the Atlantic with risk of an incident and war was an easing of relations with Japan, particularly an effort to dissociate Japan from Germany as much as possible. The Roosevelt administration began a deliberate effort in April 1941 to explore the formidable issues that divided the two countries. The idea of wide-ranging discussions with Japan was novel, for no productive diplomacy had occurred between the two nations since the London Naval Conference of 1930. Talks about specific issues occurred from time to time in the 1930s but invariably led nowhere. With Matsuoka's advent as foreign minister no discussion seemed possible.

Yet, by 1941, not impossible. An encouraging sign was the appointment of Admiral Nomura Kichisaburō as Japanese ambassador to the United States. Roosevelt had been acquainted with Nomura when the latter was naval attaché in Washington during World War I. As foreign minister in 1939, Nomura had shown a keen interest in improving relations with the United States and was understood to be associated with anti-Axis elements in Japan. To Hull he looked different from most Japanese: "tall, robust, in fine health, with an open face."[46] Hull liked him and came to believe in his sincerity if not his skill. In February and March, Roosevelt and Hull repeatedly emphasized to Nomura their rising concern over Japan's identification with the Axis, on one occasion specifically mentioning Matsuoka, "astride the Axis on his way to Berlin, talking loudly as he goes," and stressed the importance of both countries finding ways of settling their differences peacefully.[47]

Meanwhile a peculiar opportunity for opening talks arose outside the normal channels of diplomacy. In 1940 Father James M. Drought, Vicar General of the Maryknoll Society (a Catholic organization), a zealous missionary and intensely political person, seized on the idea of becoming peacemaker between Japan and the United States. Peace was essential to the furtherance of the society's missionary enterprise in the Japanese empire and particularly in China. A letter from Lewis Strauss, whose New York investment firm, Kuhn Loeb and Company, had long-standing interests in Japan, introduced Drought to

Ikawa Tadao, a Japanese banker with important connections, among them Prince Konoe. Drought hoped to serve as a go-between for the principals in both countries, bypassing rigid bureaucrats in the foreign ministries. He sought to draft an agreement and ease the path of conciliation by allowing each side to believe the other had initiated it. The Japanese army took an interest in the scheme, authorizing a staff officer, Colonel Iwakuro Hideo, to join Ikawa. The foreign ministry, while taking no responsibility and fretting that these amateur efforts would go amiss, was interested in seeing what might develop.

During the winter, Drought, with the assistance of his superior, Bishop James E. Walsh, and U.S. Postmaster General Frank Walker, a prominent Catholic layman, spun his web of accord, gaining access to the White House, drawing in Ikawa, Iwakuro, and finally Nomura himself, and testing out peace formulas. The State Department, skeptical but observant, kept in touch. On April 9, Drought delivered a draft understanding to Hull which purported to have the support not only of the Japanese embassy but the Japanese army and navy as well.[48]

The April 9 draft was far from realistic as a basis for resolving issues between Japan and the United States. It would have permitted retention of Japanese troops in China after a peace settlement for "joint defense against communism" and would have required cessation of American assistance to Chiang Kai-shek if he rejected Japanese terms. The draft in no way diminished Japan's Axis obligations, but precluded American entry into "an aggressive alliance aimed to assist any one nation against another." Even Matsuoka speaking to Steinhardt in Moscow was more flexible about Japan's Axis obligations. If Germany declared war on the United States, he hoped America would consult Japan before making any move in the Pacific. If the reverse were the case, Japan would be obligated to go to war, but would consult Germany first. The vague and hortatory language of the draft agreement reflected the amateur quality of the Drought project.[49] Nevertheless it provided a comprehensive statement of issues and thus a ready vehicle for discussion of concrete problems. The State Department could use it without having to take responsibility for its provisions or for having initiated it.

These were days of deep anxiety. From the Balkans as well as North Africa the news was, in Berle's words, "as bad as it can be." The administration was dismayed at the rapidity and effectiveness of the German attack. Yugoslav resistance, in which the administration had placed great faith, according to *New York Times* columnist Arthur Krock, was simply vanishing. The official thermometer, he said, had dropped almost to the depths of Dunkirk. Officials feared the effect of another successful blitzkrieg on Turkey, the Soviet Union, Spain, and above all on American opinion, which might well revert to isolationism.[50] Meanwhile the destroyer U.S.S. *Niblack* was venturing into U-boat waters to make a reconnaissance of Iceland for a prospective American base there under the ABC-1 plan, and navy planners were drawing up orders for American warships to patrol far into the Atlantic.[51]

On Saturday, April 12, at 9:45 a.m., Admiral Stark phoned Secretary Hull, and a busy day followed at State. At 10:05 Hull saw Welles, at 1:30 Hornbeck, Maxwell Hamilton, chief of the Far Eastern Division, and Joseph Ballantine, the officer in touch with Father Drought. At 1:40 the secretary phoned Stark, at 1:45 Hopkins, and at 1:50 the president.[52] Clearly an important issue was being decided, one involving the navy and Japan. What probably prompted these discussions was word from Stark about the president's instructions for patrolling and reinforcements from the Pacific Fleet and the navy's plans to implement them.

The idea of talks with the Japanese was already under discussion. Ambassador Grew had recently sent a series of encouraging cables reporting the rise in influence of anti-German moderates in the Japanese government and Prince Konoe's success in gaining control of "radical elements" in the army. Matsuoka, according to Grew, had failed to obtain anything in Berlin and was not likely to be any more successful on his return visit to Moscow.[53] Some Far Eastern experts at State discounted such telegrams as another bout of Grew optimism, but the information fitted with what Drought, Ikawa, and Iwakuro were saying. At the very least, Hull and his advisers might tilt the balance slightly more against Matsuoka while the foreign minister was away and against the Axis forces in Tokyo. On April 11, Hornbeck drafted a counterproposal to the Drought draft of April 9, and Hamilton advised placing the Drought plan in Nomura's lap and asking whether he wished to introduce it as his own. That day or the next, the busy Saturday, Hull arranged to meet Nomura on Monday, April 14 at 9:15 a.m., either at his apartment in the Wardman Park Hotel or at the office.[54]

On Easter Sunday, April 13, news came of the signing of a neutrality pact between the Soviet Union and Japan. This was an unpleasant surprise. As late as April 11, Steinhardt had reported Matsuoka as doubtful about securing any agreement. The pact provided that if either nation became engaged in war with a third power, the other would remain neutral, and it also mutually recognized the independence of Manchukuo—the Japanese puppet state in Man-churia—and Outer Mongolia—a Soviet satellite in central Asia—both detached from China. Matsuoka had hoped for a considerably more substantial agreement, but Moscow, in spite of deteriorating relations with Germany, was not in the least disposed to make significant concessions to Japan. Hull was correct in telling the press that the significance of the pact could be overestimated as it really did not change circumstances. Yet privately both American and British officials considered the implications "very sinister," to use Welles' words. By offering some sense of security in the north, the pact provided an important argument for the southern advance in the internal debate over Japan's course of action.

In this connection, naval intelligence noted the shortening of Japanese lines in central China, the transfer of veteran troops from there and North China to Formosa and other staging points for southward advance, and the reorganization of Japanese fleets. Some Axis move such as a drive on Singapore seemed likely in order to prevent the diversion of American naval strength to the Atlantic. The director of naval intelligence estimated that Japan "will strike and soon." Turner, War Plans director, disagreed, but most American policy-makers believed the Soviet-Japanese pact enhanced the possibility of some Japanese move southward. Furthermore, the Soviet recognition of Manchukuo was a severe blow to China; any improvement in Soviet-Japanese relations would probably result in less Soviet aid to Chungking.[55]

By Monday morning, April 14, Hull's interest in talks with Nomura, inspired by Atlantic exigencies, was spurred on by those on the Pacific side. The two met secretly at the Wardman Park. Hull established that Nomura had collaborated in framing the Drought plan and would indeed be glad to present it as a basis for negotiations. The secretary of state then set conditions. First he would want to set forth the basic principles which the United States felt must undergird a settlement. Then Nomura, if he chose, could ascertain from his government whether a basis for negotiations existed. The two arranged to meet again shortly.

Hull saw Nomura again at the Wardman Park, Wednesday evening, after consulting his Far Eastern experts at least six times, phoning Walker twice, receiving Father Drought, and seeing the president. Monday he had suggested that talks proceed by stages with agreement at each stage before proceeding to the next. This was the cautious approach recommended by his Far Eastern advisers, but it was not the way he conducted the Wednesday session. To be sure, he

repeated his precondition that Japan fundamentally change its policies of conquest and use of force. He handed Nomura a paper listing
the four basic principles of international conduct espoused by his
government which Japan must adopt: respect for the territorial integrity of all nations, non-interference in their internal affairs, equality
of opportunity, including trade, and non-disturbance of the status
quo except by peaceful means. He made clear that the two sides had
"in no sense reached the stage of negotiations," and he denied "any
commitment whatever" to the provisions of the Drought draft.

Then, however, the secretary of state proceeded to move the talks
forward by collapsing his stages. He acknowledged that if the Japanese government approved the draft and proposed it, he "individually" would accept it as a basis for "negotiations," not simply discussions. His government could readily accept some of the proposals, he
said, but of course would have to modify and reject others, and would
want to offer some of its own. Nevertheless, if Japan were "in real
earnest about changing its course," Hull concluded, he "could see no
good reason why ways could not be found to reach a fairly mutually
satisfactory settlement." He did not follow the advice of his experts
and tell Nomura that before any agreement was signed the United
States would wish to consult the British and Chinese.[56]

No evidence exists that Hull and his advisers had a strategy of settlement, a set of rank-ordered priorities and conceivable concessions.
The United States remained entirely opposed to Japan on the key
issues of China, the Axis alliance, and the southward advance. Of
course it was anxious to take advantage of any possible shift in Japanese policy. More practically, however, by conveying a positive attitude toward the Drought draft, Hull was enticing the Japanese into
diplomacy as a means of searching out the Japanese position, weakening Axis ties, and delaying a southward advance. He was not without hope of settlement but was more interested in the process than
the results.

Nomura advised his government that it must now authorize him
to negotiate on the draft proposal, adding that he had definitely
ascertained that Hull on the whole favored it. Desiring to give the
Drought plan the best possible send-off and avoid complications
raised by the American preconditions, he withheld Hull's four principles. Thus, as the authority on the subject has said, the Hull-
Nomura talks commenced upon a "fundamental misconception."
The Japanese government gained a much more positive impression
of Hull's attitude toward the Drought plan and the possibilities of
settlement than was warranted. That misconception arose from ama-

teurish diplomacy by Drought, Nomura, and their cohorts, not from deception by Hull.[57] Even so, in a moment of intense anxiety and weakness, the United States desired to get diplomacy started and succeeded.

Given the central importance of Germany in the world politics of 1941 and general uncertainty as to Hitler's intentions, the great neutrals—the United States, the Soviet Union, and Japan—were bound to keep several irons in the fire. So Japanese-American talks complemented Japanese-Soviet talks, and Soviet-American talks complemented both. Of all these dialogues the most refractory and, at this stage, unproductive was the Soviet-American.

Relations between the two nations had reached a nadir in the autumn-winter of 1939–40 with the Nazi-Soviet Pact, Soviet absorption of the Baltic states—Estonia, Latvia, and Lithuania—and the Soviet "Winter War" on little Finland, including the bombing of Helsinki. On December 2, 1939, the United States invoked a "moral embargo," urging American companies not to sell to the Soviet Union airplanes or the materials, including key metals, that went into their manufacture.

Yet the fundamental congruity of Soviet and American interests could not be ignored. Parallel with the developing German-American confrontation in 1940 were German-Soviet tensions in eastern Europe and in the Balkans and the Soviet need of American war supplies in its drive to rearm. The United States placed no little emphasis on Soviet aid to China and the Soviet role in restraining Japanese expansion from the north. In July 1940, Welles began talks with the Soviet ambassador in Washington, Constantin Oumansky, to see what progress could be made in removing the obstacles to better relations. Given the "many dangers which would affect the Soviet Union" in coming months, he told Oumansky, the logical course for the Soviets seemed to be to improve relations with the United States, from which it had nothing to fear, rather than to push those relations further downhill.[58]

The talks proved a great trial for Welles. Soviet complaint and vituperation were constant; Oumansky was almost invariably nasty and sarcastic. He stayed in close touch with the German embassy in Washington.[59] The United States had no intention of recognizing a Soviet takeover of the Baltic states, or of releasing the ships and assets of those states, which it had impounded. In responding to Soviet protests over the difficulty of purchasing American goods, it complained of the continued and indeed increasing Soviet supply of goods to Germany. Especially irritating was the fact that the Soviet Union was buying more cotton in the United States and promising more to Germany.[60] Nevertheless American officials made efforts to ease some trade difficulties and on January 21, 1941 lifted the moral embargo. In February, Welles urged that when problems appeared irresolvable, they be "left standing for the time being in the midst of the stream" while the two of them addressed issues that seemed more yielding.[61]

Particularly the United States sought to establish the identity of Soviet and American interests against Germany. On March 1, Welles passed on to Oumansky the forecast of Erwin Respondek of a possible German attack on the Soviet Union, qualified as it was. The United States, he said, had authentic information "clearly indicating" such an attack in the "not distant future." The plan was, however, contingent on "the extent to which England, supported by American endeavor, will be able to oppose not only the military strength but also the economic efforts of Germany."[62] The implication was that Russia, by supplying Germany, was only bringing down on its own head the force of German arms. Welles noticed, undoubtedly with some satisfaction, that Oumansky "turned very white."[63] On March 20 he gave Oumansky his Swedish information about German plans for attack. On this occasion Welles also stressed the common interest of the two nations in the maintenance of peace in the Pacific and the territorial integrity and independence of China.[64]

Soviet apprehension over the German forward movement in the Balkans beginning in March provided further opportunity of identifying common interests. The Soviet government expressed its displeasure on March 4 to the Bulgarian government for permitting passage of German troops. On March 11 it publicly reaffirmed its non-aggression pact with Turkey, and on March 26 the United States publicly expressed satisfaction. Then on the eve of the Nazi attack on Yugoslavia the Soviets signed a pact of friendship and non-aggression with that country.[65] In an authorized statement to Welles on March 27, Oumansky agreed that when they came to an "unsurmountable obstacle" it should be left aside. "[M]any common denominators," he said, "can be found in the long-range policy of both ... Governments." On April 9, Welles noted for Oumansky the identity of opinion of both governments regarding Yugoslavia, and they agreed on how "profoundly disquieting" the German blitzkrieg in the Balkans was. On April 18, Oumansky made what an American official regarded as the "extremely interesting" comment that American attempts to influence Soviet policy by trade restrictions seemed especially pointless since the two nations would "eventually be on the same side anyway."[66]

These were, however, hypothetical exercises. Stalin was determined to avoid provoking Germany. His support for a Balkan front, like the American, was only by gestures. In arriving at a pact of the most limited nature with Japan, the Soviet Union undoubtedly hoped to keep open the possibility of a rapprochement with the United States. On April 18, Oumansky expressed Soviet satisfaction with Hull's statement that the significance of the pact could be overestimated and assured an American official that it did not concern China at all. However, the Soviets also counted on a Japanese move southward and on rival Japanese and American "imperialisms" to protect Russia's back door in Asia while it faced the threat from Germany.[67]

With German divisions whipping through the Balkans, Stalin's attitude toward Germany became positively supine. After signature of the neutrality pact, he took the extraordinary step of going to the station himself to send off the Matsuoka party. Amid much boozy merriment and bear-hugging, Stalin threw his arm around the shoulders of the German ambassador, Count von der Schulenberg, and said, "We must remain friends ... ," and to the German military attaché, clasping both hands of that surprised officer, "friends—in any event."[68]

The sharpened danger presented by the Soviet-Japanese Pact made it all the more important to maintain existing deterrence in the Pacific. Almost as important was to avoid any seeming weakening as diplomatic conversations with Japan began. On April 17, Roosevelt decided to postpone the transfer of warships from the Pacific except for the carrier *Yorktown* and five destroyers. With these ships the president could at least sustain the carrier searches east of Bermuda, as he had promised Churchill, and the patrols into the Africa-Brazil gap.[69] Postponement of the Pacific reinforcement, did, however, force Roosevelt to restrict his plans for the Atlantic. On the weekend of April 19–21, Admiral King worked with the president at Hyde Park to revise patrol plans. The result was Western Hemisphere Defense Plan Two, which was the same as Plan One except that use of force in proximity to American territory was denied. With only two battleships available now, patrols northward toward Iceland would be few and far between, and, as Roosevelt confessed to Stimson, not much help to the British. But for now he simply could not risk war in the Atlantic, nor weaken deterrence in the Pacific. Using Admiral King's words, the president said he simply did not have enough butter to cover the bread.[70]

Chapter 3

May
Guarding the Atlantic Line

At dawn on April 6 the German army burst from Bulgaria into Yugoslavia and Greece, preceded by air attacks that destroyed the command and communication center of the Yugoslav army in Belgrade and 41,000 tons of shipping at Piraeus. This was blitzkrieg in its most stunning form carried on by fast, powerful, elite units—no less than six armored divisions, the Adolf Hitler and Das Reich SS Divisions, two other motorized divisions, and two mountain divisions—besides infantry. Checked briefly here and there by stout defense or shortage of gas, the Panzer columns probed, circled and punched, then gathered speed as the will to resist dissolved. Attacking April 6, 8, and 10 from southeast, north, and northwest, the Germans captured Belgrade on Easter Sunday, April 13, and the next day began pulling forces out of the Balkans. Two right hooks through the southern tip of Yugoslavia, wheeling southward into Greece through the Vardar Valley and the Monastir gap, captured Salonika and uncovered the left flank of the British-Greek defenses before Mount Olympus. By April 16 the British were in full retreat across the plains of Thessaly. Outflanked every time they stopped to form a line of defense, they withdrew from Greece across beaches in the south in the last days of April. But Hitler had victory in the palm of his hand in scarcely more than a week of fighting.[1]

April and May was a time of disaster for Britain, not just in the Balkans but in the Middle East as well. On March 31 at Mersa Brega, where the coastline of Libya turns from a southerly direction, leaving Cyrenaica, to a westerly one toward Tripoli, a single German division under General Erwin Rommel had tested British defenses, pressed forward and by April 3 so disorganized the British desert force that it began a harried retreat all the way back to the Egyptian border, leaving behind a besieged Tobruk. On April 3 at the other end of

"Possible Axis Moves in the Quest for Victory": *New York Times*, June 15, 1941.

the Middle East, in Baghdad, a coup brought to power Rashid Ali el-Gailani and a junta of anti-British, pro-Axis Iraqi army officers who called themselves the Golden Square. Desperate for troops, the British rushed forces from India to Basra, but before they arrived Iraqi insurgents surrounded the principal British base and airfield in Iraq at Habbaniya. By the second week of May, German planes were stopping in Vichy-held Syria en route to Iraq with supplies for Rashid Ali. Meanwhile mines dropped from airplanes interrupted traffic in the Suez Canal. Everywhere, from the Danube to the Euphrates, Tripolitania to Egypt, German power advanced; everywhere British forces were encircled, routed, or held at bay.

The shadow of the German army raced ahead of it. At a time when Rommel had one division and another moving up, the American embassy in Rome, struck by the number of troops and sand-colored tanks embarking at Naples, estimated twenty-five German divisions in Africa and another ten ready to go, with 2,000 tanks and 2,000 more to come.[2] The tendency was to exaggerate, both regarding German intentions and capabilities. Indeed the mood verged on panic. American officials in the region foresaw a German drive on Cairo, possibly by a deep encirclement through the desert to the Nile.[3] In that event and unless British tank and aircraft reinforcements arrived in time, warned the military attaché in Cairo, a disaster was "almost inevitable."[4] Americans in Cairo were warned to leave if possible; British children, it was said, were quietly being sent to Turkey. In Washington the navy's War Plans Division began considering the strategic consequences of a British defeat in Egypt and withdrawal of the Mediterranean fleet. From London came warning of a coordinated German attack on Suez and Japanese attack on Singapore. Brigadier General Miles, chief of American army intelligence, concluded that the principal theater of German operations would now be the Mediterranean.[5]

Observers saw the drive on Suez as one claw of a vast German pincer movement, the other claw striking through the northern tier of the Middle East—Turkey, Iraq, and Iran—toward India, possibly in cooperation with the Japanese. Strengthening that view was German assistance to the revolt in Iraq. It would not be unlike Germany, of course, to blackmail Turkey or Russia into permitting passage of German troops into the further reaches of the Middle East.

Washington felt growing discouragement with British military performance. So extensive and stinging was criticism among military intelligence officers that Stimson complained to Marshall. He considered them too admiring of German efficiency. The safety of the

United States, he pointed out, depended on the British fleet, which in turn depended on the preservation of the Churchill government "and the life of the promise made by Churchill last summer to keep the fleet at all odds. . . ." However, even the president was troubled by the British retreat in the desert. Symbolic of this nadir of ill fortune, this "torment of mankind," as Churchill put it that month, was the wrecking of the House of Commons by German bombs on May 11.[6]

Germany was a "military colossus" of immeasurable capabilities. General Sir John Dill, chief of the Imperial General Staff, believed nothing could "prevent the Germans from going anywhere they wish on the Continent, and this might include overrunning the Russian Caucasus." Ambassador William Phillips in Rome was impressed with how smoothly the Germans moved troops and matériel to Africa: it took only one hour to empty a ship, "and during that hour not one order was given by word of mouth!" The seemingly effortless and crushing German blitz in the Balkans was mesmerizing. Admiral Leahy noted "bitter gloom" at Vichy. Because of the rapidity of the German advances, he wrote, French hopes of a British victory had sunk to their lowest since the armistice of 1940. The Spanish press featured speeches by Charles Lindbergh, indicating the popularity of coming to terms with "conquerors," according to the American embassy at Madrid. The Swedes seemed less inclined than a month earlier to resist German demands to join the Axis.[7] A sense of impending German triumph gripped Europe. No evidence existed of American intervention in time.

In fact, the German army, so many ways impressive, was by no means superhuman and faultless. German capabilities were not unlimited. Hitler had large but sequential goals for 1941. Nevertheless, to the world he seemed headed anywhere and everywhere.

Overshadowing speculation about German designs in the Middle East were multiplying signs of a German attack on the Soviet Union. As snows melted and the campaign season approached, talk of war in the East intensified. The *New York Times* took up the possibility on three occasions in the first half of May. The London *Times* on April 20 noted Churchill's hint of German designs on "the granary of the Ukraine and the oilfields of the Caucasus." That prediction, it claimed, was confirmed by many sources in central Europe. Germany, reported the *Times*, was sending a "great army to the Russian frontier": "Trainloads of infantry and artillery equipment are rolling eastward." Factories were producing railway cars with the Russian gauge. Forced labor gangs were building roads and air bases near the frontier. Hitler, it was said in the London *Times* on May 4, would march because he required the resources of Russia and knew he could not obtain world dominion "without first [consolidating] ... his European conquests."

By mid-May it was clear from reports of American military attachés that Germany was gathering sufficient force for an attack on Russia. The attaché in Berlin placed most armored divisions in the east. Germany was training administrators for Russia, printing money for use in Russia, conducting aerial reconnaissance of the border, building military hospitals, and setting up army group commands. The illustrious Field Marshal Gerd von Runstedt was taking a command in the east.[8]

Indeed, by May preparations were impossible to disguise, for by then 300 trains a day moved eastward. German military basing in Rumania, noted the attaché in Bucharest, was aimed eastward toward Russia, not southward toward the Balkans. Motorized columns were "wending their way ... covertly by night" toward Moldavia and the Russian frontier. Trains passed due eastward from Hungary through Cluj rather than southeastward toward Bulgaria. After the Balkan blitz, attachés noted heavy traffic northwestward, especially by armored and motorized divisions, through Budapest and Vienna and then northeastward through Czechoslovakia to southern Poland. German mechanized forces were passing through the key Czech railroad junction of Bratislava night and day toward the Russian border.[9]

American estimates of the number of German divisions arrayed against the Soviet Union were close to the mark. The military attaché in Berlin arrived at a total of 89 on April 17, excluding Rumania; on May 1 there were in fact 103, including that sector. He estimated 120 on May 23, the number reached on May 20. The Russian military attaché in Berlin put the number somewhat higher. On April 21 he doubted an immediate attack, but confessed to his American counterpart that "all indications point to such an attack."[10]

Impressive as the evidence was of a forthcoming attack, most observers found it hard to believe that one would occur. The idea of an invasion of Britain died hard. At the end of April the American assistant military attaché in Berlin doubted that Germany had the means to invade Britain and "deduced" that its objective was to destroy Russia so as to dominate Europe and open the way to an attack on the empire as a means of destroying Britain at home. Yet in flat contradiction to this logic he concluded that Germany's likely course of action was to pursue these objectives in reverse order with an invasion of Britain first. At the same time, in Washington, General Miles was backing away from his Mediterranean emphasis and insisting that the British Isles was still the "decisive theater."[11]

The Berlin attaché offered a clue to this curious reasoning in a report of late March. Ordinarily, he said, the large percentage of German forces in the east would lead to the conclusion that an attack would occur in that direction, but forces facing England were still as large as could be used effectively, and air units had not been transferred to the east. "The most dangerous capability," he concluded, "is the ... one against England, and no serious error could be made by taking this stand and having Germany prosecute the ... capability against Russia." Since transfer of air units only became noticeable in late May, it is likely that this reasoning persisted.[12]

An invasion of Britain seemed more likely too because foreign observers tended to exaggerate the size of the German army. Both the Russian and American attachés estimated that the Germans had between 250 and 270 divisions, where in fact they fielded only 208. While estimates of divisions in the east were close to the mark, those elsewhere, as in France and the Low Countries, tended to be high, and German intelligence undoubtedly encouraged such exaggeration.[13] Invasion of Britain seemed the more plausible because of reports from London that reflected the British army's insistence, at least through May, that invasion was coming. General Sir John Dill, for whom the Americans had a high regard, thought it would occur about July 1. Of course, without massive preparations at the Channel ports, chances dwindled as the spring progressed, but for the first part of May at least, the cross-Channel attack possibility further confused the American picture of German intentions.[14]

While the buildup in the east was proceeding at a moderate rate, stories that this was to protect Germany's rear for the invasion of Britain or that these were troops training for that invasion or preparing for Balkan operations had some utility for German intelligence. By April, however, a new cover scheme was needed. Now the notion was encouraged that the military concentration was for the purpose of cowing Russia into making concessions.

Of course the idea of a German-Soviet settlement was not unfamiliar: the Ribbentrop-Molotov pact and subsequent trade agreements, the most recent just in January, provided historical perspective, as did the more distant Rapallo period of cooperation in the 1920s. Dictators and totalitarian regimes were expected to make unscrupulous bargains. Nothing had occurred in the Welles-Oumansky talks to provide American officials with a more favorable view, and the Soviet-Japanese Pact was hardly encouraging. Stalin, Ambassador Steinhardt reported May 5, had told one Soviet official that he expected, rather than war, satisfactory negotiations with Germany. Undoubtedly rumors that Germany intended to secure an enforced diplomatic outcome took root in the diplomatic corps of Moscow and Berlin like a weed in wet and fertile soil, an idea that German intelligence cultivated.[15]

Chargé Morris in Berlin took the bait, but he was by no means unique. He felt "impelled" to report on April 13 the revival of talk that Germany would soon attack Russia, however lacking in good authority and logic such reports were. But these rumors, he argued, were "a deliberate attempt ... to arouse the apprehension of Russia and make it more amenable to Axis demands for supplies...." These were planted stories to impress Russia or divert it from German designs in the Mediterranean. In May he noted a stream of reports that German preparations were the "spearhead" of diplomatic and military pressure designed to encourage Russian trade concessions. On May 13, Morris cabled that informants of the highest authority, including one with access to Goering, told him that preparations for invasion of Russia were complete, that an ultimatum would shortly be presented demanding control of the Ukraine and the Baku oil-fields, and that Russian refusal would lead to invasion within a fort-night. He regarded this information with reserve, but for lack of con-trary reports, the ultimatum thesis held sway.[16]

Uncertainty over German intentions is manifest in the cables from the American embassy in Moscow. On the one hand Ambassador Steinhardt made plans for evacuation of his staff in case of the Ger-man bombing of Moscow, while on the other he relayed reports indi-cating Germany would merely brandish the sword and demand concessions and that the Soviets would yield. The Soviets had their limits, but Steinhardt expected Count von der Schulenberg to keep German demands within reason.[17] The comings and goings of Schu-lenberg and the Russian ambassador in Berlin were closely watched for signs of negotiations.

Reports from other American embassies in Europe had the same purport: that the situation in the Ukraine would be settled by June, by force if necessary; that the Germans were seeking joint exploita-tion of the Ukraine, Don basin, and Caucasus; that the concentra-tions were for intimidation and that the Soviets would succumb. An intercepted message from the Japanese ambassador in Berlin argued that Stalin's assumption of the chairmanship of the Council of Peo-ple's Commissars arose from the need to make great concessions to Germany. "Stalin and Company" would have to be dealt with even-

tually, a German official release for press guidance stated, but "pressure is being exerted to feel out sentiment toward first settling with
the Bolsheviks."[18] American diplomatic reports reflected just this sort
of inspired confusion.

Meanwhile fears of a German drive to the southwest through the
Iberian peninsula to northwest Africa and the Atlantic islands had
by no means receded. Though Hitler had been keenly interested
the previous September in German navy plans for seizure of the
Canaries, Cape Verdes, and the Azores (he called the Azores the
"turntable of the Atlantic"), his mind and Germany's resources were
now concentrated on the forthcoming Russian campaign. Even so,
the Germans were happy to have the British and Americans preoccupied with grim expectations in wrong directions, so the sinister
rumors of early spring continued to flow. More was heard about
troop concentrations at the Pyrenees, German "tourists" entering
Spain, Franco conceding German troop transit, and Spain and Portugal joining the Axis.[19]

These fears applied especially to the Atlantic islands. The Portugese garrison on Terceira in the Azores numbered a mere 5,400
with no artillery. Fayal was protected by four renovated six-inch cannon vintage 1898.[20] Whichever was at the forefront of American concern—Tangier, Tetuan, Madrid, Lisbon, or the islands—resources on
the spot seemed hopelessly weak and ineffectual. Another Norway
seemed quite possible, Germany using already infiltrated agents,
small forces in innocent-looking freighters, and airborne attack.
Intimidation, fifth columns, and parachute troops would make short
work of local defenses.

The Norway model of German infiltration and seizure applied as
well to French North Africa. In April the Germans secured permission from Vichy to send an additional 130–140 officers and men, for
a total of 200, to supervise the 1940 armistice in French North Africa.
Washington immediately warned Vichy this was a violation of the
Murphy-Weygand accord, the post-armistice Franco-American
understanding about North Africa. Also at hand was a British report
that German civilians suspected of being mechanics were infiltrating
into French Morocco to take over French armored vehicles "when
the zero hour comes." Another British report, proven false, had U-
boats already basing on Dakar and using French planes for spotting
convoys.[21] The British seemed to be vying with the Germans in
arousing American security concerns regarding this region, and
aroused the Americans became.

The most dramatic confirmation of apparent German designs on Africa was pressure on Vichy through May for concessions in Africa and the Middle East, culminating in the Paris Protocols of May 27–28, 1941—described by *Time* as the "second fall of France." The final agreement was not precisely a capitulation. It did not provide Germany immediate rights to the use of Dakar, the point of greatest American concern. That concession would come into effect after July 15 and depended on German allowance of reinforcements and provision of supplies for the French army in North Africa. But the agreement fully reflected the collaborationist inclination of Admiral Jean François Darlan and the weakness of Pétain, for it stipulated that Vichy supply trucks to Rommel's army and in Syria support German efforts to sustain the revolt in Iraq.[22] If France had not yet arrived at the point where the worst American fears were realized, during May it was definitely headed in that direction.

The State Department and the president were increasingly concerned about these German pressures toward the southwest. On April 30, Hull instructed Ambassador Alexander W. Weddell in Madrid to see Franco alone and promise a broadening of trade, suggesting as a beginning the exchange of olive oil for peanut oil and perhaps 200,000 tons of wheat. Here was an inducement for Franco to resist demands for troop passage. The same day Hull directed Admiral Leahy to see Pétain alone, express American concern over German pressure for concessions in North Africa, troop transit across unoccupied France, and collaboration if not participation in the war, and offer two shiploads of food, provided of course France rejected collaboration. The Marshal gave satisfactory assurances, mentioning, however, that Darlan was then in Paris for consultation with the Germans. Roosevelt himself responded, specifically restating the French assurances, and the gloom lifted momentarily.[23]

Then on May 12 came most disturbing news. Pétain was said to be deeply depressed over decisions he would have to make in the next several days. The Germans apparently had made broad demands at Paris. The following day when Leahy saw the Marshal, though not alone this time, he met ominous words. Pétain assured Leahy only that he would not "give any voluntary active military aid to Germany," with emphasis on the word "voluntary." In response to Leahy's assertion that the United States was sure to defeat Germany in the end, the aged leader expressed "great skepticism." Clearly, said Leahy, the trend of French policy was toward collaboration. He foresaw no further serious French resistance to German demands. Admiral Darlan was making the all-too-familiar pilgrimage to Berchtesgaden. Afterwards, diplomatic circles expected a Hitler-Stalin meeting, the *New York Times* reported, to complete the economic reorganization of an Axis-dominated Europe.[24]

As of May 14 the American government was entirely confused about German intentions. Depending on whom one asked, Hitler might be sending his army in any one or two of four directions. It was confused partly because of German tactics of deception and partly because the German army, especially just then, seemed capable of almost anything. Intelligence assessments tend to reflect the course of action most feared: the British army, for example, still clung to its belief in a German cross-Channel attack.[25] The American army felt most vulnerable from a German drive through Spain toward the Atlantic islands and the African coast of the Atlantic. These were on Hitler's agenda, but only after the Russian campaign. Not knowing this, Roosevelt and his advisers concentrated on guarding the Atlantic.

A warming sun and blossoming cherry trees did not raise spirits in Washington that spring. In the case of President Roosevelt, the disheartening news and confusing intelligence from Europe arrived with a debilitating series of colds and bouts with flu, worsened by iron deficiency anemia from bleeding hemorrhoids. For days at a time in May and June he was in bed. Harry Hopkins or "Missy," Marguerite LeHand, his secretary, kept him company for dinner; an occasional adviser was allowed to lunch. April 24 he saw former ambassador William Bullitt, who made allegations of homosexuality against Sumner Welles. Roosevelt acknowledged that there was some truth in the charges, according to Bullitt, but explained that Welles' usefulness at State outweighed the security risk. Bullitt persisted, warning he could not accept further assignment so long as Welles remained, and the president abruptly terminated the meeting, saying to his military aide, General Watson, "Pa, I don't feel well. Please cancel all my appointments for the rest of the day." Mostly, according to LeHand, Roosevelt was suffering from exasperation.[26] The heart of the problem was that, faced with large and uncertain threats, he had totally inadequate military forces and was unsure what to do.

The Atlantic Fleet began patrolling under Western Hemisphere Defense Plan Two in the last week of April, but much more thinly than originally planned since most of the reinforcement from the Pacific had been postponed. The heavy cruisers *Wichita* and *Tuscaloosa* departed from Newport, Rhode Island, on April 26 for a three-week patrol, and the battleship *Texas* sailed May 5, but with the *New York* and *Arkansas* under overhaul, the next patrol was not scheduled until May 23. The Stars and Stripes would rarely be seen near the convoy routes at this rate. The carrier *Wasp* departed April 26 on a two-week cruise toward the Azores. The *Ranger* followed on May 9, and the *Wasp* was due again on May 21. The first cruise of the *Yorktown*, the only large ship so far transferred from the Pacific, would not begin until May 31, when the *Ranger* went into dock for overhaul. The great wedge of ocean assigned the carriers, lying between Bermuda, the Azores, and a point midway between the Antilles and the Cape Verdes, was largely untended. The portion of it where German supply ships were most likely to be waiting approached a million square miles in size. Further south, the first cruise into the gap between Africa and Brazil was scheduled for the *Milwaukee,* departing May 20.[27] The current ability of the fleet to spot raiders and their supply ships in the Atlantic was negligible, to say nothing of displaying force and covering landings.

These searches fell far short of what Churchill wanted. April 24 he asked for air reconnaissance south and east of Greenland, where U-boats were now hunting, and off Newfoundland, where raiders had found good pickings. He especially wanted planes from the American carriers to provide air search ahead of the convoys moving northward past the Azores and Cape Verdes. The British were prepared to send expeditions to hold these islands and prevent German capture but feared a surprise seizure before their own troops arrived. An American naval squadron roving the area might not only provide air search but also warn the Germans off and, as Churchill put it, "keep the place warm for us."[28] As it was, however, a carrier would be in the area only one or two days in every ten.

The army and its air force were even less ready. Only one army division, the 1st Infantry, was adequately trained and equipped for combat. War Department planners could list two divisions as due by May, four by July and seven by September but the actual state of training and equipping usually lagged far behind estimates. The 1st Marine Division was also a ready force, but its strength as late as November 30, 1941, was less than 10,000 men. The army air force possessed—overseas and at home, Atlantic and Pacific—53 heavy bombers, 91 medium bombers, 92 light bombers, and 327 fighters. The Germans by contrast were readying over 2,700 planes for the attack on Russia.[29] The military weakness, if not nakedness, of the United States was temporary. Vast forces were in process of formation. But for Franklin D. Roosevelt in May 1941 the cupboard was almost bare.

At this time the president had a dream which vividly portrayed the frightening circumstances facing him: with German planes threatening New York City he took refuge at Hyde Park in a bomb-proof cave provided by the Secret Service 200 feet under the Hudson cliffs, where he stayed until a German squadron passed over and departed.[30]

The one military force available to ease American security concerns on the Atlantic was the Pacific Fleet, and intense debate persisted from April into June at the highest levels over moving a portion of that fleet to the Atlantic, whether the postponed ABC-1 reinforcement or more.

At times the Atlantic and Pacific fleets seemed like different navies. The latter had power and symmetry: twelve battleships, three carriers, three divisions (four each) of heavy cruisers, three divisions of light cruisers, and fifty destroyers. Though the fleet rarely anchored, steamed, or docked all together in one mighty spectacle, it operated from one base, Pearl Harbor, and the double row of battleships alongside Ford Island, the strings of destroyers in East Loch, and the looming carriers *Lexington* and *Saratoga* were familiar sights from the main highway skirting the harbor. To a visiting British naval observer, the sight was "magnificent."[31]

The Atlantic Fleet on the other hand split into task forces in March and used several bases; its center of gravity was moving northward from Norfolk to Newport, but its missions were widely scattered and its presence no more palpable than an Atlantic fog. It was a "can-do," catch-up fleet, always short of ships, men, and equipment, improvising, straining toward war readiness. The Pacific Fleet was undergoing intensive training but operated in a more traditional, peacetime, and theoretical mode, as if preparing for a Jutland. Pearl Harbor was a scene of gleaming brass, starched white, and gold braid, of perfumed air and sunny seas. The Atlantic more often was gray and cold and hostile.

Royal Navy critics believed that, impressive as the fleet at Pearl Harbor was, the Americans had "no real idea what to do with it." Its principal function of course was to deter Japanese southward expansion, rather by its "mere existence" than by its actions. The fleet was not judged ready to display its strength in the direction of Japan or the islands in the central Pacific held by Japan under mandate from the League of Nations, and it was in any case on a short leash because of the greater strategic importance of European threats. The effect, so far as critics were concerned, was "strategic localization" if not paralysis of the fleet. If the navy had no wider scheme in mind than a "containing effect" on Japan, then it seemed reasonable to examine precisely how many ships, in particular battleships, still the standard measure of naval power, would be minimally necessary to produce that effect.[32]

Leading the charge for moving a major portion, say a half, of the Pacific Fleet to the Atlantic was Secretary Stimson. Impatient that spring with what he regarded as the dilatory and dissembling methods of the president, and increasingly apprehensive over British defeats and losses, the secretary of war believed the United States must intervene and soon. The American people in his judgment were waiting to be led. Bold, straightforward action moving a big part of the fleet against Germany would serve as a catalyst for American opinion. Sharing these views were former Rough Rider Frank Knox, who insisted the navy could clean up the Atlantic in thirty days if let loose, and General Marshall, who claimed the army air force could protect Hawaii if the fleet were withdrawn. Admiral Stark wanted a transfer but would limit it to the vessels already planned.

Stubbornly opposed was Secretary Hull, who saw the transfer not only as an encouragement to Japanese militarists but also as a weakening of his hand in the talks with Ambassador Nomura. Aligned with Hull was the president, who argued against Stimson that the fleet at Hawaii had always served as a potential striking force which "by its mere presence there" protected the southwest Pacific and Southeast Asia. Shifting it to the Atlantic would convert it to a defensive force. Stimson responded that Japan was more likely to be deterred by demonstrated American resoluteness on the Atlantic than by the current passivity on the Pacific.[33]

With Hull earnestly seeking delay, at least until the Japanese response to the diplomatic initiative of April 14–16 arrived, Roosevelt procrastinated. He asked the navy to find out British views on how much of the Pacific Fleet to shift. Should the United States, the British were asked, transfer three battleships, four light cruisers, and two destroyer squadrons as originally planned or more? If Axis pressure forced the British fleet out of the Mediterranean, where would it go? If it retired eastward to the Indian Ocean or Singapore, would it be desirable to fill the gap by American transfers from the Pacific? Knox and Stimson sounded out the British on their own, Knox suggesting, as London understood him, the transfer of all three Pacific carriers.[34]

The British response was heavily conditioned. Transfer in the original number planned was a good idea, and more too, if its Mediterranean fleet retired to the Indian Ocean, but not if Suez were blocked and it came into the Atlantic. Deterrence of Japan required either two fleets of six battleships each at Singapore and Pearl Harbor or one of nine. However, Britain could not transfer ships to Singapore unless the United States assumed belligerency in the Atlantic, so for the time being the deterrent function must be performed by the Americans and the Pearl Harbor fleet could be reduced only by the amount of the planned transfer, that is from twelve to nine battleships.[35]

The American admirals were more impressed with this exercise in classical naval logic than Stimson, who persevered for a larger shift, and than Churchill, who was horrified that the Royal Navy had discouraged sending more of the Pacific Fleet. So in this curious transnational dialogue these two Atlantic interventionists agreed upon a maximum transfer, the two navies on a minimum transfer, and the two foreign offices (at least their Far Eastern experts) on none at all, fearing encouragement of Japan. Churchill took the matter to the War Cabinet on May 1 and after consultation with New Zealand and Australia advised Washington on May 8 that "any marked advance by the United States Navy in or into the Atlantic" was more likely to deter Japan than maintenance of "the present very large" fleet at Hawaii, but nevertheless that the "force left behind" must include carriers and "impose the most effective possible deterrent upon Japan." The American problem, the British government concluded with a most thoughtfully considered blend of encouragement and reserve, "is so nicely to judge the degree of transfer that while still retaining the deterrent effect of a strong ... {fleet} in the Pacific, there will also be the deterrent effect of an increased ... {fleet} in the Atlantic."[36]

In early May a consensus was emerging to move the planned portion of the Pacific Fleet, but Hull resisted. Stimson went after the ever cautious secretary of state. He had what he considered the most serious talk ever with Hull; he had General Marshall make the case for a shift to Norman Davis, veteran Democratic foreign policy adviser, who could mediate with Hull; he worked on Dean Acheson, assistant secretary of state, who arranged for Stimson to meet Hull again at the State Department. By May 9, Hull seemed more amenable but still anxious to postpone the transfer until he received a response from the Japanese to the proposal he had wafted toward them on April 14.[37]

A Japanese response was slow in coming because Hull's opposite number in Tokyo, Foreign Minister Matsuoka, opposed the draft agreement and was making every effort to sink it. Returning to

Tokyo on April 22 from his giddy tour of European capitals, he was unpleasantly surprised to learn that official discussions he had not authorized had already begun. He eluded a liaison conference on the subject by going to the palace to pay his respects to the emperor and then sulked at home pleading illness. Matsuoka's original idea had been to work from a position of strength in the Axis alliance, accommodating the Soviets, toward a settlement with the United States that recognized Japan's leadership in East Asia. Ambassador Steinhardt and Roy Howard, head of Associated Press, had given him reason to believe he would be welcomed in Washington. Thus he would cap a stage of forceful maneuver with a tour de force of peace-making. At least this is what he seems to have dreamed. Reality now fell short. For Matsuoka the project forwarded by Nomura was ill-timed and only weakened the Axis. Success in dealing with America, he was convinced, depended on firmness. An adjustment of relations with the United States would be quite useless, he said, in fast-changing circumstances which might require an attack on Singapore or on Siberia—unnerving scenarios which led cabinet ministers to question his sanity.[38]

Though some like Matsuoka were suspicious, most Japanese officials believed Nomura had transmitted a proposal approved by the American government and were surprised at how favorable the terms were. The Japanese army and navy each viewed the matter in its own way. The army's great aims were to end the debilitating China war and to secure resources in Southeast Asia required for sustaining and protecting an autonomous empire in East Asia. It should be possible to seize British and Dutch possessions without involving the United States as long as the Americans were preoccupied on the Atlantic. To the Japanese army the draft agreement seemed to promise an acceptable resolution of the China imbroglio without destroying the Axis alliance. The navy, convinced now of Anglo-American solidarity, was more skeptical, suspecting, as one historian puts it, "that the crafty Yankees sought to delay a clash with Japan until the naval balance favored them."[39]

Since both services needed time to prepare for the southern advance, however, and gather in American oil and other strategic goods, they agreed on the need to take up the opportunity for discussions. On May 3, Matsuoka, aware of his isolation and the need for some response, agreed to offer the Americans a neutrality pact, which on May 7 Hull brushed aside. Matsuoka also instructed Nomura to present a statement warning that American intervention in the European war would only prolong world suffering, since Germany and Japan were winning. This an embarrassed Nomura quickly displayed and withdrew.[40] At the same time Matsuoka raised a more serious impediment to the discussions by informing the German and Italian ambassadors of the supposed American initiative.

The pressure on Hull for movement in the discussions he passed on to Nomura, who conveyed it to Tokyo. American public interest in escort of convoy was rising; the press speculated that the president would announce a move in that direction in a speech scheduled for Wednesday, May 14. On May 7, Hull told Nomura that all his colleagues were urging him to hasten discussions because the United States must act immediately to stop Hitler. Nomura had never seen Hull so fervent. The ambassador warned his government that in case of war with Germany and Japan, the Americans planned to bide their time in the Pacific until their "vast" navy and air force was complete and then launch a "death struggle." Those close to the president regarded an improvement in relations with Japan as desirable but not vital. Nomura urged Tokyo therefore not to miss this favorable opportunity.

Still no cable came back from Tokyo. Postmaster General Walker told Nomura that he had asked Hull if diplomacy could have a little more time, despite what Walker described as the decision of an "urgently called secret cabinet meeting" on May 8. When Nomura asked Hull if the president's speech would include any reference to the draft understanding, Hull "glowered" at him "fixedly." Nomura warned Tokyo of an "ever-stiffening" trend reflected in bellicose speeches against Germany by Stimson, Knox, and Willkie. He must have instructions at the very latest by May 9. The next day Hull extended the deadline one day. Walker passed word on May 10 that the president might change his Wednesday speech if discussions started first. Meanwhile Tokyo finally responded, and Nomura saw Hull at his apartment in the evening of Sunday, May 11.[41]

Hull's difficulty in eliciting a Japanese response was compounded by a ragged Japanese diplomatic performance. He could not always understand what Nomura was saying and, in spite of speaking "very clearly and slowly," he could never be sure that Nomura fully understood him. Furthermore, as was apparent from intercepts, the ambassador was neither reporting fully Hull's own statements nor conveying all of Matsuoka's. Translation from Japanese added to the difficulty: those done by the embassy in Washington differed from those done by the foreign ministry in Tokyo, necessitating substitutions. Tokyo followed its redraft of the understanding with a stream of revisions.[42] Nevertheless, by Monday, May 12, Hull and his advisers had a clear picture of the Japanese position, and it was very stiff.

The May 12 document was more rigorous in regard to American participation in the European war. In the original draft understanding Japan's Axis obligation would come into force only if the United States "aggressively attacked" Germany; the May 12 draft permitted no such distinction. The earlier draft obliged the United States to refrain from alliance with Britain, the later one precluded even "aggressive measures" of assistance (such as Lend-Lease). The April draft set harsh terms for ending the war in China: coalescence of the Nationalist government and the Nanking puppet regime, recognition of Manchukuo, joint defense against communism (meaning the stationing of Japanese troops in China), and withholding of American assistance to China if Chiang rejected negotiation. The May draft was even more sweeping: it pledged the United States to seek peace in China according to Japan's own publicly stated terms. The Japanese draft discarded a stipulation in the April draft that the two nations would avoid menacing deployments of their naval and air forces and weakened a Japanese pledge of peaceful intent in the southwest Pacific area. As Matsuoka explained to Nomura, and as the Americans learned through MAGIC May 13, much as Japan wished for peaceful settlements, Prince Konoe and he found it necessary at times to resort to force.[43] These were not encouraging signs.

By Tuesday, May 13, President Roosevelt was in a position to decide whether to move the fleet and how much of it to move. The Japanese by responding to the April diplomatic initiative had indicated an interest in discussions which could be encouraged so as to postpone a military move southward; yet Japan's terms were so severe that no agreement was in sight. In these circumstances removal of a portion of the fleet from Pearl Harbor was less likely to precipitate a Japanese advance or influence bargaining. The East Asian constraints on a transfer thus slackened. At the same time, deterrence of Japan would be weakened if the United States moved too many battleships while the British were unable to form their own fleet at Singapore. Moving three battleships seemed fairly safe; six would be too risky. On the other hand some transfer seemed imperative, given German menace generally and current pressure on Vichy and particularly indications Vichy was bowing. On May 13, Roosevelt ordered the transfer of three battleships, four light cruisers, and thirteen more destroyers.[44]

The transferred battleships *Idaho*, *New Mexico*, and *Mississippi* departed secretly, simply disappearing over the horizon during maneuvers, and they passed through the Panama Canal at night. Japanese agents in Panama noted the transit of some of the ships, and Tokyo was bound to learn of the absence of the rest in time. Nevertheless the secrecy of the withdrawal suggests how concerned the Americans were to maintain deterrence. Hull vetoed any mention of the transfer in the forthcoming presidential speech.[45]

For the next month and more, Stimson agitated for moving another quarter of the fleet but without success. The British were of two minds about further transfers. In Churchill's view any and all movement by the Americans into the Atlantic was welcome, but the Royal Navy was dubious. American battleships operating under the constraints of neutrality in the Atlantic were no substitute for American battleships deterring Japan in the Pacific. Damage to three British battleships in the attack on Crete at the end of May made it impossible to contemplate an Eastern fleet before August. The Admiralty even encouraged the assignment of the two new battleships *Washington* and *North Carolina*, just then commissioning at New York and Philadelphia, to the Pacific. An American navy raised on the Mahanite doctrine of fleet concentration would not lightly consider further reduction of the main fleet at Pearl Harbor. As it was, the only sixteen-inch-gun battleships in that fleet—the *Colorado, Maryland,* and *West Virginia*—were to be withdrawn one at a time for reconditioning, leaving only eight battleships at Pearl Harbor. At the White House on June 9 a worried Admiral Husband Kimmel, commander of the Pacific Fleet, gained the clear impression that Roosevelt would transfer no more ships. The location of the pair of new battleships would be decided when they were ready.[46]

More active employment of the fleet had been considered. In April, Roosevelt suggested a display of force in the North Pacific to impress on the Japanese the vulnerability of their home islands to air attack, and Admiral Stark developed a plan for dispatching a carrier, four heavy cruisers, and a destroyer squadron to the Aleutians for maneuvers, possibly with a goodwill visit by the cruisers to Petropavlovsk as an added warning. But Japanese policy appeared unsettled, so it was unclear whether a show of strength would accelerate a recession or reinforce an expansion.[47] Admiral Kimmel felt he had all he could do just to train new recruits, most easily done in the Hawaiian area. Stark urged Kimmel to plan raids on the mandated islands in case of war, but recognized the fleet must adhere to the strategic defensive. No reinforcement was planned for the Philippine garrison nor augmentation of the Asiatic Fleet. The United States was prepared to cooperate in developing defense plans for the southwest

Pacific but not to provide the British or Dutch with guarantees. Lacking such a commitment, the British could make no promises to the Dutch. "We are dead set against any commitments in the area," Colonel Joseph T. McNarney of the Army Air Corps wrote on April 7.[48]

The United States had very little to show in the place of burly warships as evidence of strength and determination in the Pacific. When the three battleships departed, twenty-one B-17 bombers arrived as partial replacement.[49] On April 14 the president licensed export of all kinds of machinery and vegetable fibers, leaving only oil unrestricted, but an oil embargo against Japan was still considered too risky. The next day he authorized military pilots to resign from their services to fly for China in a combat group that became known as the Flying Tigers. He extended Lend-Lease to China on May 6, hoping to dispel the gloom in Chungking cast by the Soviet-Japanese Pact. He was considering the appointment of Owen Lattimore as his personal representative to Chiang. It was hoped this China expert could strengthen the united front with the communists and heighten resistance to Japan.[50] Measures taken to check Japan were incremental and suggestive rather than definitive.

In these straitened circumstances a continuation of the Hull-Nomura talks was better than an impasse or break. They offered no real hope of success (Hull estimated one chance in ten) but little disadvantage. The talks might delay a Japanese advance and provide time for a weakening of Matsuoka and a reconstellation of Japanese internal forces. Meanwhile by way of MAGIC they provided insight into Japanese intentions. Above all, they offered a way to drive a wedge between Japan and its Axis partners. In pursuing this last objective Hull enjoyed some success. American pressure forced Nomura to deliver Japan's response on May 11 before Germany had an opportunity, promised by Matsuoka, to comment on the project. On this point Ribbentrop expressed intense displeasure. The United States needed a "brutally frank demonstration," Berlin warned, that if it intervened in the war Japan would join in. If Japan could not avoid negotiations, at least an American pledge not to enter the European war and a clear Japanese reaffirmation of Axis alliance obligations must be the core of any agreement. No small measure of such German dissatisfaction came to American attention through intercepts.[51] Matsuoka, while stiffening the provisions, was not prepared to show the Germans either the April draft or his response, so Berlin was left in a stew.

The opposite side of the coin was considerable embarrassment to Anglo-American relations when the British got wind of the Hull-

Nomura talks. They probably learned of them from MAGIC, which is how Stimson himself found out. Army intelligence was passing on these decrypted and translated messages to the British by an arrangement made the previous winter and approved by the president. A "rumpus" ensued when State discovered the arrangement. In any case, word of a private initiative to adjust Japanese-American relations appeared in the American press. The Canadian government, acting on a report from its legation in Tokyo, inquired about the talks on April 30.[52] So the State Department should not have been surprised when British Ambassador Lord Halifax raised the matter with Welles on May 23 and complained to Hull the next day.

Halifax, presenting a message from Foreign Secretary Eden which he had been instructed to then burn, noted that according to his government's information Germany and Italy had full reports of the conversations. The facts as he understood them were that the United States had initiated the talks, promising to take a purely defensive attitude toward the European war in return for a similar Japanese pledge regarding its Axis obligations, and that the United States would bring pressure to bear on China to make peace with Japan. Matsuoka was said to have assured Berlin that he would obtain Axis agreement before reaching any accord and that no accord would compromise the Axis. Eden believed Hull would want to know of the Matsuoka "gyrations." Hull was furious at the implication that he had been taken in by the Japanese and had somehow betrayed the British. He made, as he said, a "vigorous" denial. Foreign Office officials suspected the tantrum came from a guilty conscience. They were not unhappy to turn the tables on the State Department, which never wearied of preaching against British appeasement of the Japanese.

The trans-Atlantic squall died down May 27, when Halifax delivered a soothing message from Eden, and Hull gave assurances that no common interest or principle was in jeopardy. One satisfaction the Americans could take from the spreading word of Japanese-American talks was the "concern—even dismay" exhibited by Deputy Soviet Foreign Minister Andrei Vishinsky.[53]

Hull came nowhere near "boggy ground," to use Halifax's term. He saw Nomura, more often now with assistants on both sides, every few days for the rest of May. Rather than hand over a complete American redraft promptly, one his Far Eastern experts were perfectly capable of devising, he dragged out the talks by raising points of disagreement for discussion and submitting redrafts of particular phrases and paragraphs. He suggested language that would define as self-defense

American action to protect supplies shipped to Britain and limit Japan's Axis obligation to the case of aggressive American attack. He discussed at some length the problem posed by Japan's insistence on retaining troops in China for defense against communism, suggesting a phased withdrawal over the period of a year or so with troops in certain strategic sectors moved last. And he tried out on Nomura various formulas committing Japan to peaceful courses of action in the Southeast Asia region. Strewn along the way were warnings to Nomura that the talks had not reached the stage of negotiation and that all his remarks were unofficial and informal.[54]

As the talks proceeded the Americans laid more and more stress on the issue of Japan's relations with Germany. Not that other issues were regarded as easier to resolve or less important. Rather what preoccupied Hull was the supreme necessity of avoiding a two-front war as the United States edged toward involvement on the Atlantic. Partly, too, the conduct of Matsuoka focused attention on the issue. Receiving Ambassador Grew on May 14, for the first time since his return from abroad, Matsuoka lashed out at the American Atlantic patrols and talk of escorting convoys. Hitler's patience and "generosity" were sorely tried he warned. If any incident occurred, America would be the aggressor. The Axis alliance would come into play and war ensue. The "manly, decent" course for the United States was "to declare war openly on Germany instead of engaging in acts of war under cover of neutrality." The Japanese foreign minister's rambling and insulting language on this occasion, including speculation on his own sanity, was not likely to enhance his standing in Washington, but Matsuoka had his purposes: he showed the harsh language he used on the Americans to the German ambassador in order to recover ground with the Axis. This was his "brutally frank demonstration."[55]

The Hull and Matsuoka tantrums illustrate the increasing difficulty both Japan and the United States experienced in escaping their European connections as they confronted their separate differences. Now in his conversations with Nomura, Hull singled out Matsuoka for criticism. The stormy foreign minister was himself appearing as the main obstacle to progress; the talks were coming to be seen as a means of weakening the pro-Axis camp in Japan.

The notion that relations with Japan would improve, or at least remain tolerably bad, that issues could be set to rest for now and addressed later if only the Axis connection were broken or weakened, was mistaken. Japanese strategic policy was in process of critical change in May and June 1941, moving away from cautious southern advance sheltered by forceful Matsuoka-style diplomacy toward unabashed seizure of the western colonies in Southeast Asia not only at the risk of war but even accepting the inevitability of war with Britain and the United States. The wellsprings of Japanese aggression lay not in the German connection or in radical young military officers, as had seemed the case in the early 1930s and as American policymakers still tended to believe. The danger arose from the increasing sway of staff officers of the Japanese navy who saw Japan ever more encircled and depleted by the American-British-Dutch coalition and who argued that Japan must strike out to secure the resources, especially oil, upon which the greatness and security of the nation and the existence of the navy depended.[56] For the army the situation still appeared more obscure, the choices consequently less drastic, and the priority of interests somewhat different. Lacking consensus both services prepared, waited, and looked abroad for signs.

So did Washington, London, and Moscow. Never since Napoleon, and this time on a world scale, had one nation so dominated the currents of international life as Germany did now. In May 1941, Berlin set the beat.

Lord Halifax, reporting his lunch with the president on May 2, said his host expected American patrolling in the Atlantic to lead to an incident, which would not be unwelcome. Roosevelt, noted the British ambassador, spoke more freely than he had yet heard him about being in the war. Interventionists such as Stimson gained a similar impression and regretted the president's disingenuousness.[57] More likely his motive was simply to be encouraging. This is not to suggest that Roosevelt framed his policy on avoiding an incident. He was determined to take whatever steps were necessary to protect the Atlantic even at the cost of war. Yet, to the extent that his purposes were served without incident and war, he would gain precious time for developing war potential, maintain broad public support, avoid war with Japan, and follow his own aversion to taking any step until he had the best possible sense of the consequences.

In May the president was in fact less concerned about a U-boat incident than about German acquisition of Atlantic bases. His eyes were on Dakar and the Azores. The vital question was how much Admiral Darlan had conceded to Hitler at Berchtesgadan: Collaboration in Syria? North Africa as well? Even delivering up the French fleet? Some officials feared the worst. On May 14, Pétain was reported to have stated on the radio that France "must collaborate with Germany in Europe and Africa." Sources expected the Germans to secure airfields and ports in Spain and Portugal and a submarine base at Dakar; German shock troops were said to be moving into the Hendaye-Biarritz area close to Spain. The press was utterly pessimistic. The Darlan accord, said the *New York Times*, meant that France had turned its back on the United States and Britain: "Convinced that Germany will win the war, [France] is ready to throw in her lot and her colonial empire with Germany."[58]

The crisis in Franco-American relations was swift and acute. Shortwave broadcasts from Boston and Philadelphia heard across the Atlantic claimed that the Germans were already in Dakar. Roosevelt described Vichy as already "in a German cage."[59] He ordered the Coast Guard to take custody of the dozen or so French ships in American ports, including the huge and beautiful luxury liner *Normandie*. Pétain was to be told that his assurances of adhering to the 1940 armistice were meaningless. The president was apparently dissuaded from so strong a statement and instead warned in a shortwave broadcast to the French people that Franco-German collaboration might pose a threat to the United States and he appealed to the French people to shun the Axis. Hull told the French ambassador that the Darlan agreement gave the definite impression that Vichy had "thrown itself into the lap of Germany." Plans for shipment of food to unoccupied France and for economic assistance to North Africa came to an abrupt halt. Vichy responded with angry denials, warning that she would defend "every inch of her empire" against attack by Britain and the United States, Martinique and Dakar in particular, indeed that she was adding guns to the defenses of Dakar. That African port, according to the American consul there, was in a state of "frantic hysterical intoxication" over the crisis.[60]

In cables of May 19 and 21, Robert Murphy, who was overseeing American interests in North Africa, tried to calm American fears and put the situation in perspective. General Weygand had assured him that North Africa was not affected by the accords, that the Germans had not infiltrated into Dakar or anywhere else in French North Africa, that they were not likely to attack Gibraltar or Morocco immediately, and that they had only two divisions in Libya. Murphy found no evidence of German moves against Spanish or French territory. A German drive to the southwest would depend on their success in the eastern Mediterranean.[61]

"Leg over, leg over, the dog went to Dover": Ambassador MacVeagh had quoted the old refrain in March when the Germans were still slogging through Bulgarian snowdrifts. Now it seemed they took the next-to-last step on their way to Suez: at 8:00 a.m., May 20, German parachute and glider forces descended on the island of Crete, 200 miles from Africa and dominating the eastern Mediterranean. Ultimately 22,000 German troops landed, opposing 32,000 British and Commonwealth and 10,000 Greek soldiers. The allied forces, however, were virtually bare of air defense. By the end of the second day, after vicious fighting and severe losses, the Germans had secured the island's main airfield. On May 22 the British fleet, ordered into the Kithera Channel between southernmost Greece and Crete to destroy German seaborne invasion forces, suffered "the most severe air bombing ... naval vessels have ever experienced" from some 700 German planes massed on nearby islands and the southern Peloponnesus. German dive and torpedo bombers devastated the trapped fleet. The carrier *Formidable* lost all but four planes.[62]

For Stimson, the shadow of Crete hung over everything. To Hull, the situation seemed to be going "Hellward." At State, the capture of Suez was "just under the horizon." This with rumors the Russians had "succumbed" to German demands, suspicions that the French had given up North Africa, and fears that Japan would now strike for the oil of the Indies, indeed that the United States might soon be facing the world alone, led to feelings of the utmost depression.[63]

On May 22 a British aircraft discovered that Germany's most powerful battleship, the *Bismarck*, together with the cruiser *Prinz Eugen*, had disappeared from their anchorage in a fiord south of Bergen, Norway. The next day they were discovered hugging the ice edge of Greenland nearing a breakout into the Atlantic. In one of the rare capital ship engagements of the war, with shell splashes rising twice the height of masts, the "simply gigantic" *Bismarck*, as a Royal Navy observer described it, sank the battle cruiser *Hood*, damaged the battleship *Prince of Wales*, and, shaking off pursuers, vanished into the Atlantic. On May 26 the British navy, moving in from all directions with all available aircraft and warships, found the German battleship again and the following day cornered it. British heavy shells had a "frightful" effect: "Colossal flashes inside her ... and wretched men running hither and thither on the deck but she would neither surrender nor sink." Finally she was dispatched with two torpedoes.[64]

Watching the *Bismarck* fire at British aircraft off Greenland had been the U.S. Coast Guard cutter *Modoc. Bismarck* crossed the path of the American battleship patrol at its farthest extremity, but the old *Texas* was nearing Newport, and its sister ship *New York* was just departing. Undoubtedly cursing this bad luck, Churchill urged that the Americans be asked to play a part in the search for *Prinz Eugen* so as to provide the "incident for which the United States Government would be so thankful." And in fact an American destroyer and planes from Argentia searched the lower Davis Strait between Canada and Greenland, and for a week the *Wasp* hung about a suspected tanker rendezvous point midway between Bermuda and the Cape Verdes. The *Prinz Eugen* made for France and arrived safely.[65]

The ever worsening position of the British in the Middle East was a matter of grave concern to the American government both in terms of strategic damage done and as evidence of a general weakening of British morale with a corresponding effect on neutral nations and subjugated peoples. This concern for British morale was reflected in a Roosevelt message to Churchill on May 1 describing the intervention in Greece as a "wholly justifiable delaying action," extending Axis and shortening British lines, though he found it necessary to add, the undercurrent of concern showing, that he was sure the British would not allow any "great debacle or surrender." In the last analysis, wrote the president, the control of the Indian Ocean and the Atlantic would decide the war.

Churchill responded with one of the bleakest telegrams of their correspondence. He reflected the profound pessimism of Whitehall. Nothing in Roosevelt's recent messages indicated an inclination to intervene, and the British could not help but feel that, as one Foreign Office official put it, "in their hearts the Americans expect us to be defeated." In his message the prime minister disagreed that the loss of Egypt and the Middle East would be a "mere preliminary to the successful maintenance of a prolonged oceanic war." He could not be sure such a loss would not be "grave" (in the original "mortal"), for a war against an Axis system controlling Europe and most of Africa and Asia was a daunting proposition. Unless the United States took "more advanced positions now or very soon, the vast balances may be tilted heavily to our disadvantage." More precisely, said Churchill, in absolute frankness, the one counterbalance to growing pessimism in Europe and the Middle East would be American belligerency.

In reply, May 10, Roosevelt assured Churchill that he had no intention of minimizing either the gravity of the situation or the worthiness of the British effort. But he reiterated with a slight change his argument of May 1. No defeat in the Mediterranean, he said, could destroy their mutual interests because the outcome of the war would be decided on the Atlantic: "[U]nless Hitler can win there he cannot win anywhere in the world in the end."[66] Churchill could hardly object to this reaffirmation of America's predominant strategic conception from which flowed Lend-Lease and patrolling, but he may have sensed that this was not all the president meant in dwelling on the importance of the Atlantic. While Roosevelt unquestionably considered the Atlantic vital as a bridge to Britain and ultimately the conquest of Germany, he also regarded it as vital for protecting the safety and existence of the United States in case of British defeat. It is tempting to explain Roosevelt's public emphasis on hemisphere security in May as a rationalization for intervention in the Battle of the Atlantic on more fundamental but publicly divisive grounds of Anglo-American mutual interest. But it was not a ploy; briefly at this low point in British fortunes but authentically and intensely, the president focused on threats to the safety of the United States in a most direct and visceral sense.

The question was how to prevent German seizure of the Atlantic islands and Dakar, the bridgeheads for German access to the Americas. Crete was important as a demonstration that German power was not landlocked, that it could with control of the air leap across narrow waters and seize strategic focal points. No less important was the *Bismarck* breakout. It was a relief no longer to have to count this mammoth in capital ship balances, but the loss of the *Hood* and near escape of the *Bismarck* left Roosevelt uneasy about the Royal Navy. Above all, the rediscovery of the ship by aircraft showed that air power was critical in maintaining control of the sea, and for this bases such as Bermuda and the Azores were indispensable. Knowing the British were ready to send expeditions to the Azores and Cape Verdes in case of a German move on Portugal and Spain, Roosevelt nevertheless set out to learn whether the Portugese government in that case would accept protection of the Azores by the United States. On May 22, before learning the answer, he ordered the armed services to prepare an expeditionary force of 25,000 troops, to be ready by June 22.[67]

As usual, American capabilities fell far short of American needs. With so few troops ready for action, their disposition was a matter of the most intense concern, and with each of the islands—the Azores, Canaries, Cape Verdes, Iceland—requiring a force of at least one division, and preferably two, only one or two commitments were possible. The president was alone in his concern for the Azores. A Dakar expedition, requiring over 100,000 troops, was out of the question, but the army hoped to develop the defenses of northwestern Brazil instead and considered the Azores too distant from the Dakar-Natal bridge to justify commitment. Both services feared that tying troops down in these islands would make it impossible to fulfill the American ABC-1 pledge to send troops to Britain in case of war. No less cramping was the lack of ships. Admiral King estimated that seizure of any one island group would require two battleships, the entire reinforced cruiser strength of the Atlantic Fleet, and eighteen modern destroyers. That sort of concentration would eliminate patrolling. Furthermore, the army and navy had only enough troop transports on hand for one division. Twelve more had to be acquired and converted. Nevertheless, planning and preparations began.[68]

Along with plans for defending the Atlantic outposts Roosevelt prepared a major radio speech to the American people aimed at mobilizing support for defense policies that now frankly carried some risk of war. The press and public had been eagerly awaiting a presidential lead since cancellation of the May 14 speech. Stimson was particularly anxious for the president to set forth the basic principles which must guide the nation in this "grave crisis"; indeed, to establish the foundation on which the nation might wage war. The world was divided into two camps, he wrote the president, and "you are the leader of one camp." The American people must be led to action opposing the "evil leaders" of the other camp not by incidents involving mistake or chance but by leadership that lit the path.[69] Roosevelt set out to do just that and to convey to the American people as simply as possible the strategic insights that animated his policies.

The speech went through many drafts and did not turn out to be as explicit as Stimson hoped. It praised China's struggle but carefully refrained from mentioning Japan or the fleet transfer. Struck out were references to the Nazi-Soviet Pact of 1939, described as a "gangsters' compact," and the name of Finland from a list of victims of aggression. The possibility of Russia itself becoming a victim of aggression was not to be ruled out. The speech avoided delimitation of the Western Hemisphere because conventional definitions would have excluded the Cape Verdes and Iceland.[70] In spite of such flattenings, however, the speech, delivered appropriately before an audience of Latin American diplomats, was one of Roosevelt's most powerful and candid statements of purpose.

The president's first object was to make clear that Hitler wanted not just Europe or the Old World but the whole world. He warned of the "honeyed" words of peace after each conquest, the unlimited ambitions that lay behind them, and the sort of life Americans would lead in a Nazi-dominated world. Then he described the path of German aggression and the present threats to Spain, Portugal, northwest Africa, and the Atlantic islands. He pointed out that the Cape Verdes were only seven hours by bomber or troop-carrying plane from Brazil. The war was "approaching the brink of the Western Hemisphere itself ... coming very close to home." He stressed the importance of control of the seas. Germany recognized that it must "break through to command of the ocean" to win. Held to a continuing land war in Europe and the burdens of occupation it must lose: "[The] wider ... the Nazi land effort, the greater ... their ultimate danger."

For Americans, all freedom had always depended on freedom of the seas, from the quasi-war with France in 1799 to World War I. Now, however, with bombers and raiders and improved submarines, the problem of defending the sea routes was much greater. He described the Battle of the Atlantic, the ominous toll of British shipping and attacks on shipping "off the very shores of land we are determined to protect," creating an "actual military danger to the Americas," one emphasized by the foray of the *Bismarck* into "Western Hemisphere waters."[71]

Roosevelt now came to the essence of his argument. Iceland and Greenland in the north and the Azores and Cape Verdes in the south could serve as stepping stones for German attacks on Western Hemisphere neighbors of the United States and eventually upon the nation itself. As the Nazi seizure of Czechoslovakia began with the conquest of Austria, and the attack on Greece with the occupation of Bulgaria, Roosevelt said, the German attack on the United States could begin with the seizure of such Atlantic bases, and it would be "suicide to wait until they are in our front yard." "Anyone with an atlas" would know better. National policy, therefore, was to resist every German attempt to extend domination to the Western Hemisphere "or threaten it" or gain control of the seas. National policy was also to ensure delivery of needed supplies to Britain. That was "imperative": it could be done, must be done, would be done.

He concluded with a series of ringing assertions: that the world was divided between human slavery and human freedom, that Americans chose freedom and would not accept a "Hitler-dominated world," that (a salvo at the Japanese) the Americas could decide for themselves whether, when, and where their interests were attacked or their security threatened, and that American armed forces were being placed in strategic positions and would not hesitate to repel attack. He ended with a proclamation of unlimited national emergency which gave the president extraordinary powers over communications, public utilities, transportation, trade, and aliens.

Roosevelt's May 27 speech was a vitally important statement of policy, his only fully developed exposition in 1941 of the strategic threat as he saw it and what he was prepared to do to meet that threat. Though he did not deal with specific cases, the speech fully reflected his own conception of the problem and the plans and preparations under way to guard Atlantic outposts. His statement of imperative requirements and determination to use force if necessary gave full warning to the American people that the chosen course risked war. It was a speech that educated and led, and it received banner headlines and vociferous support in the press and letters to the White House. From April to June Roosevelt's popularity rose from 73 to 76 percent.[72]

The speech also reinforced rising public support for intervention in the Battle of the Atlantic by escort of convoy. The shift began in mid-April, most likely as a result of the blitzkrieg in the Balkans and airing of the escort issue in Congress and the press. Opinion in favor of escort rose from 41 percent April 15 to 52 percent May 13 and 55 percent June 9, while opposition declined from 50 to 38 percent.[73] Americans remained opposed by margins of three or four to one to a vote for war, but they were prepared to accept the risk of war for the vital security interests set forth by the president. He was marching with prevailing public opinion.

One unexpected result of the speech was to make the Azores operation infeasible for the time being. Only on May 26 had Roosevelt learned from the American naval attaché in Lisbon that the Portugese would accept American protection in the event they were forced by German attack to move the seat of government to the islands. But the president's explicit reference to the Azores in his speech the next day raised fears in Lisbon of provoking a German attack. The key to the precarious neutrality of Portugal lay in a tacit understanding by Germany and Britain that a move onto Portugese territory by one would lead to a countermove by the other, and so neither made the first move. Now the Portugese felt obliged to defer an invitation to the Americans. A guarantee by the British, their ancient ally, would be less provocative, and this Churchill was glad to reaffirm.[74] Roosevelt did not rest easy with these arrangements— the Azores project was not canceled—but he turned away from it to a more practical and immediately important project, the protection of Iceland.

Iceland was by no means unknown territory to Roosevelt and his advisers. The ABC-1 plan for Anglo-American joint warfare on the Atlantic gave the United States responsibility for garrisoning Iceland, and the 5th Infantry Division was preparing for the assignment—scheduled, for planning purposes, in September. The navy reconnoitered the island in April with a view to establishing a base and ordered winter clothing for battleship and escorting destroyer crews. The commander of the Atlantic Fleet Support Force, expecting to operate patrol planes from Iceland, requested a second seaplane tender. As a base, Hvalfjordur fiord ("Havafajava" in navy parlance), a "dreary and unforgiving haven" on the western side of the island, offered little enough protection from roaring gales of those latitudes, which sailors claimed blew away anemometers at readings up to 120 knots and damaged catapults and davits, as well as propellers when ships dragged anchor and went aground.[75]

Iceland offered two absolutely critical advantages to the British and American navies. Lying not far north of the usual convoy routes to Britain it provided an indispensable mid-Atlantic refueling base for destroyers in escort; the more westerly the U-boat war drifted, the more important Iceland became. In addition, Iceland controlled Denmark Strait, the passage between Greenland and Iceland favored by the German navy for raider breakouts into the Atlantic. Anxious to hasten the American arrival and straining to meet their own requirements, the British urged the Icelanders to approach the United States for protection of their shipping to North America, and on April 14 secret negotiations began with the Icelandic consul general in Washington for American protection of Iceland itself.[76]

The idea of Iceland as a terminus for an American western Atlantic convoy escort service emerged and gained increasing relevance as U-boats began hunting south of Iceland and southeast of Greenland, within the American sphere. On April 10, Oscar Cox, an assistant to Hopkins for Lend-Lease, suggested American escort of American and British ships "to the end of the Western Hemisphere" and trans-shipment of goods at some intermediate point (such as Iceland) for delivery to Britain. On April 11 the president wrote Churchill of the possibility of "sending wheat and other goods in American ships to Greenland or Iceland." On May 23 the British began destroyer escort of convoys all the way across the Atlantic. But westward expansion thinned the forces even more: escort groups operated out of St. John's, Newfoundland, at half strength. The same day Churchill described the problem to Roosevelt and asked him to move his battleship patrols closer to the convoy lanes to report sightings and make raiders and U-boats "feel insecure."[77] Neither planning nor decision had occurred, but circumstances and thinking were pointing toward American escort in the western Atlantic.

The Crete debacle and the global mathematics of naval power gave added weight to the argument for an American base at Iceland. In the Crete operation the British eastern Mediterranean fleet suffered crippling losses: three British battleships and one aircraft carrier dam-aged, three cruisers and six destroyers sunk, and six cruisers and seven destroyers damaged.[78] Even before the Kithera battle the Royal Navy had pointed out that, unless the United States took over some cruiser and destroyer tasks in the Atlantic, it would be impossible to withdraw enough of these types to establish a balanced fleet at Sin-gapore. The severe cruiser and destroyer losses at Crete added a sharp point to the British concern. The Royal Navy now asked that four American heavy cruisers be sent to Iceland for protection against raiders.[79]

The American navy was impatient with the suggestion. On account of their "rash naval action" at Crete, wrote Admiral Stark, the British would be unable to bring naval strength against Japan. When the Mediterranean fleet was intact, the Japanese would have to assume it was transferrable to the Indian Ocean. Such was no longer the case, and this weakness together with the reduction in American Pacific naval strength were encouragements for Japan to move southward. It would be impossible for the United States to transfer any more cruisers from the Pacific.[80] Nevertheless, once the four light cruisers already moving to the Atlantic arrived in mid-June to serve as escorts for the carriers, the existing heavy cruiser strength of the Atlantic Fleet would be available for service on the convoy routes and basing them or some of them at Iceland would not be illogical.

These naval considerations were undoubtedly on his mind when President Roosevelt deliberated his next step. An Iceland base would offer other advantages as well. One acute source of army and air corps discontent was that precious B-17 Flying Fortresses assigned to the British were sitting on the tarmac at the Boeing plant awaiting pilots to fly them to England. To speed up movement of these and other planes, American pilots might deliver them to the British in Labra-dor or Iceland. Furthermore, American garrisoning of Iceland would relieve British troops for reinforcement of the Middle East.[81]

Underlying argument about the positive advantages of Iceland was worry about its vulnerability. The northern flank of the Atlantic line had been a matter of concern since Germany's occupation of Den-mark in 1940. From bases in Greenland, Assistant Secretary of State Berle wrote, the Germans could bomb New York. Regarding Green-land as unquestionably Western Hemisphere territory, the Depart-ment of State sought to prevent British or Canadian occupation which might prompt a German countermove. The United States could hardly press the Canadians to desist, however, unless it took some responsibility for Greenland's defense itself. This it did by establishing a Coast Guard patrol of Greenland waters and arranging with Greenland authorities for building air bases.[82]

In 1940 the Germans had briefly established a weather station on Greenland, and President Roosevelt was acutely concerned that they might try again this summer. Until the Greenland bases were built, Iceland provided the only base for aerial surveillance of Greenland and the Denmark Strait. Air search was not enough for the president: he insisted that the navy mount an expedition to hold Scoresby Sound on Greenland's eastern coast until the end of the summer. In May 1941 German troop and ship concentrations in northern Norway became the object of American concern. Some argued they formed the northern wing of a forthcoming attack on the Soviet Union. Others were not so sure. The troops had skis, but the terrain had no snow at that time of year and was impassable by tanks. It seemed more likely to Berle they were intended for Iceland or Greenland, over which German reconnaissance planes were flying with impunity. American fears for the northern outposts were no less vivid than those for the southern. Morgenthau noted at the cabinet meeting of June 4 that the president's "whole interest ... is in the Atlantic Fleet and getting first to these various outlying islands."[83]

President Roosevelt moved without hesitation to establish an American force and base on Iceland as soon as he received strong public approval for his speech of May 27. At lunch with Lord Halifax the following day he suggested an American garrison for Iceland.[84] Churchill cordially welcomed the proposal on May 29 in a message received after the president departed for the Memorial Day weekend at Hyde Park. The day following his return, June 3, he saw Ambassador Winant and Admiral King, and in all probability the decision was made that day or the next. The army and navy received orders to mount an expedition immediately, to depart as soon as permission was obtained from Iceland. Sufficient troop lift existed for this operation but not for the Azores as well so on June 13 the latter was suspended.[85]

The German-Soviet question bore on the Iceland decision in more ways than one. Respondek's April reports to Sam Woods in Berlin, received in May, at least one of which Roosevelt saw, were increasingly positive about an attack on the Soviet Union. In order to maintain the military might necessary for extended war with the Anglo-American bloc, Respondek wrote, Germany would have to incorporate the productive forces of all Europe, especially Russia, into a general system under German control. Disappointing figures for acquisition of raw materials in April intensified the need. So "the liquidation of Russia is considered a necessity," by armored penetrations and encirclement, while a defensive front was established in the west. After capture of the principal Russian industrial and railroad centers (Baku, Grozny, Minsk, Kiev, Kharkov, Rostov, Stalingrad, the Don basin, Yekaterinoslav, the middle and southern Urals, and the Kuznetsk region), Germany would easily invade Britain and capture the Mediterranean.[86]

One indicator of the coming attack was the diminution of German air raids on Britain. ULTRA intelligence in May showed a stream of Luftwaffe units moving east. Indicating not merely intimidation but determination to attack regardless was the establishment of a prisoner-of-war cage in Poland. The British Joint Intelligence Committee remained unconvinced into June, but it is possible that Churchill provided Winant with some of the ULTRA data to take with him to Washington. Certainly the ambassador carried intelligence of great sensitivity, for his plane to Lisbon was escorted by RAF fighters and, once there, his papers were locked in the British embassy safe.[87]

For every prediction of a German attack, however, there were two of a German ultimatum and Russian submission. American embassies retailed rumors of German troops already entering Bessarabia and the Ukraine with Soviet consent, of Soviet-German agreement for joint expansion in the Middle East, and of imminent Soviet signature of the Axis pact. Rudolf Hess, Hitler's trusted lieutenant, interrogated after his dramatic flight to Scotland, admitted that Germany had demands to make on Russia which would have to be satisfied, as Churchill reported to Roosevelt on May 28. Tokyo, according to MAGIC, noted that German-Soviet relations had "suddenly cooled," but before going to war Hitler was likely to scheme for lands on the Soviet border, so the outcome would depend "upon how the Soviet acts." Adolf Berle, after lunch with the heads of British and American naval intelligence and J. Edgar Hoover, thought it "pretty clear that the Germans have already worked out some kind of agreement with the Russians."[88]

These opposing estimates—that Germany would attack and that Germany might not need to attack—both served to reinforce Roosevelt's Iceland decision. If Germany attacked the Soviet Union, the Soviets were expected to last only one or two months, a short respite but long enough to secure the Atlantic islands while Germany was preoccupied. If the Soviet Union succumbed to German demands, the respite might even be shorter and the strategic necessity would be greater.

By early June 1941 the Atlantic outpost line was clearly established in American strategy. In setting out to guard this line even at the risk of war, Roosevelt extended the sphere of American vital interest beyond territorial waters, beyond neutrality limits, beyond the mid-point of the North Atlantic, to the verges of Europe, and he gathered the warships to fulfill his aim. In the face of numbing exhibitions of German strength and widely divergent estimates of German aims, defense of the Atlantic line seemed only wise and absolutely neces-sary for the physical safety and existence of the nation. Helping England was not quite on such a fundamental level but vital too, and the Atlantic outposts could be bridges the other way.

Roosevelt was also intent upon shoring up the weakening British position in the Middle East. Alexander Kirk, a diplomat seasoned by service in two wars at Berlin, newly arrived as ambassador to Egypt, expounded in cable after cable on the desperate position of the Brit-ish there in the aftermath of Crete. He was particularly concerned with the destructive effect on British prestige in Egypt and the Arab world. At the same time, Kirk believed that British engagement of the Germans in Greece was better than declining battle for it showed the Germans that expansion did not bring peace. It was of "prime importance" for the United States to oppose Germany, he warned, if possible by war, if not by "planes and more planes." Washington responded to the need with promises of additional shipments of tanks, artillery ammunition, trucks, and road-building equipment. Supplies for the Middle East now sailed in forty-four American ships. Plans called for fifty tankers and an aircraft ferry service to the Mid-dle East by way of Brazil and Africa.[89]

By late May, Washington was oppressively warm. The president worked with his coat off and the windows of the Oval Study open. Outside the southwest window, Robert Sherwood noted, was a mag-nolia tree said to have been planted by Andrew Jackson: "It was now covered with big white blooms and their lemony scent drifted into the study."[90] This languorous seat of decision contrasted so vividly with the swift and sinister unfolding of events abroad. Choosing his way with great care among the terrible uncertainties and incapacities he faced, Roosevelt determined to control the Atlantic and placed the nation on a path risking war to ensure it. Here his stubborn cau-tion and traditional sense of American autonomy spoke. He also per-sisted in his policy of sustaining Britain in every practical way. In the

Pacific he necessarily managed a holding action with defensive fleet deployments, rhetorical support for China, and dilatory diplomacy with Japan. Mostly he waited for ships and troops and arms to mobilize and materialize and above all for German intentions to come clear.

Chapter 4

June
The Russian Factor

In June 1941 the German ground forces coiled for the greatest onslaught in the history of warfare. Last to arrive, in May and June, were the elements whose presence was most difficult to conceal: the motorized and armored divisions that formed the three great wedges to be driven into the heart of the Soviet Union, eight in the north directed at Leningrad, sixteen in the center at Moscow, and thirteen in the south at the rich agricultural and industrial region of the Ukraine and Don basin. The primary front (excluding Finland) from the Baltic to the Black Sea stretched about as far as from Chicago to New Orleans but would widen by half again as the armies moved deeper into Russia. Arrayed on this front by June 22 were 149 German divisions, two-thirds of the strength of the German army, numbering three million men, 3,350 tanks, and 2,770 planes. Providing transport were not only 600,000 motor vehicles but also 625,000 horses, indicating the great difference in mobility between the fast forces and the follow-up infantry.[1]

American and indeed all foreign observers were aware that a climax was approaching, but they remained divided almost until the last moment over whether the outcome would be Soviet submission to German demands or war. Readers of MAGIC traffic translated on June 6 would learn of Ambassador Ōshima's conviction that the German army was an "irresistible force" capable of an "annihilating movement against the Russian Army." War was not a certainty, Ribbentrop told Ōshima cautiously on June 3, and then continued more candidly that, if Japan needed to make preparations, it should do so as fast as possible. The attitude of the Soviets had become more antagonistic lately, he explained, even to the point of an armed clash at the mouth of the Danube; they seemed to be waiting for the Reich to fail. Once Germany had defeated the Soviet Union and gained

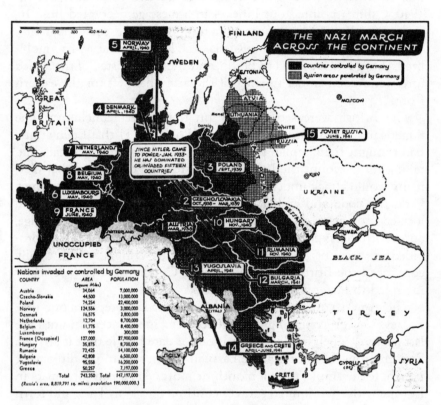

The following text appears within the map image:

THE NAZI MARCH ACROSS THE CONTINENT

Countries controlled by Germany
Russian areas penetrated by Germany

SINCE HITLER CAME TO POWER—JAN. 1933—HE HAS DOMINATED OR INVADED FIFTEEN COUNTRIES

5 NORWAY APRIL, 1940
4 DENMARK, APRIL, 1940
7 NETHERLANDS MAY, 1940
8 BELGIUM MAY, 1940
6 LUXEMBOURG MAY, 1940
9 FRANCE JUNE, 1940
3 POLAND SEPT, 1939
2 CZECHOSLOVAKIA OCT, 1938—MAR, 1939
1 AUSTRIA MAR, 1938
10 HUNGARY NOV, 1940
11 RUMANIA NOV, 1940
13 YUGOSLAVIA APRIL, 1941
12 BULGARIA MARCH, 1941
14 GREECE AND CRETE APRIL-JUNE, 1941
15 SOVIET RUSSIA JUNE, 1941

UNOCCUPIED FRANCE

Nations invaded or controlled by Germany

COUNTRY	AREA (Square Miles)	POPULATION
Austria	34,064	7,000,000
Czecho-Slovakia	44,500	13,000,000
Poland	74,254	22,400,000
Norway	124,556	3,000,000
Denmark	16,575	3,800,000
Netherlands	12,704	8,700,000
Belgium	11,775	8,400,000
Luxembourg	999	300,000
France (Occupied)	127,000	27,900,000
Hungary	35,875	8,700,000
Rumania	72,425	14,100,000
Bulgaria	42,808	6,500,000
Yugoslavia	95,558	16,200,000
Greece	50,257	7,197,000
Total	743,350	Total 147,197,000

(Russia's area, 8,819,791 sq. miles; population 190,000,000.)

"The Nazi March Across the Continent": *New York Times*, July 6, 1941.

undisputed control of all Europe, it would be untouchable by Britain and the United States. Even in terms of the war against Britain, Ribbentrop concluded, it was "imperative that the Soviet Union be beaten down now."[2]

Indeed, reported Ōshima on June 4, both Hitler and the Reich foreign minister had told him, as a matter of "gravest secrecy," that in all probability war with Russia could not be avoided. Hitler had given him advance notice of the Norway and western front offensives in 1940, Ōshima pointed out June 14 in a message decrypted June 16, so his word could be counted on now respecting the "apparently imminent" surprise attack on Russia. The Rumanian army had mobilized, Hitler had returned to Berlin, and the chief of staff of the armed forces and commander-in-chief of the army had left for the eastern front.[3]

The British were settling now on the correct conclusion. The American embassy in London reported on June 11 that Eden at first had thought the German troop concentrations were blackmail, but, taking into account the Luftwaffe transfers, he concluded that Germany would attack under any circumstances. The next day Bletchley Park, the code and cipher department of the British government, located northwest of London, between Oxford and Cambridge, apparently decrypting the same Japanese messages as MAGIC, provided an account of Hitler's interview with Ōshima which finally convinced the British Joint Intelligence Committee that "Germany intended to turn on Russia" regardless.[4]

The American government, lacking any adequate, let alone unified, system for evaluating intelligence, remained uncertain until the last minute. Much intelligence was out of date by the time it arrived. Reports from the American embassy in Berlin sent in the diplomatic pouch, for example, took a month or more. American diplomats in Europe with their limited sources continued to sway back and forth between the possibilities of German attack and intimidation, war and appeasement. By June 12 the Moscow embassy leaned to the idea of attack, but June 19 it passed on a rumor that secret negotiations were taking place in Berlin. The embassy in Berlin on June 8 found "impressive evidence" for an attack within a fortnight, but on June 21 it retailed rumors from all sides that a German ultimatum was forthcoming in the next two days. On June 7, Stockholm passed on a report of an attack in ten days, and on June 9 another that Germans were then laying down their terms in Moscow. Bucharest believed that Germany presented an ultimatum of extreme demands June 6. Rome, Budapest, and Sofia all reported rumors of a giant Soviet-German deal in the making. The Vatican, however, was understood to be expecting an attack. Both the Japanese and American governments, engaged in exploratory conversations with each other, anxiously queried their diplomatic posts respecting German-Russian negotiations.[5]

According to Lord Halifax, Welles regarded reports of a forthcoming attack as a German way of terrorizing the Soviets into submission. On June 10 he summarized Washington reports that indicated either the "imminence of hostilities, or, alternatively, of Russian surrender to Germany." To Berle on June 19 a climax seemed near. The Germans believed they could take Russia without fighting but he was not sure they could: the Russians must understand that the German object was to destroy Stalin and his regime, and that it was a case of fight or die. Stimson leaned the other way. On June 17 he wrote in his diary that it was nip and tuck whether Russia would fight or surrender, and "of course I think the chances are that she will surrender."[6]

As the climax approached, the Department of State carefully considered the position it should take. Currently Soviet-American relations were cold and distant. The Welles-Oumansky talks had marked out some common ground but also hardened disagreements, as on questions relating to the Soviet takeover of Estonia, Latvia, and Lithuania, Soviet trade with Germany, and Soviet access to American strategic goods and materials. On June 14 the United States froze the assets in America of Germany, Italy, occupied European countries, and European neutrals including the Soviet Union, explaining that the last was included because of the "interrelationship of international financial transactions" but could be freed again by assurances that the funds would not benefit Germany and Italy. The Soviet Union charged discrimination; the United States denied it. The point was clear, however, as the day of reckoning approached that the United States was not inclined to favor the Soviet Union and would retaliate in case of further Soviet-German collaboration.[7]

For Ambassador Steinhardt and the European Division of the Department of State this was precisely the correct position to take. The professional diplomats, who had hardy suspicions of all things Soviet, found the effort to improve relations entirely wrong-headed. Conciliation of the bear only made him hungrier; appeasement signified weakness. Soviet policy toward Germany was governed by fear of the German army, and no American concession could change that. Soviet psychology, Steinhardt warned, "recognized only firmness, power and force and reflects primitive instincts and reactions entirely

devoid of the restraints of civilization." Assuming no Soviet surrender to German blackmail occurred, which the United States could
not in any case prevent, then the ambassador believed the Soviets
would turn to the United States anyway to escape their folly. Only
firmness and aloofness would maintain American prestige at Moscow
and "prepare the ground for the important developments with which
we will be ultimately confronted."[8]

Specifically this policy meant treating the Soviet Union on a recip-
rocal basis, making no approaches, responding to Soviet approaches
with reserve, avoiding concessions of principle or for the sake of
atmosphere, and in general indicating that improvement in relations
was as important, if not more important, to the Soviet Union as it
was to the United States. The policy was immediately relevant to conversations in London between Eden and Ambassador Maisky, which
indicated a British willingness to recognize Soviet claims to the Baltic
states. Welles warned Halifax on June 15 against weakening the moral
principle involved and in response to the ambassador's inquiry said
that it was impossible for the United States to determine what assistance it might render if Germany attacked the Soviet Union.[9]

The Department of State was also moving to correct its position
with regard to Japan. One obvious reason was that the Hull-Nomura
talks were getting nowhere. The United States had finally set forth
its position May 31 in a redraft of the Matsuoka proposals of May
12, which in turn were a redraft of the Walsh-Drought paper of April
14. The American draft conceded nothing of significance to the Japanese. They would have to state explicitly that the Axis pact did not
apply in cases of self-defense, that is, if the United States became
involved with Germany in the Atlantic. American assistance to Britain was not banned, as in the Japanese draft. The United States
would "suggest," not "forthwith request," that the Chiang regime
negotiate peace and was not obliged to withhold aid to China if
Chiang refused. In the American draft the question of stationing Japanese troops in parts of China after a peace treaty was left for further
discussion. The United States was not required to renew its trade
treaty with Japan. Japan, however, would have to pledge that its "controlling" (not simply its "declared") policy was the maintenance of
peace in the Pacific (not just in the southwest Pacific). The Americans
desired explicit reference to the principle of non-discrimination in
trade. The status of Manchukuo (Manchuria) was left for "amicable
negotiation."[10]

During the next three weeks Japanese and American negotiators
met eight times to explore their differences and made no progress

whatsoever in resolving them. On the contrary, by June 21 disagree-ment seemed broader and more intractable. Once Hull and Nomura met alone, occasionally they met with their associates, more often the associates met without the principals. Increasing use of regular dip-lomatic personnel on both sides—in effect bureaucratizing the dis-cussions—introduced greater precision and continuity but also had the effect of more sharply registering disagreements and multiplying the number of issues. Efforts were made to shade differences by elim-inating clauses, removing them to annexes, or rewording them; but no matter how the words were squeezed and massaged, the problems remained.

The most sensitive problem was the relationship of both powers to the European war. Japanese officials, Colonel Iwakuro for one, freely admitted that the "tenor" of any Japanese interpretation of its alliance obligations was bound to be affected by the fact of any agree-ment concluded with the United States, but they were adamant in their refusal, and so instructed, to permit any language explicitly weakening the tie. Consequently the United States would have to take on faith that Japan would not declare war on the United States if the United States became engaged in war with Germany. Less salient for the moment but no more tractable was the problem of ending the war in China. To the extent that the United States was prepared to engage in that task, to the point of urging or pressing a settlement on China, it required terms it could support, and it was not prepared to support peacetime Japanese garrisons in China or, in these circumstances, to assist in legitimating the Japanese conquest of Manchuria.

It was not simply a case of circling back over the same ground: new issues arose and dormant ones took on new life. The American side began to complain about Japanese restrictions on American business in China and to harp on the need for specific statements of adher-ence to the principle of non-discrimination in trade. Questions were raised about how far Japan would go in support of its puppet regime at Nanking in the making and implementation of peace with the government at Chungking. The Japanese, mentioning the possible American use of Singapore, urged a statement renouncing acquisi-tion of new military bases. The Americans replied that, if the Japa-nese considered this a matter distinct from any renunciation of ter-ritorial designs, then indeed a new and serious question had been raised.[11] Hull spoke of the need for "clear-cut and unequivocal terms," a contradiction of the way diplomacy usually, and Japanese diplo-macy always, worked. He noted a steady winnowing of the advances made in the original scheme of April. Most important, Hull himself began wondering aloud about the sincerity of the Japanese in pursuing the negotiations. That was a concern, he told Nomura, "in the light of the loud statements which Matsuoka and others were daily making" about Japan's indissoluble ties with the Axis.[12]

Unquestionably negotiation of Japanese-American conflicts was a formidable task. Progress, however, depended on damping disagreement not broadening it, so here external influences as well as inherent difficulties must have been obstructing the path. These are not difficult to find. One factor was the declining value of the Hull-Nomura talks in driving a wedge between Japan and its alliance partners as compared with the rising embarrassment they were causing for America's own partnerships. Publicity and pointed questions led to promises of consultation and loss of flexibility on the American side. In a MAGIC intercept read on May 26, Matsuoka assured Berlin that the alliance was the cornerstone of Imperial policy. His vehement protestations of fidelity to the alliance raised the question whether it was worth continuing the talks so long as he was foreign minister, especially since Ambassador Grew was reporting that serious differences existed between the stormy petrel and Prime Minister Konoe.[13]

Another factor was disturbing information that the Japanese southward advance was about to be resumed. On June 17 a MAGIC decrypt showed that Japan was seeking German help in forcing Vichy to grant it air and sea bases in southern Indochina. These included, according to a decrypt of June 19, Saigon and the excellent harbor at Cam Ranh Bay as well as Hue, Nhatrang, Soctrang, Kompontrach, Siemriep, and Pnompenh. Alongside a disclaimer of any intention to invade the area, Tokyo said it would "take whatever measures might be necessary" to secure its aims.[14] This harbinger of further aggression came on the heels of a Dutch rebuff to Japan over Indonesian oil. On June 7, Batavia politely but firmly refused to grant Japan special privileges and more oil, ending protracted negotiations. Grew reported that Japanese extremists under German influence were demanding that Japan take strong action in response.[15] By now Americans firmly held that negotiation in the context of aggression was appeasement.

The approaching German-Soviet climax provided further reasons for disengagement with the Japanese. A pact of Soviet submission would heighten the aura of appeasement surrounding any Japanese-American agreement. Soviet-German war would bring more complex disadvantages, which were put to paper shortly after June 22 but in all probability influenced thinking beforehand. Maxwell Hamilton, chief of the Far Eastern Division, wrote that of course by freeing Japan from concern about a Soviet threat, war could accelerate the southward advance, turning any Japanese-American agreement into a scrap of paper. The alternative thesis, which enjoyed greater favor, was that Japan might join Germany in attacking the Soviets, which would make unnecessary an agreement aimed at preventing Japan's southward advance and contradict the agreement's pledge to maintain peace in the Pacific.

Walter Adams, assistant chief of the Far Eastern Division, carried this latter argument a big step further. Any advantage the United States might secure in keeping peace in the south while Japan attacked in the north would be offset, he contended, by the resulting weakening of Soviet resistance. If the American interest lay in defeating "the forces of aggression as a whole," this nation should seek to "immobilize Japan both as regards an attack upon Siberia and as regards an attack against Singapore or the Dutch East Indies." The best policy was to exhibit the same reserve toward Japan as the European Division was recommending toward the Soviet Union, though for different reasons. In this instance the object would be to deter a Siberian attack by rendering Japan "uncertain in regard to the intentions of the United States in the South Pacific."[16] That line of advice would gain increasing currency. All advice pointed toward putting diplomacy in abeyance.

Secretary Hull called Ambassador Nomura to this apartment June 21 on the eve of the German attack on Russia, handed him a statement and a rewrite of the May 31 draft agreement and proceeded to attack the Japanese foreign minister for supporting German aggression. His message here and in the statement was that the insistence by Matsuoka and the pro-Axis faction on Japan's fulfillment of its alliance obligations was making it impossible to achieve a Japanese-American settlement. In the statement and revised draft the American position was shuttered and padlocked. The secretary of state had reluctantly concluded, the statement ended, that the United States "must await some clearer indication than has yet been given that the Japanese Government as a whole desires to pursue courses of peace.... "[17] It was not a break-off; the Japanese were invited to continue. The targeting of a faction within the other government was unusual in diplomacy but the move produced what was intended, a tidy position, a pause, and the placing on Japan of the burden of moving onward.

The United States, no less than other nations, sensed that summer would bring great events which could shift the foundations of policy. Having positioned itself to widen its choices, it cleared the decks and waited.

Germany attacked the Soviet Union before dawn on June 22, 1941. Three giant wedges of armored and motorized forces, with 1,500 tanks in the center wedge and 600 on each side, punched through Soviet frontier defenses and soon were streaking across the plains of eastern Poland and the western marches of Russia. Panzer columns often advanced fifty or sixty miles a day, leaping 250 miles to Minsk and 200 miles to the Dvina, halfway to Leningrad, in the first five days. The center drove northeastward, one Panzer group the size of an army on either side of the straight road to Moscow, circling, smashing, and plunging foward in one double envelopment after another. In the first month they reached to within 130 miles of Moscow. The Russians lost over 2,000 aircraft in the first two days. North, south, and center the Russian fronts disintegrated, yielding hundreds of thousands of prisoners. At the rate of advance in the first month it was hard to imagine the survival of the Soviet Union until fall.[18]

Yet Russia was not like the other campaigns. The vastness, the unending stretches of flat plain, became awesome and disturbing. Curzio Malaparte captures the oppressive sense of space creeping into the exhilaration of rapid conquest in his description of a German column bedding down at night:

> Then the wind rises—a moist cold wind that fills one's bones with an immense numbing weariness. The wind that sweeps this Ukrainian plateau is laden with the scent of a thousand herbs and plants. From the darkness of the fields comes a ceaseless crackle as the moisture of the night causes the sunflowers to droop on their long, wrinkled stalks. All about us the corn makes a soft rustling sound, like the rustle of a silk gown. A great murmur rises through the dark countryside which is filled with the sound of slow breathing, of deep sighs.[19]

In spite of the stunning success of the Panzer columns, results of the first month's fighting fell far short of German expectations. Most significant were the instances of tenacious Russian resistance, even counterattacks. Pockets of surrounded Red Army troops held out; guerrilla warfare began along the lengthening German supply lines. No less, German intelligence had underestimated the quality of Russian arms and the amount of war industry within reach of the initial German thrusts. Critical were German supply deficiencies. The fast forces carried adequate supplies only for their first deep penetrations into the Soviet Union. After some 300 miles the tanks had to pause for resupply and for the infantry to catch up. Lacking sufficient motor transport of its own, the German army scrounged among stocks of defeated countries, gathering over 2,000 different kinds of vehicles requiring over a million spare parts for Army Group Center alone. The different track widths of Russian and European railroads, the muddled German army system of supply control, the lack of hard-surface roads in Russia, the weather, and lack of motor oil began to slow the advance. Within the month half of Army Group South's trucks were out of action.[20]

A further problem was the lack of any clear-cut strategic consensus, leading to growing differences among the generals and between them and Hitler as to which of the three army groups and which of the objectives—capture of the great cities or destruction of the Red Army—should be given priority. As the front widened, leaving flanks hanging in the air, the distance between tank columns and foot soldiers lengthened. The Dvina-Smolensk-Dneiper line was attained, but fighting continued west of it and the high season of campaigning slipped by.

This vast distant drama of space and time captured American attention. After banner headlines June 23 and 24, the *New York Herald Tribune* maintained average daily headlines four columns wide during July. Since both sides denied foreign newsmen access to the front and manipulated the facts of fighting in a "war of communiqués," only the sketchiest of pictures of the tide of battle emerged, with gross exaggerations of enemy casualties and prisoners taken. Yet with all the distortion and dimness, the titanic proportions of the struggle were apparent.

The first feeling was one of relief and not a little glee. Ambassador Grew expressed a common belief when he said the new war was "the best thing that could have happened. Dog eat dog. Let the Nazis and the Communists so weaken each other that the democracies will soon gain the upper hand or at least will be released from their dire peril." Stimson reported to the president the view of the War Department that Germany would have to postpone invasion of Britain and slack off on plans and campaigns elsewhere. It could not interfere with the forthcoming American occupation of Iceland. The door was now open, he advised, for the president to lead the way into winning the Battle of the Atlantic. Harry Hopkins was reported to have said that the war would further scatter German forces and complicate the German position. Vichy officials conveyed a more sanguine view. They had thought Germany could get what it wanted without war. Failure to do so was an indication of weakness, that Germany feared American participation, even that it had lost the war. Now was America's chance to act, said one French official.[21]

President Roosevelt was among the optimists. It is impossible to say whether or not he shared the general view that Hitler would make demands and Stalin would submit, but once the invasion began he took a consistently positive view of developments. "Now comes this Russian diversion," he wrote Leahy on June 26. "If it is more than just that it will mean the liberation of Europe from Nazi domination.... " At the same time, inclined to view Soviet policy as more pragmatic than ideological, he did not think the democracies needed to worry about Russian domination of Europe. He could see no "intellectually satisfying" explanation for Hitler's attack, he told Lord Halifax on July 7. If the main purpose was to gain world sympathy by war on Communist Russia, then Hitler's sense of public psychology was wrong and he had made "his first big political miscalculation," while the free world had gained precious time.[22]

Just how much time was anyone's guess. The Berlin embassy reported German predictions that Russian resistance would be crushed by August 1. British intelligence anticipated that the Germans would reach the Moscow-Rostov line in three weeks. A British informant of the embassy in Moscow estimated on June 30 that they would reach Moscow in five days. Ambassador Steinhardt believed Moscow would fall in much less than sixty days; Sir Stafford Cripps, the British ambassador, saw not less than sixty. The War Department predicted from one to three months. Military intelligence measured German progress by comparing daily advances with those in France in 1940, Stimson objecting that the conditions were different.[23] Estimates fluctuated even day to day, but a trend emerged. In the first week the universal view was dark. The main question, said General Marshall, was whether the Russians would manage to withdraw and avoid encirclement. The Germans had struck early enough so that the crops were too green to burn. Ultimately, he said, the area between Moscow and the Black Sea was the key to Russia. To the chief of staff, the Russians, lacking high officers of quality, were showing no signs of skillful maneuver. In the first days of July, Stimson was more discouraged than ever by the progress of the "German Moloch."[24]

The American embassy in Moscow, affected by tremors of fear at the capital and making plans for evacuation, was consistently gloomy. German progress seemed less than expected July 2, but more because of German caution than Soviet resistance. On July 3 it reported the German offensive "completely successful" and a week later nuanced that estimate slightly on the negative side: German losses were indeed severe and Russian resistance "considerably greater" than the Germans expected, but even so there was no evidence "that the German offensive has encountered any serious setbacks." Meanwhile, as women and children began to leave Moscow, the embassy reported fears of a huge German envelopment of the city. On July 17, German fast forces were understood to be within 75 miles of Moscow. On July 19, Soviet troops and supplies were said to be moving *east* of Moscow. On July 22 the city was bombed for the first time. Steinhardt's view of Russian resistance was more negative than that of his Japanese colleague, who spoke of serious German difficulties.[25]

Outside Russia as the mists lifted slightly in July, the idea of a short war began to fade. On June 30 the American embassy in Berlin noted that the Germans were facing "stubborn and even desperate opposition and enormous tactical difficulties." Even German propaganda spoke of fanatical Soviet resistance. The American legation in Switzerland gave high and indeed exaggerated figures for German losses (one million casualties in the first three weeks, for example). Its sources reported that the German General Staff had grossly underestimated Soviet fighting capacity and leadership, and that the invasion was running behind schedule. Vichy officials believed that Hitler had made a "serious psychological error" in expecting the Russian people to rise.[26] London was encouraged: the Germans would have to postpone an invasion of the island, even though only temporarily. At the Foreign Office a German defeat by Russia even entered the realm of the conceivable. The battle in Russia, wrote one prognosticator, might well be an epic of war, dimming Britain's lonely struggle and reviving the Russian "mystique."[27] That sort of thinking would have seemed madly optimistic to American officials, but if A. A. Berle is at all representative, they began to doubt a German invasion of Britain and to accept that German casualties were greater than anticipated and progress less. But, Berle added, "no living being can tell what will wash out of this."[28] The one big change in American perceptions of the conflict at the end of the first month was the realization that Germany faced a costly and difficult struggle.

Summing up one month of the war, the *New York Times* pointed out that Hitler had unleashed "the eternal war" between Teuton and Slav. The Germans recklessly engaged themselves with their "natural enemy" in battle of "unprecedented ferocity." Six hundred miles into Russia the invaders were only on the margins, and the supposedly "annihilated" Red Army kept reforming itself. "Nazi tanks go where the Golden Horde once ruled but the dust and mud may swallow them up too."[29]

Now that war had come, Soviet-American relations looked entirely different from the way they had looked before June 22 when the question was appeasement or war. Now the posture of cool reserve urged by the European Division seemed quite mistaken, at least to the White House. Churchill, knowing that every day of Soviet resistance postponed a German invasion just that much, made an immediate offer of cooperation and assistance. The American statement of policy, made by Acting Secretary Welles at a press conference June 23, was by no means comradely. It dwelt on German treachery (and the implicit folly of relying on non-aggression pacts with Hitler) and on American revulsion for Soviet denial of freedom of worship. Soviet Communist dictatorship was just as alien to the American people as Nazi dictatorship. But the issue at the moment facing a "realistic America," the statement continued, was the defeat of Hitler's plan of world conquest and "any defense against Hitlerism, any rallying of the forces opposing Hitlerism, from whatever source these forces may spring" enhanced American security.[30] This was not an offer of aid to the Soviet Union, but it sought to prepare the way by urging Americans to set aside their profound aversion to that nation and consider their national interest. Despite the icy tone it went substantially beyond the posture American diplomats recommended before the German attack.

In subsequent weeks Roosevelt took a number of steps to implement the offer. He exempted the Soviet Union from the order freezing assets. He ruled against invoking the neutrality act and inclusion of Soviet ports in combat areas. A number of minor problems were resolved and one difficult one was buried: the Soviet embassy was firmly told not to raise the issue of the American sequestering of Estonian, Latvian, and Lithuanian ships. The State Department set up machinery for expediting Soviet orders and investigated means of payment.[31] On July 10 the president, who always seemed one step ahead of informed opinion on the possibility of prolonged and prolonging Soviet resistance, saw Soviet Ambassador Oumansky for the first time in 1941. Just in was an encouraging report from London on the Russian fighting. He promised to fill the most urgently needed Soviet requests, provided the British approved and they could be shipped to reach the front before October 1 and the onset of winter. The more machines the Germans used up in Russia, he added, the more certain and rapid the German defeat, since German production was not as great as supposed.[32] Clearly the president was moving to aid the Russians, indeed accelerating and setting the pace in the administration. Even so, he was covering his bets: what could be sent immediately was not necessarily what the Russians were asking for (machine tools, gasoline refineries, explosives plants), and he had not given Soviet requirements priority over all other demands.

Very little entered the supply pipeline to Russia that first month— only $6.5 million worth of goods—as a result of the president's over-tures. In fact the United States and the Soviet Union were just com-ing face to face with the problems of supply: the remoteness of the Soviet Union, the lack of transport and communication, American public opposition to including the Soviet Union in Lend-Lease, dis-inclination to reveal production and weapons secrets to the Soviets, refusal of the Soviets to help in establishing priorities by explaining the use intended for the goods, and lack of specificity in Soviet orders. One fundamental problem underlay all difficulties: allocation of the limited output immediately available among Great Britain, the Soviet Union, the American armed forces, and other friendly nations. The president required a system for doing so, beyond that a review of strategic priorities in the light of the new situation, and beyond that an estimate of how much American war production would be required to defeat the nation's enemies. July 9 he ordered the War Department to begin this study of arms requirements, work-ing from the battlefield back to the factory, the results of which were known as the Victory Program.[33] Not so much the German attack as Russian resistance opened entirely new vistas of war and policy for the United States.

The American perspective on the future of Europe was changing. A central question of July was how to deal with the emerging alliance between Great Britain and the Soviet Union. In spite of its predica-ment, Moscow lost no time in asserting its interest in a boundary with Poland not far removed from that of the Nazi-Soviet pact of 1939. Various reports and remarks roused suspicions at the State Department that Britain would accede to such demands as an induce-ment for Russia to continue the war. In conversation with Welles, for example, Lord Halifax had encouraged the idea of accepting Russian domain over the Baltic republics, to the disgust of Berle, who saw this as the old Foreign Office practice of engaging in "polite dishonor" when it served British interests. In the same vein, an Associated Press dispatch carried a statement by the head of the Yugoslav government-in-exile that Britain and the United States had guaranteed not to dismember Yugoslavia at the end of the war and that Britain had promised Trieste to Yugoslavia. A declaration by Eden promising independence to recently captured Syria, formerly a French mandate of the League of Nations, suggested British unilateral commitments in the Middle East as well. Further cause of American concern was evidence that Britain was taking the lead in organizing the governments-in-exile of occupied Europe for gathering, sharing, transporting, and distributing food and raw materials when they were liberated. Granting humanitarian intent, Berle also saw a British effort "to channelize the trade and economics of this area through London when the war is over" and to exclude the United States.[34]

Negotiations were indeed under way between Moscow and London. Stalin was insisting on a formal understanding between the two nations for mutual assistance and no separate peace. He was not asking the British for territorial commitments, and the British, though anxious to close, were keeping Washington fully informed. The British were also mediating for an agreement between the Polish government-in-exile and the Soviet Union. Here the main issue was territorial. The Poles wanted Soviet recognition of Poland's prewar boundary defined by the Treaty of Riga of 1921 when Polish forces supplied from the West had driven the Bolsheviks far to the east of the boundary considered ethnographically Polish by the Paris Peace Conference. The Soviet Union was prepared to renounce the Nazi-Soviet Pact of course and revert to an ethnographic frontier, but in fact the two boundaries were much closer to each other than to the Riga line. The Poles in fear sought American intervention to secure the larger interwar Poland. Stalin also wanted to set up national committees of Poles, Czechs, and Yugoslavs in the Soviet Union, giving rise to concern that these might become Soviet-sponsored shadow governments competing with the exile regimes in London.[35]

On July 14 the president, warned by Berle, cabled Churchill that it was much too early to make territorial or economic commitments. He referred to rumors of "trades or deals" which the British were alleged to be making, citing as examples the "stupid" stories about Yugoslavia and reminding Churchill of the "serious trouble" such promises to Italians and others caused in 1919. He dwelt on the virtues of plebiscite and wondered whether, Croat and Serb hating each other so, it might not be applied in Yugoslavia. Behind the banter this was a sharp and disagreeable message. No wonder Churchill did not answer it personally. Implicitly it raised a question about every European frontier and political understanding. It was in effect the "general caveat" Berle had called for, a Roosevelt restatement of the non-recognition policy.[36]

So a sudden storm arose in British-American relations. American policymakers were immediately reminded of the secret treaties which so bedeviled Wilson's diplomacy in World War I. At the Foreign Office, British officials drew on the same historical analogy but with the opposite fear, that Roosevelt, like Wilson, saw himself as world peacemaker.[37] The price of an independent policy was exclusion from the councils of those engaged together, with all the suspicion thereby engendered. This was particularly the case for the United States now that two great powers, Britain and Russia, were collaborating.

The problem posed by the new rhythms of European diplomacy was not confined to bureaucratic definitions of national interest. Roosevelt feared that, in setting precedents for postwar settlements, Britain might undermine the political foundations upon which the anti-Axis forces could most effectively wage war and which he required to lead the American people into war if necessary. Not that he or the American public had a clear idea of the sort of peace they wanted. Certain Wilsonian principles were basic: self-determination, non-use of force in international disputes, non-interference in the internal affairs of other nations, freedom of trade, and so forth. How these principles might apply to specific situations neither the president nor the State Department was ready to say. Recognizing that European frontier definitions tended to divide Americans, the president was exceedingly reluctant to make commitments at this stage and was greatly disturbed over the possibility of being presented with faits accomplis. Any agreement diminishing the national estate of an occupied country would equally diminish its will to engage in resistance against the Nazi conqueror. The president's object was to keep public expectations high by keeping political issues open.

The United States had two frameworks of policy in 1941: one internationalist looking toward cooperation with other nations great and small, free and occupied, in destroying the Nazi scourge; the other nationalist, focusing directly on the safety and survival of the United States and protection of the Western Hemisphere. In the spring, when the German threat seemed so stark and terrible, the nationalist framework predominated. Now as the balance righted and coalition opportunities beckoned, the internationalist framework moved to the fore. Roosevelt recognized that in order to protect his position he would have to collaborate more actively with the belligerents and especially with Britain; the makeweight to the new Russian factor would be greater Anglo-American political intimacy. On July 11 the president dispatched Harry Hopkins to London to arrange a meeting with Churchill.[38]

Churchill was probably not unhappy that Anglo-Soviet diplomacy was drawing the Americans closer. With Hopkins in personal consultation by July 17, the British worked to ease American concerns. Eden assured the House of Commons that the Anglo-Soviet agreement of July 14 contained no territorial guarantees or recognition of territorial changes. The Poles were distressed by their failure to secure explicit Soviet recognition of their prewar boundary, but they gained the solatium of a note from Eden that Britain would not recognize territorial changes resulting from the Nazi-Soviet Pact and which pledged that Britain had given no territorial guarantees in its own agreement with the Soviets. The Department of State would have preferred a response by the prime minister to the president's message of July 14 but professed itself satisfied with the assurance to the Poles. The general issue of postwar territorial guarantees remained on the agenda for a meeting of the principals.[39]

Just as the problem of adjusting American policy to the shifting political relations of Europe prompted closer collaboration with Great Britain, so developments in the Battle of the Atlantic drew the two nations deeper into a working partnership. Both broad avenues of policy pointed toward a summit.

As German armies began their drive eastward, the naval reinforcements from the Pacific were preparing to enter service on the Atlantic. The battleships and cruisers transited the Canal by June 9 and filtered into fleet missions as they readied over the course of the next six weeks. The *Idaho, New Mexico,* and *Mississippi* joined the *Texas, New York,* and *Arkansas* so that by the end of July two battleships were always on the mid-Atlantic sentry line, steaming to and fro between a point southeast of the Grand Banks and the southern extremity of the German blockade zone around Iceland. Three carriers operated out of Bermuda—the *Yorktown, Wasp,* and, while the *Ranger* was under overhaul, the escort carrier *Long Island*—but their light cruiser escorts from the Pacific were waylaid for troopship escort and did not all join the carriers until August. Only then could all the heavy cruisers join the battleships in their assigned positions near the convoy routes.[40] Steaming back and forth across the Atlantic these summer days was pleasant enough, the ship lit up at night with a searchlight on the flag. So far as the records show, no German raiders or supply ships were encountered.

In fact the patrols made a substantial contribution just by their presence. On June 19 the *Texas* reached the northern extremity of its patrol at the edge of the blockade zone and turned back. Unknowingly it was hunted that day and the next by U-boat 203 which never gained a good firing position because of the battleship's speed and zig-zag course.[41] German submarines had been under orders not to attack American merchant or naval vessels except in the blockade zone. On the eve of BARBAROSSA, Admiral Karl Doenitz issued orders first allowing, then disallowing, attacks in the blockade zone. The near-incident with the *Texas* settled the matter: stringent orders from the Fuehrer forbade any and all attacks on American men-of-war. Hitler was determined to avoid war with the United States until victory in Russia was assured. U-boats were to confine their attacks, inside and outside the blockade area, to cruisers, battleships, and aircraft carriers clearly identified as enemy. "[E]very incident involving the USA is to be avoided." On July 9, Hitler informed the navy that he wished to avoid war with the United States for another month or two.[42] Thus the intervention of American warships had the effect of making the North Atlantic more problematical and less profitable for U-boats.

The carrier searches from Bermuda toward the Azores and the patrols by four-stack cruisers into the gap between Africa and Brazil may have had a similar effect on German supply vessels. Close coordination of the two navies was easily effected at Bermuda. On June 4, in the midst of a widespread search for supply ships sent out for the *Bismarck*, the *Yorktown* took aboard a British naval officer, presumably to communicate any sightings to a British cruiser lying in wait as a "killing force," to use Churchill's words. The carrier found nothing, but northwest of the Azores, outside the *Yorktown*'s reach, lay two German supply ships which the British sank June 5 and 6.[43] At the same time the *Milwaukee* cruising near the equator passed near two German tankers without locating them. Again, the British sank these June 5 and 6. Undoubtedly American patrols made untraveled pockets of the North Atlantic less secure for German ships, but credit for the clean sweep of German supply ships in the Atlantic during June is due ULTRA, which made it possible for the British, beginning in May 1941, to read German naval communications currently.[44] With precise locations of German ships already in hand, the British cruisers did not need American eyes.

By July 1941 the United States and Germany had reached a stand-off in the Atlantic, though a tenuous one entirely dependent on the progress of German arms in Russia. On June 14, Roosevelt learned of the sinking in May of the American merchant ship *Robin Moor*. He toyed with the idea of asking Brazil to release a German vessel it was holding so it could be seized in retaliation, but the sinking was several weeks old, so it undoubtedly seemed wiser to let sleeping dogs lie, at least until American troops had arrived safely in Iceland.[45]

On July 1, agreement was finally reached with the government of Iceland for the United States to assume responsibility for defense of that island. While Iceland was by no means averse to American protection, it was anxious to avoid the ambiguity of joint Anglo-American defense, especially since one was a belligerent, the other not. On the other hand, President Roosevelt, who had originally spoken of relief rather than reinforcement of the British garrison, by June 28 shied away from taking sole responsibility. The complexities of the Iceland expedition were becoming apparent: the shortage of troop transports, the precious few American divisions ready or near-ready for active service, the legislative restriction against use of draftees outside the Western Hemisphere, and the likely storm of criticism if he sought to lift it. He simply could not afford to assume sole responsibility. The issue was resolved by agreement that the American forces would supplement and "eventually" replace the British. But the president was determined that Iceland be more secure than before, so he pressed his reluctant advisers to increase the American contingent from 7,500 to 10,000 and insisted on sending a squadron of fighter planes.[46] In spite of the German invasion of the Soviet Union, Roosevelt in early July remained primarily concerned with guarding the Atlantic line. In fact his first reaction was to seize the opportunity to enhance the immediate physical safety of the nation.

Iceland was a new departure as well. More than the Azores it was the turntable of the Atlantic, sitting astride broad avenues of entry into that ocean from German-controlled waters and convoy routes to Britain and possibly the Soviet Union. This was the first American military expedition outside the hemisphere since World War I. With it the nation ventured into deeper waters of great power combination and quasi-war. Task Force 19 carrying the 1st Provisional Marine Brigade, waiting at Argentia for completion of the agreement with Iceland, sailed at once. On this mission the Atlantic Fleet was not patrolling on the margins of U-boat operations but cutting directly through the convoy lanes. To ensure safety the troop transports were escorted by two battleships, two cruisers, and thirteen destroyers.[47] The task force arrived at Reykjavik on July 7 after an uncontested passage.

The president was thrilled, "just riding on the waves." Three days later word came that the brand-new *Tirpitz* was loose and headed for Iceland or Greenland. What the *Bismarck* had done to the *Hood* seemed destined for the World War I battleships *Texas* and *New York* at Reykjavik. The disparity in maximum range of the big guns was at least 4,000 yards, to say nothing of the German advantage in modern fire control. All heaved a big sigh of relief when the German monster was found to be still at Kiel.[48]

In the course of July, Atlantic jitters subsided. Accompanying the next contingent to Iceland were the modernized battleship *Mississippi*, two heavy cruisers, and the *Wasp*. Heavy bombing severely damaged the *Scharnhorst* and *Gneisenau* at Brest. Reports of the establishment of German U-boat bases in West African ports proved false; chances of an attack on Gibraltar or Spain declined as the Germans extended themselves in Russia. On June 3 at Vichy, General Weygand had launched a "scathing attack" on Darlan's collaborationist policy and by June 6 had forced a reconsideration of the Paris Protocols. Murphy reported that French North African policy had suffered no change after all.[49] Hitler on the eve of BARBAROSSA was in no position to bring Vichy to heel. Meanwhile war in the desert was at a stalemate: a British offensive in June had stalled but it had sufficiently damaged Rommel's forces, which were denied reinforcement, to immobilize him. Further east the British put down the revolt in Iraq and defeated the Vichy French in Syria. A German thrust through Turkey no longer seemed imminent: American military intelligence considered danger to the Middle East to be materially reduced by the war on Russia.

This stabilization occurring in June and July, after months of crisis and disaster, enabled the American government to come to grips with the problem it had been forced to sidestep since April: the central strategic question of protection of convoys against the U-boat. Indeed, with troops on Iceland, it would have to begin running and protecting convoys in the western Atlantic. Early in July, probably July 1 by phone from Hyde Park, the president authorized the navy to begin planning for escort of convoy.[50]

By June 1941, convoy and escort in the North Atlantic had evolved substantially into the system that continued through the war. Merchant ships now received protection all the way from North America to the Western Approaches of Great Britain, divided into slow (SC) convoys averaging six and one-half knots and fast (HX) convoys averaging nine. Escort groups, at this time composed of a destroyer and several corvettes, changed hands at a Mid-Ocean Meeting Point (MOMP), the relieved group continuing to Iceland for refueling and the relievers shepherding the fifty or sixty merchantmen onward. The convoy route depended on the season and the location of U-boats. In summer, with drift ice receding, the best route lay to the north close to Greenland and Iceland and as far as possible from German aircraft, though no route was ideal and this one entailed laboring through heavy beam seas. At any time the convoy might be diverted to avoid U-boats. The Royal Canadian Navy operated the western leg from St. John's, Newfoundland, and the Royal Navy the eastern.[51]

In formulating a plan for the president the navy found itself divided on Atlantic strategy. In mid-June, the Admiralty, picking up on Roosevelt's suggestion of using Iceland as a transshipment point, suggested that, given the westerly drift of the Battle of the Atlantic, the ABC-1 agreement be changed to assign the Support Force destroyers to St. John's, Newfoundland, home base for convoy escorts in the western Atlantic, instead of to the United Kingdom. American assumption of escort responsibility from North America to Iceland would release British and Canadian escorts for thicker protection in the eastern Atlantic and on other routes.[52] Now skeptical of an American declaration of war implementing ABC-1, the hard-pressed Royal Navy preferred a bird in hand to two in the bush.

With this recommendation Admiral King agreed, but for different reasons. He faced a task of growing difficulty in husbanding the Support Force destroyers for service in British waters while allowing for necessary yard work, "working up," and providing escort for his own warships. This was not all. King had been chief of staff to Vice Admiral Henry T. Mayo, commander of the Atlantic Fleet in World War I. Mayo had strongly objected to the establishment in Britain of an independent naval command under Admiral William Sims subordinated to overall British direction. Stark had been on Sims' staff and history seemed to be repeating itself.[53] On July 2, King wrote Stark that in his view the dispatch of American forces to Europe under existing war plans was outdated by extension of the escort system to North America and American occupation of Iceland. Following the cardinal principle that coordination of naval forces depended on each having its own defined sphere of operation, the British and American navies should switch tasks, the Americans taking over escort in the western Atlantic and the British the American war assignments in the eastern.[54] King had opportunities of presenting his views to the president, who was by now accustomed to dealing directly and alone with the admiral. King, who wore the Navy Cross and Distinguished Service Medal with Gold Star, and harbored "a storm within him," was not one easily to acquiesce in withdrawal of ships from his command.[55]

Admiral Stark and his staff disagreed with King and the Admiralty. British survival, they believed, depended on the earliest possible American entry into the war and implementation rather than change of the ABC-1 agreement. Iceland was strategically significant primarily as it related to Britain, Stark insisted, and to antisubmarine warfare conducted in the Western Approaches, which remained the area of greatest danger and where the Support Force belonged. This was a view to which Churchill and Stimson, in their anxiety for American entry into the war, heartily subscribed.[56] Stark and Turner now opposed establishing a base and garrison on Iceland.[57] The island looked to them like a dead end. Escort in the western Atlantic would be useful only so far as it promptly produced an incident—and war—which propelled the navy into British waters.

Admiral Stark warned the president that "every day of delay" in getting into the war was dangerous. Only a "war psychology" in America would lift production to necessary levels. He urged Roosevelt to "seize the psychological opportunity presented by the German-Russian clash and announce and start escorting immediately and protecting the Western Atlantic on a large scale." Western Hemisphere Defense Plan Three, formulated while the president vacationed at Hyde Park and vetted by the Admiralty and Churchill, embodied this all-out approach. According to the draft plan, the United States would escort all shipping—American, Icelandic, and British—as far as Iceland and destroy Axis forces encountered anywhere in the Western Hemisphere. Suspected Axis supply ships would be searched. British escorts would be withdrawn except for five merchant cruisers and twenty Canadian escorts. To these would be added twenty-seven old and twenty-seven new American destroyers (six squadrons) organized in escort units of five or six each. The six battleships and five heavy cruisers of the Atlantic Fleet would be available for convoy protection when raiders were loose. Action along these lines, Admiral Stark believed, "would almost certainly involve us in war."[58]

The Atlantic Fleet was not prepared to go into action in any such numbers immediately. The twenty-seven destroyers of the Support Force were ready to fight, but at the moment thirteen of them were escorting the marines to Iceland, not returning until July 21, and one was under repair. A third of the Atlantic Fleet destroyers, including all but two of the Pacific reinforcements, were required just to escort carriers, battleships, and cruisers. Newly completed destroyers of Squadron 11 were assigned to the Support Force but some were filling in as carrier escorts for destroyers undergoing overhaul. Destroyer Squadron 13, also assigned to the Support Force, was still completing; its first ship would be ready July 20 and all vessels would need weeks for trials and "working up." Squadron 27, old destroyers in the Caribbean, the last addition to the Support Force, required extended refit. One division (four ships) would be ready early in September, the other in October. On July 9 fifteen destroyers were immediately available. By August the fleet could call on twenty-nine, by September forty-three, and by October fifty. The force contemplated for merchant convoy escort would not reach its promised strength of fifty-four until the end of October.[59]

The Atlantic Fleet was still in transition, absorbing vessels from the Pacific Fleet, reshuffling ships, divisions, and squadrons for compatibility and suitability to assignment, overhauling, refitting, and repairing. Most of the fleet now operated from Newport, Rhode Island. Argentia in Newfoundland opened as a naval base July 15, but Iceland still lacked American base facilities. None of the logistical services and only part of the elaborate communications networks necessary for an international trade escort system were in place. Planning was just beginning.

The immediate capabilities of the Atlantic Fleet were not of critical concern to Stark and his staff because they did not envisage a sustained independent role for it, but rather a transitional one, triggering war and leading to combined operations with the British. Their preferred course was Western Hemisphere Defense Plan Three with its all-out escort and hemisphere-wide state of belligerency. On July 9, Stark presented the president with three alternatives. Roosevelt may have requested options or the navy deemed it prudent to offer them. In any case he could choose Plan Three or one of two less drastic schemes: first, escort limited to American and Icelandic ships bound for Iceland with attack on German submarines and raiders which sought to interfere; and, second, the same limited escort with attack on German forces anywhere in the Western Hemisphere.[60]

Roosevelt was not ready for all-out measures. Admiral King, who was at the White House on July 9 and 17, probably resisted an immediate all-out solution, arguing the unreadiness of his fleet. Time was needed to sort problems and, in King's words, "get correctly started on this complicated situation."[61] Operational limitations went hand in hand with the president's inclination to take one step at a time. That step he took, however. Roosevelt's decision was, as usual, a blend of advice, yet peculiarly his own: American naval protection would be restricted to convoys under American control and formed on American and Icelandic ships, but British merchant ships could join up. This more limited and, as the British said, "cumbersome" approach became Western Hemisphere Defense Plan Four. One advantage of the plan, aside from providing convoys with a figleaf of American nationality, was that it provided for as many convoys as the Americans could escort, not necessarily as many as sailed.[62]

Designing an escort system under Plan Four proved to be immensely difficult. With protection limited to convoys on the line of communication to Iceland, planners had to determine how far from a convoy U-boats posed a threat justifying attack by escorts. By June the Admiralty was providing the Navy Department in Washington with daily convoy and U-boat locations.[63] How was Washington to keep the American convoys and escorts informed? Who would divert convoys from newly discovered U-boats? How would British ships and American convoys meet up? Who was responsible for the safety of British ships joining a convoy? Who would make British and American convoy schedules jibe and keep a ready supply of escort vessels? Who would deal with a breakout by the *Tirpitz*? How would Plan Four, restricting protection to convoys, square with American responsibility under ABC-1 for the western Atlantic as a whole, a command arrangement, by the way, which the Canadians bitterly resisted?[64]

British, Canadian, and American naval officers labored through the July heat in Washington to find answers to these questions. The fellow traveler idea pressed by Harry Hopkins, providing an American-flag service which coincided with British convoys, proved impossible: the Americans could not cover every convoy. Admiral King, consulting with the president, then devised a plan for alternating convoys with the Canadians, each navy contributing thirty escorts, and agreement along these lines was reached July 22. However, the president reversed himself and through Admiral Stark rejected the agreement on the ground that it was impossible to enter into formal undertakings with foreign authorities for the operation of American naval forces, and so when Plan Four went into effect July 24, provision for combined convoys was withheld.[65]

A plan that would meet the president's requirement of cooperation but not combination proved impractical; a practical plan did not meet the president's requirement. The Americans were discovering that escort of convoy was so intricate an operation, especially when multinational, that it could only be effected on a basis of political intimacy of the powers involved. Once that was plain, Roosevelt postponed putting into effect an integrated convoy system until his meeting with Churchill at Argentia. Only after he had established common peace aims with Churchill and thereby the political basis for risking and waging war could he move to co-belligerency on the Atlantic.

Postponement did not seem too harmful because the Battle of the Atlantic turned sharply in Britain's favor during the summer. U-boats faced short summer nights that curtailed the gathering of the pack and less hunting time the further westward they cruised. ULTRA provided the British and Canadians a supreme advantage by near-current location of most submarines permitting diversion of convoys around them. The Germans ascribed British knowledge of their whereabouts in part to reports from American naval patrols, which, they complained, "greatly hampered" operations. Discouraged by slim pickings from North American convoys and constraints imposed by the Fuehrer, the German navy shifted U-boats closer to Europe and Africa where Luftwaffe planes could spot convoys. The elimination of German supply vessels on the Atlantic in June made further attacks on convoys by German heavy ships "almost impossible." In addition, BARBAROSSA drew the Luftwaffe away from British ports and, as the summer passed, released British destroyers from invasion guard. With these favoring conditions as well as end-to-end escort, completion of new corvettes, transfer of American Coast Guard cutters, more patrol planes, and fewer independently routed ships, sinkings sharply decreased. Tonnage lost plummeted from 432,025 in May to 120,975 in June. In fact, no ships in North American convoys were lost from the end of June until the second week of September.[66]

In the weeks before the Argentia Conference the Atlantic Fleet expanded operations, but slowly, a step at a time. On July 30 the battleship *New Mexico*, reaching the northern end of the patrol line, kept on to Iceland instead of turning back. Thereafter battleships ceased patrolling and stood guard at the Iceland base of Hvalfjordur and at Argentia, though precisely what they were guarding remained unclear. On August 5, possibly for experimental purposes, the Support Force formed its first unit of old and new destroyers, a mixture required for merchant convoy service so that if old destroyers ran low on fuel and broke off, the convoy would not be left unprotected. On August 9, American ships moved directly into the convoy lanes.

Powerful, heavily escorted task forces and small groups of Icelandic ships or navy supply and auxiliary vessels, usually guarded by two destroyers, passed close to British convoys but only seldom and then briefly, almost coincidentally, traveled in company with them.[67] Training and preparation for active service continued intensively, but otherwise the fleet was mostly marking time, waiting for the summit.

Many circumstances inhibited American intervention in the Battle of the Atlantic. Certainly Roosevelt had to move cautiously in the face of opposition in Congress to the extension of Selective Service and the dispatch of troops outside the Western Hemisphere to Iceland. Even so, given his other constraints, the president probably considered that taking a step at a time but moving was a broadly wise and prudent course and one generally congruent with existing public sentiment. Hadley Cantril polls taken July 11 and 19 and sent to the White House showed that the German-Russian war had not decreased the percentage favorable to assisting Britain even at the risk of war. Seventy-two percent wanted Russia to win and 4 percent Germany. Further reason for caution was interception of more Japanese messages indicating an impending move into Indochina. Roosevelt would not want to overreach in the Atlantic while a crisis brewed in Southeast Asia and would have all the more reason to underscore the defensive character of any move.[68]

Chapter 5

July
The Containment of Japan

The outbreak of war between Germany and the Soviet Union faced Japan with a most severe dilemma. The lie of Japanese policy had been increasingly toward the south, for resource acquisition and imperial self-sufficiency, for sealing off China, for Axis collaboration against Britain. The Imperial Army and Navy may not have had the same reasons for supporting the southward trend, but they had reasons running in the same direction, and these jibed with Matsuoka diplomacy, as evidenced by his pact with the Soviet Union. Now in June 1941 the global balance had shifted as rudely as earlier it had, in the opposite direction, with the Nazi-Soviet Pact of 1939. Now Axis collaboration pointed northward. The Soviet Union, instead of being neutralized, would in all likelihood join hands with Britain and the United States, increasing the isolation and encirclement of Japan. Only three months earlier Matsuoka had dreamed of arraying Japan with Germany and the Soviet Union; now the one had attacked the other with only the briefest intimation of its intentions. For ten days after June 22 the Japanese government struggled to regain consensus and adjust its policies to the vastly altered circumstances.

Important elements swung behind an attack on the Soviet Union. Russia had always been the Japanese army's traditional foe and most likely antagonist. Leading officers were sorely tempted to strike while the Red Army was beset by invasion from the west. If the Soviet threat were eliminated, the resources of eastern Siberia secured, Moscow's aid to China cut off, and the Anglo-Americans became preoccupied with an all-powerful Germany, then the southward advance could safely proceed. This seizure of the initiative was termed the policy of the "green persimmon," from the notion that the persimmon was better secured by shaking the tree while the fruit was green than by waiting for it to ripen and fall. Matsuoka, once he had caught

118

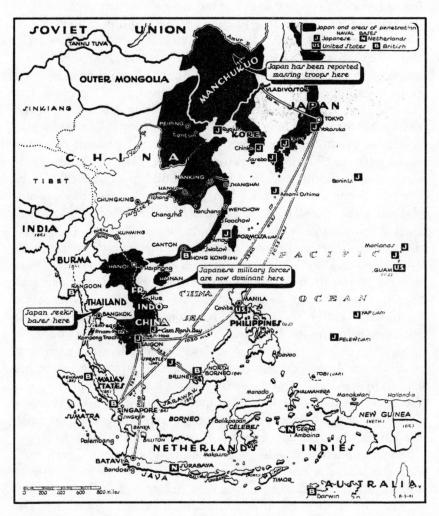

"East Asia—From Which Japan Would Carve a 'Co-Prosperity Sphere'": *New York Times*, August 3, 1941.

his breath, hastened to join the early harvesters, indeed to lead them, as adherence to the alliance with Germany was the centerpiece of his diplomacy.

Not all the generals and colonels were so bold. Soviet Far Eastern forces had dealt severely with the Japanese Kwantung Army in border fighting at Changkufeng in 1938 and Nomonhon in 1939. Moreover, in June 1941 twelve Japanese divisions and 800 planes faced thirty Russian divisions (twenty-six by July 2) and 2,800 planes. Even allowing for the larger Japanese division, the Kwantung Army was badly outnumbered and not yet deployed or supplied for attack. Followers of the "ripe persimmon" strategy argued that mobilization and reinforcement must come first. The general staff's *Kantokuen* plan called for beefing up the forces in Manchuria to twenty-two divisions, with 850,000 men, requiring 800,000 tons of shipping, for operations beginning August 29. This buildup would still not be enough; conditions would not be ripe for attack unless the Russians also withdrew a major portion of their Far Eastern forces: one-half their divisions and two-thirds of their planes. Accordingly, Japan's decision for war in the north, which would have to be taken by August 10 to allow completion of operations before winter, would depend on the course of the German-Soviet war and what demands it made on Soviet forces in the Far East. Unless conditions to the north were "extremely favorable" for attack, mainstream opinion in the army held, the southward advance should proceed. Japan should in any case choose its avenue of advance independently of Germany.

While the Japanese army could visualize an attack on the Soviet Union in certain circumstances and made preparations, the navy was totally opposed, not the least of its motivations being that a land war would enhance the army's call upon national resources and diminish the navy's. Of wider import was the navy's argument that the Soviet Union was likely to coalesce with Britain and the United States and that war with the one would lead to war with all three, whereas a southward advance leading to war with Britain and the United States was not likely to bring in a Soviet Union beset by Germany. The fleet's carriers would not be available to protect Japanese cities from Soviet air power, naval officers pointed out to their army counterparts.

A pliant naval leadership strongly influenced by aggressive subordinates on the naval war plans committee insisted on pursuing the southward advance. The navy was determined to break out of what it saw as ever-tightening Anglo-American-Dutch encirclement. It took very seriously the offensive capabilities of the American fleet at

Pearl Harbor, which, in war games of 1940, effectively attacked while the Imperial Navy invaded the Dutch East Indies. From this lesson the navy planners moved to the assumption that at some point the southward advance would trigger an American embargo, that this would force Japan to seize the Dutch East Indies for oil, and that war with the Americans as well as the British and Dutch was bound to result. This path of reasoning, always circling back to the presumption of war with the United States, pushed Japan's navy toward acceptance of general war as a matter of planning and policy. Large threats justified larger allocation of war resources, especially steel for new ships, and the navy was not backward in its claims in policy debates, contributing more than its share to the creation of a crisis mentality. At the same time the navy needed time to prepare and it recognized the risk of war with the United States, so accompanying this fatalistic thinking and feverish argument was a sizable if subdued strain of caution.

The army, for that matter, was not lacking in enthusiasts for a southern policy. Key generals recognized the danger of a diffusion of Japanese strength between north and south and the necessity of coordinated army and navy action in the south. The next step in the southward advance, acquisition of bases in southern Indochina, would yield critical staging areas for an attack on Malaya and Singapore. Pnompenh, Kompong Trach, and Siem Reap—Cambodian sites for air bases—lay less than 400 miles across the Gulf of Siam from invasion beaches at Singora, Pattani, and Kota Bharu. Beyond the slender isthmus of Kra, which joined Malaya to the Asian mainland, lay the Indian Ocean, Burma and the back door to China. Projecting into the South China Sea like a clenched fist, southern Indochina outflanked the Philippines and would carry Japanese power to the very edge of the resource-rich Indies. In addition to the Cambodian bases, the operation required sites in what is now southern Vietnam: Saigon and Cam Ranh Bay as naval bases and Da Nang, Soc Trang, Nha Trang, and Bienhoa as air bases. The army insisted on moving in troops as well, peacefully if the French acquiesced and by force if they refused. The painstaking process of balancing opposing views and stakes culminated July 2 in an Imperial Conference decision (the emperor present) that Japan would prepare in the north and attack if the Germans were clearly winning. Meanwhile they would secure a final departure line for attack in the south.[1]

While the Japanese government deliberated, American officials speculated. They did not doubt that the new tide of war in Europe could have large repercussions in East Asia, but they found it very difficult in spite of MAGIC to fathom what was, after all, a highly conditional and ambiguous Japanese policy. They were aware of conferences to thrash out differences day after day in Tokyo. Writing the day before the July 2 Imperial Conference, President Roosevelt saw what he described as a "real dragdown and knockout fight" going on, the Japanese "trying to decide which way they are going to jump—attack Russia, attack the South Seas (thus throwing their lot definitely with Germany), or whether they will sit on the fence and be more friendly with us."[2] While the president viewed the question broadly as a choice between two camps, his subordinates dwelt on more discrete Japanese choices: attack on the Soviet Union, seizure of bases in southern Indochina, attack on Malaya and the Dutch East Indies, watchful waiting, improvement in relations with the United States, or some combination or sequence of these.[3]

Initially, the predominant feeling among military and diplomatic officials was that Japan would attack the Soviets. The opportunity to remove the perpetual menace in the north, if feasible, would prove enormously tempting. This view was strongly reinforced by decryption of a message from Matsuoka to Berlin for Ribbentrop just after the Imperial Conference of July 2. Japan, it said, was "preparing for all possible eventualities" and "keenly watching developments" in eastern Siberia so as to join Germany in "combatting the Communist menace." British officials, who must have decrypted the same message at the same time, correctly emphasized the "preparing" and "watching" and concluded that Japan would not move northward "for the present."[4]

The Americans, especially the navy, were less conditional.[5] The commandant of the Third Naval District in New York reported that a source close to the Japanese business community there expected a war on Russia about July 20. Reports from China also indicated an attack northward.[6] In this forecast of northward advance the influence of Admiral Kelly Turner is apparent. The dogmatic and domineering chief of War Plans, who insisted on control of intelligence as well, became all too confident of his knowledge of Japanese ways acquired from a whirlwind ceremonial visit to Japan in 1939 as captain of the cruiser *Augusta*. Believing that the admirals he met then were not inclined to risk war with the United States, and dedicated to the Europe-first strategy, Turner was easily swayed by evidence of a northward thrust.[7] But the Japanese admirals he met in 1939 were not of the same ilk as those in control in 1941.

This early sense of imminent Japanese-Soviet war diminished as July wore on. British advice that Japan would wait and see and the fact that the Kwantung army was not strong enough yet led to the correct conclusion that the northward advance was dependent on the progress of the German invasion of Russia, though at what point Japan would feel confident enough to attack was impossible to say. Perhaps the fall of Moscow.[8]

At the same time, however, reports from American consuls in Mukden, Dairen, and Harbin provided impressive evidence of the seriousness of Japanese preparations. Beginning July 18, these told of a swelling stream of Japanese infantry, cavalry, and artillery troops arriving in Manchuria and, using coolies and draft animals, passing north to strategic locations within reach of the Soviet border. The embassy in Tokyo reported a large-scale secret mobilization of reserves. Grew asked for information about the progress of the German offensive, as this, the embassy believed, would determine the Japanese attitude.[9] Throughout July a large question mark hung over Japan's intentions in the north.

On the other hand, British and American officials had no doubt about Japanese intentions toward southern Indochina. MAGIC provided a full account from Tokyo's messages seeking Vichy's consent: that an expeditionary force of 40,000 troops was being sent, that Japan would use force if Vichy refused, that Vichy must respond by July 20, that the French did indeed bow to Japanese demands that day, that an agreement was worked out July 23, and that Japanese troops were prepared to disembark July 24—which they did.[10]

Nor did officials doubt that southern Indochina was the penultimate and not the ultimate stage of the southward advance. Suggestive of Japanese army thinking was a MAGIC intercept translated July 19 which reported that military authorities in Canton considered that the object of the Indochina occupation was "to launch therefrom a rapid attack" on Singapore with an ultimatum to the Dutch. This telegram especially worried Stimson because it implied that Singapore could be taken by only one division, but he was reassured by his staff that the Malay Peninsula was so narrow that two divisions could hold the Japanese and that they would have to attack Hong Kong and the Philippines at the same time, landings beyond the capabilities of the Japanese navy.

Japan did not seem likely to take the final step immediately. American naval intelligence knew that the bulk of the Japanese fleet was in home waters. It lay anchored in full view of the public at Yokohama on July 8, and the captain of an American ship sighted three carriers and seven battleships maneuvering off the southern tip of Kyushu on July 16. The Japanese government sought to reassure the

British and Americans that their intentions were limited to Indo-china; the bases in southern Indochina were not "jumping off places." Hollow as these assurances sounded for the future, they seemed to put a period on Japanese advance for the moment.[11]

Yet MAGIC was a source of daily disquiet. According to inter-cepts, Japan was ordering its shipping in the Atlantic to hasten to the Pacific, clearing the Panama Canal by July 22. A probable reason was fear of seizure in American ports in reprisal for the Indochina advance, but it also seemed likely that the ships were needed for troop lift to Manchuria or some other large-scale impending opera-tion. On July 5, American officials detained a Japanese freighter at Manila with a cargo of chrome for the United States but with sched-uled intervening stops at Japanese ports. Messages passed back and forth between Tokyo and Japanese embassies and consulates con-cerning disposal of codes, documents, and property if "worse came to worst." Japanese intelligence designated Mexico City as headquarters for reporting about the United States in case of a break in relations. It suggested ways of tying down American forces: for example, by fomenting rebellion in Guatemala, leading to American armed inter-vention. Intercepts of messages between Tokyo and the embassy in Washington discussed use of American blacks as spies and agitators. The time had come to send home portraits of the emperor, which held a revered place in every Japanese mission abroad. From U.S. Treasury officials came word that Japanese firms were liquidating their assets in the United States. Apprised of some of this intelligence by Welles on July 10, Lord Halifax concluded that the situation with Japan was "deteriorating rapidly."[12]

MAGIC gave the impression of a Japan on the move, one way or the other, or both, not immediately but soon. It reflected the oppor-tunism of Japanese policy and its dependence on external develop-ments, as well as the sense of urgency and of momentous departure that prevailed in Tokyo. What MAGIC could not capture were the fissures, doubts, crossed purposes, least-worst choices, and misappre-hension that shaped the Imperial decision of July 2. The result, even taking into account the north-south ambivalence, was a picture of a more confident and resolute and therefore more fearsome Japan than was really the case. Yet it is hard to imagine how the truths might have been discovered, given the secrecy of Japanese policymaking and the virtual elimination of American embassy contacts with influ-ential Japanese. Ambassador Grew, nine years in Japan and sup-ported by an excellent staff of foreign service officers, many of them fluent in Japanese, despaired: he had never had "greater difficulty" in keeping his government informed.[13]

So far as diplomacy was concerned, Japanese-American relations were a wasteland in July 1941. No sooner did sprigs of flexibility and interest in negotiations appear than they were scorched by the increasingly confrontational postures of the two powers. And these sprigs were scarcely promising to begin with.

At least Matsuoka was no longer an obstacle. The high-rolling foreign minister had put himself out of favor with the military by insisting on an immediate attack against the Soviet Union and, given the Hull statement of June 21, he was regarded as an insuperable obstacle to further talks with the Americans. He symbolized the German connection, which so far had produced nothing but unpleasant surprises for Japan. On July 16 the Konoe cabinet resigned and was reconstituted without Matsuoka.[14] Before this, in an interview with an American newsman, Prince Konoe had stressed the defensive nature of the Axis alliance and his desire to improve relations with the United States.[15] Ambassador Nomura, in a talk with Admiral Turner, insisted that Japan held in its own hands the decision as to when the military claims of the alliance came into effect. Japan would in any case act only for its own (and not Germany's) purposes.[16] Hull, at the request of the Japanese embassy, withdrew his offending statement of June 21 aimed at Matsuoka, and Tokyo sent a revision of the April draft understanding; the way seemed clear for resumption of diplomacy.[17] In Tokyo, Grew had been encouraged by the cabinet shift. The new foreign minister, Admiral Toyoda Teijirō, who spoke English well, seemed keenly interested in improving relations. Grew concluded on July 23 that Japan would adopt a less dynamic and more independent foreign policy. He would not venture to predict a new orientation or rapprochement with the British and Americans, but he mentioned it.[18]

This was the day before Japanese troops landed in southern Indochina. A MAGIC intercept of a July 19 message reassured Germany that the cabinet shift had not changed Japan's foreign policy and that it remained "faithful to the principles of the Tripartite Pact."[19] On July 23, Acting Secretary Welles, in his most solemn and Olympian manner, informed the Japanese counsellor of embassy that the occupation "constituted notice ... that the Japanese Government intended to pursue a policy of force" and was the last step before conquest of territories in Southeast Asia. In view of these considerations and at the request of Hull, he concluded, the American government could see no basis for the continuation of the Hull-Nomura talks.[20] The following day Roosevelt, anxious not to close all doors, made one more gesture, suggesting to Nomura the neutralization of Indochina, but acknowledged the proposal might be too late. Nomura barely mentioned it to Tokyo.[21]

Not only was diplomacy impossible in the context of armed advance but also the Japanese-American agenda, as it had year after year in the past, was lengthened by one more knotty problem. Increasingly British and American officials turned to consideration of military and economic measures for stopping Japan's advance in any direction. They were affected not simply by the increased threat from Japan and the poverty of diplomacy. They were also impatient. Preoccupied with the greater threat of Germany and in particular by the large strategic consequences and possibilities of the German invasion of Russia, they found Japan's new intents immensely provoking. The evidence these provided of further strains in the Axis alliance was reassuring, but a Japan pursuing a more independent—and unpredictable—course was in some ways more disconcerting. A dramatic change in fortune of the European war was in the making, either for much the worse or much the better, along the roads to Leningrad, Moscow, and Kiev. The Americans were on the point of intervening in the Battle of the Atlantic, but could not fight two wars at once. Somehow Japan must be boxed in and neutralized; East Asia must be disconnected from the central problems of war and defense.

One obvious course was to deter Japan by strengthening and, so far as possible, combining the East Asian forces opposing Japan: the British Commonwealth, the Dutch in the East Indies, and the Chinese. The possibilities for coalition-building had greatly improved. The threat of a Soviet-Axis combination, which lurked in the background of Matsuoka diplomacy, had disappeared. Not that Russia was joining the anti-Japanese front; it was preserving the strictest neutrality. But the rapid development of Soviet ties with Britain and the United States had to weigh in Japanese calculations. The German-Soviet war provided Roosevelt with a superb opportunity to do what he did so well, to enlarge the realm of common values and friendly relations for the United States. At the same time it left Japan more isolated.

MAGIC provided abundant evidence of Japan's sense of encirclement by enemies. For example, Japanese officials reported 431 American aviators and technical experts had arrived at Chengtu on July 15 and another 450 were at Manila en route to China. Ten B-17 bombers were said to have arrived at Rangoon for shipment to China, together with 220 trucks. The Americans were building air bases in southwest China, according to an intercept from Nanking. Tokyo noted a great disparity between what Chungking was asking for and what it was getting, but the ties seemed closer. Shanghai heard rumors of a secret Chinese-American understanding for the expansion of the Chinese air force and American use of Chinese bases. A secret agent reported that B-17s had the range to fly to Tokyo from China, raid the city for two hours, and return. The appointment of Owen Lattimore as Chiang's personal aide meant more British, American, and Soviet assistance for China, Shanghai reported, and more cooperation between Kuomintang and Communist forces. Tokyo warned of an American-British-Dutch-Chinese bloc which could join with the Soviet Union in attacking Japan. Nomura despaired of the increasing determination of the Dutch, British, and Americans to protect the "Malay Barrier" with "concerted air and submarine defense." Japanese officials in the Dutch East Indies, according to MAGIC, noted the presence of American naval officers in Soerabaja and of British and Australian army officers in Batavia. The British and Americans were, in Tokyo's words, "acting like a cunning dragon seemingly asleep." This stream of intelligence reflected and enhanced Japanese fears that their nation had enemies in all corners.[22]

From the American point of view this Japanese talk of encirclement was absurd, for they were having the greatest difficulty building what would later be described as "situations of strength" against Japan. The British and American navies could not agree on a combined plan for the defense of the "Malay Barrier." The ADB-1 plan, formulated by British Commonwealth, Dutch, and American military representatives at Singapore in April, found little favor in Washington. Stark and Marshall rejected it July 3, hastening perhaps to ensure that the British did not act during the crisis on the assumption of greater American support than they were going to get. The plan was too slanted toward British imperial interests: Singapore, Burma, the Indian Ocean trade routes, and Australia. It reflected London's east-west strategic perspective, whereas the Americans operated on a north-south axis. With Japanese naval power in the mandates between the Philippines and Hawaii, American access to its colony in war was necessarily from the southwest Pacific; Admiral Hart was expected to retire southward through the Makassar Strait and the Moluccas toward the arc of islands forming the Dutch East Indies. The ADB plan, however, would send him, train and all, west to Singapore under British command.

Furthermore, ADB was much more positive about the Philippines than the Americans felt at the moment. It urged the building of air bases there for the bombardment of Japan, a form of warfare which Japan with its inflammable cities "particularly fears." The current American view was the traditional one: that the islands could not be held for long. They could be outflanked by Indochina on the west and the Palaus on the east. The U.S. Pacific Fleet was a deterrent of course, but remote from defense of the "Malay Barrier."

The failure of ADB planning did not mean the absence of cooperation. The navies were getting to know each other and each other's bases and waters. An ADB communication system linking naval contingents, based on a Dutch machine cypher, was established and arrangements for exchange of encrypted Japanese intercepts and decrypted values were being made. Furthermore, ADB conceptions were beginning to influence American strategic thinking about the Philippines. Even so, at the moment the coalition was a hollow shell.[23]

No British or American battleships—and only one 10,000-ton British carrier—were stationed between Alexandria and Pearl Harbor. At the "Malay Barrier" the American-British-Dutch coalition could muster eight cruisers (with another six in Australia and New Zealand) and twenty-four destroyers, the American portion being one heavy cruiser, one old light cruiser, and thirteen World War I four-stack destroyers.

However, the battleship situation in the Atlantic was beginning to improve, and the British were raising their eyes at last to the formation of an Eastern fleet. Once the Americans took responsibility for guarding Denmark Strait, which awaited Roosevelt's conference with Churchill, four old British battleships on convoy duty in the western Atlantic could be refitted and sent to the Indian Ocean. The new American battleships *North Carolina* and *Washington* were undergoing trials, and H.M.S. *Duke of York* was due for completion by the end of the year.[24] Admiral Stark took up with the Admiralty once more the question of assigning American battleships to Gibraltar to relieve British capital ships for the east. The American navy may have had in mind sending the new battleships when completed to Iceland and the *Idaho*, *New Mexico*, and *Mississippi* to "the Rock," their original assignment under ABC-1, but without Mediterranean responsibilities.[25] These prospective reinforcements, together with completion of repairs on other British battleships and bomb damage to the *Gneisenau* and *Scharnhorst*, would turn the naval balance in the Atlantic in Britain's favor. And so combined naval planning against Japan was not as futile as it seemed.

While prospects brightened for an Eastern fleet, the defense of its base, Singapore, seemed ever more problematical. Lacking enough troops to defend the 500-mile-long Malay States colony, the British had decided in 1940 to rely on air power to keep the Japanese at a distance, but then found it possible to gather only 180 of the 336 aircraft required, and most of these were obsolete. The small and only partially trained army—three divisions and one brigade—with little artillery and no tanks had to spread out through jungle country, with few roads, to defend the airfields. Japanese landings at Singora and Pattani on the Thai peninsular coast just north of Malaya, from which beachheads they could strike south along the main line of communication and outflank the airfields, would be impossible to prevent unless Britain pre-emptively invaded Thailand at least four days before the Japanese struck. Such an operation not only posed logistical problems; it also raised the question whether the United States Congress would be prepared to declare war and join forces in the event of *British* aggression. No solution to these strategic dilemmas was in sight. Furthermore, first claim on British reinforcements was held by the Middle East Command, which planned an offensive for November.[26]

The British desperately needed help as the Japanese approached the doorstep of the British empire in July 1941. The Chiefs of Staff and defense committee of the War Cabinet debated the next move. How could Japan be deterred? By a warning that the next move would mean war? But where to draw the line? At Malaya, all of Thailand, or the southern tip of Thailand? Should Britain now promise assistance to the Dutch? Could Britain take any measures without a guarantee from the United States? Would any warning have effect if not joined in by the United States? As officials of the Foreign Office, the military and the cabinet went round and round these questions, it became clearer that the key to Southeast Asian defense for Britain was a joint British-American warning to Japan based upon obtaining an American guarantee of help. Soundings were taken in Washington.[27]

The view from outside the war was very different from inside it. American officials were disinclined to bring matters to a head with Japan. What mattered were outcomes in Russia and on the Atlantic. A sense of weakness in East Asia and fatalism about the probable course of events there prevailed. The Department of State briefly considered a suggestion from Winant for a regional defensive alliance. If the imperialist stigma could be removed by elevating India to dominion status, then a coalition of British Commonwealth nations and China would be sufficiently attractive to the American public to allow a pledge of support.[28] This was cast aside, undoubtedly because it was inconceivable that Churchill would permit a change in the status of India. Welles allowed that the United States would inevitably be involved if the Japanese attacked Singapore or the Dutch East Indies, but not necessarily if they attacked Thailand. This was a personal opinion, he said, not a governmental promise. The Americans ruled out minatory language.[29]

Nevertheless, in spite of all this negativism, the American strategic view of Southeast Asia was beginning to change. The shift was detectable not in broad theater terms but on the narrower question of reinforcement for the Philippines.

Gradually, barely perceptibly at first, the United States Army was coming to view the Philippines not as a strategic liability after all but as an asset. The generals and colonels had to come far. In the traditional view the islands were indefensible and not worth a large military investment. American army officers and men there numbered less than 11,000. All the airplanes, about 165, were obsolete. The largest American infantry unit was the 31st Regiment. At the last it would defend the beaches of Corregidor, denying Manila Bay to the enemy for as long as possible, but, as everyone understood, not long enough for the Pacific Fleet to arrive in time.[30] A naval observer reported to Admiral Stark that the army planned in the event of war to tell the Japanese that Camp John Hay and Fort McKinley were non-military zones for women and children.[31] The army believed that American forces in the islands together with the Philippine Scouts would delay and to that extent perhaps deter a Japanese attack on Singapore and the Dutch East Indies. The British Chiefs of Staff disagreed: the Philippines was not a serious deterrent so long as the United States would not reinforce it.[32]

The strategic shift had begun early in 1941. A War Plans Division recommendation of October 1940 for withdrawal of American armed forces from the islands for lack of a policy for holding them met with strong dissent in the General Staff. As War Plans had pointed out, the world situation and defense spending were changing the premises, creating perhaps the need and before too long the capability of a firmer stand. In January, Washington approved an increase in the strength of the 31st Regiment from 1,107 to 1,653, and the Philippine Scouts from 6,415 to 12,000, together with an increase of 1,500 in coast artillery troops.[33] In February 1941, General Douglas Mac-

Arthur, military adviser to the Philippine government, offered a plan for the defense of most of the Philippines. He had the quaint idea of defending the Visayas, the host of islands lying between Luzon and Mindanao, by guarding the passages inward from the oceans with coastal defense guns, mines, and torpedo boats. The 12-inch guns he requested were unavailable, but Marshall and the president approved 8-inch and 155-caliber substitutes.[34] Each month the gates opened a little wider; by July even scarce, modern P-40 fighters were approved.

American determination to achieve more credible deterrence and the increasing availability of matériel and manpower in 1941 partially explains this new disposition to reinforce. But equally significant was a rising determination in the face of increasing Japanese threat to defend American interests and possessions in East Asia. Strategic write-offs seemed irrelevant; the fundamental human passion for defending one's own was aroused. Nations seeking American help and protection would not be impressed by abdication of responsibility for defense of the Philippines.

The Japanese advance into southern Indochina brought a new stage of American commitment. On July 26 the president, following plans laid earlier, called the Philippine army into service and placed it with United States Army forces in a new combined command. The same day MacArthur was recalled to duty in the American army and appointed commander. The immediate substantive difference was negligible since the Philippine units had little in the way of officers, weapons, and training. And Washington had no intention of reinforcing by as much as an infantry division; Europe retained its strategic priority. Nevertheless, the raising of an army of 120,000 in the Philippines and the more direct American responsibility for their defense were evidence of a new determination and were intended to be.

An anti-Japanese coalition was inconceivable without China, which so absorbed Japanese manpower and resources, including one and a half million casualties in four years of war.[35] China's plight was painful and worsening: a drying up of aid from Russia since the Soviet-Japanese Pact, accelerating inflation, demoralization of the army, and still only a trickle of supplies finding their way through from the United States. Washington pressed on with existing programs such as currency stabilization, improvement of the Burma Road, and Lend-Lease supplies. In July, Claire Chennault's Flying Tiger pilots were sailing for Rangoon and China aboard a Dutch ship escorted through the Japanese Mandates by two American heavy cruisers. At the same time, in American priorities China always ranked after Britain, and now after the Soviet Union with its vast needs, and, since supply was too small for these and American needs, China got the left-overs. American dissatisfaction with Chungking's slack prosecution of the war, the persisting failure of the Kuomintang and the Communists to unite and turn on the enemy, importunate and ill-considered requests for supplies—such as tanks too heavy for Chinese bridges—Chinese corruption, and the daunting size of China's needs shrank enthusiasm for new undertakings. Roosevelt offered praise and encouragement at every opportunity but kept his distance. He never answered Chiang directly, he told Morgenthau on July 10. He urged transmission of reports of Japanese troop and plane withdrawals from the Chinese front (probably for redeployment to Manchuria) to the Chungking government with the suggestion that "one or two powerful attacks on weakened Japanese positions might do real good at this time." An astute British observer described Roosevelt as "willing to give Chiang Kai-shek just enough, but no more than enough, aid to continue the war and counteract the defeatists in Chungking."[36]

A stimulus for Chinese morale seemed essential, nonetheless.[37] On July 23, Roosevelt approved the sending of an American military mission in China to assist in procurement, transportation, and use of Lend-Lease war matériel. Though the mission would act under cover of the military attaché's office for the time being, it established for the first time a direct military connection with China. Roosevelt also approved the dispatch of 269 additional fighters and 66 bombers to China and promised to train Chinese pilots to fly them. All the planes were marginal or obsolete so far as the British and American services were concerned and none would be ready until November. The Chinese spoke longingly of B-17s but none were available. Even so, the inclusion of bombers, an offensive weapon, meant another firebreak had been crossed. Gaining ground was the idea of using China as a base for bombing attacks against Japanese cities, particularly incendiary raids. Japanese fears that the United States would use China against them, at least looking ahead to 1942, were not entirely misplaced.

In contrast to the military program of the ABCD coalition, which for the time being was more show than substance, American economic measures against Japan were a tightening band of steel. The settled policy of not cutting off export of oil for fear it might precipitate Japanese seizure of the Dutch East Indies remained in effect, but step-by-step curtailment in the spring of 1941 steadily reduced the flow. Earlier restrictions had been ineffective. After the prohibition against export of aviation-grade gasoline and lubricating oil in July 1940, Japan greatly increased its purchases of all other petroleum products, including especially gasoline of an octane rating and oil of a viscosity just below the prohibited levels, which could either be used in Japanese airplanes or converted for such use.

Evidence of Japanese stockpiling prompted export control officials to seek further restrictions on quality and a reduction in the quantity permitted to peacetime levels, before the war with China. While awaiting a policy decision, they withheld approval of new export licenses. None had been issued since April 8. At the same time the government, concurrently with the British, exerted pressure on oil companies to withdraw tankers under foreign charter from the Japan trade. With American-flag tankers already unobtainable, the Japanese had to depend on their own fleet and in fact were unable to move all the oil for which they had licenses. A sizable freighter traffic in oil was sharply reduced by a ban on export of steel drums. A further impediment arose from American assistance in hauling British oil from the Caribbean to East Coast ports to compensate for heavy British tanker losses to U-boats. The resulting gas shortage in the Atlantic and Gulf states led to a ban on oil exports from there to other than British Empire ports. By July the cumulative effect of these measures was a decline in oil exports to Japan, and in fact in Japan's oil stockpile as well.[38]

But perception lagged behind restriction: Japan seemed to be getting more oil than ever. In the ten months after the aviation-gas embargo the Japanese took away almost four times as much gasoline as they had taken in 1939 and almost three times as much lubricating oil. Five million licensed gallons awaited shipment. Two million more gallons had been applied for. Shipments from California in May were the highest in ten months—over two million barrels—on account of a coincidence in tanker sailings, according to the board chairman of Stanvac.[39] Photographs and stories of Japanese ships loading oil infuriated Americans, who were reported to be two to one in favor of taking steps to keep Japan from becoming more powerful, even at the risk of war. They bitterly criticized continuing shipment of oil to Japan. It was "incomprehensible." Why should people in the eastern United States give up their Sunday drive so Japan could carry on war with American oil "to extinguish the lamps of China"? It was "ghastly" how we were letting Japan "pile up" oil to attack us with, said Morgenthau.[40]

Once Japan's purpose in Indochina became evident in July, the sentiment for oil sanctions became overpowering. Cabinet hawks—

Stimson, Ickes, and Morgenthau in particular—led the way. Hull was a distant, wavering voice from White Sulphur Springs. His Far Eastern Division, steadfastly a restraining influence, was weakening. Only the navy held out against shutting off Japan's oil. Admiral Turner in a memorandum circulated to the president and Welles argued that a Japanese attack on Russia was more likely than on the British and Dutch, in which case the United States could intervene in the European war without concern for the Pacific. However, a complete embargo was likely to send Japan south and possibly lead to a Pacific war, which would be contrary to American strategic interests.[41]

Roosevelt seemed at first to lean against further restrictions. Would it be advisable, he asked Lord Halifax, to exert maximum economic pressure now? Would it "work as a deterrent"? Or would it precipitate Japanese action southward? The United States, he reminded the British ambassador, could not fight both wars at once. Dearly wishing to know which way the president's mind was working, the British replied that their strongest card was Japan's fear of war with the United States. It was imperative to choose a course that would maintain Japan's uncertainty about oil supply.[42]

The president's concerns were many and contradictory. He was anxious to deter an attack on Malaya and the Dutch East Indies, which he regarded as vital because of their resources and British supply in the Middle East, but he was not prepared to make a critical issue of southern Indochina itself, which seemed important only as a stepping stone. To draw the line precisely, the American response would have to come after the Japanese moved into southern Indochina. Economic pressure had not been ineffective in the past according to Stimson and Morgenthau, who in 1940 had pointed out that in 1918 during the joint Japanese-American intervention in Siberia, restriction on the export of American cotton had made Japan more cooperative.[43] Yet Roosevelt did not want to precipitate a further advance by cutting off Japan's access to oil entirely, nor anger Japan with a formal embargo. If Japan was to have some oil, a rationale and prescription of quantities and qualities were necessary. On the other hand, public prescription was something of a commitment, making oil policy less unpredictable and more difficult to change.

Thanks to MAGIC, Roosevelt had two weeks to ponder these conflicting objectives and sift suggestions from two Cabinet meetings, consultation with the British and discussions among State and Treasury officials. On July 12 Tokyo instructed its ambassador at Vichy to see Pétain and present Japanese demands for bases in southern Indochina. Military occupation would take place in any event, the

Marshal was warned; if the French wished it to be peaceful they must accept the demands. Vichy acquiesced. Japanese troops landed at Saigon July 24. By the time of Vichy's capitulation Roosevelt was ready with a response.

He put together a three-tiered system for the control of trade with Japan. At the public level he froze Japanese assets in the United States, just as in June he had frozen German and Italian funds. The Japanese now not only had to secure a license from the agency responsible for controlling export of products related to national defense; they also had to secure a license approved by an interdepartmental committee to unblock dollars to pay for the oil before it could be shipped. But no embargo: no new prohibitions, quotas, restrictions; indeed no public guidance at all as to what the trader might or might not ship; in short maximum uncertainty.

At the policy level, but not publicly, Roosevelt did indeed plan new restrictions reducing the quality of gasoline and lubricating oil and the quantity of other petroleum products permitted. These, as soon as they could be drawn up, would guide the decisions of the export control authorities. A system would exist for Japan to get oil but the Japanese could only guess what kind and how much from transactions approved or disapproved. Finally, at the operational level, the means would exist to halt shipments abruptly without notice or change of regulations. As E. H. Foley, a Treasury official, pointed out, the freezing control was "a very flexible instrument." For now, licenses for dollars would be granted as export licenses were presented, but "any day," the president said, funds could be denied, with immediate effect on shipments. The new system was decided upon at the Cabinet meeting of July 24 and the freezing order promulgated on Friday, July 26, after the president had left for a weekend at Hyde Park.[44]

The British and Dutch followed suit but in a state of puzzlement and annoyance. They welcomed the firming trend of American policy but feared it would not be carried far enough to stop the Japanese in their tracks but far enough to bring the Japanese down on them. They wanted close consultation, joint action, and American guarantees of support. This would be the moment for a joint warning.[45] Roosevelt, as he demonstrated July 24 in disapproving plans for a combined convoy system, was not ready for close collaboration with Britain before meeting with Churchill at Argentia. At the moment he was intent on establishing a trade control system, not an embargo, and was divulging to no one—probably was himself unsure—how far he would carry it. Thus the British and Dutch had no idea what they were tying onto. In fact each cable from the British embassy in Washington left the Foreign Office more confused. Rather than be accused of weakness, however, they renounced their trade treaties with Japan, froze Japanese accounts in sterling and guilders, and settled down to see what the United States would do next.[46]

The democracies had yet to bite, but the implications for Japan still were enormous. American ownership of much of the oil in Latin America and the Good Neighbor policy of consolidating relations—military, political, and economic—with Western Hemisphere nations ensured that Latin American policies would move more or less in step with the United States. American, British, and Dutch companies owned all the oil of southeastern and southwestern Asia and were working in the closest collaboration with their governments.[47] With the British Commonwealth, the Dutch East Indies, and the Western Hemisphere in a position to stop doing business with Japan, and with access to Germany closed, Japan risked having all trade cease beyond the zone of its military control.

While the United States was beginning to "stiffen things up all along the line" against Japan, to quote A. A. Berle, the German offensive in Russia was losing momentum.[48] Army Group North faced an ever-widening front and thick, swampy forests. Panzer leaders Rheinhardt and Manstein waited impatiently at the Luga River, eighty miles from Leningrad, for infantry and supplies to catch up. The Panzer groups of Army Group Center had encircled Smolensk, but Guderian's had become embroiled with a ragged but fierce Russian counterattack to the southeast in the Yelnya-Roslavl area. Movement along the high road to Moscow had ceased. Army Group South, on the other hand, was now making rapid progress. Kleist, having concentrated his three Panzer corps west of Kiev, sliced southeast, and soon his tank columns were combing the Ukrainian wheatlands. Beyond the Dneiper lay the rich Don basin, boasting "wheat as tall as a shaft and potatoes big as a wheel," but Kleist had yet to cross the river in force.[49]

In late July the German army was worn but not severely damaged. It had reached its first-stage objectives and was capable of further enormous strides and annihilating blows. But it had failed to destroy the Red Army in the frontier battles. It had used up its rations and left is railheads and supply dumps far behind. The army was so short of trucks that it was using Russian horse-drawn wagons. Army Group Center was receiving only eight to fifteen of the twenty-five provision trains it daily required. By mid-July the wear on machines and men was beginning to tell. Exhausted tank crews fought for days with hatches closed. Engines, sprockets, and tank treads were giving out. The combat strength of the fast forces in Army Group Center was 60 percent of normal, that in Army Group South 40 percent.[50]

On July 19, Hitler ordered a halt in the advance on Moscow and sent the fast forces of Army Group Center north to assist in the attack on Leningrad and south to join in the envelopment of Kiev. Generals of that army group, particularly Guderian, strongly objected, arguing that it was vital to smash on and capture Moscow. In fact, Moscow was beyond the reach of the Germans for the time being. The shock of discovering that the Red Army was much bigger than expected and was feeding fresh divisions constantly into the battle; the widening gaps between formations as the front broadened, leaving Russian armies, however disorganized, wedged into the open flanks; guerrilla attacks in the rear; the chilling expanse of Russia; and the bravery and stoicism of the Russian soldier—all these factors dampened enthusiasm for smashing eastward immediately. But most important, the supply situation made a pause for replenishment not only advisable but inescapable. During the last ten days of July this "monstrous awe-inspiring war of movement" became relatively static.[51]

President Roosevelt learned of these developments the way most Americans did, by reading the newspapers. The American embassies in Moscow and Berlin were slow to pick up the trend, in the former case because of a tendency to discount Soviet claims, and in the latter because information was so scarce. Newspapers, lacking correspondents at the front, depended on war communiqués. In the battle of the communiqués the Germans for once had little to offer, leaving the field to the Soviets, who were not slow in grabbing the headlines to claim full credit for stopping the German offensive. And these claims were eye-catching, usually in four- to six-column headlines. Berlin only enhanced their impact by alluding to fighting around Smolensk as the "greatest and bloodiest battle in history."

First reports of the stalemate arrived July 21. The *New York Times* headline that day was RUSSIANS REPORT NAZI DRIVES HALTED IN FOUR SECTORS WITH HEAVY LOSSES. Competent observers were reported to have said that the blitzkrieg had been braked. The Russians had stood their ground near Smolensk for five days now, the *Times* reported. Could they hang on until autumn? In June the time until the autumn rains and first frosts had seemed unimaginably long. Now one could count the weeks; comparisons with Napoleon's campaign appeared.

Every day now reports of German difficulties and Russian resis-tance appeared. On July 24, in the headline announcing Vichy's sur-render of bases in southern Indochina was word that NAZIS ADMIT RUSSIANS SLOW DRIVES. Berlin acknowledged "extremely fero-cious counterattacks" by fresh troops. Over the weekend, while the president was at Hyde Park, the Russians were said to be holding firmly, in fact to have smashed three German divisions. Monday, July 28, a Soviet spokesman described the blitz as a "washout." The Ger-mans had captured Paris in thirty-six days, he pointed out, but were nowhere near victory on the thirty-seventh day of their Russian cam-paign. So far, the *New York Times* wrote, the Germans had failed to capture Leningrad, Moscow, Kiev, or Odessa and had suffered losses beyond expectation. This was indeed "slow-tempo Blitzkrieg."

On July 29 the Russians made their first direct and positive claim that the German offensive had failed: NAZI DRIVE BROKEN, RED ARMY ON OFFENSIVE, RUSSIANS SAY was the four-column *Washington Post* headline. German losses were said to be "staggering," the invasion timetable "completely upset." Hanson Baldwin that day, under the headline "Winter Looms as Red Ally," wrote: "The future history of the world is being written in the struggling melee of tanks and planes and men on the 2,000-mile front." The *Washington Post* now considered June 22 possibly the most significant date in World War II. Unless the Germans could get another equally big offensive going, it claimed, they might have to fight General Mud and General Frost.[52]

Reports from American diplomatic missions, few as they were, con-firmed news accounts of a stalemate. The State Department was reduced to pleading with its legation in Bern, Switzerland, a key news center, for any information, no matter how exaggerated or unfounded, about the progress of the campaign and German reac-tion to it.[53] The embassy in Moscow dwelt on the Soviet evacuation of that city, but Rome reflected Italian pessimism: to officers returning from the front Russia looked like a "second China." Vichy consid-ered the Red Army to be proving stronger than anyone suspected. Admiral Darlan said German soldiers were exhausting themselves "simply shooting down the masses of men thrown against them."[54]

Washington was impressed. Berle, warning against sentimentalism about the Russians, conceded on July 31 that the German invasion was "already a failure." He estimated German losses at 900,000. In fact that day they reached 213,301.[55] Stimson, who received an intelli-gence briefing from General Marshall on July 28, was somewhat more cautious: the Germans seemed to have "stubbed their toe" but suffered a half-million to a million casualties. He likened Russian guerrilla resistance to the French ambush of General Braddock in the French and Indian War. Colonel Philip Faymonville, the army's expert on the Soviet Union, expected organized groups of Russians to hold out indefinitely.[56]

Marshall also briefed the president, who impressed Morgenthau as being "much more forceful" than he had seen him for some time. According to Marshall's information, Roosevelt said, German tank engines wore out after 200 hours or forty days' use because of inferior lubricating oil. Whether the technical information was accurate or not, the president had hit upon a key problem of the German army in Russia at that moment. It is possible that Roosevelt also saw at this time a memorandum by former ambassador to the Soviet Union Joseph E. Davies, who had access to the White House. In this paper he emphasized how much Soviet industry lay far to the east between Kuibyshev and Krasnoyarsk, beyond the immediate reach of the Germans. The week of July 28 a Soviet military mission was in Washington and lost no opportunity of stressing Soviet determination and confidence. The "charm and optimism" of its leader, Lieutenant General F. I. Golikov, did much to offset the pall cast over relations by Oumansky. From all sides President Roosevelt was receiving information and assurance that the Soviet Union had a good chance of surviving the German onslaught until the rains and snows came.[57]

Roosevelt returned Monday, July 28, from his long weekend of rest and thought at Hyde Park with his interest in aid to Russia greatly intensified. He learned that most Soviet requests were stalled. In some cases the American cupboard was bare; in others the British or American armed services retained priority. Soviet orders were hasty and improvised, numbing in their extent, vague in particulars and generally confusing. Ambassador Oumansky was consistently boorish in seeking help, and many American officials remained profoundly suspicious of all things Soviet in providing it. Nevertheless, it was hard to deny that the German-Soviet war provided "the longest and the deepest front and the fiercest fighting known in this or any other war," as Oumansky claimed, and that the Soviet Union was bearing "the brunt of the German might."[58]

Morgenthau expressed the view now held by the president that "this was the time to get Hitler." The Russians "have just got to get this stuff and get it fast," wrote the Treasury secretary:

We will never have a better chance. ... [S]omebody has been looking over this country and the good Lord has been with us, but we can't count on the good Lord and just plain dumb luck forever.

The president let fly at the Cabinet meeting on August 1. For forty-five minutes he lectured his principal advisers and especially a "thoroughly miserable" and smoldering Stimson on speeding up aid to Russia. He accused them of giving the Russians the runaround. He was "sick and tired of hearing that they are going to get this and they are going to get that," he said in a rare outburst of anger. "Whatever we are going to give them has to be over there by the first of October, and the only answer I want to hear is that it is under way."[59]

On July 26 the president had approved Hopkins' request to fly on from London to Moscow to learn what the situation on the Russian front was and what they needed most. He was received with extraordinary attention by the Soviets, indicating "the extreme importance ... attached to his visit." Hopkins cabled on August 1 that he was "ever so confident about this front," mentioning the "exceptionally good" morale of the Russians and their "unbounded determination to win." The next day, in the absence of Hopkins, the president put Wayne Coy, one of his best administrators, in full charge of expediting aid. "Use a heavy hand," he ordered Coy, "—act as a burr under the saddle and get things moving." He had told the Russians, he added, that he was dividing aid into two categories: high-priority matériel that could get there for use in battle before October, and the rest later. After October 1 the weather would curtail operations, and "if Germany can be held until then, Russia is safe until spring." Closing his orders to Coy he said, "Step on it!"[60]

Coy got some results, but weapons could not be made out of thin air. The Russians asked for 3,000 P-40 fighter planes and were promised 200, of which 141 came from British stocks; the rest were shipped August 25, lacking spare parts. Scrambling, Coy found some toluol (for explosives), aluminum, and machine tools—but in nominal quantities. Most valuable were authorized shipments of 315,000 tons of aviation gas together with lubricating oil and tetraethyl lead, as well as encouragement in Soviet chartering of American tankers to assist in delivery. What the left hand was denying the Japanese the right hand was providing the Russians. The Russians asked for 3,000 bombers and got five. They asked for 20,000 anti-aircraft cannon and machine guns and got none, 5,000 anti-tank guns and got none, 25,000 M1 Garand rifles and got 1,000.[61] For waging a battle he regarded as decisive, the president had painfully little to offer besides tokens and promises.

In the light of this intense new interest in the survival of the Soviet Union which arose in the last days of July, Roosevelt and Welles were loath to permit any shipments of oil which might encourage or permit a Japanese attack on the Soviet Union. Ten Japanese divisions— 300,000 soldiers—were now reported to be in Manchuria, and there was talk of a Japanese blockade of Vladivostok. Even restricting Japan to the average petroleum purchases of 1935–36 would permit shipment of over five million barrels of crude and 445,000 barrels of gasoline in the balance of 1941.[62] A shipment now would be the first authorized since April and would be regarded as an affirmative statement about Japanese-American relations. In any case, officials engaged in export control considered a delay of two weeks advisable before any exchange permits were approved, in order to devise quotas and quality standards and coordinate policies with other governments.[63]

On July 29, Acheson informed the Foreign Funds Control Committee that he had discussed the matter with Welles, "who thought that for the next week or so the happiest solution with respect to Japanese trade would be for the Foreign Funds Control {sic} to take no action on Japanese applications." A week later the president and Welles would be on the way to Argentia and so the likely intent was to extend the withholding of action at least until the Roosevelt-Churchill conference. On August 1 all valid licenses for export of petroleum products were revoked. As Lord Halifax saw American oil policy on the eve of the president's departure, the intention was not to be lenient, but to "keep the Japanese in a state of uncertainty." He detected an "overriding wish" in spite of quotas to deny certain qualities of oil to Japan, especially California crude and blending agents.[64] American officials were already considering the Soviet Union as a silent and limited partner in the containment of Japan. On July 4, Grew was instructed at the special request of the president to inform Prime Minister Konoe personally of American concern at reports that Japan had decided to embark on hostilities against the Soviet Union. He was to to warn the Japanese that any such move would "render illusory" American and Japanese efforts to strengthen "the peace of the Pacific." A week later, to Halifax, Welles confided that a Japanese attack northward no less than a move into southern Indochina would bring on an American embargo.[65]

Roosevelt undoubtedly believed that he would be in a better position to decide just how much oil to allow Japan after reviewing this and all the other connecting problems with Churchill and their advisers. Delay, of course, made any affirmative action on oil more difficult and a de facto embargo would increase the risk of war with Japan. On the other hand, there were reasons for believing that an embargo might not precipitate a Japanese attack southward. Hamilton pointed out on July 31 that Japan was weaker economically and now open to attack from all sides. Grew reported that the new Japanese foreign minister, Admiral Toyoda, was greatly distressed and dejected by the freezing of assets. He had hardly slept in the past few nights. Roosevelt wired Churchill in satisfaction that their concurrent action seemed to be "bearing fruit": "I hear their Government much upset and no conclusive future policy has been determined on."[66] A policy of maximizing Japanese uncertainty and insecurity seemed to be having a useful effect. It would certainly have public support. The State Department noted that editorials were making an "almost unanimous and very insistent demand for a firmer stand in the Far East."[67] Even some risk would be worthwhile if a Japanese attack on the Soviet Union could be prevented. Any security Japan might find in resumption of oil shipments or in fact any improvement in its relations with the United States might encourage it to move with Germany against Russia, the survival of which now, at the end of July, was a matter of vital importance to the United States.[68]

This new strategic conception enhanced the importance of the Philippines. The president saw Marshall and Stark on July 30. The following day at his staff conference the general said that it was "the policy of the United States to defend the Philippines," an unexceptional statement in itself, but in the shifting strategic context one of significance. Clearly the White House meeting had produced a change of attitude, not to the extent that Far Eastern defenses would be allowed to "jeopardize the success of the major efforts made in the theater of the Atlantic" by so much as the dispatch of an infantry division, for example, but at least to a new sense of the value and possibilities of holding the Philippines.[69] Central to this new confidence was the idea of using the islands as base for strategic air power against Japan.

The early summer of 1941 was an important moment in the history of the United States Army Air Forces. The air branch was gaining greater autonomy thanks to reorganizations instituted by Stimson, Marshall, and Assistant Secretary for Air Robert Lovett.[70] Production of modern airplanes was just beginning to rise: B-17s from six a month at the end of 1940 to twenty-five in June; P-40s from nineteen in February to 126 in May and sixty-eight in June. In May the president ordered production of heavy bombers increased to five hundred a month. He considered no single item more important.[71] Yet the British, Chinese, and now the Russians were siphoning off new production. Enthusiastic exponents of air power, committed to precision daylight attacks by large formations of heavy bombers, Air Corps leaders, such as Major General Henry H. Arnold, were unable to gather and retain enough planes to form a central strategic command. At one point that year GHQ Air Force had three pilots for every plane.[72] In war the air force would have a central role to play in the destruction of German industry. Short of war it lacked a strategic mission and was vulnerable to pressure from the navy for a larger proportion of aircraft production facilities.

Air Corps hopes and plans centered on the B-17 heavy bomber, the Flying Fortress, twenty of which had been sent to the Royal Air Force. Officially and publicly they were a success, but General Arnold knew better: reports of misuse, malfunction, and aborted missions began arriving in May. This early version had too few machine guns and flew at great heights to escape the Messerschmidt 109s, so high that bombing was less precise, windows frosted over, guns jammed, and oxygen equipment failed. British crews lacked adequate training, Air Corps officers believed; they failed to fly in tight formation; they were using an inferior bombsight: American frustration mounted with the criticisms. As of the end of July no mission had been a success, and eight of the twenty planes had been lost or disabled. The British were using the other heavy bomber sent, the B-24, to ferry air crews and matériel across the Atlantic or to hunt submarines.[73]

In March, Arnold, in a complaint not unlike that of Admiral King about destroyers, had warned Marshall that "piecemeal reinforcement" of the British violated General Pershing's principle that Americans must fight in American units under American command. It prevented formation of our own "striking force," he complained to Lovett in May.[74]

Once the army began to take an interest in the defense of the Philippines, the islands' advantages for projection of air power became evident. The navy had been urging a buildup since early 1940.[75] Crete provided army war planners only the latest proof that no seaborne expedition could succeed without command of the air. The Norwegian campaign and Battle of Britain in 1940 were other examples. "The best protection against hostile landings consists of well-sited air bases and a powerful, balanced, intrepid air force," advised the military attaché in Cairo after a study of the Crete campaign.[76] Such a force in the Philippines seemed perfectly situated not only to defend the archipelago but also to interdict hostile movements across the South China Sea aimed at the Dutch East Indies and Borneo. Shuttling between Manila and Singapore, Batavia, Darwin, and Port Moresby on New Guinea, B-17s could provide a web of air power that might give meaning to the concept of a "Malay Barrier" and supply the deterrent force which the British and American navies were unable to provide. Furthermore, southern China, Formosa, and, with use of Soviet bases, even the home islands of Japan would lie within range of B-17s based in northern Luzon. In the Philippines project the Air Corps saw the opportunity to protect its position, prove its principal weapon and advance its central doctrine. Stimson, Marshall, and the planners were ready to be convinced.

On July 16 the intelligence section of the Air War Plans Division advised the development of mid-Pacific island airfields for heavy bomber passage. It considered inadequate a policy which "in the light of the present international situation," failed to develop and make use of "airdromes for land-based aviation in the Far East and Australia." On July 18, General Arnold recommended allocating four heavy bombardment groups (272 B-17s with 68 in reserve) and two more pursuit groups (130 P-40s) to the Philippines, as they became available in the next eight months.[77]

Before making such a large commitment, Marshall and undoubtedly the president wanted to await strategic discussions with the British at Argentia. The Air Corps would have to prove it could fly them there too, but it was confident: the B-17s of the 19th Bombardment Group had flown as long a leg as was needed when they successfully completed a flight from California to Hawaii in May. Various routes to the Philippines were considered: Nome-Vladivostok-Changsha, and Brazil-Freetown-Khartoum-Karachi-Singapore. The most promising appeared to be Hawaii-Midway-Wake-Port Moresby-Darwin, and officers were immediately dispatched to investigate landing conditions and fuel supply at these points.[78] A squadron of B-17s from Hawaii was designated to pioneer this air route. "The presence of a squadron of those big ones would give the Japanese some bad moments," observed General Marshall.[79]

July was a wonderfully clarifying month to Roosevelt and his advisers. The German attack on the Soviet Union together with mounting evidence of the Russians' ability to sustain resistance made it conceivable to marshal forces sufficient to defeat Nazi Germany. Where in the spring the forces of aggression had seemed awesome

and victory imponderable, it now seemed a realistic, calculable objective. On July 9 the president ordered the services to estimate how
much total production would be required to defeat the nation's
potential enemies.

The incalculable component of this global scheme of ordered force
was Japan. The German-Soviet war had intensified Japan's expansionism, its opportunism, and also its unpredictability. Whether
Japan went north or south it threatened to upset the improving balance of forces. This careening expansionism must be stopped. Japan
must be boxed in, contained, immobilized. The strongest weapon was
economic: embargo was a deterrent, or, if stringently applied, powerfully coercive. Coalition diplomacy, military aid, demonstrations of
firmness, and deployment now and in coming months of naval and
air reinforcements would, it was hoped, keep Japan within bounds.
The risks of war would increase, but the risks of inaction, in the
global calculus, seemed greater.

Roosevelt could see the whole picture now. In July he was forceful,
impatient with delay, pressing upon events, so different from the
reserved, withdrawn president of the spring. His decisions were still
tentative, depending on the outcome of his conference with Churchill, but he knew what direction he wanted to take. Would they find
a satisfactory peace program justifying the risk of war by intervention
in the Battle of the Atlantic? How much of the still slender product
of the "Arsenal of Democracy" should go to the desperate Russians,
and how much to the British and the increasingly insistent American
armed forces? How rigorous should the embargo against Japan be?
These were questions to turn over as Roosevelt entrained for New
London the evening of August 2 to begin his journey to Newfoundland and the Atlantic Conference.

Chapter 6

August–September
Crossing the Threshold

At New London on Monday, August 4, President Roosevelt boarded the yacht *Potomac* ostensibly for a cruise along the New England coast, but after a day of well-publicized boating and fishing in Buzzards Bay he slipped into nearby Vineyard Sound to rendezvous with Admiral King's flagship *Augusta*. Early the next morning he boarded the heavy cruiser, which, with another heavy cruiser and five destroyers, immediately departed for Newfoundland. Steaming at high speed in spite of fog, the task force arrived at Argentia on August 7, one day before Churchill's earliest possible arrival in the *Prince of Wales* and two days before the scarred British battleship entered the bay.[1] Though the American Lend-Lease base was on British territory, Roosevelt was determined to welcome the prime minister to North America.

During the trip and the wait, the president received radio messages corroborating news accounts of the German slow-down in Russia. Welles arrived by air on August 8 with the latest intelligence. Dispatches indicated that the cool and skeptical attitude maintained by the embassy at Moscow was changing. On August 2 it had reported that the German drive had halted or slowed and that the Russians were manifesting "definite optimism." Three days later it judged that "determined and courageous Soviet resistance" as well as the need for resupply had brought a respite, which the Soviets were likely to put to good use and further delay the German advance. Such a delay, the embassy concluded, would have a vital bearing on the "ability of the Soviet armies effectively to engage the bulk of the German armies until the advent of winter" and if necessary to withdraw eastward while continuing to fight.[2]

The embassy at Berlin sounded an even more positive note. Heavy as Soviet battle losses appeared to be, it reported August 2, the "stop-

146

"The German-Russian Front After Three Months of War": *New York Times*, September 21, 1941.

ping even temporarily of the German offensive" more than compen-
sated for them. On August 6 the embassy conveyed information
from a source it considered reliable that Hitler had turned over the
Russian campaign to the high command and left for Obersalzburg to
plan future operations. The German schedule for defeat of the Red
Army by August 15 and occupation of European Russia by September 30, it was said, had been modified "owing to unforeseen stubborn
Soviet resistance." Especially disturbing had been the discovery of a
second Soviet defense line of more than 100 fresh Soviet divisions
east of the so-called Stalin Line. Now the Germans aimed for the line
of the Volga by winter, still a vast ambition but short of victory. German propaganda, the embassy reported on August 7, had been coun-
teracting public uneasiness over the "unexpected difficulty" of the
eastern campaign and the prospect "which has only recently been
widely realized within Germany that the war as a whole will go into
another winter." On the basis of this sort of information, British
intelligence officials were concluding that a German invasion in 1941
now seemed very unlikely and that the German objective in Russia
would be consolidation.[3]

On arrival at Argentia the president called a conference of his military advisers, including Marshall, Stark, and Arnold, and gave them
a glimpse of his intentions. Prominent in the review was his decision
to increase the number of B-17s in the Philippines from a squadron
of nine planes to a group of thirty-six. "That was a distinct change
of policy," Arnold later reminisced. "It was the start of a thought to
give General MacArthur weapons for offensive operations." A
squadron of B-17s could do little more than assist in the defense of
the islands, but a group could attack or threaten Japanese territory.
To use General Marshall's words to his British opposite, General Sir
John Dill, at the coming conference, the reinforcement of the Philippines would act as a "serious deterrent" to Japan, especially in the
winter months which were more suitable for high-altitude bombing.
Roosevelt furthermore stated his intention to send twenty-eight P-
40s a month to Russia for September, October, and November. That
the Philippines project was linked in the president's mind with the
Russian situation is indicated by the fact that Arnold in his outline
notes of the meeting placed the dispatch of the B-17s alongside the
dispatch of the P-40s to Russia under the overall heading of "Russia."
The object was not simply to deter a southward advance but a northward advance as well.[4]

Boarding the *Augusta* immediately upon arrival in the *Prince of
Wales* was "Hurry Upkins" with full reports of his talks in Moscow.

Wasted by illness but fiercely determined, Hopkins had flown back to Scotland in time to join Churchill for the voyage to Argentia. In conversations on July 30 and 31 he had found Stalin cooperative, forthcoming, and vitally concerned to secure help from the democracies. Hopkins undoubtedly found it curious to hear the leader of the Soviet state, which Churchill had described that spring as "an amoral crocodile lurking in the depths," condemn Hitler Germany for lack of moral standards, but now, at least, views of Germany coincided.[5]

At their second conference, with Maxim Litvinov as translator the only other person present, Stalin gave the first detailed exposition of the progress of the war so far provided the West. "Merely because German forces pierce the Russian line does not mean the Russians are lost," he pointed out. Soviet mechanized forces were fighting far forward of their lines and with partisans were seeping in between the Panzers and the follow-up infantry. This infiltration forced the Germans to disperse their tanks and infantry to protect their lines of communication. With this difficulty and the lack of good roads, the Germans were finding that "moving mechanized forces through Russia was very different than moving them over the boulevards of Belgium and France."[6]

Pressure on his army in the last ten days had considerably lessened, Stalin went on; the Germans were tired. It would be difficult for them to continue the offensive after September 1 when the heavy rains began, and after October 1 they would have to go on the defensive for the winter. "He expressed great confidence that the line during the winter months would be in front of Moscow, Kiev and Leningrad—probably not more than 100 kilometres away from where it is now." To capture the bulk of Soviet munitions plants, German forces would have to move 150 miles east of these centers. For the May 1942 campaign Stalin expected to mobilize 350 divisions. In rough comparison (the U.S. division was bigger), Roosevelt expected to have twenty divisions ready by the end of 1941.[7] Stalin's assessment contained much that was true about the battle at the moment. Needless to say, it was as positive as he could make it and far more positive in claims for the future than the staggering losses and bad generalship of the Red Army and the strength of the replenishing Wehrmacht justified.

The most urgent Soviet needs, according to Stalin, were light anti-aircraft guns, aluminum for planes, machine guns and rifles, and for the longer term tanks, planes, steel, oil, and other matériel already requested. Stalin urged American entry into the war and the most intimate cooperation, even to the extent of welcoming an American army on the Russian front and sharing Soviet tank designs. But by the next spring, he said, the problem of supply would be acute.

Hopkins carried out the president's instruction to deal with Soviet requests for aid in two categories: what could be delivered immediately—largely token quantities; and what could be shipped for a war that lasted into 1942. Long-term needs, Hopkins advised the Soviet leader, could be addressed at a conference in Moscow, at which American, British, and Soviet representatives would allocate munitions according to the strategic value of each front as well as national interests. Taking his cue from Stalin's statement that the Soviet front should be stabilized by October 1, and mindful that it would be "very unwise" to hold a conference until it was established "whether or not there was to be a front," Hopkins tentatively suggested a meeting about that date. The Russians were to be given maximum encouragement to fight on with token American assistance now and hopes for 1942 until the immediate outcome was clear. What could then be offered would be far more substantial and encouraging than the pittance that could be provided now.

Hopkins also conferred with Foreign Minister V. M. Molotov about Japan, the latter betraying considerable unease about the possibility of a Japanese attack on Siberia. He gave Hopkins the impression that "the Japanese would not hesitate to strike if a propitious time occurred." The one thing which would prevent it, said the Soviet, was some kind of American warning—meaning, Hopkins supposed, a statement that the United States would come to Russia's assistance if Russia were attacked by Japan. Hopkins replied that his government shared these concerns but had no desire to be provocative. Nevertheless, he would convey this message to the president.[8]

The dominant cast of Argentia was gray, from the bleak, misty hills and cove to the warships riding at anchor. Enlivening the scene were pinpoints of color in flags, uniforms, and gleaming brasswork and the hum of small boats scuttling between the British battleship and the American cruisers. In spite of the convenience of the remote spot as a secret rendezvous, the symbolic value of an Atlantic meeting, and the delight both principals took in a naval encounter, the disadvantages were considerable. The difficulty of shuffling officials between ships, the constant burden of protocol for dignitaries aboard warships, and the wariness each side had of the other—strangers with differing purposes, one at peace, the other at war—led to a feeling of disorganization and desultory, fragmented decision-making. This sense of aimlessness, however, and the lack of immediate dramatic results should not belie the significance of the conference.

Argentia was a critical juncture in the evolution of Roosevelt's world policies. Churchill was right in saying that something big was happening, "something really big," and it was not just the cementing of personal ties from the principals on down and the tears welling up during the singing of "Onward Christian Soldiers" at a common divine service on the afterdeck of the *Prince of Wales*, with American and British sailors intermingled under the big guns. The importance of Argentia lay not in radical departures and vivid consequences but in the congealing of tentative policies devised in response to the recent great changes in world politics and the balance of forces.

Roosevelt's chief purpose at Argentia was to establish the political basis for waging and winning the war. Not that he was seeking war. Rather, he was about to embark on courses of action in the containment of Japan and protection of the Atlantic which carried distinct risks of war, but which he nevertheless regarded as crucial for the nation's security. He desired a public declaration of fundamental American convictions about the conditions of peaceful world order, the sort of peace his countrymen would feel justified entry into the war. At the same time he wanted it framed as a joint statement with Great Britain, not issued unilaterally like Woodrow Wilson's Fourteen Points. He sought an international standard, a banner for the anti-Axis coalition to rally around, and a promise for subjugated peoples.

But first he wanted an answer to his question of July 14 as to whether Britain had made any secret commitments to the Soviet Union or any of the governments-in-exile regarding postwar territorial changes. London's silence on this score was disturbing. However, Sir Alexander Cadogan, permanent under secretary of the Foreign Office, came with assurances. In a long talk with Welles on the first day of the conference, only a short time after the president and prime minister had first met, he said Britain had promised Yugoslavia in March to allow reconsideration of the status of Italian-owned Istria after the war, hardly a "firm commitment," he pointed out, but he solemnly pledged that this was the only territorial undertaking his government had made. Welles and Roosevelt were satisfied.[9]

Negotiation of a joint declaration of purpose was not completed until the day of departure, but there was never any likelihood of failure; that, said Hopkins, was "inconceivable." The Atlantic Charter, as it came to be known, was mostly a restatement of familiar Wilsonian principles: non-aggrandizement, self-determination (with the "wish" for restoration of sovereignty and self-government to peoples "forcibly deprived of them"), freedom of trade, freedom of the seas, abandonment of force, disarmament, and ultimately, in some form, a world security organization. Point Six offered a gentle vision of world peace after the destruction of "Nazi tyranny," one providing "all nations the means of dwelling in safety within their own boundaries, and ... assurance that all the men in all the lands may live out their lives in freedom from fear and want." The only serious disagreement arose over free trade, with Churchill insisting that he must make an exception for existing agreements for trade preference within the Commonwealth, and Welles representing the deep-set convictions of Hull and his advisers in favor of an unconditional open door. Roosevelt settled the matter by siding with Churchill.[10]

The Atlantic Charter was unremarkable because most people in the United States and Britain took for granted most of what it said. No other vision of world order had any standing. The strength of the Charter lay in the sharp contrast it drew between the multilateral world vision of the democracies and the self-serving aims of the Axis.

Churchill's chief purpose at Argentia, of course, was to range the United States as closely as possible with Britain, and it was his particular concern to do this in respect to Japan. The British government's preferred course of action was to secure a guarantee of assistance from the United States, give one to the Netherlands for the East Indies, and use these as the basis of an explicit warning to Japan of war against further encroachment. Churchill expressed the view of the Foreign Office when he said that the way to deal with Japan was to use the "firmest language and strongest combination." Indeed, some in the Foreign Office argued for "even hastening the issue" seeing this as the time, while Russia held out and the United States tightened the economic screws, "to settle accounts with Japan." Australia pressed for an American guarantee for the opposite reason, the glaring weakness of British defenses in Southeast Asia. Of particular concern at this time were Japanese designs on Thailand, the next domino after southern Indochina. The British reported they had a secret message from the Thai prime minister that the Japanese were demanding under threat of force military as well as economic concessions. Japanese bases on the Kra isthmus would uncover the defenses of Malaya. The War Cabinet in London understood that Congress, not the president, had the power to declare war, but still believed (and so informed Churchill aboard the *Prince of Wales*) that Roosevelt might be induced to present an oblique war warning which they could join in.[11]

Churchill agreed. The Americans were told that Britain had just given a pledge of assistance, limited to the forces at Britain's disposal in the region, to the Netherlands in case of Japanese attack on the East Indies. Now how far could the Americans go respecting an attack on the Dutch and a movement into Thailand? Churchill proposed simultaneous British, American, and Dutch warnings to Tokyo that any further encroachment by Japan in the southwest Pacific would result in countermeasures by those countries even though these might lead to war. Further, according to the Churchill draft, the United States would warn Japan that if the British went to the assistance of the Netherlands, the president would request authority from Congress to give them aid.[12]

Roosevelt preferred a less precipitate approach. He had not changed his mind about the need for firmness in dealing with Japan. The period of "extreme patience" had come to an end, Welles told Cadogan. Roosevelt was expanding the air reinforcement of the Philippines. He promised Churchill to maintain trade restrictions in full force, though he did not explain what that meant, whether limiting Japan to peacetime use of oil or continuing to withhold funds for any oil exports. The trick, as it must have seemed to him, was to curtail oil exports as much as possible without provoking Japan by a formal ban. Furthermore, while at every step now Roosevelt was stiffening policy, he was one to preserve as much flexibility as the situation permitted. The British did not learn then or for some time thereafter that trade had been suspended just before he left Washington.

In Welles' view the time for warnings had passed. Only a few days earlier he had pointed out to the minister-counselor of the Japanese embassy, who was returning to Japan to report personally to Prince Konoe, that if Japan persisted in its drive for overlordship in East Asia and the south Pacific, hostilities were bound to ensue between their two countries. Given its recent sharply increased opposition to Japan, Welles told Cadogan, the American public was not likely to tolerate a Japanese attack on the East Indies.[13] Of course the American was describing an historical process whereas the British, seeking deterrence, wanted sterner stuff. Nevertheless, a warning on the British model would in fact have been superfluous, for the principal Japanese decision-makers had already concluded that an attack on Malaya or the Dutch East Indies was bound to lead to war with the United States.

Roosevelt understood that a Japanese attack on the Dutch East Indies would result in war. He said as much on the eve of the conference: if Japan attacked there, "we are vitally interested and will do

our utmost to get them out."[14] But he was also undoubtedly influenced by his belief that the American people had not reached the
point of supporting a declaration of war against Japan or Germany
and that it would be unwise to commit them farther down this road
than they had reached by themselves. It seems unlikely, however, that
he regarded this as a hindrance, for it fitted his own fundamental
belief that sound policy derived from American interest. British and
American interests, while congruent, were not identical. He spoke of
a vital interest in the Dutch East Indies but not in Singapore. He
preferred to take responsibility for escort operations in the western
Atlantic rather than to send an American destroyer force to the British Isles and to set his own course in adopting sanctions against
Japan. Yet he was not a nationalist rather than an internationalist;
he was both. He sought the most intimate cooperation, in fact coordination, with Churchill. But he resisted formal combination and
commitment. Always he insisted on preserving control of the allocation of American resources and the timing and nature of American
responses to Axis aggression.

Roosevelt's main difference with Churchill was his reluctance to
bring matters to a head. He wanted a drying up of Japanese oil supplies rather than a formal severance of trade, a sobering realization
not a sudden shock. A war warning, too, might precipitate matters
when delay was vital. He wanted at least thirty days for Anglo-American reinforcement, in which the first echelon of Flying Fortresses
might reach the Philippines and, as Churchill reported, "we may
improve our position in the Singapore area."[15]

An opportunity to play for time had just appeared. On August 6,
Nomura had delivered to Hull, now back at his desk, a Japanese reply
to the president's suggestion of the neutralization of Indochina,
which had been lost in the swirl of events at the end of July. The
Japanese picked up Roosevelt's proposal and offered a deal: Japan
would promise not to extend its military presence beyond French
Indochina and would remove its troops from Indochina upon settlement of the China war provided the United States would halt its
military buildup in the region, restore normal trade relations, and use
its good offices to bring about negotiations with Chiang Kai-shek.[16]
This would have been the worst kind of Munich. In return for America's relaxing all pressures, Japan would promise no further expansion. But the southern Indochina move would have to be accepted—
and thus somewhat validated—until the United States facilitated an
end to the China war. Roosevelt and Churchill agreed the terms were
impossible, but Roosevelt was interested in the fact that the Japanese

couched their proposal as a response to his own and that they offered negotiations. He proposed to take up the offer and enter into discussions on condition that the Japanese make no move while the talks were in progress. He would make no concessions and relax no pressures but, as a Foreign Office official described it, "keep the Japanese in play" for the next one to three months.[17]

Although he had no intention of appeasing Japan, Roosevelt finally concluded he had to appease Churchill. After divine services on the *Prince of Wales* the prime minister cornered Welles and pleaded with him "in the most emphatic manner" for a "clear-cut" warning. This was the only hope of preventing a war, he warned, in which Japanese cruisers would play havoc with British imperial communications in the Indian Ocean. Such a blow "might be almost decisive" to his government.

The next day, Roosevelt outlined his delaying tactics and then agreed to a war warning substantially in accord with Churchill's draft. He would tell Nomura that, if Japan refused these conditions for talks or made further advances, "in his belief" the United States would take certain steps in spite of his realization that these "might result in war."[18] The warning was not quite as unconditional as the British desired, but it used the word *war*. Furthermore, the president included Thailand in his neutralization proposal, in spite of the fact that before the conference he affirmed that an advance into Thailand should not be occasion for war. Presumably he was being educated on the strategic importance of southern Thailand. And he was prepared to extend the warning to include a Japanese attack on the Soviet Union and to so inform Moscow. Welles, however, more interested in the negotiations than the warning, advised a weaker statement of unlimited applicability. The two principals approved. No verbatim copy of the intended warning was given Churchill, but Roosevelt assured him "on more than one occasion," said Churchill, that he would use the prime minister's warning. "One would always fear State Department trying to tone it down," Churchill radioed the War Cabinet August 12, "but President has promised definitely to use hard language," and in this apprehensive yet hopeful frame of mind he left the issue. A message of his August 15 noted that the promised American warning also covered the Soviet Union, so "perhaps Stalin will line up, too.... " Such a combination, with the Dutch and Chinese, he believed, would keep Japan quiet for a while.[19]

Roosevelt went to Argentia fully expecting to confirm the taking over of convoy escort operations in the western Atlantic. This was to be a fruit of the conference, a result of agreement about war aims, and so it was. Churchill took the initiative in his enthralling review of the war situation aboard the *Augusta* the first evening of the conference. The Royal Navy, he said, needed to withdraw its fifty-two destroyers and corvettes from escort operations in the western Atlantic to bolster convoy protection along the Gibraltar and West African routes where submarines were now concentrating. The Americans readily agreed. Roosevelt had told his advisers before Churchill arrived that the United States must protect cargoes as far as Iceland, in fact east of Iceland. Upon sending Hopkins to London in July he had given him a map torn from the *National Geographic* upon which he had drawn a line encircling Iceland some 200 miles to the east, about halfway to the Faroe Islands, and then running west and south as before along the 26th meridian. This was to be the zone of operations. Each convoy must contain at least one American or Icelandic-flag ship. American war vessels would be restricted to convoy protection, a responsibility broadly though vaguely defined: it would be too late for escorts to start shooting after an attack began, the president told his advisers. The two navies aimed at starting American escort on September 1.[20]

Iceland had manifold strategic advantages: as a base for North Atlantic escort operations, as a link in the bomber ferry route, and now as the staging point for Arctic convoys to Russia. This last was a perilous route funneling a thousand miles between the Arctic ice and German air and naval forces in northern Norway, but in Stalin's judgment it was the best. Vladivostok, he told Hopkins, was too far from the scene of battle, and it was obviously vulnerable to Japanese attack. The Persian Gulf–Iranian route was undeveloped. The Arctic passage was at least more direct, Murmansk was ice-free, and the coming fall and winter nights were protectively long. A British squadron was already reconnoitering the route. By taking over convoy protection in the western Atlantic, the United States would help open up a British convoy route to Russia for American and British war material.[21]

Iceland was also the northern bastion of the Atlantic line described in Roosevelt's speech of May 27. The new front in Russia eased but by no means dissolved the president's concern for protection of the Atlantic. A stabilization of the front in the Soviet Union during the winter, the desired outcome, would have the disadvantage of permitting Hitler to withdraw the few divisions needed for a campaign through the Iberian Peninsula to northwest Africa. The situation in Spain, Churchill warned, was going from bad to worse. Hopkins returned from Argentia "much churned up over the likelihood of the Germans or Spain making a drive to the south, including the Atlantic islands—the Azores, Canaries, Cape Verdes."[22]

No less concern was expressed over French North Africa. The Germans appeared again to be pressing Vichy for bases, and American fears for Dakar once more intensified. Japanese "joint defense" arrangements with the French for southern Indochina could serve as a model. The Germans were said to be annoyed at Weygand's collaboration with the Americans and to be pressuring Vichy to remove Murphy from the North African scene. Murphy himself, the coolest of observers, in an August 2 cable credited reports that "the tide in Vichy is running rapidly in the direction of concessions to the Germans in French Africa." Stimson fanned public concern August 15 in a radio address noting German efforts to secure an invitation to Dakar. The government had reason to believe, he said, that a "major advance" would be made by Germany into North Africa.[23] In fact the Germans had no such immediate intentions. It was an artificial crisis probably stirred up by the French North African authorities to gain American economic aid and by the Germans as well to divert attention from the Russian front.

Roosevelt, however, was not prepared to second-guess such reports. The Atlantic barrier was no less a matter of vital interest to him in August than it had been in May. From Argentia he ordered implementation of plans to augment the Iceland garrison in early September. Numbers were less a problem, however, since the British, with invasion fears eased, were willing not only to retain their own contingent but also slightly reinforce it. Now only 5,000 instead of 10,000 American troops were needed to reinforce the Marine brigade already present.[24]

Security of the Azores presented less a problem as well. Portugal's President Salazar was now willing to accept American in place of British protection in case of German attack. The British could now transfer their attention to the Canary Islands, which, Churchill informed Roosevelt, they were preparing to seize after the September full moon on the assumption that Hitler would "almost inevitably" occupy Spain and Portugal, rendering Gibraltar unusable.[25]

Little more could be done to cobble up the southern approaches to the Western Hemisphere. The army was planning expeditionary forces for the Azores as well as Recife and Natal at the northeast extremity of Brazil, the ports nearest Africa, but the troops and transports were nowhere ready. Admiral Stark told Admiral Pound, the First Sea Lord, that he still planned to send a task force to Gibraltar as provided for in ABC-1. Or if that base was unusable, to Freetown

or South American ports. He was considering assigning the new battleships *Washington* and *North Carolina* to this southern blocking
force. They would in any event be held in the Atlantic.[26]

The *Prince of Wales* left Argentia on August 12 escorted by American as well as British destroyers. Memory of this heartening naval
clasp was soon lost in the North Atlantic mists as the British party
and, later, official circles in London, weary of two years of war and
one year of lonely struggle, canvassed the meager concrete benefits
of the meeting. The Soviet bid for vast quantities of American war
matériel along with their own needs and those of the American
armed services added up to far more than the Americans could produce. The two leaders followed Hopkins' advice in suggesting to Stalin a meeting at Moscow about October 1 to decide how, when, and
where among the three nations war supplies should be allocated. Russia was indeed a "welcome guest," as Churchill said, but it was a "hun-
gry table," and in view of the president's passionate concern to sustain the Soviet war effort, British leaders were deeply worried about
having their own requirements met, especially for their forthcoming
Mideast offensive.[27]

The Atlantic Charter and the promised war warning were fine, but
where was the substance? The United States Navy was taking over
convoy protection in the western Atlantic—where U-boats were
scarce. The Stars and Stripes would not be flying at Londonderry and
Gare Loch after all, though work on the bases would continue. The
destroyers as well as long-range submarines of the ABC-1 war plan
would remain closer to home. No more Catalina patrol planes, the
type that had spotted the *Bismarck*, were available.[28] Furthermore, the
new American battleships would not be available for assignment to
Gibraltar or anywhere else until the end of the year. In builder's trials
the new lightweight machinery and hull form of the *Washington* and
North Carolina had produced severe vibration in the propeller shafts
at high speed which affected the fire control systems. "The problem
must have been terrifying," says one authority, because all battleships
being built and some cruisers were following the same design.
Experts advised substituting new propellers with fewer blades.[29]
These experiments would take months. So with no more American
battleships coming from the yards or the Pacific, the Royal Navy
would gain no substitutes for any battleships it might send to Singapore. It was not difficult to imagine that Roosevelt intended to supply the war to a limited extent indeed and otherwise stand on the
sidelines.[30]

The East Asian picture was no more encouraging. The Americans were asking the British to reduce their allocations of certain items to permit strengthening of the Philippines, which they argued would assist Singapore. The Admiralty doubted the practical value of the B-17 reinforcement of the Philippines. Americans had, they thought, "rather exaggerated hopes of the effect of operations, particularly air, from the Philippines against a Japanese expedition to the South China Sea."[31] Given the American refusal to accept plans for the defense of the "Malay Barrier" and British ignorance of how far Roosevelt was prepared to go in restricting oil shipments to Japan, the party aboard the *Prince of Wales* may well have voyaged eastward with a sinking feeling.

Yet it would have been the wrong feeling. The importance of Argentia was less what the two leaders agreed to than what Roosevelt himself concluded. A burgeoning but still tentative interest in supplying the Soviet Union became a firm determination. In fact, maintaining a Russian front against Hitler became the centerpiece of his world strategy, with large consequences in all theaters. He was ready to enter the Battle of the Atlantic at the risk of war, tipping from most benevolent neutrality to active belligerency, in order to forward supplies to the Soviet Union no less than Britain. He was taking advantage of Hitler's drive to the east and refusal to accept the American challenge on the Atlantic to intervene with less risk of war. Avoiding a confrontation with Germany reduced the chances of war with Japan. He thereby kept in abeyance the vast claims on American production a declaration of war would entail. But it is hard to believe that he did not understand that sooner or later, one way or the other, this course of action would lead to war.

So far as Japan was concerned, he had three possible courses of action: the passive, the soft, and the hard. The passive route was simply to do nothing to provoke Japan, either by an oil embargo or by Asian reinforcements, in order to bring the full weight of American power to bear against Germany. But he undoubtedly perceived this to be the riskiest course, for it not only left the resources of Southeast Asia and Britain's connections to Australia and New Zealand at Japan's mercy but also offered no discouragement to a Japanese attack against the Soviet rear. The soft choice meant coming to an agreement with Japan which at least offered the possibility of preventing a further southward advance by some concession ending the China war, but at great cost to the American reputation as guarantor of nations resisting aggression, and probably with heightened risk of a Japanese attack northward once its southern flank was secure. He was moving along the third course, the hard policy, estimating it no doubt the least risky: severe containment of Japan risked war, but in that event more likely a southward than the more critical northward attack. Meanwhile, the draining of Japan's oil supplies would progressively reduce its capacity for war. The risk would decline as American military power increased and in time far surpassed that of Japan.

The decisions of the Atlantic Conference period were bold departures, and President Roosevelt surely did not take them without trepidation. So far American public opinion had been mobilizing behind his policies. However, administration confidence in public support received a rude shock on August 12, the last day of the conference, when word came that the House of Representatives had extended the Selective Service Act by a margin of one vote. The slimness of victory did not really signify a relapse into isolationism, but it indicated the limits of interventionism. Extension of the draft was an issue of great political sensitivity because many felt honor-bound to the conscripts to limit their service to the original term of one year. The vote drew these as well as hard-core isolationists, most Republicans and all Roosevelt-haters.[32] It also drew the complacent. News readers of later July and early August could gain the impression that the Germans had met their match in Russia and that maintaining a large army for defense of the Western Hemisphere, which after all was the rationale for the draft, was no longer urgent. So the temptation to turn a deaf ear to Roosevelt's and Marshall's warnings and entreaties was powerful.

Still, a margin of one was enough. American mobilization stayed on course. According to a *Fortune* poll, 72 percent of Americans believed Hitler would try to conquer the world and 58 percent that armed intervention was necessary to defeat him. A poll in Montana indicated that the most outspoken isolationist, Senator Burton K. Wheeler, would be defeated in an election now by at least 100,000 votes. The index of production rose steadily. The steel industry reached full capacity and mills worked through the July 4 weekend. Shortages began to appear. In two instances, at North American and Federal Shipbuilding, the military services took over plants to prevent longer work stoppages.[33]

Public opinion and domestic political considerations generally could not be ignored. Neither could international political and strategic requirements and military capabilities. So far Roosevelt had managed to keep his various autonomous imperatives in rough harmony. As he moved to a global framework of policy, this became increasingly difficult to do.

The president returned to Washington on Sunday morning, August 17, refreshed and buoyant from his ocean voyage and settled course of action. Preceding him was Welles with the war warning and preceding Welles was a message asking Hull to set up a meeting with Nomura. The secretary of state, who was naturally averse to show-downs, and his advisers strongly disapproved of the warning for the same reason the president had been dubious about it: threatening language risked provoking Japan in a situation in which delay seemed imperative. Hamilton and Joseph Ballantine of the Far Eastern Division took out their pencils, and by the time the president returned the warning was a pale imitation of the Churchill original.

Roosevelt agreed to the change, but for him the critical factor now was materialization of a better basis for conducting discussions with the Japanese, one requiring softer language.[34] The Japanese government had now asked for a conference between Premier Konoe and President Roosevelt in Hawaii. The idea was not new: it had been among Father Drought's proposals in the spring. Ambassador Nomura, who doubted that the Americans would be moved by anything but concrete proposals, had reintroduced it in a conversation with the secretary of state on August 8, but so gingerly that Hull virtually ignored it. MAGIC, however, showed that Nomura was acting under instructions and that his government attached great importance to the proposal. According to intercepts, the Konoe cabinet believed that the only way to relieve the "critically tense" situation was for the leaders to meet, "lay their cards on the table, express their true feelings, and attempt to determine a way out.... "[35] On August 16, Nomura urged on Hull a return to the more comprehensive framework of the conversations conducted in the spring and interrupted in July as a preliminary to a leaders' meeting, and indicated that his government "would make concessions in order to avoid war."[36]

It was very hard to say no. Conceivably the Japanese were having a change of heart, though Roosevelt doubted it. They were more influenced by the sway of battle in Russia than by regard for the United States, he told Lord Halifax.[37] Even so, finding out seemed wise, and resuming the talks offered the further opportunity of weakening Japan's ties with the Axis at the delicate moment when the United States was intervening in the Battle of the Atlantic. Above all, a return to the Hull-Nomura format of the spring, in all its complexity with the added inducement of a culminating leaders' meeting,

was likely to win more time for containment than discussions pivot-
ing on the neutralization of Indochina. The previous talks had, after
all, consumed three months. But a blunt war warning was not likely
to create a mood conducive to extended discussions, so Roosevelt
accepted the weaker version.

The president saw Nomura on Sunday afternoon, August 17, only
a few hours after his return. The meeting really consisted of two conversations divided by a pause: one admonitory, the other concilia-
tory. First Roosevelt read the State Department's version of the warning, which no longer insisted upon an unconditional Japanese
commitment to remove its forces from Indochina, nor referred to the
Indochina neutralization proposal and British support for it, nor
warned against advance in specific places or directions. Most important, the warning itself did not use the word "war" or "conflict." It
simply said that, if Japan made any further advances, the United
States would have to take whatever steps were necessary to safeguard
the rights and interests of its citizens and its safety and security.[38]
And by commenting on the text, thereby distancing himself from it,
Roosevelt gave Nomura the clear impression that he was reluctantly
but dutifully conveying a message the bureaucrats had devised. He
even left some doubt as to whether he was delivering a written communication at all, for he denied it the status of a diplomatic note,
describing the warning as "merely what we want to say," and "reference material," yet insisting that "it should be expressed in writing."[39]
The president went to extraordinary lengths to sugar-coat the pill.

Moving to the second part of the conversation, Roosevelt showed
how the Japanese move into southern Indochina had led to a break-
down in diplomacy, then painted a fair picture of the possibilities for
peace on American principles and an open door for trade and
resources in the Pacific region. If Japan was prepared to abandon its
expansion and embark on such a program, Roosevelt went on, his
government would, as requested, consider resumption of the Hull-
Nomura conversations and seek to arrange a time and place for a
meeting of high officials. The president said he preferred San Francisco or Seattle because a journey to Hawaii would take too long and
he was not permitted to fly. Juneau or Sitka in the Alaska panhandle
might be an alternative, he said. But while dangling the hope of a
leaders' meeting before Nomura, Roosevelt let it be known that distance was a problem, and he could not promise attendance. Furthermore, a critical condition, first the United States required a "clearer
statement" of the Japanese government's "attitude and plans."[40]

To the British, Roosevelt tried to minimize his weakening of the warning. Informing Lord Halifax of the proposal for a meeting with Konoe, he claimed that the warning he delivered was similar to the Argentia draft. But Halifax checked the wording with Welles, and Churchill soon knew better.[41]

Publicly the prime minister gloried in the common aspirations and promised cooperation of Argentia: as he had journeyed home, he said, "overhead the far-ranging Catalina airboats soared, vigilant, protecting eagles in the sky." "We shall not be denied the strength to do our duty to the end," he assured his war-weary countrymen. Turning to Asia he scathingly denounced Japanese military "factions" which were "seeking to emulate the style of Hitler and Mussolini as if it were a new wave of European revelation." Japanese armies had been "wandering" about China for years bringing "carnage, ruin, corruption." Now they threatened the southwest Pacific and he was "certain that this has got to stop." Cleverly placing America out front as Japan's principal antagonist, he praised the "infinite patience" with which it was trying to work out a settlement, but if trouble came, he warned, Britain would "of course" range itself "unhesitatingly at the side of the United States." The Japanese press reacted to the speech with "almost unprecedented violence in tone," Grew reported.[42]

Churchill was depicting in rhetoric the common front he had failed to secure in secret diplomacy, and with some success. The *New York Times*, under the four-column headline CHURCHILL WARNS JAPANESE TO "STOP" OR FACE BRITISH-AMERICAN COALITION, commented that the British leader had confirmed what many suspected: that the two governments had decided at Argentia to take the "strongest sort of line" with Japan.[43]

Behind these rhetorical flourishes, the British government grew increasingly critical as it examined the American backslidings and the paltry tangible results of Argentia. Particularly disillusioning were Roosevelt's frequent public assurances that he had not made any commitments at the conference and that the nation stood no closer to war. On August 28, Churchill, aiming at Roosevelt, wrote Hopkins a most despondent letter. He spoke of a "wave of depression" in the cabinet and informed circles over apparent American disinclination to become involved. "If 1942 opens with Russia knocked out and Britain left again alone all kinds of dangers may arise," he warned. That night, he said, thirty U-boats lay in a line from eastern Iceland to northern Ireland but east of the 26th meridian, beyond current American responsibility. In the past two days submarines had sunk 25,000 tons of shipping. The implication was clear that the Battle of the Atlantic could still be lost while Americans guarded its western reaches. He ended by saying that he would be grateful for "any sort of hope." If the British ever reached the conclusion that the United States would not somehow, sometime join the fray, Hopkins warned Roosevelt, "there would be a very critical moment in the war and the British appeasers might have some influence on Churchill."[44]

Churchill was keeping one step ahead of the American navy, which was moving as fast as possible to enter the Battle of the Atlantic within the limitations agreed to at Argentia. The president, having taken his decision, left implementation to the navy; admirals were not summoned to the White House in August as they had been in July. Nevertheless, over a month passed before escort began. The navy planned to start September 1, but administrative and logistical problems forced postponement.

The "Washington machinery" was not ready, Admiral King explained to a subordinate.[45] He undoubtedly meant the special staff and communications network to control convoys and escorts in the western Atlantic. American escort operations entirely depended on British experience and sophisticated facilities, on the ULTRA decryption work at Bletchley Park, on the Operational Intelligence Center, Trade Plot, and Submarine Tracking Room at the Admiralty, and on the Western Approaches Command at Liverpool. Multinational escort required the most intimate cooperation with the Royal Canadian Navy at Ottawa and St. John's, Newfoundland, and coordination with the system for forming up, routing, and dispatching convoys from American ports and Sydney and Halifax, Nova Scotia. The Office of the Chief of Naval Operations in Washington, hub of American escort communications, had to tie into London's routing and tracking systems and expedite information to Atlantic Fleet headquarters and the various destroyer escort bases and forces. Information about U-boat and convoy locations requiring the tightest secrecy had to be disseminated in cyphers accessible to headquarters of three navies. American command in the western Atlantic had to be instituted and escort units inserted without disrupting the schedules of convoys, six to eight of which at regular intervals were passing back and forth across the ocean on any given day.[46]

Great difficulty occurred in getting ships to the right place at the right time. Icelandic and American-flag merchantmen, one of which Roosevelt still insisted had to provide a figleaf of neutrality for each convoy, were a particular problem. Adequate numbers of American vessels only began departing from New York on August 27. Some

Icelandic vessels were so slow they endangered their escorts; others ignored escorts and steamed off alone.

A division of responsibility was arranged with the Americans taking fast (HX) convoys and the Royal Canadian Navy the slow (SC) from a point south of Newfoundland to a rendezvous with British escorts south of Iceland and then back again with convoys of empty ships. But the Canadians, with too few vessels and too few with adequate range, had to retain some of the British escorts to carry out their side of the bargain.

The measured activity of the Atlantic Fleet before the Argentia conference gave way to a rush for position afterward. Within a week Admiral King ordered the fleet train from Newport to Casco Bay, Maine, the nearest American anchorage to the convoy routes. The Support Force commander established himself at Argentia. Destroyer tenders, repair ships, oilers, and other auxiliaries followed or moved on to Iceland. At Casco Bay, King set up a destroyer pool, dissolving the neat division and squadron organization, so that escort units could be filled out on the basis of readiness and a mixture of old and new destroyers. From there units moved up to Argentia near the convoy meeting point or were pre-positioned in Iceland for the westbound convoys.

By mid-September thirty-three destroyers, every one the Atlantic Fleet commander could get his hands on, and the Coast Guard cutter *Campbell* were ready for merchant vessel escort at the northern bases. Another sixteen were due by the end of October and six more by the end of the year, leaving a bare minimum to escort warships, one division (four ships) to patrol the Caribbean, and a sonar training division at Key West which Admiral King coveted. He had barely enough vessels to begin the task: six escort groups of five destroyers each. Canadian units had even fewer. King planned to increase the number to seven groups of at least six each, and allow a layover in Boston, but storm damage and machinery breakdowns were constantly whittling down the number available to meet the inexorable convoy schedules.[47]

So urgent was the need for destroyers that peacetime criteria for efficiency were dispensed with. Gunnery proficiency was below that of the Pacific Fleet and, for recently completed destroyers, unsatisfactory. In machine gun practice in August even veteran Support Force squadrons were scoring virtually no hits because of lack of practice ammunition. U.S.S. *Ericsson*, *Nicholson*, and *Mayo* reported for escort duty with no gunnery practice at all. Injuries among crews unfamiliar with weapons and equipment were "far too many in number." Few destroyers were equipped with radar and fewer still experienced in its use. U.S.S. *Babbitt,* hurrying to duty, received its underwater sound detection gear not in a dockyard but at Casco Bay from a tender.[48]

As the fleet readied, the war moved back toward it. The number of operational U-boats increased from sixty-five in July to eighty in October and the number on station rose past thirty, permitting the U-boat command to form a wolfpack of fourteen boats, Group Markgraf, for Greenland-Iceland waters. These began entering the western Atlantic on August 18 and by early September were neatly positioned in rank and file to sight any plume of smoke in the hundreds of miles of convoy routes lying southeast of Greenland and southwest of Iceland. At the same time the German naval command began super-encyphering U-boat locations within encyphered messages, delaying ULTRA by as much as four days and temporarily masking U-boat deployment. Atlantic Fleet destroyers were entering far more dangerous waters than could have been imagined a month earlier.[49]

The nearly inevitable encounter occurred September 4 some 125 miles southwest of Iceland between U.S.S. *Greer,* a World War I destroyer, and U-652, cruising on the northern flank of Group Markgraf. *Greer* was sailing alone carrying mail and officer passengers to Reykjavik from Boston and Argentia. Informed by a British patrol bomber of a submarine in its path it proceeded to hunt and find the boat and pursue it tenaciously for the next several hours, in full compliance with orders to trail and report U-boats in the American defense zone. U-boats were forbidden to initiate attacks on American warships, but the submerged U-652, unable to identify the nationality of its pursuer and believing depth charges dropped by the plane had come from the destroyer, finally fired two torpedoes in self-defense, which *Greer* dodged. The American destroyer responded with depth-charge attacks and further pursuit until called off at twilight. The quarry, shaken but not damaged, continued westward to join in a pack attack on September 9-11 on SC-42, which was desperately trying an end-run to the north, close to Greenland. U-652 claimed as probably sunk two of the sixteen vessels lost from that devastated convoy.[50]

The *Greer* incident greatly facilitated arrangements for escort of convoy. The incident allowed removal of the restrictions under which it would be conducted. President Roosevelt on learning of the encounter immediately ordered the navy to "eliminate" the submarine, and destroyers were ordered down from Iceland before the search was called off.[51]

The following day, September 5, the president met with Admiral King and Admiral Stark among others and authorized the beginning of outward-bound escort September 16 and escort back from Iceland of the first convoy available whether fast or slow. Destroyers were ordered out again from Iceland on September 12 to assist battered convoy SC 42. Then Roosevelt permitted destroyers to escort convoys without American or Icelandic-flag ships and the Royal Canadian and Royal navies to escort American ships as far as Iceland. A few days later he authorized attack on German and Italian warships anywhere in the western Atlantic, including Iceland and a broad belt of ocean to its east. Mere presence of a submarine or raider was now grounds for attack. By September 16, when the first American escort group, Task Unit 4.1.1, met the first American-escorted convoy, HX 150 out of Halifax, the United States Navy was in a state of full belligerency in the western Atlantic.[52]

As he had done in his radio address of May 27 before the Iceland venture, so now before taking this next big step Roosevelt made a powerful presentation of his views and intentions to the American people and sought their support. His plans for a broadcast were interrupted by the failing health and then death of his mother the weekend of September 6–7. He was with her when she died at Hyde Park on Sunday, and he remained for her funeral. Meanwhile the speech went through draft after draft at the State Department and White House. Hopkins brought the latest draft to the presidential train in New York as it was returning to Washington, and that evening and the next morning Roosevelt refined it and tested it on congressional leaders.[53] On Thursday evening, September 11, he broadcast a major state paper setting out the basis for intervention in the Battle of the Atlantic and, if that followed, war with Germany. The speech went out in his familiar, reassuring voice and vivid, colloquial idiom to a nation of family homes gathered around their radios. He aimed his message abroad as well, to the nations and peoples fighting Hitler and particularly to the British, described by Churchill as so very discouraged with the lack of tangible results from the Atlantic meeting.

Claiming correctly that the submarine fired first on the *Greer* and with deliberate intent to sink it, the president was silent about what the U-boat captain must have regarded as hostile pursuit. Roosevelt did not rest his case on the ambiguities of the chase, however, but placed the incident in the larger context of German U-boat warfare and American devotion to the freedom of the seas. The *Greer*, he insisted, was on a "legitimate mission" to Iceland, an American out-post protecting waters through which passed ships of many flags car-rying food and war matériel provided by the American people as an essential part of their own defense. If the U-boat had been unable to identify the destroyer, as the Nazis claimed, and still fired, this reflected a policy of indiscriminate violence, as proven by such other attacks as the sinking of the *Robin Moor* and stalking of the U.S.S. *Texas* in June, and the recent sinkings of the Panamanian freighter *Sessa* and the American freighter *Steel Seafarer*.

These acts of "piracy" were all part of a Nazi plan for domination of the seas wherein no American ship could travel without the "con-descending grace of this … tyrannical power." A counterpart was Nazi subversion of governments in Latin America aiming at ultimate control of the Western Hemisphere and a "permanent world system based on force, terror, and murder." The Monroe Doctrine was too self-limiting for Roosevelt, however; the immediate issue, he insisted, was freedom of shipping on the high seas, the settled policy of the United States since Presidents John Adams and Thomas Jefferson cleared the Caribbean of privateers and the Mediterranean of cor-sairs. The line of supply to the enemies of Hitler would be maintained at all costs and by active defense: "When you see a rattlesnake poised to strike, you do not wait … you crush him." The American navy would protect "not only American ships but ships of any flag" in American defensive waters. "Let this warning be clear," he concluded: "From now on, if German and Italian vessels enter the waters, the protection of which is necessary for American defense, they do so at their own peril." ROOSEVELT ORDERS NAVY TO SHOOT FIRST, the banner headline of the *New York Times* reported the next day.

The president was evasive about the precise manner in which the navy would provide protection. In fact Stimson himself did not learn of the escort system until September 25. Nonetheless the determi-nation to use force and the justification for it had been forthrightly declared to the American people, and their reaction was powerfully supportive. Approving "in general" the "shoot on sight" directive were 62 percent of those interviewed by Gallup, disapproving 28 percent.[54]

Once restrictions on escort eased, the British, Canadian, and American navies were soon getting much "mixed up together," to use Churchill's apt phrase.[55] Even before the *Greer* incident, the battle-ship H.M.S. *Rodney* teamed up with the American carriers *Wasp*, *Yorktown*, and *Long Island* in search of a German raider, possibly the cruiser *Prinz Eugen,* which British intelligence feared had broken out again and which had been supposedly sighted east of Bermuda. The search was in vain.[56] The president's orders to shoot on sight in the western Atlantic included German surface raiders as well as aircraft overflying Iceland.[57]

On September 17 the Admiralty proposed that the United States Navy take over formal responsibility for guarding Denmark Strait, explaining that an important operation in the Mediterranean required withdrawal of heavy units from the Home fleet. This was Operation HALBERD, a vital supply convoy to Malta guarded by *Prince of Wales, Rodney,* and *Nelson.*[58] Admiral King agreed, and within ten days nearly all the ships of the Atlantic Fleet were at the northern bases or headed there. They included one old and two modernized battleships, three heavy cruisers, and a carrier at Hvalfjordur; and one modernized and two old battleships, a carrier and two light cruisers at Argentia with a third carrier and a light cruiser headed there. Altogether some fifty destroyers were escorting warships or merchant convoys in northern waters. In addition, the new battleship *Washington,* though still not fully ready, was in a back-up position at Rockland, Maine.[59] On September 27 the commanders of the Home fleet and the Western Approaches, Admirals Sir John Tovey and Sir Percy Noble, arrived in Iceland in H.M.S. *King George V* to see for themselves that Denmark Strait was locked tight and to work out ways of improving communications between the British and American fleets.[60] By October the American naval concentration against Germany in the northern reaches of the Atlantic was not far smaller than the Pacific Fleet itself.

During the same September 5 meeting with Admirals Stark and King at which the president concluded his decisions on escort of convoy, he also considered a recent request from Churchill for troop transports and cargo ships to move 40,000 British troops from the United Kingdom to the Middle East. The purpose was not further reinforcement of the British forces in Egypt, however, but building strength through the Persian Gulf in Syria, Iraq, and Iran. By suppressing the Iraqi coup in May and defeating the Vichy French in Syria in July, British forces closed up to the southern border of Turkey. On August 25 Soviet and British forces by mutual agreement moved into Iran to prevent a pro-German coup at Teheran like the one in Iraq and to establish a supply corridor to the Soviet Union across the Caucasus. The object of the reinforcement, Churchill explained, was to sustain the "Russian reserve positions in the Volga basin" and encourage Turkey "to stand as a solid block against German passage in Syria and Palestine."[61] What had inspired this urgent dispatch of regular British divisions to a front so far from battle was dismal news from the Russian front.

Shortly after Argentia, the German offensive resumed and soon sweeps and plunges by Panzer and motorized forces were taking huge bites out of the Red Army. The Soviets now were paying the price for the rest and replenishment of German forces in late July and early August. Army Group North cut Leningrad's communications, besieged the city and prepared to storm it. In the center the decision was to defer the attack on Moscow. Guderian's Panzer army swung south and with easier supply on a lateral front drove in behind the massive, inert concentration of Soviet forces—two-thirds of a million men—at Kiev. Opposite him, from Army Group South, Kleist's Panzer group crossed the Dnieper and gathered mass to strike north, meet Guderian, and seal off Kiev. Further south, Runstedt's columns fanned out across the Ukraine to encircle Odessa, cut off the Crimea, and capture the great bend of the Dnieper where it pokes eastwardly toward the industries of the Don basin. Beyond the Don lay the Caucasus and the Volga. Every major city of European Russia was imperiled except, for the moment, Moscow.[62]

Western observers were slow to grasp the grim reality as the optimism of early August persisted. The American embassy in Moscow, now determinedly hopeful where it had been persistently skeptical, considered the reverses in the Ukraine as no worse than one battle lost. It warned that the capture of Rostov, where the Germans could turn the corner into the Caucasus, would be most serious, but pointed out on August 23 that winter would begin in sixty days. Soviet destruction of the great dam at Zaporozhe on the Dnieper, their emblem of proletarian progress, showed that Stalin's scorched earth policy was in "deadly earnest." The American legation in Switzerland, estimating German casualties of 1,400,000 (British estimates were 2,000,000), saw no sign of the breaking of Russian morale, fronts, or command. General Mason-Macfarlane, the British observer at Moscow, reported after a visit to the front that Russian morale and equipment were excellent, though he acknowledged that the situation in the south was "precarious." The New York Times reported the Russians holding or gaining on August 24, 25, 28, 31, September 1, 3, and 4. Only the American military attaché in London, with access to British intelligence, which in turn was based partly on ULTRA, pointed out the grave danger of the envelopment of Kiev.[63]

So after weeks of sanguine reports, news of this "lurch into disaster in the Ukraine," as one authority has described it, came as a shock to

Roosevelt, especially delivered as it was in a letter from Stalin to Churchill which was passed on to Washington on September 5. The situation, the Soviet chief said, had "considerably deteriorated" in the past three weeks because the Germans had transferred thirty to thirty-four divisions and great numbers of tanks and aircraft from the west. They did so "with impunity," he continued acidly, because they recognized that the danger in the west was a bluff. Their strategy was to smash their enemies singly, first the Soviet Union, then Britain. Now more than half the Ukraine was gone, and the enemy was at the gates of Leningrad. He ticked off the losses: the Krivoi Rog iron-ore district and metallurgical works in the Ukraine. Out of production for months because of evacuation were an aluminum factory on the Dnieper, another at Tikhvin in the north, an automotive factory and two aircraft factories in the Ukraine, and two automotive factories and an aircraft factory in Leningrad.[64]

The only answer to this "mortal menace" was a British second front in the Balkans or France, a guarantee of 30,000 tons of aluminum by October, and monthly shipments of 400 aircraft and 500 tanks. Without this help, the Soviet dictator concluded in brutal candor, Russia would be defeated or so weakened it would be unable to help its allies by active operations. In conveying the message, Churchill informed Roosevelt that Soviet Ambassador Ivan Maisky in London had used language "which could not exclude the impression that they might be thinking of separate terms." With that language the American government was already familiar. In a dispatch Washington received August 27, Anthony Biddle, ambassador to several governments-in-exile in London, had reported Maisky as saying that the Soviet Union would make peace unless the United States entered the war and the British opened a second front.[65]

Churchill responded to Stalin with equal candor that a second front that year was impossible and the next year indeterminable. The best he could offer was a buildup of forces in the Middle East, which, after the defeat of Axis forces in Libya, would "come into line on your southern flank," some undefined operation "in the extreme North when there is more darkness," and further battering of Germany from the air. Lacking a fighting front to offer, the British government stretched itself on war supplies. Churchill said he would try to expedite the Moscow conference on supply and promised on the spot, from British production, one-half of Stalin's request for tanks and planes with the hope that the Americans would supply the other half. He apologized to Roosevelt for presuming on American aid, explaining that the "moment may be decisive."[66]

These were the exigencies when Roosevelt met with the admirals on September 5 to decide arrangements for escort of convoy. On the immediate issue of reinforcing the Middle East the president decided to meet the prime minister halfway: he would provide transports for one division and ten to twelve cargo ships. The troop ships would be the navy's largest and fastest: the former luxury liners *United States, America,* and *Manhattan.*[67]

Roosevelt was no less determined to provide the Soviet Union with all possible war matériel than he had been before the Argentia conference. Upon his return from Argentia in the wake of the House vote barely extending the draft, he warned reporters against a natural tendency to slacken in delivery of goods when the Russians were succeeding. This, he said, was "terribly, terribly dangerous." He established the priority of Russian supply in the most authoritative and deliberate way in a letter to Stimson on August 30: "I deem it to be of paramount importance for the safety and security of America that all reasonable munitions help be provided for Russia, not only immediately but as long as she continues to fight the Axis powers effectively."[68]

The problem was that demands had carried beyond any reasonable expectation of supply. Aside from the Russians, the British were counting on about one-third of American aircraft and one-half of American tank production, the latter especially important for CRUSADER, their impending offensive in Libya.[69] The Middle East command was a favorite whipping boy of the U.S. Army; its deficiencies, whether in command, supply or tactics, were always being paraded through the General Staff. But Roosevelt unwaveringly supported its reinforcement on the ground that "the enemy must be fought wherever he was found."[70] To these demands were added those of the burgeoning American armed services, to say nothing of voices offstage such as China's.

The war and America's relationship to it had changed faster than estimates of what it would take to win it. The army and navy were still at work on the estimates, known as the Victory Program, which the president had asked for July 9. On August 30 he directed Stimson to submit by September 10 his recommendations regarding allocation of war production through June 1942 among the United States and forces opposed to the Axis, and also his estimates of the production required for ultimate victory. Lights burned late at the War Department. On September 8, Roosevelt agreed with Churchill on an earlier date, September 25, for the Moscow conference on supply which they had planned at Argentia. The president suggested that their delegations first meet in London a week hence to coordinate allocations and estimates, immediate and ultimate. He sent the unwelcome news (by way of a letter over Hopkins' signature) that American supply commitments to Britain would have to be reviewed in the light of Soviet requirements.[71] The urgency of the situation described by Stalin only intensified Roosevelt's determination to send all possible aid as soon as possible.

The competitors for American supply were in fact "dividing a deficiency."[72] War production in 1941 was still less than 10 percent of total production and less than two-thirds of British-Canadian, which it would not surpass until the last quarter of 1942. Because of design changes, B-17 production halted and the United States produced exactly one heavy bomber in July 1941. Better than half the military planes produced were trainers, and there were scarcely any spare parts. The United States had on hand eighty medium tanks and expected to complete 450 in the July-September quarter as against 10,790 by the end of 1942. It expected to produce 230,000 tons of shipping in the same quarter; the army calculated that defeat of Germany would require the 10.8 million already planned through 1943 and an additional 13.1 million tons.[73]

From September 8 to the end of the month, intense and at times bitter struggles over priorities and allocations occurred between the White House and the army, the army and navy, the Americans and British at London, and the Anglo-Americans and Russians in Moscow. Roosevelt carefully monitored the action and imposed his will at crucial moments to ensure that the outcome would be acceptable to the Soviet government.

Bitterest of all was the battle over tanks. Stalin asked for five hundred a month, or 4,500 through June 1942, and the British promised half. Under pressure to match the British offer of 2,250, the U.S. Army agreed to stretch out the equipping of the 3rd, 4th, and 5th Armored Divisions and fifteen independent tank battalions and postpone activation of the 6th Armored Division. This sacrifice and severe cutbacks in British allocations yielded 1,524 medium and light tanks, or precisely two-thirds of the matching offer. The British protested, whereupon the president ordered a doubling of tank production and an increase of 25 percent in deliveries, to the anguish of the U.S. Navy, which feared that a higher priority for tanks would reduce the armor plate available for warship construction. With a greater supply promised, at least on paper, the British agreed to make up the difference in immediate deliveries in return for a larger quota of American tanks later. On this basis Stalin's demand for 500 tanks a month could be met. In the meantime the Soviet demand had risen to 1,100 a month, but in the end Stalin settled for five hundred.[74]

With this sort of juggling and some highly speculative promissory notes on future production and delivery, the British Commonwealth and United States came forward with responsive offerings at Moscow on September 28. They would meet Stalin's original requests for aircraft and tanks in full. Canada would provide one-half the aluminum sought, and the Americans would study the possibility of providing the rest. Counterbalancing modest amounts of other weapons, the British and Americans offered 90,000 jeeps and trucks, as well as a wide array of finished metals and raw materials, and large amounts of wheat and sugar. Britain and the United States assured production but not delivery, leaving the enormous problem of transportation to joint responsibility and the future. Payment was a problem since Roosevelt was not quite ready to extend Lend-Lease to the Soviet Union on account of anti-Soviet public opinion, but by patching together credits and old purchases the Treasury Department tided over the interim. Stalin sent word he was "much gratified."[75]

Whiffs of the battle over allocations began seeping into the press. Correspondents Walter Lippmann and Ernest K. Lindley, writing independently, set forth the opinion of the British and of the American navy that the United States should rely on sea and air power and on its manufacturing capacity to constrict and batter Germany into submission rather than build a huge army for the invasion of Europe. Pressure actually arose to reduce the size of the army. Stimson, Marshall, Lovett, and McCloy vigorously resisted the idea, contending that the United States must ultimately "come to grips with and annihilate" the German war machine. They pointed to existing commitments for task forces and bases and to what might happen if "Hitler gets his feet out of the bog in Russia." On September 22, Stimson and Marshall went to the White House to defend the army's current strength and projected size of 215 divisions under the Victory Program. The outcome was a presidential decision to defer further expansion of the army after February 1942 in order to release munitions for allies. That this represented Roosevelt's choice of the navy's rather than the army's concept of defeating Germany seems unlikely. Roosevelt chose not to choose, dwelling on the immediate, imperative need to ensure Soviet survival into 1942. On September 20 the press reported the German capture of Kiev. The military attaché in London reported "definite disintegration" along the entire Russian front. The president was determined to provide aid to the Soviet Union so substantial that Stalin would not only gain concrete assistance but also the conviction that Britain and the United States were allies he could count on.[76]

The competition among the Soviets, the British and the American armed services for American aircraft production, no less severe than that for tanks, had significant strategic consequences. The 1,800 planes promised the Soviet Union for the next nine months, consisting of fighters and medium bombers but not any heavy bombers, would come from British and U.S. Army allocations. The British insisted on American heavy bombers in compensation. Stimson, Marshall, and the Army Air Corps bitterly resisted. They were displeased, to be sure, with British handling of the few precious B-17s sent earlier, but, more important, they believed it was high time for the United States to develop its own heavy bomber forces. From August 1940 to June 1941, top priority had gone to building 1,221 planes for the navy.[77] On August 25, Stimson and Marshall witnessed the first B-17Es coming off the assembly line at the Boeing plant in Seattle. This version of the Flying Fortress was much more heavily armed, with top, rear, and belly rotating powered turrets for twin .50 caliber machine guns. The Air Corps, with only 108 heavy bombers as of June 30, was determined to get as many of them as it could.[78]

The argument for building American strategic air power increasingly turned on the air reinforcement of the Philippines. On August 11 a group of army officers left Hawaii by navy patrol plane for Australia to prepare the way for trans-Pacific flights of B-17s. On September 5 nine B-17s took off from Hickam Field, Hawaii, for Midway and Wake islands. From Wake at high altitude and at night they overflew the eastern Carolines, Japanese mandated islands, headed for Port Moresby in southeastern New Guinea and hopped from there to Darwin, Australia, and Clark Field near Manila, arriving September 12.[79] Difficult and dangerous as this pioneering flight was, it solved the problem of moving large aircraft across the Pacific quickly and opened the door to a buildup of strategic air power in Southeast Asia.

Stimson was enthusiastic. The arrival of the B-17s, he wrote on September 12, demonstrated American ability to position air power in the narrow seas of Southeast Asia to cut the line of communications of any Japanese expeditionary force sent southward. He spent a good part of the day September 16 poring over maps to see "how far our planes would reach." Stimson and General Marshall understood Roosevelt's concern for aid to the Soviet Union and his disposition, as Churchill explained to Stalin on August 28, "to take [a] strong line against further Japanese aggression whether in the South

or in the Northwest Pacific." Marshall aimed his argument for holding on to American bombers and developing American strategic air
power directly at these presidential concerns. In his brief for a conference with the president on September 22, next in priority after
preparing task forces for defense of the Atlantic islands was the air
reinforcement of the Philippines. The brief read: "Rush buildup of
air power to Philippines ... to restrain Japan from advance into
Malaysia or Eastern Siberia."[80]

What American planes might deter heavily depended on how far
they could reach. The B-17C, the version sent in September, had a
combat radius with a half-load of bombs of 900 miles. Formosa,
Shanghai, even Okinawa, were within striking distance, but not the
home islands of Japan. The B-17E, however, the new version to be
sent thereafter, had a somewhat longer reach which might place Kyushu, the southern island of Japan, within striking distance. The
army's War Plans Division began a special study of these and other
strategic possibilities of air power in the Philippines on September
16.[81]

Enthusiasm for the project did not wait. The B-17s authorized at
Argentia, which would bring the total in the Philippines to thirty-
five, prepared to move in October. The day the first nine B-17s
arrived in the Philippines, Marshall ordered a second group of thirty-
five across in December—as soon as it had new planes—for a total of
seventy. The Air Corps was pressing for more, asking MacArthur
how many could be accommodated on existing fields in three months
and how many in six.

Bombers alone, of course, would be helpless. The Air Corps
received authorization September 12 for a broad-based buildup
including a group of fifty-four dive bombers and an additional group
of fighters (130), as well as reconnaissance, air warning, command,
ordnance, and engineering units. The army was preparing to send
the tanks, artillery, and anti-aircraft guns authorized in August. This
was the sort of power, Stimson believed, that would "keep the fear of
God in Japan." Not infantry yet, however: the army was considering
sending a National Guard division but asked MacArthur's views on
the subject, warning that the demand for shipping was heavy.[82]

The oil embargo and air reinforcement of the Philippines were
both meant to halt Japanese expansion but there the similarity ends.
The reinforcement project aimed at making a Japanese attack northward or southward too costly and risky. This deterrent effect itself
was speculative and would not in any case be fully realized for several
months when runways were extended and planes, ground personnel,

munitions, and gasoline arrived. Therefore it might prompt Japanese action before the military capability was in place. Nevertheless, the aim of the reinforcement was to encourage Japanese inaction. The oil embargo, however, if fully implemented and joined in by the British and Dutch, would have an immediate and growing impact and carry beyond deterrence to coercion. The clock would be ticking toward the moment when Japan would lack the fuel to send armies and fleets into battle and it would have to attack, change its aims, or subside in influence. It would suffer severe penalties from inaction.

The decision on an oil embargo was closely held and deviously managed. Action proceeded not in the formal realm of peacetime quotas and proclamations restricting export, for on paper Japan was supposed to receive some quantities of some kinds of oil, but in the shadowy world of inaction, circumvention, and red tape.[83]

Upon the freezing of Japanese assets in July, the United States required both export licenses and licenses to withdraw funds to pay for the exports. Before leaving for Argentia, Welles had directed Acheson to withhold action on exchange licenses for the time being, in effect while the president and he were absent. Most export licenses were denied, but a few were approved, and these came before the Foreign Funds Control Committee, which before long would have to give reasons for delay. Then, as Dean Acheson later explained to Sir Ronald Campbell of the British embassy, the committee "discovered by accident the technique of imposing total embargo by way of its freezing order without having to take decisions about quotas for particular commodities."[84] In anticipation of the freezing order, Japanese banks had sequestered dollars in the United States and Latin America. Aware of this plunge into cash and foreign accounts, the committee insisted that these funds be used before releasing frozen assets. The Japanese demurred.

This was the state of affairs Acheson reported to Welles the day before the president returned from Argentia.[85] Undoubtedly either by phone or in person on August 21 or 29, when he saw the president alone, Welles reported the situation to Roosevelt, and no countervailing directive was issued.[86] Japanese trade, Acheson noted on August 20, was "a matter of confidential discussion between the President and Secretary Hull." On September 5, a day Hull had lunch with the president, the secretary of state gave departmental sanction to these stalling maneuvers. The United States had imposed an embargo without saying so. It was in a position, said Acheson, to point out to the Japanese that they had "imposed {an} embargo upon themselves by their lack of loyalty to [the] American freezing order."[87]

The de facto embargo worked this way. The Japanese embassy asked Foreign Funds whether it would accept payment for pending oil shipments by assets transferred from Brazil. The answer was that this was a hypothetical question. The Japanese would have to transfer the funds, risking their being frozen, and then apply. The Japanese offered silk for cotton and oil and were told the United States did not need silk. They then offered release of exports to America which they had halted in retaliation, but were asked to present a list and then told the list was incomplete, and that in any event an exchange was impossible because there were no Japanese purchases which had been paid for. The Japanese proposed to ship dollars from Japan, but Foreign Funds wanted proof these were legally obtained abroad. The Japanese suggested gold in payment and received no answer. They then returned to the idea of remitting balances from South America and met silence again. Finally, in early November two Japanese tankers on the West Coast, which had been "gathering oysters" on their propellers awaiting cargo since July, weighed anchor and returned to Japan empty.[88]

Trade did not stop immediately. One ship was allowed as ballast a cargo of low-grade lubricating oil, asphalt, cotton, and cocoa beans. Some iron ore moved to Japan from the Philippines, some cotton to Japanese-occupied China. Dollars and yen were unfrozen to pay diplomatic staffs.[89]

The stall only gradually surfaced. For weeks the British and Dutch were left in ignorance of the American intent. They learned September 13 that the embargo was "practically absolute" but that Hull wanted no publicity "which might demonstrate the completeness of the present embargo or suggest greater severity." On September 26, Acheson apologized for the problems caused by the "somewhat opportunist measures" he had been obliged to follow, and he finally explained to the British and Dutch how the embargo worked and urged them to achieve the same result. They were already well on the way. Certain Indian trade with Japan posed a problem, and Britain was anxious to secure as much magnesium as possible from Japan for the making of incendiary bombs, but Japan's trade outside its orbit in East Asia had been practically closed down by October.[90]

With the single exception of a stringent war warning, Roosevelt by October had fulfilled the commitments he made at Argentia. He had reaffirmed and indeed reinforced and extended the new policy directions he had chosen in the wake of the German attack on Russia. He had entered the Battle of the Atlantic, though on his own terms, extended the best aid possible to the Soviet Union, begun the buildup of a deterrent force in the Philippines, applied maximum economic pressure against Japan, and entangled the Japanese in complex and prolonged diplomatic talks. He had established, if not a formal alliance, an intimate political relationship with Great Britain. He had chosen courses risking war in the belief that alternative courses seemed riskier to American vital interests. The central dynamic of his policies was the conviction that the survival of the Soviet Union was essential for the defeat of Germany and that the defeat of Germany was essential for American security. This more than any other concern, to his mind, required the immobilization of Japan.

No single decision or day marked the point when Roosevelt crossed over from benevolent neutrality to belligerency and risk of war. The process was complex and extended from late July to mid-September. One particular day, however, seems to epitomize the transition: Friday, September 5, 1941. This was the day following the *Greer* incident when he ordered the start of convoy escort, the day he received Stalin's ominous message and promised his three best transports for reinforcement adjacent to the Russians in the Middle East. It was also the day Secretary Hull formalized within government the undercover embargo and when the first B-17s departed for Manila and the 19th Bombardment Group was ordered to follow in October.

Chapter 7

October–November
Race Against Time

In early August, just as President Roosevelt was deciding that the Soviets might survive the German onslaught, the Japanese government was reaching the same conclusion. Ironically the United States then took steps to prevent a Japanese attack northward at precisely the moment Japan decided to postpone it. On August 9, the day before the start of the Argentia conference, the Japanese government formally decided against operations in Siberia that year.

Besides offering surprisingly strong resistance in the west, the Soviet Union was slow to withdraw its forces from the Far East. The Soviets maintained some thirty tough, experienced divisions, three cavalry brigades, sixteen tank brigades, and 2,000 tanks and aircraft east of Lake Baikal, most of the infantry manning extensive fortifications along the Ussuri and Amur rivers on the northern and eastern borders of Manchuria. Japanese intelligence noted a westward movement of forces in July, but only a few formations and these from the Baikal area rather than the more critical Amur-Ussuri front, which in fact was being strengthened. A decision for war by August 10 was necessary for an attack at the end of the month and completion of the campaign by mid-October, when the bitter cold and snows of the Siberian winter would set in.[1]

Along with fading prospects of quick success in the north came the "staggering blow" of American sanctions.[2] Some of the more cosmopolitan officials in finance, foreign affairs, and the navy had feared some such severe American response to the move into southern Indochina, but the army as a whole and the militant elements of the navy in the vanguard of the southern advance movement were taken entirely by surprise. Japanese insiders, aware of the hesitations and divergent ambitions composing the southern Indochina decision, found it hard to understand the severity of the American response

180

The German-Russian Front: *New York Times*, November 9, 1941.

but were quick to assume the worst, that the embargo was total. While testing American regulations for whatever oil might still be obtained, the Japanese government was of one mind: exchange controls that placed the American government in a position to turn the tap at will, on or off, day to day, were intolerable.[3]

The Japanese nation, in the eyes of its leaders, faced a supreme crisis. Access to the world's resources was suddenly disappearing. Gone now was Japan's trans-Siberian link to Germany and supplies of key metals and machinery. Denied access to oil outside the empire, Japan had two years' supply in stockpile, and less under the demands of war. As it was, the supply was diminishing by 12,000 tons each day. A feeling of desperation took hold: Japan was "like a fish in a pond from which the water was gradually being drained away."[4]

The Tokyo atmosphere was heavy with the paranoia of encirclement. Japanese could gaze upon Soviet and American-chartered tankers plying La Perouse Strait between Hokkaido and Japanese-held southern Sakhalin with oil products for Vladivostok. Consuls reported the opening of an American naval air base at Dutch Harbor in the Aleutians, the arrival of a Soviet air mission in the United States and its inspection of an American heavy bomber. They speculated on the possibility of the United States supplying airplanes to the Soviet Union by way of Alaska and even eventually establishing a bombing force in Siberia. Japanese consuls also reported construction of an airfield at Davao in the Philippines suitable for use by bombers and the arrival of American reinforcements at Manila. A British warship was noted visiting Manila as well as the cruisers *St. Louis* and *Phoenix* from Hawaii, which, according to rumor, departed for Singapore. Japanese intelligence noted the arrival in China of American pilots and planes and construction there of new air bases with British, American, and Russian help.[5] The oil embargo seemed to be, in the words of one authority, the "final, major link in a chain of encirclement" by the ABCD powers, a culmination of years of effort on their part "to deny Japan her rightful place in the world by destroying her only available means of self-existence and self-defense." Unless Japan could break the "circle of force" by diplomacy and quickly, the reasoning went, it must fight.[6] President Roosevelt had succeeded better than he knew in preoccupying Japan with the south.

The Japanese army was of one mind on the necessity for attack southward including war with the United States. Even proponents of an attack northward were converted by the necessity of first securing adequate resources in the south. Further negotiation seemed futile but was tolerable so long as a decision for war was reached by early October for attack in November.

The position of the navy was more complex, but the upshot was the same. Whereas the army required Imperial sanction and a long lead time to gather and deploy forces and transports for attack, and therefore required an early formal decision for war, the navy was already close to a war footing and could move quite soon after a decision. So it could allow diplomacy more time. Japan's navy was also dissatisfied with the army's plan of attack: it wanted the army to commit more divisions and include initial landings in the Philippines to forestall American use of the islands.

If not more sanguine about negotiations, the navy was more serious.[7] Although war enthusiasts on the naval general staff tended to ignore or underestimate America's war production capability, leading admirals were aware of the huge building plans of 1940–41, including seventeen battleships completing, abuilding, or ordered, and twelve attack carriers. The American navy would add 178 destroyers to the fleet in 1942 and 1943. By current Japanese navy estimates, the United States had not far from three times the warship tonnage under construction that Japan did. A few admirals such as Yamamoto Isoroku, commander of the Combined Fleet, warned that the prospects in a long war were very bleak.

Naval leaders, then, hoped against hope that some further shift in the fluctuating and unpredictable balance of world forces or in American intentions would open the way for a Japanese-American compromise that guaranteed Japan access to oil and other war resources. Less involved in China, the navy was more flexible than the army on the issue of retaining troops there. It stood more strongly for trying diplomacy before reaching a decision for war.

Yet the current was flowing toward war in the navy, too. The other side of the coin in the Japanese-American naval balance was that at the moment, in late summer 1941, the Imperial Navy outnumbered the Anglo-American-Dutch forces facing it eleven to nine in battleships and ten to three in carriers and that the enemy forces were scattered from Singapore to Pearl Harbor. Against the American building program, however, Japan's advantage would steadily decline, and after 1943 precipitously. Never would Japan have a more favorable moment to strike. For the navy, dwindling oil supplies made all the difference between taking to the blue waters and rusting in port. Control of East Indies oil, staff officers argued, would enable Japan to fight a protracted war. A psychology of desperation, characterized by "do or die," "fight or surrender," and "now or never" dichotomies, percolated upward from middle echelon officers to Admiral Nagano Osami, chief of the general staff, and Admiral Oikawa Kojirō, navy minister.

The same sense of desperation affected the civilian leadership of Japan but led to a different conclusion: somehow diplomacy must be made to work so as to avoid war. Prime Minister Konoe, monitoring the military's turn toward the south in the wake of the American embargo, decided to play his high card: a bid for a meeting with the American president. Thus Ambassador Nomura's suggestion of August 6 met by Roosevelt's seemingly encouraging response of August 17.

It was a move founded on hope, not substance. This melancholy nobleman, on whom the emperor and court had lavished such hopes for wise leadership, had already proven to be a weak reed for peace. His first and second cabinets had led Japan into the war in China, the Axis alliance, and the southward advance—in short into the predicament it now faced. Disdainful of Western liberalism and much taken by the expansionist notions of the thirties, he was ambivalent about power and flaccid in its use.[8] Konoe now suddenly determined to reverse the tide by a supreme act of political will and skill. The army was certain he would fail, the navy only less so. At the least the premier's initiative would quiet uncertainties about going to war while preparations for attack continued. Japan's terms for peace must remain the same, however, the army insisted. Konoe could offer no substantial concession and must promise that if diplomacy failed he would not resign but lead the nation into war.

On the basis of these understandings between the armed services and between them and the cabinet, the government met in Imperial Conference September 6. Hara Yosimichi, president of the privy council, pointed out that plans placed greater emphasis on war than diplomacy, and, when neither of the uniformed chiefs of the armed services responded, the emperor himself intervened with a rebuke to the supreme command. He read from a poem of his grandfather, the Emperor Meiji:

> Throughout the world
> Everywhere we are all brothers
> Why then do the winds and waves rage so turbulently?

After a stunned silence Admiral Nagano insisted that Japan would choose war only as an "unavoidable last resort."[9] On that basis the conference concluded that, if early October brought no prospect of Japan's demands being met, the nation would then decide to go to war with the United States, Great Britain, and the Netherlands. This was the same day (September 5, Washington time) on which American policy respecting the Battle of the Atlantic, aid to Russia, the oil embargo, and reinforcement of the Philippines solidified all across the line.

Meanwhile the Japanese were not finding prospects for a leaders' meeting encouraging. Nomura saw the president on August 28 and September 3, each visit sandwiched between talks with Hull. Roosevelt had suggested a mid-October rendezvous. The ambassador urged September 21. The president had engagements in late September. The Japanese said the meeting was an essential first step, a means of discussing all issues from the broadest standpoint and exploring every means of "saving the situation." The Americans regarded the meeting as a last step, to be devoted to ratification of agreements previously reached on all fundamental questions. Discussion along these lines, a continuation of the Hull-Nomura format of the spring, Konoe warned, "did not meet the need of the present situation which is developing swiftly and may produce unforeseen contingencies." First, the Americans insisted, the Japanese government must show it stands "earnestly" for the principles the United States had been proclaiming and the practical application thereof. Then the British, Chinese, and Dutch would have to be "prevailed upon."[10]

Publicity about the Hull-Nomura talks created a further obstacle. Churchill's broadcast on August 24 alerted America's partners, no less than Japan's, to the pourparlers and roused anxieties. The White House made no attempt to keep Nomura's visit of August 28 secret, and Nomura himself, upon emerging from the president's office, told newsmen that he had delivered a message from Premier Konoe. The same day Wilfred Fleischer, formerly a journalist in Tokyo and now correspondent for the *New York Herald Tribune,* stopped at the Japanese embassy to say that he gathered from an interview with the president several days earlier that Konoe would like a meeting in Hawaii. A chorus of newspaper speculation followed.[11] At the same time Tokyo made no secret of its displeasure over shipments of American oil to Vladivostok and Washington responded with disdain for Japan's complaints.[12] On September 4, Nomura reported to Tokyo his impression that the American attitude had "very much stiffened."[13]

On the evening after the Imperial Conference of September 6, Ambassador Grew and Counselor of Embassy Dooman, who was fluent in Japanese, dined with the premier at Prince Konoe's invitation. Every precaution was taken to keep the meeting secret: use of the home of a friend, license plates removed from the car, servants sent away. Konoe began by saying he desired that his statements be conveyed directly to the president. While it was true, he said, that he was fully responsible for the deplorable state of relations between the two countries, it was equally true that only he could repair the damage, and he was determined to spare no effort to succeed.

The American government seemed to doubt his ability to carry a peace program against the military, but it was mistaken, he insisted, because army and navy leaders had from the beginning supported the talks in Washington and had promised to send high-ranking officers with the premier to a meeting with President Roosevelt. Konoe said he believed that a basis already existed for agreement, but he added as further encouragement his personal, and therefore his government's, hearty concurrence with Hull's four principles: the territorial integrity and sovereignty of all nations; non-interference in the internal affairs of other nations; the open door for trade; and preservation of the status quo except for change by peaceful means. He "repeatedly stressed," Grew reported, that time was of the essence. The two governments must reach an overall accord now and work out details later. The reverse approach, working out all details first, might take them past the time when he could put an agreement into effect.[14]

Konoe's initiative was strongly reinforced by Grew in a flow of telegrams during September and a personal letter to the president. Seeing war clouds looming as he had in Berlin, where he served as counselor of embassy on the eve of American entry into World War I, the ambassador urgently and eloquently pressed the case for a leaders' meeting. American firmness and the German attack on Russia had thoroughly discredited Matsuoka diplomacy, he argued, generating a fundamental realignment of Japan's policies and a recrudescence of moderate and liberal leadership. He had been told that in a personal encounter with Roosevelt, Konoe would be in a position to make "far-reaching concessions" and with the emperor's support enforce these on the army and navy. A meeting, he believed, would at least produce explicit assurances effectively ending Japan's Axis connection and begin a process of regeneration in Japanese-American relations. But the American government must not expect satisfactory specific commitments in advance of a meeting, for these could be used by pro-Axis elements to prevent one; it must trust Konoe and the process of step-by-step conciliation. The alternative, he warned, was replacement of the Konoe cabinet by a military dictatorship and a steady drift to war.[15]

The State Department was not impressed. The man who had been prime minister when the China war started, when Japan moved into northern and southern Indochina, and when Japan joined the Axis did not seem likely to be able to force the Japanese army to withdraw now. Grew was an old hand at diplomacy and had an expert staff, but he had a record of periodic overoptimism about the forces of restraint and moderation in Japan. Weakening Grew's argument now was his failure to provide any concrete illustration of how the two sides might bridge their differences.[16]

As the Japanese position unfolded under persistent American probing during September, it became evident that these differences were especially great on China issues; in fact Japan's terms were stricter in September than they had been in May. The Konoe government still insisted that the United States cease assistance to China and that any settlement permit the stationing of Japanese troops in China. Now, however, it also stipulated that, while American trade in China would be permitted on an "equitable" basis, Japanese trade there would proceed under the principle of "geographical propinquity," a characteristic Japanese and imperialist euphemism for hegemony. Furthermore, the United States would have to cease all military preparations in the region and restore normal trade before Japan reached a settlement in China and withdrew its forces from Indochina.[17]

Despite the apparent stiffening, from the State Department's perspective the slender possibility of a shift in the Japanese position justified the tedious process of discovery. But discovery also assisted the more fundamental object of delay. The trick, Stimson believed, was to string out the negotiations without letting them ripen into a leaders' meeting.[18] As September passed and impatience and despair mounted in Tokyo, Hull and his Far Eastern experts—Hamilton, Ballantine, and Max Schmidt, as well as Grew and Dooman in Tokyo—questioned, compared, and criticized the Japanese terms. Somewhat like the Foreign Funds Control Committee in the matter of shutting down trade, they kept asking for further clarification and explanation without registering either progress or impasse.

For example, in one important respect Japanese terms of September were an improvement over those of May: they stressed Japan's independent interpretation of its obligations under the Axis alliance in case of war between Germany and the United States. Matsuoka had resisted any such weakening. Clearly Japan would not let its relationship with Germany stand in the way of an improvement in relations with the United States, provided that East Asian problems could be resolved. The State Department was silent on the shift until October 2, when it noted this step "with appreciation" but asked for "additional clarification" on Japan's ties with the Axis.[19]

Tokyo's shifting tactics and the ineptitude of its diplomats greatly facilitated delay. On September 6, Foreign Minister Toyoda, trying to avoid becoming bogged down in details, presented through Nomura the outline of a possible bargain, concentrating on the main issues in contention. Was this not a narrowing of Japan's position, the Americans asked, compared with the comprehensive draft understandings of April and May and Prince Konoe's assurances to Grew of adherence to American principles? In the September 6 proposal Japan promised to make no military advance from Indochina or southward generally. What about attacks northward, the Americans wanted to know. The Japanese promised an open door for trade in the southwest Pacific region, but what about the Pacific as a whole? Ambassador Nomura tangled communications himself on September 4 by presenting his own unauthorized proposal, couched in the comprehensive format of the earlier discussions. The American embassy in Tokyo was still trying to sort out the resulting confusion two weeks later.

Finally on September 25 through Grew and on September 27 through Nomura, Toyoda presented Japan's position in the established comprehensive format and most urgently requested an explicit American response setting a date and place for a leaders' meeting. With the president's approval, the State Department prepared its first written response to the Japanese proposals, which Hull delivered on October 2. Japan's offer was a disappointment, it said, because it seemed to narrow and qualify the principles and assurances upon which the talks were being conducted. If that impression was correct, the statement asked, would a meeting of leaders "be likely to contribute to the advancement of the high purposes which we have mutually in mind?" The American government invited "renewed consideration of these fundamental principles" and offered the "earnest hope" that this would lead to the desired meeting. Well into October the Japanese persisted in trying to elicit American counterproposals, both through Grew and Nomura, without success. On October 16 the Konoe cabinet, with nothing to show for its diplomacy and riven with dispute over further pursuit of it, resigned. Roosevelt had hoped to gain from thirty to sixty days by talks. As he wrote Churchill, they had gained "two months of respite in the Far East."[20]

The attention of Washington was devoted less to the tottering Konoe cabinet, however, than to the crumbling outer defenses of Moscow. On October 2, German Army Group Center launched a giant offensive to encircle Moscow and "finish the Russians off."[21] Already strongest in Panzer forces, Von Bock's group was further reinforced for this final blow by transfer of all the armor from the northern group of armies and a Panzer corps from the southern. Attacking on a 150-mile semicircular front west of Moscow were six German armies. The plan was to punch a hole in the middle of the Russian defenses, between Bryansk and Vyazma, to sweep in behind these twin citadels on the road to Moscow and destroy the main forces defending it, and then to send the flanking Panzer armies of Hoth and Guderian north and south of the capital in a climactic encirclement.

The German tanks broke through quickly and completely. In the Bryansk and Vyazma pockets more than 500,000 Russian troops were lost. Guderian, circling to the south, seized Orel and moved on Tula, due south of Moscow, while Hoth took Kalinin, opening the way to the Moscow-Volga Canal, and Moscow from the north. Between these pincers German infantry and armor, against desperate Russian resistance, fought their way eastwards along the Smolensk road as far as Mozaisk, fewer than fifty miles from Moscow. There at night they could see the glow of anti-aircraft fire over the capital. Radio Moscow admitted that the inhabitants were in "immense danger."[22] Fear filtered into the city, leading to wild rumors, evacuation of government offices, looting, and panicky flight by some Moscovites. The embassies moved with the foreign ministry to Kuibyshev, more than 500 miles southeast of Moscow.

To Berlin, victory seemed almost in the palm of the hand. Nazi propaganda boasted of motorized columns "streaming four abreast" down highways toward Moscow. At the front, however, a deepening sense of foreboding accompanied the exhilaration of conquest. Each encirclement led only to new Soviet defense lines. The Russians fought savagely and, after Marshal Georgi Zhukov took command of the front October 10, more resiliently. The Soviet T-34 outperformed the heaviest German tank. At Mozaisk, German troops in summer denim first encountered hardy Siberian troops in their white, quilted winter clothing. They also encountered worsening weather, now heavy cold rains, mud, and impassable roads, now frost and the first light snow. The last leaves were off the birches, maples, and oaks, and "ominous black clouds would build up far in the distance, towering high above the steppe," harbingers of the "ice wind, now gathering strength over the Aral Sea."[23] These, however, were portents not deeds.

The German drive on Moscow came as a distinct shock to Washington. Signs of an offensive were not lacking: a warning on October 1 from London based on ULTRA, Hitler's reference on October 3 to a "vast drive" in progress, an American diplomat's glimpse on October 6 of a Finnish war map showing "two German pincer thrusts in the direction of Moscow."[24] But the Germans were tight-lipped, and it was not until October 8, when the Vyazma and Bryansk encirclements were complete, that they beat the victory drums. Then banner headlines (six columns in the *New York Times*) brought a frightening sense of the size and import of the battle. The British War Office considered the whole Russian war now "at crisis." The Germans appeared to be throwing "their entire war machine into this all-out effort to take Moscow at any price." A usually optimistic Churchill estimated the chances of the Germans taking Moscow as even, his director of military intelligence as slightly better than even. When would winter in the Moscow region begin "in earnest," the prime minister asked? American army intelligence expected that the loss of Moscow would result in a "radical change of regime." At risk, too, were the supply routes from the West through Archangel and the Persian corridor, for the Germans were also racing toward Rostov. News from Russia, Stimson noted October 10, was "very bad": it was "nip and tuck" whether the Germans would not finish their war before winter. Even the imperturbable Berle confessed anxiety.[25]

As the German-Soviet war provided the central dynamic in world power relations, the repercussions of this October crisis were far-ranging. Fears revived of German attacks elsewhere, especially in the Middle East, once Moscow fell and the eastern front stabilized.[26] The failure of Britain to meet urgent Soviet requests for dispatch of British forces to the Russian front, either in the north or in the Caucasus, left British-Soviet relations "badly strained," Steinhardt reported. A sullen Molotov complained that such American P-40 fighter aircraft as had been delivered had engine defects. Leahy reported that Britain's failure to help its ally at this critical moment was having a great effect on Vichy, always a barometer of Axis military fortunes. France now expected a German victory in Russia and new pressure for German bases in French Africa.[27]

Of immediate importance to the American government was the possible effect on Tokyo of either the fall of Moscow or the withdrawal of Soviet Siberian armies to prevent its fall. Would Japan attack northward? Barring a Soviet collapse, Japan had no such intention. By October, Moscow knew this from definitive reports of Richard Sorge, a spy on the staff of the German embassy in Tokyo, and began to withdraw about half the divisions as well as 1,000 aircraft and 1,000 tanks from its Far Eastern command for the Moscow battle.[28] Washington, however, did not know. True, American consular reports from Harbin, Mukden, and Dairen showed that reinforcement of the Kwantung Army in Manchuria had practically ceased, but this fact could be taken to mean that preparations for attack were complete.[29]

The fall of the Konoe cabinet on October 16 (the same day diplomats evacuated Moscow) and appointment as prime minister of General Tōjō Hideki, previously war minister, intensified concern. Tōjō was known for his "particular dislike of the Russians" and his prediction in 1938 that Japan would have to fight the Soviet Union.[30]

Most observers believed that Japan would wait for a decisive turn of events on the European front, but on October 17 high Chinese military officers, upon learning of a reduction in Soviet Far Eastern forces, predicted an attack in a few days.[31] Winter was a limitation, but the possibility remained, and was discussed, of an attack aimed only at an isolated Vladivostok.[32] On October 21, army intelligence judged the Kwantung and Siberian armies as roughly matched, but a reduction providing the Japanese with a two-to-one superiority would probably lead to a Japanese attack and three-to-one would certainly do so. The navy, strongly influenced by Admiral Turner's conviction that Japan would turn north rather than south, warned that hostilities between Japan and the Soviet Union were now a "strong possibility."[33] Roosevelt himself told Lord Halifax on October 10 that he feared a Japanese attack on Vladivostok. On October 15 he wrote Churchill that the "Jap situation" was "definitely worse" and that he thought they were "headed North."[34]

Evidence was not lacking, however, that the Japanese might choose to attack southward. On October 3 the French governor-general of Indochina told the American consul in Hanoi that the Japanese had demanded four more air bases in Cambodia and expressed his "grave apprehension" of further Japanese advances to the south. Soon after, Grew reported preparations to send an additional 50,000 troops to Indochina. Worrisome, too, was a public statement by the director of Japanese navy intelligence that his service was "itching" for action against the Americans. The Japanese navy, it seemed to Stimson, was "beginning to talk almost as radically as the army," and the time had come to draw lines which, if crossed, would manifestly justify a military response.[35] These southern threats, however, seemed still somewhat distant and directed toward Yunnan province (as the Japanese hoped they would seem) or Thailand. Naval analysts accepted that Japan was mobilizing for war, but was not yet ready. At the moment naval forces were moving from southern areas back to home waters, not the other way around. Most observers probably agreed with a British War Office estimate that the Japanese would prefer to avoid the danger of involvement with Britain and the United States.[36]

Discordant signs in MAGIC intercepts failed to attract special attention, such as a request that Japanese agents in Manila investigate coastal defenses on Luzon and the sending of a ship to bring Japanese home from the Middle East, India, and East Asia by November 20. An order decrypted and translated October 9 directed the consul in Honolulu to report the precise location of Pacific Fleet vessels in Pearl Harbor with greater attention to those in fixed and predictable positions such as wharves, docks, and buoys than those at anchor. Yet intelligence fitted this into the category of typical, widespread reporting of American ship movements.[37]

Reasoning as to which way Japan might jump was speculative, in the category of the possible rather than the probable. Minds leaning one way did not rule out the other. The only conviction was an exasperated apprehension over Japan's undifferentiated and opportunistic expansionism. Nevertheless, the conjunction of the German threat to Moscow with the fall of the Konoe cabinet gave greater prominence in American official minds to the northern vector than the southern.

The question returned of how to get Japan "off Russia's back," as Norwegian diplomat Trygve Lie put it.[38] Roosevelt confided to Halifax on October 10 that sometime earlier (possibly in a verbal message delivered by Harriman) he had advised Stalin that in case of an acute crisis on the German front he should withdraw his troops from Siberia and not worry too much what the Japanese did, because any incursion could be corrected later—how, Roosevelt did not say.[39] The president was hard to pin down. Shortly after the fall of the Konoe cabinet, Halifax pursued the question. What would the United States do in the event of a Japanese attack on Russia, an event the Foreign Office considered possible given "the stimulus of the German advance on Moscow, the pressure of our economic measures, and the likelihood that Japan would wish to avoid a head-on collision with the A.B.C.D. Powers by moving southward"? But the Americans as usual avoided commitments.[40] On October 22, through Winant, Maisky urged a British-American warning against an attack on the

Soviet Union, but Hull was not prepared to go beyond the general-ized admonition he had given in the past.[41]

To the British mind, the German attack and Japanese cabinet shift called for the utmost firmness in diplomacy. The trade embargo was "slowly strangling" Japan, British diplomats believed, forcing it sooner or later to "break out or give way."[42] Whether or not Japan attacked depended on the solidity of the democratic front. The Brit-ish no less than the Commonwealth and Chinese governments were deeply apprehensive that the Hull-Nomura conversations would lead to some kind of appeasement of Japan and a weakening of that front, but they were at a loss to know what to do, for the discussions were entirely in the hands of the State Department, which did not take kindly to advice.[43]

They had nothing to fear; as seen before, the Americans had no intention of offering concessions. Hull and Stimson agreed between themselves that if the Japanese threw in their hand they might be allowed to keep Manchuria, but should be required to evacuate the rest of China and guarantee Soviet borders. An army intelligence estimate of October 2 warned against an agreement ending the war in China and permitting Japan to withdraw the bulk of its army: "Any action on our part ... which would liberate Japanese ... forces for action against Russia's rear in Siberia would be foolhardy." The object of policy must be to assist China in its efforts to "contain" the Japanese army.[44] Army War Plans advised a continuance of existing pressures "with a view to rendering Japan incapable of offensive operations against Russia or against possessions of the associated powers in the Far East."[45] Roosevelt and Hull repeatedly assured friendly ambassadors that no concessions would be made. Not for the last time, coalition diplomacy powerfully reinforced United States firmness.

The only further means of immobilizing Japan, so far as Roosevelt and his advisers could see, was to strengthen American military power in East Asia. That could most effectively and quickly be accomplished, the War Department believed, by speeding the air reinforcement of the Philippines.

American plans for deploying air power to East Asia had steadily expanded in August and September: first a squadron, then a group, then two groups. This was "great strength" to General Marshall, though not the four groups envisaged by the air staff in July. Seventy B-17s were to be in the Philippines or on the way by January 1, 1942. Thirty-five B-24 Liberators, a four-engine bomber with a slightly longer range, would leave for Manila by February 1. Between April and October 1942 the total force would rise to 136 operating heavy bombers and thirty-four reserves together with additional dive bombers and fighters.[46] These numbers, of course, were ever in jeopardy from a president listening to the urgent pleas of the British and Russians. The more were Stimson and the army anxious to stress the strategic importance of an American air mission in East Asia.[47]

On October 16, in the wake of the fall of the Konoe cabinet, Roosevelt called an emergency meeting of his military advisers. It seems most likely that at this meeting he decided to accelerate Philippine reinforcement plans. Thirty planes of the 7th Bombardment Group were now to leave one month earlier than scheduled, by December 1, the remaining five with thirty more by January 1, and another thirty by February 1, together with thirty-five B-24s. Under this speeded-up delivery schedule, by March 1942 the Far East Air Force would muster 165 heavy bombers.[48]

Now the Philippines would have an air force headquarters, with bomber and interceptor commands, to be led by Major General Lewis H. Brereton, who, as Marshall pointed out to MacArthur, had a "keen appreciation ... of the potentialities of air power." Now also for the first time the army committed an additional ground combat unit to the Philippines, an infantry regiment, together with another tank battalion, an anti-aircraft regiment, and a field artillery brigade. Together with more air and ground service units, prospective reinforcements would add 44,000 Americans to the Philippine garrison.[49]

The navy, too, contributed to the reinforcement of the Philippines by sending Submarine Squadron 2 from the Pacific Fleet to the Asiatic Fleet. These twelve newly commissioned vessels joined eleven modern and six old boats at Manila to form the largest submarine force in the navy. Submarines seemed ideally suited to the straits and restricted shipping passages surrounding the South China Sea. The navy had great faith in new torpedoes which were designed to explode simply by passing through a warship's magnetic field.[50]

As the American air commitment grew, so did the concept of its use. Bombers which could fly 2,000 miles need not be restricted to one base. B-17s and B-24s using Darwin, Singapore, a base in the Dutch East Indies, and the Philippines could command the myriad of narrow seas, archipelagos, peninsulas, and islands that lay between Asia and Australia. The navy began delivering bombs to Singapore. Roosevelt encouraged the Australians to move squadrons up to North Borneo. From Davao in the Philippines and Rabaul on New Britain the bombers could reach the Japanese Mandates and prevent a Japanese flanking of the Philippines from the east.[51]

The ferry route across the central Pacific and the Japanese Mandates being too vulnerable, the army and navy began development of a more southerly route, with shorter hops to accommodate medium bombers as well. This line of communications consisted of Palmyra and Christmas Islands, due south of Hawaii, the Phoenix group (Canton, Howland, Phoenix) southwest of there, then the Samoan Islands, the Fijis, the New Hebrides, New Caledonia, and Rockhampton on the northeast coast of Australia which would serve as a major air depot and distributing point.[52]

As the effort to establish American air power in East Asia accelerated and expanded in October, the American military leadership warmed to the idea. The army's War Plans Division study encouraged by Stimson concluded that "strong offensive air forces" in the Philippines, prepared to operate from British and Soviet bases, would provide a crucial deterrent to Japanese expansion in any direction. Japan would be unable to undertake any southward advance without first removing the threat in the Philippines, but attacking these islands would be a major operation requiring carrier planes and air support from Formosa. Japan, they were confident, would hesitate to try it except as a last resort.

Deterring a Japanese attack on Siberia would be major American, British, and Dutch forces in its rear, the possibility of American entry into the war, and the use of Russian bases for bombardment of Japan's highly inflammable cities. Even if the United States did not enter the war, the American commitment to supply the Soviet Union would serve as an implicit threat to a Japanese attack northward. General Arnold, chief of the Air Corps, wrote MacArthur that B-24s from northern Luzon could reach as far as Nagasaki and, if arrangements could be made to use Vladivostok, operations from there could cover most of Japan.[53]

Stimson's vision was even more sweeping. The bombers, he said, were the country's "big stick." They "revolutionized" the strategy of the Pacific, carrying American power to the Philippines for the first time since the aftermath of World War I, when Japan secured the central Pacific islands and the United States agreed at the Washington Conference to limit the size of its fleet. "From being impotent to influence events in that area," he wrote Roosevelt, "we suddenly find ourselves vested with the possibility of great effective power." Time was needed; the deterrent threat was still "imperfect." Even so, it "bids fair to stop Japan's march to the south and secure the safety of Singapore."

The secretary of war allowed to Harriman that he was not so sure about deterrence northward, but that advance he considered unlikely at the moment. In arguing for the reinforcement to the president, however, Stimson was more sanguine. He related it directly to preservation of Russian defensive power in Europe. With the Archangel route in jeopardy and the Persian corridor undeveloped, Vladivostok was crucial. He presented an exciting picture of heavy bombers shuttling from the Philippines across Japan to bases at Vladivostok and thence onward to Alaska and back, after the fashion of the German Condors flying between bases in western France and Norway. That sort of capability would have "immense powers of warning to Japan as well as of assurance to Russia." Hull was said to be cheered too. The air move had "really given a punch to his own diplomacy in the Far East and ... opened the door to Vladivostok...."[54]

The austere General Marshall was obviously excited by the possibilities he described for Admiral Stark on the phone:

> The conception is that if we can build up quickly, considering the fact those planes can operate from Fort {sic} Darwin and Australia, from New Britain; from Singapore and the Dutch East Indies; possibly even Vladivostok, we can cover that whole area of possible Japanese operations.... And we stick to it into the Mandated Islands. {This} would exercise a more determining influence on the course of events right now than anything else.... Because it practically backs the Japanese off and would certainly stop them on the Malaysian thing. It probably would make them feel they didn't dare take the Siberian thing and I think it has a better than 50% chance of forcing them to practically drop the Axis.

By acting with rapidity the United States might give the Japanese "a complete pause."[55]

As the army became increasingly aware, this vision of power overcoming distance did not extend to the supply and service functions which made it possible to put these planes in the air. The transport shortage, aggravated by commitment of the biggest ships to the British, slowed reinforcement. So did the navy's insistence on escorted convoys for troop transports and vital cargo ships and for roundabout routing, southward from Hawaii and then close to Australia, for all other vessels. Lacking fuel storage along the air route and in the Philippines, the air force had to supply gasoline in drums, which themselves were in short supply, and reserve cargo space for bulky storage tanks. Departure of the 19th Bombardment Group in October was delayed by the need to reinforce the cabins to withstand the recoil of added machine guns. Stimson became so impatient with postponements that on October 16 he ordered the first flight of B-17s to take off the next day or explain in writing to him why not. The air force provided daily reports on their progress across the Pacific.[56]

The British were making similar calculations of deterrence at the same time. The Admiralty had been planning gradually to form an Eastern fleet of six battleships, a battle cruiser, and an aircraft carrier over the next six months. Since August, Churchill, seeking to instill fear in the Japanese and encouragement in the Dominions, had been pushing for immediate dispatch of a small, powerful force centering on a modern battleship of the King George V class. The Admiralty, anxious to keep its best battleships in the Atlantic against the *Tirpitz* and its fellow raiders, was reluctant.[57]

The fall of the Konoe cabinet and what Eden described as the "Russian defeats" and what the Admiralty described as "the deterioration of the Russian situation" brought the issue to a head. These events were bound to encourage Japanese "extreme elements," the foreign minister pointed out, in which direction it was not yet clear, but "the stronger the joint front that the A.B.C.D. Powers can show, the greater the deterrent to Japanese action." Sending a capital ship would make a difference, a Foreign Office diarist noted, for the Japanese were "so hysterical" they might "rush themselves off their feet."[58] Availability of more capital ships from speedy repairs, near-completion of the battleship *Duke of York*, and American acceptance of defense of Denmark Strait against raiders strengthened the case.

At an October 17 meeting of the cabinet's Defense Committee, Eden, Clement Attlee, and Churchill carried the day, and the Admiralty reluctantly ordered H.M.S. *Prince of Wales* immediately to join the battle cruiser *Repulse* in the Indian Ocean. The new carrier *Indomitable*, working up in the Caribbean, was to follow in late November, and four old "R" class battleships to arrive by the end of the year. Admiral Tom Phillips, vice-chief of naval staff, was ordered to command.[59] Churchill informed Roosevelt of the dispatch of the *Prince of Wales* with delight. Here was "something that can catch and kill anything." "The firmer your attitude and ours," he urged, "the less chance of their taking the plunge."[60]

Two reversals of long-term power deficits in East Asia were taking place, at least in the Anglo-American official mind. An air armada in the Philippines would not only at last make possible a defense of the archipelago but could be used there for deterring, and in the event of war attacking, Japan. The new Eastern fleet would finally make

Singapore the mighty bastion of naval power it was supposed to be. And the Anglo-American strategic discordance seemed to be mending too. The Admiralty suggested the use of Manila as an advanced base for the Eastern fleet. To Admiral Stark and his advisers this degree of cooperation and forward staging seemed premature, but they were enthusiastic over the transfer, urging the British to go further and send cruisers and destroyers and more fighters and long-range bombers to Malaya.[61] Admiral Thomas Hart, commander-in-chief of the U.S. Asiatic Fleet, decided in October to fight from Manila Bay instead of withdrawing southward, as he was authorized, and Stark promised in case of war to send eight destroyers from the Philippines to the Eastern fleet.[62] The two navies were operating on the principle of cooperation rather than unified command—leaving to their Asiatic commanders the problem of working out a combined operating plan—but American objections to the original ADB scheme were being met, one by one.[63] The invention of the Philippines as a strategic asset was overcoming the Anglo-American planning impasse of the spring and summer.

The Soviet strategic connection was a different matter. The use of Soviet bases was a highly speculative proposition. Obviously these would not be available unless Japan attacked, for neither the Soviets nor the Americans had any desire to provoke a northward advance. Deterrence, then, would depend on whether the Japanese in deciding about the north would take into account threats from American bombers at the limit of their range in the south or possibly moving to bases in the north.

The Anglo-American reinforcement spasm of mid-October 1941 was replete with errors: placing excessive confidence in the symbolic deterrent effect of battleships and heavy bombers—the shadow of power—before they were fully emplaced, protected, and ready for use; exaggerating the capability of weapons (high altitude bombers against dodging ships; the effective range of bombers); simultaneously employing economic coercion, which would force action, and deterrence, seeking to forestall or delay action; grossly underestimating Japanese military capabilities, determination, and desperation.[64] The Air Corps vision and doctrine of strategic air power and determination to protect its growth was an important factor in the American augmentation. Principally, however, both strategic deployments responded to threats that Japan appeared to pose, particularly to the Soviet Union at a critical point in the German invasion. Convinced that Soviet survival was essential to winning the war against the main enemy, Germany, and otherwise virtually helpless in providing immediate assistance, the United States and Britain determined at the very least to attempt to keep Japan off Russia's back, even at some risk to themselves, a greater risk than they knew.

The Japanese were not in the least deterred. The fall of the Konoe cabinet was, to be sure, due to the hesitation of the prime minister and navy minister to take the final plunge, a decision for war after the failure of diplomacy by the deadline, but these ministers worried about Japan's ability to win a long war, not about the dispatch of British and American forces (which after all had not arrived). And to the extent that "ABCD encirclement" was evidently tightening, it only heightened the resolve to break out before it was too late. At the same time, as long as preparations for war continued, the armed services were content to allow diplomacy to proceed.

The emperor, however, was anxious to start from scratch and have the entire question of going to war reconsidered, as if the decision of the September 6 Imperial Conference had never been taken. General Tōjō, so informed, agreed to this unprecedented command and led an intensive canvass from October 23 to November 2 of all relevant factors and possible courses of action. In the discussion the navy insisted it needed more steel for ship construction to wage war successfully, and when the army relented the admirals in effect signed up for war. The oil embargo "hovered over the conference table like a demon."[65] The players were somewhat different from September's, but the stockpiles were lower, the urgency greater, and the predominant military and bureaucratic perspectives no less narrow and opportunistic. Unlike Konoe, Tōjō, characterized by his biographer as "blunt and decisive, forthright and assertive, naive and aggressive," was prepared to lead the cabinet to a clearcut decision and the nation to war.[66] At an Imperial Conference on November 5 the government agreed to make a decision for war if diplomacy had not succeeded by December 1.

War plans were integrated and polished. Centerpiece for the navy was a bold plan of Admiral Yamamoto, which the navy general staff adopted October 19, for a carrier raid on Pearl Harbor to eliminate the possibility of the American fleet interfering with southern operations. These operations would begin with simultaneous invasion of the Philippines, mounted' and supported from Formosa and the Palaus; of Malaya, staged through and covered from Indochina; and of Thailand and Burma, from Indochina. Wake Island and Hong Kong would be subdued along the way. At a later stage Japanese forces would concentrate on the Dutch East Indies and Burma. These immensely complex and risky operations would require every ship the navy could send to sea but would need less than one-fourth of the Japanese army. As November unfolded, the various forces moving into position for attack would become increasingly evident to ABCD intelligence.

The diplomatic plan of the Tōgō government was more a repackaging than a revision. Foreign Minister Tōjō Shigenori offered two approaches. Plan A was a restatement of the Japanese position for a comprehensive settlement, only now more precise about the question of troops in China. Japan would remove its forces after a peace settlement but insist on retaining garrisons in Hainan, North China, and Inner Mongolia for a prolonged but finite period. Plan B, a fallback option in case Plan A failed, would put the China problem aside and seek a partial settlement by a return to the conditions existing prior to the Japanese advance into southern Indochina.

Discussions resumed in Washington on November 7 along the lines of Plan A and continued every few days, twice at the White House, to November 18. This phase of the everlasting Hull-Nomura talks was quite distinctive, and not just from the urgency with which the Japanese pressed their case. Hull was different: more impatient, critical, and intrusive, altogether more "preachy," he flogged the tired old issues again and again. On the Axis alliance he pushed harder than before. Could the ambassador assure him, Hull asked, that if his government entered into a settlement with the United States the Axis alliance "would automatically become a dead letter," "automatically disappear"? No Pacific settlement was possible with Japan "clinging to her Tripartite Pact."[67]

Nor would a settlement in China be possible so long as the United States continued to assist Chiang, dragging out negotiations forever, the ambassador pointed out. China would then, just on the troop issue perhaps, hold the key to Japanese-American relations "which might result in war." Hull asked how many soldiers Japan wanted to retain in China and was told about 10 percent of those currently present. It was a situation full of trouble, the secretary of state responded, "one of Japan's own making and it was up to the Japanese Government to find some way of getting itself out...." If only the Japanese people could get "war and invasion out of mind."[68]

Hull seemed to be emphasizing differences as if to bring matters to a head instead of stringing out the talks for maximum delay, as he had in September and October. But the matter he wished to dispose of was not the talks themselves but the idea of a comprehensive settlement, as represented in Plan A. In November with increasing urgency the American government sought a partial, temporary settlement with Japan, a *modus vivendi*. It did so in the growing realization of a shift in strategic circumstances.

The German offensive against Moscow had bogged down at the end of October. German propaganda admitted on October 27 that "weather conditions have entailed a temporary halt in the advance."[69] In the following several weeks the German command reshuffled armies and replenished divisions for one final heave at Moscow on November 15, which the Soviets knew was coming and braced for.

The hopes of British-American observers for German failure before Moscow outpaced reality. *New York Times* dispatches were consistently optimistic from November 1 to 20. German sources reported the weather "miserable beyond all conception"; roads "simply disappeared" in "one great indivisible quagmire." The "fabled Russian winter" was "closing in," then gripping "Nazi armies," killing German soldiers. "Stalemate," "standstill," "floundering," and "failure" were words used to describe the German offensive. The Russians were said to be halting, holding, or beating off the Germans, even gaining ground, pushing on, beginning a "sustained counteroffensive." The Soviet regime would never permit a lull in battle, said the *Times*, and so the Eastern front was now a "permanent factor" in the war.

Official reports were more guarded but increasingly hopeful. Some said the offensive had been stopped, others that it was too early to predict. According to the American embassy at Kuibyshev on October 28, the Soviets apparently did not expect to hold Moscow but would make the Germans pay the highest possible price for it. Still, the weather at Moscow was "thickening." November 9 the embassy reported that Vladimir Dekanozov, former Soviet ambassador to Berlin, believed that if Leningrad and Moscow could hold out another month the Germans would be stalled for the winter. Though large Soviet forces had been withdrawn from the east, he assured the embassy that enough remained for a stubborn defense in case Japan attacked. On November 13 the embassy reported that the fall of Moscow was no longer considered inevitable. Churchill was now said to have reversed his odds: he was waging five to four on the Germans' being stopped.[70]

Whereas American officials in October considered a Japanese attack northward the most likely possibility, in November that eventuality seemed farfetched. American consuls in Manchuria had nothing to report. In a November 7 dispatch, Grew found "no indications" the Tōjō government contemplated such action. The appointment of Tōgō, former ambassador to Moscow, as foreign minister seemed to indicate, on the contrary, a constructive attitude toward the Soviet Union. The *Japan Times and Advertiser*, regarded as a mouthpiece of the foreign office, doubted the collapse of the Soviet Union even if Moscow, Leningrad, and the whole of European Russia were conquered. Japanese forces in Manchuria were sufficient, the American embassy in Tokyo believed, to take advantage of a Soviet collapse, but not to take on an "intact Soviet Far Eastern army and air force." Japan, Grew believed, would persist in a policy of "watchful waiting."[71]

Japanese military movements were, if anything, southward, not northward. The American consul in Saigon reported an increase in Japanese troops in Indochina in the latter part of October. Airplanes, tanks, artillery: "military equipment of all kinds" was arriving. Construction of air bases, radio stations, piers, and barracks was preparing the way for "accommodation of a large army." Under instructions to monitor the buildup closely, the Saigon and Hanoi consuls reported further increases in the first week of November to approximately 50,000 troops with the majority in southern Indochina, some arriving there from Hanoi by rail. The naval attaché in Tokyo expected a buildup of 100,000 and occupation of Thailand.[72] Concentrations were beginning to occur at sea too: troop transports off Hainan, according to the Chinese, and communications intelligence of naval, air, and base force movements to the Mandates. Two new carriers had joined the fleet which was gathered at Kure.[73]

This apparent southward drift of Japanese power was accompanied in Tokyo by a virulent anti-American press campaign. The United States had "the soul of a prostitute," said Tokyo's *Nichi Nichi*. According to Domei, the official news agency, Japan was completing its "war structure" for a seemingly inevitable "armed clash in the Pacific." The American oil embargo was forcing the nation to "drastic action" for self-defense. A newspaper close to Japan's foreign office insisted that peace hinged on "America's sincerity in understanding and recognizing Japan's immutable national policy."[74]

The anger and fatalism of these public expressions of Japanese policy worried Grew. On November 3 he sent a powerful telegram to the State Department based in part on a draft by Eugene Dooman, his counselor of embassy, who had grown up in Japan and been educated in the same school as many of Japan's civilian leaders. That economic coercion could bring about Japan's collapse as an aggressive power was an "uncertain and dangerous hypothesis," Grew warned. The failure of conciliation begun by the Konoe cabinet could well produce an abrupt swing of policy in the opposite direc-

tion to an "all-out, do or die attempt, actually risking national hara-
kiri, to make Japan impervious" to foreign economic pressures. He
was anxious to avoid any misconception of "Japan's capacity to rush
headlong into a suicidal struggle with the United States," or the dis-
counting of current preparations as mere "saber rattling." The primary question in this "grave and momentous subject" was whether
war with Japan was justified by American national objectives, and
that was a question on which the sands were "running fast." "Action
by Japan which might render unavoidable an armed conflict with the
United States may come with dangerous and dramatic suddenness."[75]

MAGIC intercepts conveyed the same sense of impending finality.
On November 2, Tokyo made it very clear to Nomura that the Plan
A/Plan B proposals were a "last effort." Tōgō used the language of
ultimate crisis. The situation was "very grave," relations had "reached
the edge." Without "quick accord," negotiations would "certainly be
ruptured." Japan was gambling its fate "on the throw of this die,"
"showing the limit of our friendship," "making our last possible
bargain."[76]

Taken altogether this intelligence was puzzling. On the one hand,
Japan and the United States seemed to be on a collision course unless
saved by diplomacy. On the other hand, the only Japanese threat
which had materialized so far, the Indochina concentration, did not
seem to justify America's going to war. The strategic and policy implications of that concentration were debated at the State Department
and within the military early in November in response to an urgent
plea from Chiang Kai-shek for a warning to Japan and dispatch of
American and British air units to assist in repelling what he took to
be an imminent Japanese attack from Indochina into Yunnan province. Japanese capture of Kunming, he warned, and closing of the
Burma Road—China's only remaining supply line from the West—
would lead to China's fall. The State Department was impressed and
asked the military what support could be given.[77]

The answer, concurred in by Roosevelt, was none. The army was
skeptical of a Japanese thrust into Yunnan: the terrain was rugged,
the defensive possibilities excellent and the forces presently in northern Indochina insufficient. They would need twice as many troops,
ten divisions, and two months to mount a Yunnan offensive. The
embassy in Tokyo, the consul in Hanoi, and the military attaché in
London, reflecting British estimates, were also dubious.[78] An alter-
nate hypothesis was that Indochina was a staging area for an attack
on Malaya, but the army's War Plans Division considered this highly
unlikely because landings along the eastern coast of Malaya would

be difficult "while the northeast monsoon beats upon the shores of the China Sea from November to February."[79]

More likely, Japanese forces in Indochina were intended for a third alternative, the invasion of Thailand next door, which would pose a vital security threat only if extended to the Kra isthmus. Even that possibility was discounted by Admiral Ingersoll, vice chief of naval operations, who argued that Japan's next move if it occurred would not be a one-country operation but an all-out attack on the Philippines, Malaya, and the Dutch East Indies. Army War Plans considered this beyond Japan's means: Malaya would require ten to twenty divisions and the Philippines ten, but Japan had only ten to twelve for southern operations altogether. An attack on Siberia was not considered a serious possibility now; an attack on Hawaii was not considered.[80]

The army and navy recommended on November 5 that, unless Japan attacked British, Dutch, or American territory, the United States take no action which might precipitate war. This was not a time "to get brash," said Ingersoll. The Pacific Fleet was inferior to the Japanese fleet to begin with, and currently major units were in the yards or escorting convoys. War in the Pacific would have to be waged with long lines of communication and inferior East Asian bases. Above all, offensive operations would require a major diversion of merchant shipping to the Pacific, most likely resulting in loss of the Battle of the Atlantic and the supply lines to Britain and Russia. Neither the army nor navy had any intention of altering the strategic priority of Europe.[81]

With only a little more time, however, the strategic situation in East Asia would improve. By mid-December, or more precisely December 10 in General Marshall's accounting, the reinforcement of the Philippines would have reached "impressive strength," posing a "positive threat to any Japanese operations south of Formosa." By then thirty-five B-17s of the 7th Bombardment Group were due to have arrived, doubling the number of heavy bombers in the Philippines, along with 145 P-40 interceptors and 54 dive bombers. MacArthur estimated that all elements of ten Philippine divisions and three regiments of constabulary would be mobilized and housed by December 15. By February or March, American power in the Philippines conjoined with British naval increases would reach the deterrent level. The situation called for delay by "clever diplomacy," in Marshall's view, with some minor concessions to the Japanese, such as relaxing oil restrictions.[82]

So far the Americans had enjoyed the luxury of balancing potential power against threat without a time limit. But as the November 5 recommendation was going to the president, so was a MAGIC intercept informing Nomura that all arrangements for signing of an agreement must be completed by November 25.[83]

The pace accelerated. On November 6, Ambassador Kurusu Saburō was reported in the press to be rushing to catch the Pan American Clipper at Hong Kong with "last" proposals for the United States. On November 8, Marshall directed that reinforcements for the Philippines "be expedited in every way." On November 10, Churchill boasted publicly of sending a "powerful naval force of heavy ships" for service in the Indian and Pacific oceans. On November 11 the *New York Times* reported the crisis was "now held acute." On November 14 the president ordered withdrawal of the remaining Marines in China. On November 15, from MAGIC, Tokyo confirmed November 25 as the final date and described it as "absolutely immovable." On November 17, Grew warned that on account of the inability of the embassy to monitor Japanese military activity, it might not be able to provide adequate warning of Japanese actions outside the China theater "exploiting every possible tactical advantage such as surprise. . . . " The sands were indeed running, and fast.[84]

So Japan's plan was to go southward, and it involved the United States. For three months Roosevelt's foreign policy had sought to prevent Japanese movement in any direction, north or south. Now, with Soviet survival into 1942 seemingly assured, an easing of Japan's problems in the south was not likely to encourage an attack on Siberia. With the Soviet factor disengaged, American strategic thinking reverted to the familiar balancing of interests between Atlantic and Pacific represented in the ABC talks and RAINBOW plans. In November the necessities and opportunities of the Battle of the Atlantic made it seem all the more imperative to maintain a strategic defensive in Asia and if at all possible to avoid war with Japan.

Waging antisubmarine warfare in the Atlantic had proved to be more difficult than expected. Stimson gathered from Knox that the navy was "thoroughly scared about their inability to stamp out the sub menace." Planners noted an alarming increase in the number of U-boats completing and coming on station. Admiral King was trying to get his hands on any ship over 600 tons which could make twelve knots and steam 3,000 miles or more to fill out his hard-pressed escort units.[85] On October 17 the U.S.S. *Kearny* was hit while assisting a badly disorganized convoy under heavy attack. A torpedo blew out the forward boiler room, killing seven, but the ship limped back to

Iceland safely. On October 31 HX 156 chanced upon a U-boat pack in transit, and the U.S.S. *Reuben James* was sunk with 115 hands.[86]

Despite these losses and the unremitting misery of escort duty on the North Atlantic in winter, the outlook was, for the moment, improving. October's losses were less than September's, and U-boats sank only thirteen ships in November. One important reason for this success was the transfer of ten U-boats from the Atlantic to the Mediterranean to protect the supply route to Rommel's army in Africa, with more to follow.[87] On November 7 the Soviet Union became eligible for Lend-Lease. On November 13, Congress rescinded the remaining neutrality laws, though by slender majorities, permitting the arming of merchant ships and their entry into combat zones. Now, besides assisting in British supply, American and American-controlled tonnage could carry war materials for the 1942 campaigning season directly to the Soviet Union by way of the Arctic convoys. Should German raiders break into the Atlantic, the Admiralty was informed on November 6, American forces would not be constrained by hemispherical boundaries.[88]

Typical of 1941 was the swaying balance between current Anglo-American naval weakness and approaching strength. On November 3 the carrier *Indomitable*, assigned to the Eastern fleet, went aground in Jamaica. Ten days later the *Ark Royal* was sunk in the Mediterranean. Norfolk quickly repaired the *Indomitable*, but she was too late to sail with Phillips and was held in the Atlantic probably because — on account of refits and repairs — the Royal Navy was down to one fleet carrier. On November 25 a U-boat sank the battleship *Barham*.[89] The balance was due to tip favorably again soon with new ships reporting for duty, but for the moment the margin of advantage on the Atlantic seemed very slim.

So far the Hull-Nomura talks had been a matter of discovery and delay, not bargaining. Now the United States seriously considered what concessions it might make to avoid war. Roosevelt showed his interest in a *modus vivendi* the day after he learned of the November 25 deadline. On November 6 he sounded out Stimson on the idea of a truce with no further military buildup or troop movement for six months or until the Chinese and Japanese arrived at a settlement. The secretary of war promptly disposed of that sort of bargain by pointing out how it would let the Chinese down and cut short the reinforcement of the Philippines.

At his November 10 meeting with Nomura, Roosevelt twisted the conversation around to drop in a word about the *modus vivendi* as an instrument of diplomacy, it "being not merely an expedient and temporary agreement, but also one which takes into account actual and human existence." Nomura was bewildered but determined to find out whether the president had in mind a provisional agreement.[90] The Hull-Nomura conversations now entered a curious bilevel phase: discussion continued on various aspects of a comprehensive settlement, punctuated now and then with sallies into a temporary agreement.

The Americans preferred to have the Japanese take the initiative for a *modus vivendi* to gain bargaining advantage and to keep their own record clear of any taint of appeasement. A Japanese initiative seemed a practical first step too, since, as the Americans knew, they had Plan B in the wings. This proposal, sent November 4, decrypted and translated the next day, would pledge Japan not to advance beyond Indochina and to withdraw her troops from there upon reaching a settlement with China in return for American restoration of trade and agreement to "engage in no activity which might put an obstacle in the way of Japan in her efforts to make peace with China."[91] Nomura and his new colleague Kurusu, who arrived November 15, saw no hope for such an American engagement and, though instructed to present the plan, devised a formula of their own. In this they were encouraged on November 17 by word from a cabinet member, undoubtedly Postmaster General Walker, that the president wanted an understanding but needed something concrete, such as Japanese evacuation of Indochina.[92]

On November 18, steering clear of a Japanese troop withdrawal contingent on peace settlement elsewhere, the two ambassadors suggested to Hull a return to the status quo of July, before the Japanese advance into southern Indochina and the freezing of assets. Hull was not displeased, but Tōgō was. The foreign minister reproved Nomura and ordered him back to Plan B, but with changes, notably a pledge to evacuate southern Indochina, an important concession, Tōgō pointed out. This was the Plan B presented November 20, Thanksgiving Day.[93]

The ball was now in the American court. Plan B had improved but still had the impossible requirement that the United States suspend assistance to Chiang during Sino-Japanese peace negotiations. New ideas were needed. Hull had already asked his advisers to explore all possibilities. The Japan desk officers sent up a set of terms; another set from Treasury would solve in one swoop all Japanese-American problems back to the turn of the century. The air was charged with reciprocity. Maxwell Hamilton, the sober, meticulous chief of the Far

Eastern Division, in a moment of giddiness suggested a swap of New Guinea, or parts of it, for Japanese ships.[94]

Even Roosevelt tried his hand, giving Hull an outline *modus vivendi* on November 17.[95] The president, as before, had in mind a six-month agreement exchanging relaxation of trade restrictions ("some oil and rice now—more later") for pledges by Japan not to send more troops north or south and not to invoke the Axis alliance in case the United States became involved in war with Germany. The United States would bring the Japanese and Chinese together for peace talks but take no part in them. The outline undoubtedly spurred the search for a *modus* but it was outdated by the Nomura-Kurusu proposal the next day and unhelpful on specific issues. Roosevelt was content to leave the management of this diplomatic initiative to Hull and his experts. He offered guidelines, he nudged the process along, but he kept his distance from a project that risked accusations of appeasement.

The Friday and Saturday after Thanksgiving, Hull and his Far Eastern advisers, taking the various drafts from all sources, including Plan B, put together two new sets of proposals, a *modus vivendi* and a comprehensive agreement. The short-term proposition would prevent any further Japanese cross-border military encroachment but not affect American-British-Dutch reinforcements or existing Japanese deployments except in Indochina. It adopted the revised Plan B idea of a return to the status of July in Indochina with a limit of 25,000 Japanese troops in the north. In return the United States would modify its trade restrictions to allow export of certain non-defense commodities such as food and raw cotton and, on a month-by-month basis, lower-grade petroleum products in quantities appropriate to civilian use. The proposal was silent on the Axis alliance, reflecting the failure of Roosevelt and Hull to secure any Japanese concession on this issue at least for a *modus vivendi*. The duration of the agreement would be three months, gaining the needed time for reinforcement of the Philippines at the least cost in replenishing Japan's oil stocks.

On the crucial issue of peace in China the proposal broached the idea of bringing the two sides together for talks in the Philippines. The United States would not look with disfavor, it even suggested, upon an armistice, raising the possibility which that term implied of a suspension of American aid to China during the talks. But Chinese-Japanese peace talks were not a necessary condition of the *modus*, and neither therefore was suspension of American assistance to China, which was a requirement of Plan B. So, while the two sides were moving within negotiating range of each other, fundamental difficulties remained, not only the question of aid to China but also the question of how much of what kind of oil.

Whereas the *modus* reduced the framework of discussion, the comprehensive proposal extended it beyond the most exhaustive restatements of the American position, such as those of June 21 and October 2. Japan would have to withdraw from China and Indochina, recognize Chiang's as the only legitimate government of China, negotiate the Manchurian question with Chungking, give up (with the Western powers) its extraterritorial rights and concessions in China, sign a multilateral non-aggression pact, guarantee the neutralization of Indochina, and make a dead letter of the Axis pact as the price for restoration of trade and for peaceful settlement.[96]

Although the draft comprehensive proposal and the draft *modus vivendi* were annexed to each other, it seems very unlikely that they were supposed to be presented together to the Japanese, for the stringency of the former would wither the latter. Instead they were alternates. They would be combined for presentation to the allies, as a means of reassuring them about the *modus* and of making a record, and then one or the other would be handed the Japanese depending on circumstances and allied approval. On November 22, Hull met with the British and Chinese ambassadors and the Dutch and Australian ministers to launch the *modus*.

First reactions were on the whole encouraging. The secretary of state seems to have been hoping for quick approval of the American lead without getting into fine print. He described Plan B, gained approval for offering a substitute rather than improving the Japanese draft, and then gave a "rough sketch" of his own *modus* and a quick reading of the comprehensive plan without presenting copies to the envoys. Halifax was cautiously supportive: an agreement which got the bulk of Japanese troops out of Indochina without giving too much economic relief seemed sensible. Churchill's first reaction was similar. Hu Shih, the Chinese ambassador, agreed that removal of the troops would be a great relief but asked whether the military standstill applied to Japanese troops within China, to which Hull was forced to respond in the negative. Hu said China regarded the embargo as vital and "would be very reluctant to see it seriously reduced." On that note the diplomats left to seek instructions from their governments.[97]

These were mostly negative. At the Foreign Office in London firmness in dealing with Japan was the rule, and greater firmness the more threatening Japan became. British officials wished to avoid another war, needless to say, and were determined to stay exactly in the shadow of American policy. But they had always been suspicious of the Hull-Nomura conversations, a suspicion heightened by Hull's high dudgeon at the least bit of criticism and his failure to take them into his confidence. For some the *modus vivendi* smacked all too much of appeasement. Others looked to growing strength: the *Prince of Wales* was noticed at Capetown on November 23. The Dominions were informed, and the War Cabinet met to decide.

Britain chose an oblique response, urging a toughening rather than a rejection of Hull's proposal. Our demands should be pitched at a higher level, the Foreign Office advised. Japan should be required to remove all its forces of all kinds, including air, from Indochina and suspend advances in China. Relaxation of trade curbs, not to include oil, should occur only after a Japanese withdrawal and on condition of progress toward a general settlement. It is impossible to say from available sources what the British knowledge of Japanese intentions was at this point, but the implicit assumption was that time remained for bargaining. The Foreign Office simply did not share the American apprehension, derived from MAGIC, of imminent Japanese operations in the south.[98]

The Chinese response lacked all subtlety. Chiang Kai-shek was determined to defeat any possibility of a temporary arrangement with Japan. By all channels of communication—the Chinese ambassador in London, Hu-Shih and T. V. Soong in Washington, and Owen Lattimore, the Generalissimo's personal American adviser—China sounded its dissent. Chiang scarcely paused with an objection over the number of troops Japan would be permitted to keep in Indochina. Any relaxation of economic pressure "while leaving Japan entrenched in China" would make the Chinese people feel "completely sacrificed" by America. By putting aside the Chinese question, the United States "was still inclined to appease Japan at the expense of China." The agreement would destroy American prestige in Asia just as surely as the closing of the Burma Road had destroyed British and would lead Japan and Chinese defeatists to urge "oriental solidarity against occidental treachery." Supplementing official objections were leaks to the press, one, for example, to a United Press correspondent by the Chinese embassy in London. Readers of the November 25 *New York Times*, for example, learned the essential provisions of the *modus vivendi*.[99]

Contrary to public claims of ABCD harmony, there was indeed "a rift in the alphabetical lute." Looking for support, Hull called the ABCD envoys back on Monday, November 24. Only the Dutch minister was instructed, though he was positive. This time Hull permitted the representatives to copy the proposals. Halifax asked to refer the detailed provisions to the Foreign Office for study. Questioning and argument continued until Hull complained of his partner governments' "lack of interest and lack of a disposition to cooperate" and on that sour note the meeting broke up.

That night to ensure prompt consideration at the highest level, the president at Hull's request sent a copy of the *modus vivendi* proposal to Churchill. The following day Halifax gave Hull detailed and severe Foreign Office criticisms of the proposal. During the following night, November 25–26, Churchill's reply arrived. "[O]nly one point ... disquiets us," he wrote. "What about Chiang Kai-shek? Is he not having a very thin diet?" Should China collapse, "our joint dangers would enormously increase." Churchill was sure that American "regard for the Chinese cause" would govern action. The prime minister seems to have concluded that a firm ABCD front was Britain's safest bet because it made most likely American participation in any war begun by Japan, and more likely thereby American entry into the European war. The course of settlement, however temporary, risked that combination and made it more likely that the United States would stay on the sidelines. By this skillful thrust the onus for killing the Hull proposal would fall on the Chinese more than on the British.[100]

The *modus vivendi* was failing rapidly by Monday and Tuesday, November 24–25. Hardly encouraging were three MAGIC intercepts translated on Monday, all instructions to Nomura and Kurusu that cessation of American aid to China during peace negotiations was essential. Chiang Kai-shek must be "made" to propose an end to hostilities. On November 22, Hull learned that the deadline for a Japanese-American agreement had been extended from November 25 to November 29. Monday he learned that the extension was in Tokyo time, meaning Friday, November 28 in Washington.[101]

Accompanying this terminal date for diplomacy was increasing evidence that Japanese forces were moving up to a starting line for attack: reinforcements to the Mandates, increased naval activity at Truk and Jaluit, an expeditionary force in the Palaus, surveillance of American supply routes to Australia, accelerated troop debarkation at Haiphong, 20,000 soldiers landed at Saigon. Hanoi heard from a reliable source that the Japanese would attack Thailand, including the Kra isthmus, on December 1.[102]

Of particular concern was the embarkation of Japanese troops at Shanghai. The assistant naval attaché there reported intense activity since November 15, with the arrival and loading of many ships including troop transports and vessels carrying timber trestles (for pier or bridge construction) and landing craft. On November 19 ten transports sailed, and in the following week many were sighted by ship captains between Shanghai and Hong Kong on a course for Indochina. Similar information came from British intelligence. These were troops intended for Malaya. The United States Navy was coming alive to the probability of amphibious landings, but the army was more complacent. Stimson's mind was still set on Indochina, where, he recalled, the Japanese had informed French authorities they would be moving 50,000 more troops. They were talking evacuation and stuffing more troops in. This for Secretary of War Stimson was perfidy—typical Japanese perfidy stretching back to the Manchurian crisis of 1931. Early on November 26 he warned the president of the Japanese troop movements.[103]

This suddenly rising storm found the Philippines reinforcement in disarray. A stream of heavy bombers, now amounting to forty-eight planes, was scheduled to depart December 3–10. Another eighty-two would fly out in the following ten weeks. Fifty-two dive bombers, delayed at Hawaii two weeks and then placed in a slow convoy, would not arrive until Christmas Day. One pursuit group of 105 P-40s had arrived; half of a second was at sea and the other half would depart on December 5. Due to sail in early December were aircraft maintenance, command, and warning units, together with field artillery and signal battalions, a cavalry troop, an infantry regiment, and medical detachments, altogether 21,000 troops, by far the largest reinforcement yet. To the question whether they would arrive in time now was added the question whether they would arrive safely. So worried was the navy at the incompleteness of Philippine defenses that it denied Admiral Hart permission to stay and fight at Manila Bay, and so the cruisers and destroyers of the Asiatic Fleet began moving southward out of reach of Japanese air strikes.[104]

East Asia did not supply the only ration of bad news. On November 21 the press reported the ousting of General Weygand as Vichy's supreme authority in Africa—at the express demand of Hitler, it was said. This opened the way to further Nazi penetration of Africa and left in tatters Washington's policy of encouraging French North African autonomy. On November 18 the British forces in Egypt launched their long-awaited offensive against Rommel. They plunged deeply behind German-Italian lines but soon were locked in a "brutal slugging match," an armored "battle of Kilkenny cats," which destroyed most of the tanks on both sides. London was now "putting a brake on overoptimism." By November 26 Roosevelt himself was wondering whether the British could sustain the drive.[105]

The outlook on the German-Soviet front now seemed absolutely precarious. The final German push on Moscow began on November 15 and was soon making substantial progress over the frozen ground. Panzer armies striking southeast captured Klin, Solnechogorsk, and Istra by November 25, opening a breach for an "armored jemmy of tremendous strength that soon threatened to break open the whole Russian position in the northwest." The 7th Panzer Division struck for the Moscow-Volga Canal, "the last major obstacle before Moscow was completely outflanked from the north." To the south of Moscow, Guderian swung east of Tula, captured Venev on November 25, and made for Kashira on the Oka River, loss of which would open the road to the capital and its encirclement. Along the Black Sea, Kleist's Panzer group captured Rostov and an intact bridge across the Don on November 20. From this gateway to the Caucasus the road seemed open to Astrakhan on the Caspian or the Maikop oil fields.[106]

The press learned enough of the savage fighting to grasp the significance of this "doom-laden final week of November," as John Erickson calls it. The *New York Times* described the attack as "overpowering," "the like of which has not been seen." The flanks of Moscow's defenses were "yielding." The Germans were straining with every ounce to capture Moscow at any cost. On November 23 the Russians admitted the situation was "gravely worsened" on the northern sector and even more critical on the southern. On November 25 the Nazis were reported thirty-one miles from Moscow; the Germans claimed eighteen. The Red Army was fighting "one of the most critical battles of its history." The moment of greatest danger in the five-month war had arrived. The Russian situation, Roosevelt told Morgenthau on November 26, was "awful": Moscow was "falling."[107]

The *modus vivendi* had no hope in this moment of pervasive and deadly threat. Stark and Marshall undoubtedly made the argument for delay to Hull and Roosevelt in their meetings November 25. The director of the army's War Plans Division stated the position bluntly to Hull on November 21: the army considered it a matter of "grave importance to the success of our war effort in Europe that we reach a *modus vivendi* with Japan."[108] The negative case became overwhelming, however. The Chinese attack on the *modus*, abetted by the British, was right on target. Roosevelt had to consider the implications of a partial settlement for the anti-Japanese and anti-German coalitions. Japanese deadlines, deployments, and stiff bargaining terms, as revealed by MAGIC, did not encourage diplomacy. The supreme crisis in Russia and discouraging news from Africa called for solidarity and steadfastness. Above all, the movement of Japanese troop convoys into the South China Sea had a crystalizing effect on the president, for conciliation in the presence of aggression was appeasement. Roosevelt and Hull decided to drop the *modus vivendi* and present in its place, with full recognition they had come to the end of diplomacy, the comprehensive proposal which predicated any settlement on a total Japanese withdrawal from China. This Hull did on November 26.

Epilogue

Japan Attacks

For Washington, the days following Hull's comprehensive note to the Japanese of November 26, his so-called Ten-Point program, were filled with excruciating uncertainty. The steady southward progression of Japanese forces indicated an attack soon, but officials were at a loss to know where the blow would fall or what more might be done to prevent it. How to respond depended on where the Japanese attacked. The response to an attack on American territory was obvious, but if British or Dutch territory were involved and not American, a question would arise, and if, say, Thailand alone were the victim, many doubts as well.

The most likely outcome still seemed to be a move into Thailand. More and more Japanese troops landed in neighboring Indochina, the total in the southern part rising from 50,000 to 90,000 just between November 21 and 29, according to the American consul in Saigon, and with them came large numbers of trucks and aircraft. Some intelligence officials inferred that these were the troops which had embarked at Shanghai (which in fact were harboring at Hainan Island in the Gulf of Tonkin).[1] A move on Thailand seemed to fit Japanese behavior: step-by-step encroachment taking advantage of developing opportunities but avoiding head-on collision. It opened the way to Malaya and to Rangoon, port of entry for the Burma Road.

Japanese preparations seemed more extensive than required for the seizure of Thailand, however, as if the next step, not the next but one, would provoke war. In a speech reported in the American press on November 30, Premier Tōjō condemned Britain and the United States for "fishing in troubled waters" by pitting Asians against each other. On December 1 the Japanese navy changed its radio call signs, the first time it had done so twice in a thirty-day period, and sharply reduced its radio traffic, indicating concern for the secrecy of impending naval operations. American intelligence had lost track of the air-

215

craft carriers.² The Japanese appeared to be forming new task forces in the South China Sea and the Mandates, indicating "major opera-tions" in the Indochina-Thai area soon, possibly including a descent on Borneo.³ Meanwhile MAGIC was decrypting instructions from Tokyo on destruction of codes, and Japanese nationals were hurrying home from British and Dutch territories. Guam and the British Gil-bert Islands sighted Japanese reconnaisance planes.⁴

Was all this activity and secrecy directed merely at the Thai oper-ation or were there ulterior objectives such as the Kra isthmus, Sin-gapore or the Dutch East Indies? How could Japan possibly attack such objectives across the South China Sea without dealing first with American power on its flank in the Philippines? But why would Japan force a war with the United States when its every interest lay in avoiding consolidation of its enemies and engagement with a power of such enormous latent strength? These questions circled through the minds of tired American officials as they fretted over the weekend of November 29–30 and into the following week.

On November 27 the army and navy sent out war warnings to relevant commands including Hawaii but especially directed to the Philippines. An "aggressive move by Japan" was expected in the next few days, the navy warning read, against "either" the Philippines, Thailand, the Kra isthmus, or Borneo. The military view was that, if Japan invaded the main body of Thailand or through Thailand China, the United States should stand still, allowing further rein-forcement of the Philippines. However, if Japan attacked the south-erly extension of Thailand, the Kra isthmus, thereby imperiling Malaya, or other British or Dutch territory, America must resist.⁵

The distinction between Thai and other possible ventures seemed increasingly artificial, however. Britain urgently needed to occupy the beaches in the southerly portion of the Kra isthmus inside Thai-land to protect Malaya but would only invite Japanese occupation of Bangkok and become cast as the aggressor if it moved first. A Japa-nese first move would remove that inhibition and bring in the Brit-ish. Given this likely sequence, either a clash between Japan and Brit-ain would occur in Thailand or the Japanese would preempt by striking the Kra first. This at least appears to be the strategic logic that Roosevelt gathered from discussions with his closest advisers and Halifax.

On December 1 the president called in the British ambassador for a critical conversation. In case of a Japanese attack on Thailand, the president said, he would support British action, meaning the move-ment of British troops into the Kra. The British must do what was strategically necessary, he said. As to how and how soon he would provide support he was not so clear, but he would need a few days to "get things into political shape." Respecting the case of a direct Japanese attack on British or Dutch territory he spoke more plainly, though in a typically informal manner. In that event, he said, "we should obviously all be together." On December 3, this time with Welles present, Roosevelt assured Halifax he meant armed support and assented to the British plan for a preventive occupation of the Kra area. The British government now authorized its Malaya command to initiate this plan, called MATADOR, to forestall a Japanese landing on that shore or as a response to any Japanese incursion into Thailand. It now also gave the Dutch a formal guarantee of armed support. Admiral Phillips, his capital ships having arrived in Singapore, flew to Manila to coordinate naval action with the Americans. Admiral Hart ordered Destroyer Division 57 at Balikpapan in Borneo to sail for Singapore.[6] Thus ABDA seemed finally locked together.

This new solidarity was reactive not preventive, however. The British still hoped for an Anglo-American warning to Japan. Stimson urged the president to draw a line, transgression of which would lead the United States to fight. Roosevelt consistently resisted, sensitive to the Constitutional limitations he had already exceeded by his promise to Halifax, but above all ever-cautious, unwilling to confront the public and Congress until he knew which eventuality he faced. He intended to make an appeal for peace to the Emperor of Japan, but apparently only at the last minute when reconnaissance showed an attack coming. His main object probably was to establish a formal interest in protecting Thailand, Malaya, and the Dutch East Indies in case he needed to ask Congress for a declaration of war.[7] As the first week of December wore on, with American policy settling into this passive vein and the South China Sea still largely empty, an eerie stillness overhung the Pacific and East Asia.

From another part of the world came decisive and welcome news. By December the German campaign against Moscow was finally petering out from exhaustion and icy cold. On December 1, word arrived that the Soviets had retaken Rostov, saving the Caucasus.[8] On the night of December 4 the Red Army, stiffened by its Siberian divisions, launched a counteroffensive on the Moscow front, and BARBAROSSA went into winter quarters.

On December 1, Tokyo time, the Japanese government in Imperial Conference confirmed the decision for war. Only some positive outcome of the Hull-Nomura negotiations could have possibly forestalled that decision. The Hull note of November 26 made it apparent that further negotiation was hopeless. The attack on Pearl Harbor by six carriers, the heart of the Imperial Navy's air arm, would go forward. On December 3 this Pearl Harbor Striking Force, which had sortied from the Kurile Islands on November 26, crossed the International Date Line south of the Aleutians in its passage across the barren, stormy North Pacific toward Hawaii. On December 4 (Tokyo time) nineteen Japanese transports departed from Hainan and gathering contingents from Cam Ranh Bay and Saigon and covering forces from Mako in the Pescadores headed southwest into the South China Sea. On December 6, British reconnaissance aircraft sighted these convoys as they rounded the southernmost tip of Indochina into the Gulf of Siam.[9] Before the RAF could find out whether they were headed for the Kra coast and Malaya or Bangkok, they were lost in monsoon clouds. When Roosevelt learned of the report the following day, December 6 (Washington time), he sent his plea for peace to Emperor Hirohito.

Around midnight December 7/8 (Singapore time), Japanese transports arrived at Kota Bharu in the northeast corner of Malaya and Patani and Singora on the Kra isthmus and began landing troops. At approximately the same time, dawn December 7, 275 miles north of Hawaii, the Striking Force launched more than two hundred planes against the United States Pacific Fleet at Pearl Harbor and an hour later sent off 170 more. In the following hours occurred air raids on Singapore, the Philippines, Guam, and Wake and an assault on Hong Kong. Japanese air power, whether aboard the Striking Force, situated on Formosa and the southern Indochina coast, or quickly landed in Malaya and the Philippines, devastated British and American defenses.

At Hawaii surprise was complete. The Japanese immediately attacked the airfields at Pearl Harbor and nearby, gutting hangars and aircraft neatly lined up on taxiways for better security against sabotage. They left seventy-nine usable army airplanes out of the original 231. At Pearl Harbor, high-level bombers, dive bombers, and torpedo planes concentrated on Battleship Row, where, singly and in pairs, the pride of the Pacific Fleet was moored. They sank five. Bombs ignited the forward magazine of *Arizona*, shattering the battleship. *Oklahoma* capsized, trapping hundreds of seamen inside. *West Virginia* and *California* settled in the mud upright. *Nevada*, attempting to escape the harbor, was beached in flames. *Pennsylvania*, *Tennessee*, and *Maryland* suffered damage but remained afloat. *Colorado*, undergoing modernization on the West Coast, escaped altogether.

Otherwise damage was relatively light. No aircraft carrier was in port: *Lexington* and *Enterprise* were delivering planes to outlying bases and *Saratoga* was on the West Coast. One heavy cruiser present, *New Orleans*, was peppered with fragments, the other, *San Francisco*, was unharmed. Of six light cruisers, one was sunk, one heavily damaged, one lightly damaged, and three were unscathed. Only three destroyers were put out of action. The power plant, repair shops, and oil storage tanks were spared. Nonetheless, the Japanese now had every reason to believe that their attacks southward would not be threatened from the Pacific flank.

Dawn came to the Philippines several hours later but in spite of forewarning, the American command was caught with its planes down. It delayed action for hours, lulled by the belief that the airfields of central Luzon were beyond reach of Japanese air power and torn between sequestering its precious B-17s and hurling them against Japanese air concentrations on Formosa. Shortly after noon that day, eighty-eight Japanese naval bombers and Zero fighters, with engines modified to extend their range, attacked Clark Field. Half of the thirty-five B-17s in the Philippines, arming and fueling for a mission to Formosa, were destroyed. Within the first day, half of the modern fighters were gone too. Having promptly seized command of the air, Japanese forces were in a position to destroy or force the withdrawal of American air and naval power from the Philippines, leaving the islands open to invasion.

The night after these attacks, H.M.S. *Prince of Wales* and *Repulse* with four destroyers left Singapore and steamed north to pounce on Japanese transports off Singora. Sighted by Japanese aircraft, Admiral Phillips wisely turned about. Then what proved to be a false report of Japanese landings further south diverted him to the coast and delayed his withdrawal long enough for the Japanese to spot him again. At 11:00 a.m. December 10 local time, eighty-eight naval bombers and torpedo planes from Indochinese bases attacked, again operating well beyond their expected range. They methodically destroyed the battleship and battle cruiser, sending them down with 840 men and Admiral Phillips. The blow to British morale and prestige in East Asia was immense.

The British and Americans consistently underrated the Japanese and failed to appreciate the defiant, do-or-die mentality of its current leadership. Western defenses were still weak, weapons ineffective or obsolete, and leadership mostly mediocre. The rituals and routines of peace prevailed; minds were not at war pitch. These Western weaknesses in no way detract from the brilliance and daring of the Japanese plan and the effectiveness of the wide-ranging Japanese attacks. Imperial headquarters riveted Western attention on the preliminaries that could not be concealed—the staging of forces to Indochina and the Gulf of Siam—keeping their ultimate destination ambiguous, while moving in on the Americans by stealth. Japan obtained its immediate objectives. The way was open for conquest of a broad domain from the borders of India to the mid-Pacific and from the Aleutians to New Guinea.

The day after Pearl Harbor the United States, powerfully united and vowing vengeance, declared war on Japan. Hitler, delighted to find the United States weakened, its forces divided, and anxious to sustain Japan and prevent any possible rapprochement between the Pacific antagonists while he finished off Russia in 1942, declared war on December 11. He undoubtedly believed he had little to lose, given existing American engagement in the Battle of the Atlantic, and he had much to gain by turning loose his submarines on unprotected American commerce along the East Coast. The U-boat fleet had nearly tripled in size during 1941.[10] Italy followed Germany, and the United States instantly responded with a declaration of war on both. December 11 was nine months to the day since the passage of Lend-Lease. Now the great neutrals had joined the fray, by choice and force of circumstance. The questions that overhung international relations in March of global alignment and balance of forces had all been answered: The world was at war.

Notes

MID	U.S. Army Military Intelligence Division
NA	National Archives, Washington
NHC	U.S. Naval History Center, Navy Yard, Washington
NHOB	U.S. Naval History Operations Branch, Federal Record Center, Suitland, MD
NOA	U.S. Navy Operational Archives, Navy Yard, Washington
NWPD	U.S. Navy War Plans Division
OCS	Office of Chief of Staff, U.S. Army
OF	President's Official File, FDRL
ONI	U.S. Navy Office of Naval Intelligence
OPD	U.S. Army Operations Division (successor to War Plans Division)
OPNAV	Office of U.S. Chief of Naval Operations
PHA	U.S. Congress, *Hearings on the Pearl Harbor Attack*
PPF	President's Personal File, FDRL
PREM	British Prime Minister's office records
PRO	Public Record Office, Kew, United Kingdom
PSF	President's Secretary's File, FDRL
PW	740.0011 Pacific War file, RG 59
RG	Record Group
SecState	U.S. Secretary of State
SOPD	Strategical and Operational Planning Documents, NOA
SPDR	U.S. Navy Strategic Plans Division records
SPENAVO	U.S. Special Naval Observer, London
SRDJ	Translations of Japanese diplomatic messages, (MAGIC)
SRGN	German navy U-boat messages
WPD	U.S. Army War Plans Division

Prologue

1. Walter Consuelo Langsam, *The World Since 1919* (New York, 1948), 77.

2. Gerhard L. Weinberg, *The Foreign Policy of Hitler's Germany: Diplomatic Revolution in Europe, 1933-36* (Chicago, 1970), 7; Weinberg, *The Foreign Policy of Hitler's Germany: Starting World War II, 1937-39* (Chicago, 1980), 657-59.

3. On Roosevelt's foreign policy: Robert Dallek, *Franklin D. Roosevelt and American Foreign Policy, 1932-1945* (New York, 1979).

4. Michael A. Barnhart, *Japan Prepares for Total War: The Search for Economic Security, 1919-1941* (Ithaca, 1987), 144-46.

5. C. Vann Woodward, "The Comparability of American History," Woodward, ed., *The Comparative Approach to American History* (New York, 1968), 4-5.

6. James C. Fahey, *The Ships and Aircraft of the United States Fleet: Victory Edition* (New York, 1945). Actual building did not begin until later, in some cases several

years later, as dockyard space became available. Not all were completed; seven battleships were scrapped, for example.

7. Lauchlin Currie memo for president (cited as FDR), 16 July 1940, President's Secretary's File (cited as PSF): Currie, Franklin D. Roosevelt Library (cited as FDRL), Hyde Park, NY.

Chapter 1. March 1941: The Aura of German Power

1. Minister in Bulgaria to Secretary of State (cited as SecState), 6 March 1941, 740.0011 European War 1939 (cited as 740.0011 EW)/8861, central files of the Department of State, Record Group (cited as RG) 59, National Archives (cited as NA), Washington; *New York Times*, 2 March 1941.

2. On German plans for 1941: Larry H. Addington, *The Blitzkrieg Era and the German General Staff, 1865-1941* (New Brunswick, 1971), 178-90; Barry Leach, *German Strategy Against Russia, 1939-1941* (Oxford, 1973), chaps. 3-5; Martin Van Creveld, *Hitler's Strategy: The Balkan Clue, 1940-1941* (London, 1973).

3. Adolf A. Berle, Jr., diary, 9, 14, 24 Feb. 1941, Adolf A. Berle, Jr., papers, FDRL; Henry L. Stimson diary (microfilm), 8, 11, 17-21 March 1941, Henry L. Stimson papers, Yale University Library, New Haven; *Washington Post*, 17, 18 March 1941.

4. This is a necessarily impressionistic account of internal problems in early 1941, though Stimson's diary and the President's Secretary's File at Hyde Park are informative, and Dallek, *Roosevelt Foreign Policy*, is helpful, especially p. 267. The definitive work on isolationism is Wayne S. Cole, *Roosevelt and the Isolationists, 1932-45* (Lincoln, NE, 1983). The literature on prewar mobilization is scanty. I am indebted to comments by Arthur M. Schlesinger, Jr., on this score, but I do not mean here to represent his views. On the economy I used *Time* and *Fortune* magazines.

5. Waldo Heinrichs, "President Franklin D. Roosevelt's Intervention in the Battle of the Atlantic, 1941," *Diplomatic History* (Fall 1986), 10:316; Frank Freidel, *Franklin D. Roosevelt: Launching the New Deal* (Boston, 1973), 269. Information here and subsequently on whom the president saw is from: president's appointment diaries, 1939-1944, President's Personal File (cited as PPF) 1-0(1), FDRL; White House usher's diary, 1941, White House: Office of the Chief of Social Entertainments, box 320, ibid.

6. Stimson diary, 7 Nov., 17 Dec. 1940, 21 Jan., 17 Sept. 1941.

7. David Reynolds, *The Creation of the Anglo-American Alliance 1937-41: A Study in Competitive Cooperation* (Chapel Hill, 1981), 182.

8. Roberta Wohlstetter, *Pearl Harbor: Warning and Decision* (Stanford, 1962), 180.

9. Richard Dunlop, *Donovan, America's Master Spy* (Chicago, 1982), 283-84. A sampling of boxes in RG 226, records of the Office of Strategic Services, NA, suggests that the office of the Coordinator of Information (predecessor to OSS) began receiving reports from other agencies in Oct. 1941. Berle diary, 7 March 1941; Stimson diary, 17 April 1941 (Miles).

10. An example of Roosevelt's interest in figures is: FDR memo for Hull and Welles, 8 April 1941 enclosing Anthony Drexel Biddle, Jr., to FDR, 26 March 1941, PSF:State Dept., FDRL. Henri L. Claudel to FDR, 10 Feb. 1941, enclosing excerpt of letter from Paul Claudel, 12 Jan. 1941, author's translation, President's Personal File (cited as PPF):5847, FDRL; transcript of oral history of Vice Admiral Walter S. Anderson (Oral History Research Office, Columbia University, 1966), 230. Between March and November 1941 for the army and May and November for the navy,

Roosevelt was denied MAGIC documents because of lax security at the White House, but briefings from the intercepts continued: Ruth R. Harris, "The 'Magic' Leak of 1941 and Japanese-American Relations," *Pacific Historical Review* (Feb. 1981), 50:77,93; "Dissemination to the White House," A.D. Kramer memo, 12 Nov. 1941, U.S. Congress, *Hearings of Joint Committee on the Investigation of the Pearl Harbor Attack*, 79th Cong., 1st sess. (39 parts; Washington, 1946) (cited as PHA), 11:5475–76.

11. Respondek was the anonymous German friend of Woods referred to by Hull in his memoirs: Cordell Hull, *The Memoirs of Cordell Hull* (2 vols.; New York, 1948), 2:967–68. His reports, Hull asserted, provided "excellent reason to believe Hitler would attack Russia" and served as a basis for an American warning to the Soviet Union of such an attack (see Chapter 2 below). William L. Langer and S. Everett Gleason considered the report which Hull claimed to have received in January "of truly staggering import" for it "transmitted what was obviously a copy of Hitler's directive for the attack on Soviet Russia.... ": *The Undeclared War, 1940–1941* (New York, 1953), 336–37.

New evidence has come to light which requires modification of these conclusions. A memorandum by Woods, written after World War II, detailing his relationship with the German source but not naming him, has been found in the Hull papers: "Memorandum for Honorable Cordell Hull," "Undated" folder, box 56, microfilm reel 27, frame 569ff, papers of Cordell Hull, Manuscripts Division, Library of Congress (cited as LC), Washington. From the language and details of his memoirs it is clear Hull used the Woods memo as the basis for his own account. Woods, who by this time had only his recollections of the reports to base his account on, accurately described the BARBAROSSA plan but not the 3 Jan. 1941 report. The latter was buried in Military Intelligence Division files: military attaché Berlin, report of 17 Jan. 1941, No. 17875, 2016-1326/7, Military Intelligence Division files (cited as MID 2016-1326/7), entry 65, records of War Department General and Special Staffs, 1920–1941, RG 165, NA. The Fuehrer directive for BARBAROSSA, however, was available to Woods in 1946: Fuehrer Directive No. 21, 18 Dec. 1941, Doc. 446-PS, U.S. Department of State, Office of Chief of Counsel for Prosecution of Axis Criminality, *Nazi Conspiracy and Aggression* (8 vols.; Washington, 1946), 3:407–9. Langer and Gleason, not having seen the 3 Jan. report, probably concluded from Hull's (Woods') account that Woods' source had secured and transmitted the BARBAROSSA directive itself, but he had not.

The first to identify Woods' source as Respondek was Professor William E. Griffith of Massachusetts Institute of Technology: Barton Whaley, *Codeword BARBAROSSA* (Cambridge, MA, 1973), 38, 277, fn 48. Griffith guesses, though he cannot be certain, that Respondek was the one: Griffith to author, 4 Nov. 1985. He says, however, that in 1945 or 1946 he did meet Respondek, who said he had given Woods a German occupation bank note printed in advance. Woods' memo notes that "Ralph" (the cover name of his source) gave him a 1000-ruble note. Furthermore, Respondek's curriculum vitae in a directory of Reichstag members, fits with the description of the source in Woods' memo and in the American military attaché's introduction to the 3 Jan. report: *Verzeichnis die Mitglieder des Reichstags* (Berlin, 1932), 180. Barton Whaley pointed to Respondek as an informant of Woods but described Hans Herwarth von Bittenfeld, a career diplomat then serving in the army, as a more important one: *Codeword BARBAROSSA*, 38. Herwarth strongly denied this in a letter to the author, 8 Nov. 1985, a denial also made in his memoirs: Hans von Herwarth with

S. Frederick Starr, *Against Two Evils* (New York, 1981), 177–78. He had met Woods but his "reports" were only conversations. Professor Harold C. Deutsch of the U.S. Army War College has stated that he was told by Charles A. Bohlen, a friend of Herwarth, that Woods' informant was Erwin Respondek: copy of Deutsch letter, "To Whom It May Concern", 6 Dec. 1982, enclosed in Herwarth to author, 8 Nov. 1985.

The 3 Jan. report, as stated, and several other reports of May 1941 from the same source have been located in Military Intelligence Division files: MID 2016-1326/ 7,20,23, RG 165. The bulk of the reports, however, together with material relating to their verification, have been found in the papers of Breckinridge Long: "Bonsal, Steven—Translations—Complete Set" folder, box 258, Long papers, LC. See also Breckinridge Long diary, 21 Feb., 11 March, 4 April 1941, ibid., and Fred L. Israel, ed., *The War Diary of Breckinridge Long; Selections from the Years 1939–1944* (Lincoln, NE, 1966), 182–84, 188–89. Several of the State Department reports refer to the 3 Jan. report in the MID files.

On German general staff planning in the period July–Dec. 1940: Leach, *German Strategy*, 70–123.

12. Berle diary, 9, 24 Feb., 5 March 1941.

13. Steinhardt to SecState, 26 Feb., 24 March, 1941, U.S. Department of State, *Foreign Relations of the United States, 1941* (cited as FR) (7 vols.; Washington, 1956–63), 1:702–3, 133–34. See also 740.0011 EW/8769, 9288, 9589, RG 59.

14. Gunther to SecState, 25 Feb. 1941, FR 1941, 1:290 and 18 March 1941, 740.0011 EW/9137, RG 59; FR 1941, 1:129–31, 274–76, 280–81, 285–87, 291–92; military attaché Bucharest, report of 17 Feb. 1941, MID 183–316, RG 165.

15. Van Creveld, *Hitler's Strategy*, 135, 138; Winston Chruchill, *The Grand Alliance* (Boston, 1950), 356–57; F. H. Hinsley, *British Intelligence in the Second World War: Its Influence on Strategy and Operations* (3 vols.; New York, 1979–84), 1:370–71, 451–52; Earle (Sofia) to SecState, 27 March 1941, 740.0011 EW/9368, RG 59.

16. Military attaché Bern, Switzerland, reports of 20 Feb.–3 April 1941, MID 2074-151/34–38, RG 165; Leahy to SecState, 14, 22 March 1941, 740.0011 EW/9047, 9262, RG 59. See also naval attaché Berlin, reports of 26 March, 5 April, 1941, #194, #211, Probability of War reports, vol. 1, PSF:subject files, FDRL.

17. MID 2074-151/38, 2657-230/16–22, 2016-1297, 2016-1326, RG 165; 740.0011 EW/8604; Office of Naval Information, *Fuehrer Conferences on Matters Dealing with the German Navy, 1941* (2 vols.; Washington, 1947), 1:entry for 2 Feb. 1941.

18. Military attaché Berlin, reports of 24 Feb., 21 March 1941, MID 2657-230/18, 2016-1077/171, RG 165; Military Intelligence Daily Summary, 21 March 1941, MID 2657-234, ibid.

19. U.S. Department of State, *Foreign Service List, January 1941* (Washington, 1941).

20. Henderson to Laurence Steinhardt, 31 March 1941, box 33, papers of Laurence A. Steinhardt, LC; memo by Wallace Murray, 8 March 1941, 740.0011 EW/8769, RG 59.

21. Foreign Office Record Group (cited as FO) 371/26518, C2222/19/18, C2317/ 19/18, C2919/19/18, Public Record Office (cited as PRO), Kew, London.

22. SRDJ 8811, 9405, 9544, 9749, 9842, 9987, 10179, 10455, 10766, copies of Japanese diplomatic messages intercepted, decrypted, and translated, RG 457, NA.

23. On German deception operations for BARBAROSSA and rumors: Whaley, *Codeword BARBAROSSA*, chap. 7.

24. Charles B. Burdick, *Germany's Military Strategy and Spain in World War II* (Syracuse, 1968), 117–23; Langer and Gleason, *Undeclared War*, 76–85, 360–65.

25. 740.0011 EW/8575, 8629, 8655, 8898, 8910, 8927, 9045, 9099, 9179, 9238, 9241A, 9258, 9320, 9346, 9361, 10750, RG 59; Berle diary, 14 Feb. 1941; Sherman Miles memo for Chief of Staff (cited as COS), 10 March 1941, box 5, PSF:safe file (cited as safe), FDRL; William L. Langer, *Our Vichy Gamble* (Hamden, CT, 1965), 135–41.

26. Stimson diary, 20 March 1941.

27. Air Bulletin: Air Operations 1 Nov. 1940–15 Jan. 1941, 740.0011 EW/8616, RG 59.

28. Military attaché Berlin, reports of 18 Jan.–24 April 1941, MID 1833-316, RG 165; Fuehrer Directive of 28 Feb. 1941, as quoted in J.M.A. Gwyer and J.R.M. Butler, *Grand Strategy* (London, 1964), 3 (Part 1):10; *New York Times*, 14 March 1941; (London) *Times*, 15–22 March 1941. On the "night blitz": "Air Operations, 1 Nov. 1940–15 Jan. 1941, 740.0011 EW/8616, RG 59; Hinsley, *British Intelligence*, 1:315, 318, 329–30; Churchill, *Grand Alliance*, 42–44; Basil Collier, *Defense of the United Kingdom* (London, 1957), chaps. 17, 18; Angus Calder, *The People's War: Britain, 1939–1945* (New York, 1969), 210–21; W. K. Hancock and M. M. Gowing, *British War Economy* (London, 1949), 240–80; Captain S. W. Roskill, *The War at Sea, 1939–1945* (3 vols.; London, 1954–61), 1:610 (Appendix O).

29. Calder, *People's War*, 214; *Washington Post*, 24 March 1941.

30. Military attaché London, report of 17 March 1941, 740.0011 EW/9296, RG 59, report of 20 March 1941, MID 2060-1236/6, RG 165; military attaché Berlin, report of 12 March 1941, MID 183-316, ibid.; Stimson diary, 25 March 1941; *Washington Post*, 20, 24 March 1941; Gwyer and Butler, *Grand Strategy*, 3 (Part 1):9; H. H. Arnold *Global Mission* (New York, 1949), 218–19.

31. Military attaché London, report of 1 April 1941, MID 2062-1236/7, RG 165; Calder, *People's War*, 212–13.

32. Roskill, *War at Sea*, 1: chap. 16, 349–50.

33. On U-boat warfare in early 1941: ibid., 343–65, 451–64; *Fuehrer Conferences*, 1:entry for 20 April 1941; Churchill to FDR, 4 April 1941, C-77x, Warren F. Kimball, ed., *Churchill and Roosevelt: The Complete Correspondence* (3 vols.; Princeton, 1984), 1:161–62; "Convoys: Abstract of Admiralty History of Atlantic Convoys As Communicated to S. E. Morison July 13, 1942, by Commander W. B. Rowbotham," box 11, office files of Rear Admiral S. E. Morison, 1911–1969, Naval Operational Archives (cited as NOA), Navy Yard, Washington.

34. L. E. Denfeld to Chief of Naval Operations (cited as CNO), 22 April 1941, EA–EZ folder, box 96, Strategic Plans Division records (cited as SPDR), NOA; American naval attaché London (cited as ALUSNA) to Naval Operations Office (cited as OPNAV), 24 March 1941, series 1, records of Commander Naval Forces Europe (cited as COMNAVFOREUR), NOA. On the former American destroyers: ALUSNA to OPNAV, 8 Jan. 1941, ibid.; Heinrichs, "Roosevelt's Intervention," 317.

35. Cajus Bekker, *The German Navy, 1939–1945* (London, 1972), 16, 19, 33, 57; Roskill, *War at Sea*, 1:367–87.

36. Estimating losses for any given period is difficult because the data cover different periods for different kinds of losses. These estimates are based on Roskill, ibid., 362–64, 371–76, 379, 616. See also: Office of Naval Intelligence (cited as ONI) memo for Secretary of Navy, 27 March 1941, A4-3/CV-EF53 folder, box 220, secret correspondence of the office of Chief of Naval Operations (cited as CNO secret), RG 80, NA; Hancock and Gowing, *British War Economy*, 349–67; Gwyer and Butler, *Grand Strategy*, 3 (part 1):9–10.

37. ALUSNA to OPNAV, 17 March 1941, series 1, COMNAVFOREUR records, NOA; Winant to SecState (Churchill for Hopkins), 28 March 1941, 740.0011 EW/9415, RG 59; *New York Times*, 11, 13, 18 March 1941; *Washington Post*, 19 March 1941; Roskill, *War at Sea*, 1:609 (Appendix O).

38. Samuel I. Rosenman, comp., *The Public Papers and Addresses of Franklin D. Roosevelt: 1941* (13 vols.; New York, 1950), 10:63; *Washington Post*, 16 March 1941; *New York Times*, 16, 19 March 1941; Robert E. Sherwood, *Roosevelt and Hopkins; An Intimate History* (New York, 1948), 267.

39. Director of War Plans to CNO, 12 March 1941, A16-3/FF, box 91, SPDR, NOA; CNO to directors of divisions, OPNAV, 18 March 1941, ibid.; *U.S.S. Benson* to Commander Destroyer Squadron (cited as COMDESRON) 7, box 1, Commander-in-Chief Atlantic Fleet (cited as CINCLANT), World War II message files, Naval History Operational Branch (cited as NHOB), Federal Record Center, Suitland, MD (cited as FRS); King to Stark, 16 March 1941, A14-5/FF13, box 232, CNO secret, RG 80; Historical Section, Office of Commander-in-Chief Atlantic Fleet (cited as CINCLANT), "U.S. Naval Administration in World War II: Commander-in-Chief, U.S. Atlantic Fleet," 128, microfiche, U.S. Navy Historical Center (cited as NHC), Navy Yard, Washington; *New York Times*, 15 March 1941.

40. Harold Ickes, *The Secret Diary of Harold L. Ickes* (3 vols.; New York, 1955), 3:469.

Chapter 2. April: Balancing Risks

1. Hosoya Chihiro, "The Japanese-Soviet Neutrality Pact," in James William Morley, ed., *Japan's Road to the Pacific War: The Fateful Choice, Japan's Advance into Southeast Asia, 1939–1941. Selected Translations from Taiheiyō sensō e no michi: kaisen gaikō shi* (New York, 1980), 71. On the Matsuoka trip: ibid., 64–85.

2. The following works have been helpful in arriving at this description of Japanese decision-making, though the author takes full responsibility for it and it may differ substantially from any one of them: Barnhart, *Japan Prepares for Total War*; James B. Crowley, *Japan's Quest for Autonomy: National Security and Foreign Policy, 1930–1938* (Princeton, 1966); Crowley, "Japan's Military Foreign Policies," in James William Morley, ed., *Japan's Foreign Policy, 1868–1941: A Research Guide* (New York, 1974), 3–117; Morley, ed., *Fateful Choice*; Usui Katsumi, "The Role of the Foreign Ministry," and Asada Sadao, "The Japanese Navy and the United States," in Dorothy Borg and Shumpei Okamoto, eds., *Pearl Harbor as History: Japanese-American Relations, 1931–1941* (New York, 1973), 127–48, 225–59; Shumpei Okamoto, *The Japanese Oligarchy and the Russo-Japanese War* (New York, 1970), 230–32.

3. Irvine H. Anderson, Jr., *The Standard-Vacuum Oil Company and United States East Asian Policy, 1933–1941* (Princeton, 1975), 146–57.

4. Waldo H. Heinrichs, Jr., *American Ambassador: Joseph C. Grew and the Development of the United States Diplomatic Tradition* (Boston, 1966), 325–28.

5. Tokyo to Singapore, 20 March 1941, SRDJ 10589, Taihoku to Batavia, 4 Feb. 1941, SRDJ 10660, Berlin to Tokyo, 26 March 1941, SRDJ 10684, RG 457.

6. SecState to Grew, 5 April 1941, FR 1941, 4:931; naval attaché Tokyo, report of March {n.d.} 1941, box 122, SPDR, NOA; Captain R. E. Schuirmann, Central Division, OPNAV, to State Department, 18 Feb. 1941, 740.0011 EW/8675, RG 59.

7. Freidel, *Launching the New Deal*, 121–23.

8. Ernest R. May, "Foreword," May and James C. Thomson Jr., eds., *American-East Asian Relations: A Survey* (Cambridge, MA, 1972), xiv.

9. Waldo H. Heinrichs, Jr., "The Role of the U.S. Navy," Borg and Okamoto, eds., *Pearl Harbor as History*, 220, 223.

10. Dorothy Borg, *The United States and the Far Eastern Crisis of 1933–1938: From the Manchurian Incident Through the Initial Stage of the Sino-Japanese War* (Cambridge, MA, 1964), 522–25.

11. As quoted in Heinrichs, "Role of the U.S. Navy," 212–13.

12. Stark to Admiral Husband Kimmel, Commander-in-Chief, Pacific Fleet (cited as CINCPAC), 10 Feb. and 25 Feb. 1941, enclosing Stark memo for FDR, 11 Feb. 1941, PHA, 16:2147–49; Stark to Admiral Thomas Hart, Commander-in-Chief, Asiatic Fleet (cited as CINCAF), 16 Oct. 1940, A16-3(15), CNO secret, RG 80; CINCPAC to CNO, 28 March 1941, A16(R-3), ibid.; Capt. Tracy B. Kittredge, "United States-British Naval Cooperation, 1940–1945," microfilm NRS II-226, chap. 13, 308–22, chap. 13 notes, 267–70, 294–96.

13. Stark memo for Knox, 12 Nov. 1940, PSF (safe): Navy, FDRL. Also: CNO to Secretary of Navy, 17 Jan. 1941, A16-3/FF Warfare-U.S. Fleet, box 91, SPDR, NOA; Stark memo, 21 Dec. 1940 enclosing "Study of the Immediate Problems Concerning Involvement in War," War Plans Division numerical files, 1920–41 (cited as WPD), 4561, RG 165; director, navy War Plans Division (cited as NWPD) to chairman, General Board, 2 April 1941, A16-1, CNO secret, RG 80. Until the adoption of the Rainbow 5, ABC-1 strategy in the spring of 1941, the dominant planning concept in the navy was Rainbow 3, which aimed at securing control of the western Pacific but only as rapidly as possible consistent with protection of the Western Hemisphere. Assuming defense in the Atlantic, Rainbow 3 was not far different from the initial stage of Rainbow 5. The various Rainbow plans are described in Maurice Matloff and Edwin M. Snell, *The War Department: Strategic Planning for Coalition Warfare, 1941–1942* (Washington, 1953), 7–8.

14. G. C. Marshall memo, 17 Jan. 1941, of White House conference same day, exec. #4, item #11, box 21, executive files, Operations Division (cited as OPD), RG 165.

15. Lt. Cdr. R. Mason, report on Singapore, 23 Nov. 1940, box 71, SPDR, NOA; statement by U.S. staff committee, "U.S. Military Position in the Far East," box 118, ibid.; minutes, 7 Feb. 1941, minutes of U.S.-British staff conversations, box 119, ibid.; questionnaire submitted by U.K. delegation, 29 Jan. 1941, reports of U.S.-British staff conversations, ibid.; Maj. Gen. Stanley D. Embick et al. memo for COS, 12 Feb. 1941, exec. #4, item #11, OPD, RG 165; Stark to Hart, 12 Nov. 1940, correspondence of Rear Adm. Robert L. Ghormley, subject files, COMNAVFOREUR records, NOA; Ghormley memo of conversation with Adm. Sir Dudley Pound, 19 Nov. 1940, ibid.; Rear Adm. Roger Bellairs to British Chiefs of Staff, 11, 15, 23 Feb. 1941, FO 371/26147, A685/G and A875/11/45, FO 371/26219, A1134/384/45, PRO; James R. Leutze, *Bargaining for Supremacy: Anglo-American Naval Collaboration, 1937–1941* (Chapel Hill, 1977), chaps. 14, 15; Heinrichs, "Role of the U.S. Navy," 221–23.

16. FDR to Grew, 21 Jan. 1941, PSF:Japan, FDRL, also in Joseph C. Grew, *Turbulent Era: A Diplomatic Record of Forty Years, 1904–1945*, Walter Johnson, ed. (2 vols.; Boston, 1952), 2:1259–60. See also Hornbeck memo, 4 Dec. 1940, "Far East (Before Dec. 7, 1941)" folder, box 4, RG 107, NA.

17. The key documents on the navy's recommendations for intervening in the Battle of the Atlantic are: Knox to FDR, 21 March 1941, A16-1/FF13, CNO secret, RG 80; Knox to FDR, 20 March 1941, Navy Department folder, box 10, RG 107;

memo {n.a.}, "Ocean Escort in the Western Atlantic," PHA, 16:2162–63 (The date of this memo is probably 1 April 1941. See copy indexed to that date in Adm. Richmond Kelly Turner Papers, box 20, director NWPD special file #2, item 25, NOA). On the U.S. Navy and the Battle of the Atlantic: Samuel Eliot Morison, *The Battle of the Atlantic, September 1939–May 1943* (Boston, 1947); Patrick Abbazia, Mr. *Roosevelt's Navy: The Private War of the U.S. Atlantic Fleet, 1939–1942* (Annapolis, 1975).

18. Secretary of Navy Charles Edison to FDR, 24 June 1940, PSF: Navy Dept., FDRL.

19. U.S. Atlantic Fleet Operating Plan 0–3, 23 March 1941, supplementary plan, A16/FF13, CNO secret, RG 80; "Are We Ready?" vol. 2, 1940–1941, box 90, SPDR, NOA; Bellairs to British Chiefs of Staff, 15 Feb. 1941, FO 371/26219, A827/384/45, PRO. On distribution of U.S. Atlantic Fleet and plans for it: British printed copy of ABC-1 and ABC-2, box 116, SPDR, NOA; minutes and reports of U.S.-British staff meetings, Jan.–March 1941, boxes 118, 119, ibid.; "Disposition and Location of U.S. Naval Forces," 5 Feb. 1941, Annex A, box 118, SPDR, NOA. I am grateful to Vice Adm. Edwin B. Hooper, USN (Ret.), who was gunnery officer of the U.S.S. *Washington* in World War II, for his estimates of the relative power of American and German battleships.

20. Bellairs to British Chiefs of Staff, 17 Feb. 1941, FO 371/26147, A939/11/45, PRO; CNO to directors of Ship Movements, Fleet Maintenance, Fleet Training, 15 Feb. 1941, box 81, SPDR, NOA; director NWPD to CNO, 3 April 1941, ibid.; Rear Adm. Mark Bristol to Turner, 28 March 1941, A16-3/FF, box 91, ibid.

21. Churchill to FDR, 19 March 1941, C-69x, Kimball, ed., *Churchill-Roosevelt Correspondence,* 1:149–50.

22. Churchill to FDR, 9 Jan. 1941, C-53x, ibid., 126–27; memo (n.a., n.d.), exec. #4, item #11 (ABC file), box 21, OPD, RG 165; John McCloy to Knox, 27 March 1941 and enclosure, A16-1/EF13, CNO secret, RG 80; Stimson diary, 24, 25 March 1941; *New York Times,* 9, 16 March 1941; *Washington Post,* 22, 26 March 1941; Sherwood, *Roosevelt and Hopkins,* 257.

23. Welles to FDR, 27 March 1941, 740.0011 EW/9201G, RG 59; Churchill to FDR, 6 April 1941, C-78x, Kimball ed., *Churchill-Roosevelt Correspondence,* 1:164.

24. Halifax to Churchill, 18 April 1941, and Churchill to Halifax, 12 May 1941, FO 371/26148, A3375/11/45, PRO; Long diary, 17 April 1941.

25. Director NWPD to CNO, 14 March 1941, A3-1/DD, CNO secret, RG 80.

26. COMDESRON 2 to CNO and director, Fleet Training, 10 May 1941, box 3278, Commander Destroyers Atlantic Fleet (cited as COMDESLANT) general administrative files, 1941–1944, RG 313, FRS; director NWPD to CNO, 23 April 1941, box 95, SPDR, NOA. Information on ship movements, schedules, and assignments here and elsewhere in this study, unless otherwise cited, comes from: Ship Movements, Daily Movement Series, World War II command files, NOA; Information Relating to Change of Status of Naval Vessels, A4-1, box 3272, RG 313, FRS; Availability for Operations, Schedules of Employment, A4-3#4, box 3273, ibid.; Atlantic Fleet Weekly Operations Sheets and Lists of Predicted Ship Locations, A4-3(1)#3, ibid.

27. CNO to CINCLANT, 22 May 1941, A3-1/DD, CNO secret, RG 80; CNO to CINCLANT, 1 April 1941, "New Construction #2" folder, box 36, Ship Movements Division general correspondence, 1920–1942 (cited as SM), RG 38; CINCLANT to OPNAV, 25 April 1941, "CINCLANT" folder, box 61, ibid.; deck log of U.S.S. *Texas,* 9 May 1941, Ships' Deck Logs, RG 24, NA.

28. "Are We Ready?" vol. 2, box 90, SPDR, NOA; CNO to chiefs of Bureaus of Ships and Ordinance, 9, 30 April 1941, box 95, ibid. The tension is well illustrated in Admiral King's memorandum to the fleet, "Making the Best with What We Have," in Morison, *Battle of the Atlantic*, 52–53.

29. J. M. Haines, "Anti-Submarine Warfare, 7 Dec. 1941–7 Dec. 1942," antisubmarine ordinance and equipment folder, box 23, Tenth Fleet files, NOA; reports of Task Units, 4.1.5 and 4.1.8, A14-1, CNO secret, RG 80; Commander Destroyer Flotilla 1 to ships of Flotilla 1, 13 June 1941, box 6, Rear Adm. Paul R. Heineman Papers, NOA; COMDESRON 27 to commander Support Force, 29 Aug. 1941, box 25, CINCLANT message files, NHOB, FRS; director, Fleet Training, memo, 19 Sept. 1941, A5-A5/1, CNO confidential files, RG 80; memo for president [n.a.], 21 March 1941, A16-1/EF13, CNO secret, RG 80; director NWPD to CNO, 10 Feb. 1941, A16-3/FF, box 91, SPDR, NOA. See reports of poor gunnery practice, boxes 3279, 3280, 3297, RG 313, FRS.

30. Stimson diary, 2 April 1941.

31. Berle diary, 16 March 1941; *Washington Post*, 16 March 1941; Butler, *Grand Strategy*, 2:457.

32. Stimson diary, 27 March 1941; MacVeagh to FDR, 8 March 1941, PSF: Greece, FDRL (Eden).

33. *Washington Post*, 29 March (Lippmann), 3 April, 1941; Engert, Beirut (Kirk) to SecState, 740.0011 EW/8865, RG 59; Berle diary, 6 Feb., 17 March 1941.

34. FDR to Hull, 11, 20 Feb. 1941, PSF:Turkey and PSF: Hull, FDRL; military attaché Athens, report of 26 March 1941, MID 183-316/145, RG 165.

35. "Ocean Escort in the Western Atlantic," [1] April 1941, PHA 16:2162–63; CNO to CINCPAC, 7 April 1941, ibid., 11:5503; Morgenthau to FDR, 19 Feb. 1941, PSF: Charts Folder, FDRL; "U.S. Naval Shipbuilding Program—Combatant Vessels," A1-3, CNO confidential, RG 80.

36. Stimson diary, 4 April 1941; Ickes, *Secret Diary*, 3:473; 21 March, 7 April polls, George H. Gallup, *The Gallup Poll: Public Opinion, 1935–1971* (3 vols.; New York, 1972), 1:270, 273.

37. As quoted in William L. Langer and S. Everett Gleason, *The Challenge to Isolation: The World Crisis of 1937–1941 and American Foreign Policy* (New York, 1952), 597, based on authors' conversation with Stark, 18 Feb. 1948.

38. CNO to CINCPAC, 7 April 1941, PHA, 11:5503.

39. Stimson diary, 10 April 1941.

40. Roosevelt did not authorize escort of convoy and then change his mind; he did not authorize it in the first place. The source for historians on this point has been Kittredge, "U.S.-British Naval Cooperation," 414. Kittredge correctly states that two Western Hemisphere defense plans were formulated at this time, but, apparently lacking a copy of the first, he identifies it with the navy's proposals of 20 March and 1 April for escort of convoy. The correct Western Hemisphere Defense Plan One is: [n.a.] memo for Secretary of Navy, 14 April 1941, director NWPD folder, special file #1, box 20, Turner papers, NOA, with revisions by FDR, incorporated in memo for Secretary of Navy, 16 April 1941, ibid.; the document is also in A16/QG2, CNO secret, RG 80. On task force assignments: CINCLANT Operation Plans 3-41, 4-41, 18, 21 April 1941, "CINCLANT (through May 1941)" box, strategical and operational planning documents (cited as SOPD), NOA; briefing charts for July 1941, briefing chart file, July–Dec. 1941, NOA; Stark to Kimmel, 19 April 1941, PHA, 16:2163.

41. Press conference #758, 25 April 1941, *Complete Presidential Press Conferences of Franklin Delano Roosevelt* (25 vols. in 12; New York, 1972), 17:285.

42. FDR to Churchill, 29 March 1941, R-29x, R-30x, Kimball, ed., *Roosevelt-Churchill Correspondence*, 1:153–54.

43. Halifax to FDR, 11 March 1941, PSF: Great Britain, FDRL; Hopkins memo for FDR, {n.d.} PSF:Hopkins, ibid.; Ingersoll memo for Capt. Daniel J. Callaghan, 21 Feb. 1941, PSF: Navy, ibid.; FDR to Knox, 1 April 1941, ibid.; *(Illustrious)* military attaché in Athens, report of 3 Feb. 1941, MID 183-316, RG 165; naval attaché London, reports, n.d. and 24 March 1941, file #2, series 1, COMNAVFOREUR records, NOA; C-70x, C-78x, R-28x, R-29x, R-30x, Kimball, ed., *Roosevelt-Churchill Correspondence*, 1:150–51, 153, 157, 164; Kittredge, "U.S.-British Naval Cooperation," 418.

44. Hancock and Gowing, *British War Economy*, 258.

45. Welles to FDR, 24 March 1941, 740.0011 EW/9201D, RG 59; Harriman to SecState, 24 March 1941, Harriman folder, box 8, RG 107; Langer and Gleason, *Undeclared War*, 433–34.

46. Hull, *Memoirs*, 2:987; Hilary Conroy, "Nomura Kichisaburō," Richard Dean Burns and Edward M. Bennett, eds., *Diplomats in Crisis: United States-Chinese-Japanese Relations, 1919–1941* (Santa Barbara, 1974), 297–316; Heinrichs, *Grew*, 294–99.

47. Hull memo of conversation, 14 March 1941, U.S. Department of State, *Foreign Relations of the United States, Japan: 1931–1941* (2 vols.; Washington, 1943) (cited as FR Japan), 2:398; ibid., 387–96.

48. R.J.C. Butow, *The John Doe Associates: Backdoor Diplomacy for Peace, 1941* (Stanford, 1974), Parts 1–2; Hosoya Chihiro, "The Role of Japan's Foreign Ministry and Its Embassy in Washington, 1940–1941," in Borg and Okamoto, eds., *Pearl Harbor as History*, 150–51; Yoshitake Oka, *Konoe Fumimaro: A Political Biography*, tr. Shumpei Okamoto and Patricia Murray (Tokyo, 1983), 119–25. Awareness of the Walsh-Drought mission by the Japanese foreign ministry is evident from a MAGIC intercept: Tokyo (vice minister of foreign affairs) to Washington, 6 March 1941, tr. 12 March 1941, SRDJ 10331, RG 457. The names in this message had been withheld by the U.S. government, but were released 9 Feb. 1984. The vice minister stated: "Lately we have heard various sorts of rumors concerning Ikawa, and I fear that if Walsh's and Drought's {sic} work is not to get off to a bad start, you {Nomura} will have to give Ikawa some instructions."

49. Proposal presented 9 April 1941, FR Japan, 2:398–402; Steinhardt to SecState, 11 April 1941, FR 1941, 4:936–37.

50. Berle diary, 15 April 1941; *New York Times*, 13 April 1941.

51. Abbazia, *Mr. Roosevelt's Navy*, chap. 17. *Niblack* in fact thought it was encountering a submarine on 11 April and dropped depth charges. However, it did not report the incident until returning to Newport 28 April. No U-boat reported an encounter.

52. Hull desk diary, 12 April 1941, reel 39, Hull papers.

53. Grew to SecState, 10 April 1941, FR 1941, 4:140; ibid., 128–29.

54. Memos by Hornbeck and Hamilton, 11 April 1941, ibid., 142–47; Hull desk diary, 14 April 1941, reel 39, Hull papers. The appointment would not have been entered on Easter Sunday nor with a question about locale on Monday. Thus the appointment was made before word arrived of the Soviet-Japanese Neutrality Pact.

55. Steinhardt to SecState, 11 April 1941, FR 1941, 4:937–38; SecState to Steinhardt, 15 April 1941, ibid., 948–49; Hosoya, "Japanese-Soviet Neutrality Pact," 74–79; Halifax to FO, 14 April 1941, FO 371/27956, F2964/421/23, PRO (Welles); A. H.

McCollum memo, 17 April 1941, with comments by Turner and Capt. Alan C. Kirk, PHA, 15:1853–55 (naval intelligence); FO 371/27957, F3581/421/23 and FO 371/27956, F3128/421/23, PRO; 740.0011 Pacific War (cited as PW)/196,222, RG 59; FR 1941, 4:947–8, 961–65; *New York Times*, 13 April 1941.

56. Hull memos, 14, 16 April 1941, FR Japan, 2:402–10; Hull desk diary, 15, 16 April 1941, reel 39, Hull papers; memo for Hull {n.a.} {15–16 April}, FR 1941, 4:153–54.

57. R.J.C. Butow, "The Hull-Nomura Conversations: A Fundamental Misconception," *American Historical Review* (July 1960), 65:822–36; Nomura to Tokyo, 17 April 1941, tr. 19 April 1941, SRDJ 11118, RG 457.

58. As quoted in Langer and Gleason, *Challenge to Isolation*, 725. On Soviet-American relations in 1939–40: ibid., 312–42, 638–51, 723–28.

59. J. Edgar Hoover to Berle, 4 Dec. 1940, MID 2657-278, RG 165; Hoover to Berle, 12 March 1941, 740.0011 EW/9785, RG 59.

60. FDR to Hull, 3 March 1941, PSF:Hull, FDRL; Steinhardt to SecState, 11, 20 Jan. 1941, FR 1941, 1:121, 126–28.

61. Loy Henderson memo, 27 Feb. 1941, ibid. 708; Langer and Gleason, *Undeclared War*, 335–45.

62. SecState to Steinhardt, 1 March 1941, FR 1941, 1:712–13.

63. Sumner Welles, *Time for Decision* (New York, 1944), 171.

64. Welles memos, 20 March 1941, FR 1941, 1:723 and fn. 25, 4:920.

65. Steinhardt to SecState, 12 April 1941, 761.62/895, RG 59; FR 1941, 1:296, 301, 611–12.

66. Memos by Henderson, 27 March, 18 April 1941, ibid., 728, 742; memo by Welles, 9 April 1941, ibid., 735–36.

67. Peter Berton, "Introduction" to Hosoya, "Japanese-Soviet Neutrality Pact," Morley, ed., *Fateful Choice*, 10; memo by Henderson, 18 April 1941, FR 1941, 1:741.

68. Schulenberg to Foreign Ministry, 13 April 1941, #333, U.S. Department of State, *Documents on German Foreign Policy, 1918–1945* (12 vols.; Washington, 1962), Series D (cited as DGFP), 12:537; Herwarth, *Against Two Evils*, 190.

69. Stark to Kimmel, 19 April 1941, PHA, 16:2163–64; CNO to CINCLANT, 17 April 1941, box 81, SPDR, NOA.

70. Stimson diary, 24 April 1941; CINCLANT Operation Plan 4-41, 21 April 1941, "CINCLANT (through May 1941)" folder, SOPD, NOA; CINCLANT, "U.S. Naval Administration in World War II:CINCLANT," 145–47, microfiche, NHC; Kittredge, "U.S.-British Naval Cooperation," 414.

Chapter 3. May: Guarding the Atlantic Line

1. Van Creveld, *Hitler's Strategy*, 153–66.

2. Naval attaché Rome, report of 20 April 1941, 740.0011 EW/10426, RG 59; Phillips to SecState, 25 April 1941, ibid./10334; ibid./10426, 10506, 10524.

3. Ibid./10288, 10345, 10493, 10961; military attaché Cairo, report of 25 April 1941, 370.2, box 486, Army Intelligence Project decimal file, 1941–45, RG 319, FRS.

4. Military attaché Cairo, report of 30 April 1941, MID 2657-298/5, RG 165.

5. Kirk to SecState, 27 April 1941, 740.0011 EW/10388, RG 59; military attaché Ankara, report of 24 April 1941, ibid./10496; "Estimate of Future British Action in Middle East," 23 April 1941, director NWPD special file #1, box 20, Turner papers,

NOA; military attaché London, report of 13 April 1941, 740.0011 EW/10174, RG 59; Engert (Beirut) to SecState, 21 April 1941, ibid./10201; Miles to COS, 16, 20 April 1941, MID 2016-1297, RG 165.

6. Stimson diary, 15, 17 April 1941; Churchill to FDR, 19 May 1941, C-88x, Kimball, ed., *Churchill-Roosevelt Correspondence,* 1:190.

7. Engert to SecState, 21 April 1941, 740.0011 EW/10201, RG 59 ("military colossus"); military attaché London, report of 20 April 1941, ibid./10513 (Dill); Phillips to FDR, 18 April 1941, PSF: Phillips, FDRL; Leahy to SecState, 16, 21 April 1941, 740.0011 EW/10022, 10196, RG 59; Weddell (Madrid) to SecState, 25 April 1941, ibid./10375; Sterling (Stockholm) to SecState, 19 April 1941, ibid./10107.

8. Military attaché Berlin, report of 15 April 1941, received 7 May 1941, MID 2016-1077/183, RG 165.

9. Gunther to SecState and military attaché reports, Budapest and Bucharest, 24 April 1941, 740.0011 EW/10377, 10428, 10516, RG 59; military attaché Bucharest, report of 6 May 1941, #6095, MID regional files, 1933–44, RG 165, FRS; military attaché Moscow, report of 12 May 1941, MID reports, Harry Hopkins papers, FDRL (Bratislava); 740.0011 EW/10466, 10625, 11077, 11078, RG 59; Van Creveld, *Hitler's Strategy,* 171.

10. Military attaché Berlin, reports of 17 April, 23 May 1941, 740.0011 EW/10345, 11269, RG 59; ibid., report of 21 April 1941, MID 2657-230/30, RG 165; Leach, *German Strategy Against Russia,* 169.

11. Military attaché Berlin, report of 21 April 1941, MID 2657-230/30, RG 165; Miles to COS, 23 April 1941, MID 2657-229, I.B. 31–33, ibid.

12. Assistant military attaché Berlin, order of battle report as of 15–20 March 1941, 740.0011 EW/10637, RG 59; Hinsley, *British Intelligence,* 1:466.

13. Military attaché Berlin, report of 17 April 1941, 740.0011 EW/10345, RG 59; Leach, *German Strategy Against Russia,* 94, fn. 4. On deception operations by German intelligence: ibid., 169; directive of High Command of Wehrmacht, 1 May 1941, #431, DGFP, 12:685; Whaley, *Codeword BARBAROSSA,* 170–75, 247–51.

14. Winant to SecState, 27 April 1941, 740.0011 EW/10405 1/3, RG 59; military attaché London, report of 17 April 1941, ibid./10272.

15. Steinhardt to SecState, 5 May 1941, FR 1941, 1:141; Whaley *Codeword BARBAROSSA,* 175–82; Hinsley, *British Intelligence,* 1:483. Hinsley argues that the story of an enforced diplomatic settlement could not have been a German deception device because it could not have fooled the Russians, whom the Germans needed to mystify most. Whaley argues persuasively that the story probably started as speculation in the diplomatic community and then was picked up and fed by the Germans to sow confusion. For the Russians, the fact that no negotiations were under way would not necessarily weaken the story because they would always expect, and indeed appear to have been always expecting, a German statement of terms or ultimatum.

16. Morris to SecState, 13 April, 13 May 1941, FR 1941, 1:139–43; Morris to SecState, 7, 14 May 1941, 740.0011 EW/10703, 10975, RG 59; Morris to SecState, 1 May 1941, 761.62/918, ibid.

17. Steinhardt to SecState, 30 April 1941, FR 1941, 1:879–81, 20 April 1941, ibid., 4:959–61, 21 April 1941, 740.0011 EW/10176, RG 59.

18. Ibid./10596, 10680, 10687, 10913, 10932; Ōshima to Tokyo, 9 May 1941, SRDJ 11724, RG 457; military attaché Berlin, report of 28 April 1941, 2657-B-765/19, 000.7, box 459, RG 319, FRS (press guidance).

19. Memo of conversation between Hitler and Darlan, 11 May 1941, #491, DGFP, 12:771 ("turntable"); 740.0011 EW/10345, 10516, 10531, 10713, 10797, 10844, 11173, RG 59; SRDJ 11216, RG 457; MID 2074-151/39, RG 165; *New York Times*, 4 May 1941; Holger H. Herwig, *Politics of Frustration: The United States in German Naval Planning, 1889–1941* (Boston, 1976), 211–16.

20. 740.0011 EW/9961, 10912, RG 59.

21. Leahy to SecState and SecState to Leahy, 17, 18 April 1941, FR 1941, 2:291–93; 740.0011 EW/10423, 10487, 10696A, 10736, RG 59.

22. "Protocols Signed at Paris May 27 and 28, 1941," #559, DGFP. 12:897–900; *Time*, 26 May 1941.

23. SecState to Weddell, 30 April 1941, FR 1941, 2:893–95; SecState to Leahy, 30 April 1941, ibid., 158–60; Leahy to SecState, and SecState to Leahy, 8 May 1941, ibid., 160–63.

24. Leahy to SecState, 12, 13 May 1941, ibid., 165–70; *New York Times*, 13 May 1941.

25. Ernest R. May, ed., *Knowing One's Enemies: Intelligence Assessments Before the Two World Wars* (Princeton, 1984), 541; Hinsley, *British Intelligence*, 1:467.

26. Sherwood, *Roosevelt and Hopkins*, 293; editor's note, Kimball, ed., *Churchill-Roosevelt Correspondence*, 1:185; Jim Bishop, *FDR's Last Year* (London, 1974), 5; William Bullitt memo, 23 April 1941, Orville H. Bullitt, ed., *For the President: Franklin D. Roosevelt and William C. Bullitt* (Boston, 1972), 512–14.

27. Ghormley to Pound, 9, 22 May 1941, Admiralty records, ADM 205/9, PRO; Rear Adm. Jonas Ingram to King, 23 May 1941, box 8, Admiral Ernest J. King papers, LC; operation orders for Task Forces 1, 2, 3, "CINCLANT (through May 1941)" box, SOPD, NOA; W. C. Ansel to Turner, 28 May 1941, A16-3/A7-3, box 91, SPDR, NOA; Commander Aircraft Atlantic Fleet to CINCLANT, 5 May 1941, A4-3, box 108, RG 313, FRS; CINCLANT to Commander Aircraft Atlantic Fleet, 17 May 1941, box 1, CINCLANT message files, NHOB, FRS.

28. Churchill to FDR, 24 April, 1941, C-81x, Kimball, ed., *Churchill-Roosevelt Correspondence*, 1:172–74.

29. WPD 4402-89, RG 165; Assistant Secreatry of War Robert Lovett to Stimson, 14 May 1941, box 1, Stimson safe file, RG 107; Churchill, *Grand Alliance*, 378; Richard M. Leighton and Robert W. Coakley, *The War Department: Global Logistics and Strategy, 1940–1943* (Washington, 1955), 61, 71–75; Lt. Col. Frank O. Hough et al., *Pearl Harbor to Guadalcanal: History of the U.S. Marine Corps in World War II* (Washington, 1959), 56.

30. Berle diary, 26 May 1941.

31. Captain Victor Danckwerts to Pound, 17 April 1941, ADM 205/9, PRO.

32. Ibid.; Halifax to FO, 17, 25 April 1941, FO 371/26220, A2782/384/45 and A3015/2368/45, PRO.

33. Stimson diary, 15–29 April 1941; Halifax to FO, 29 April 1941, FO 371/26220, A3153/384/45, PRO.

34. Stark to FDR, 29 April 1941, PHA, 19:3456; minutes of War Cabinet meeting, 30 April 1941, Cabinet records, CAB 69/2, PRO.

35. Halifax to FO, 29 April 1941, FO 371/26220, A3153/384/45, PRO.

36. Ibid.; Stimson diary, 2, 5 May 1941; Knox to FDR (n.d.) enclosing Danckwerts memo, 8 May 1941, PHA, 19:3461.

37. Stimson diary, 5–10 May 1941.

38. David J. Lu, *From Marco Polo Bridge to Pearl Harbor: Japan's Entry into World War II* (Washington, 1961), 166–70; Hosoya, "Role of the Foreign Ministry," Borg and Okamoto, eds., *Pearl Harbor as History*, 152–53.

39. Barnhart, *Japan Prepares for Total War*, 205.

40. Hull memo, 7 May 1941, FR Japan, 2:412.

41. Nomura to Tokyo, 7–10 May 1941, SRDJ 11523, 11544, 11546, 11572, 11607, 11637, 11638, RG 457; Tokyo to Nomura, 9 May 1941, SRDJ 11617, 11622, ibid. The document presented Hull on 11 May was a less polished version of the 12 May Japanese draft understanding. Copies of the document and the "Explanation" were made before the documents were returned at Nomura's request: 711.94/2086, RG 59. The word used in the translated intercept (SRDJ 11523) was "enthusiastic" but "fervent" seems more appropriate.

42. Hull memos, 7, 11 May 1941, FR Japan, 2:415–16; SRDJ 11542, 11616, 11625, 11626, 11629, 11699, 11700, RG 457.

43. Proposal of 9 April 1941 and draft proposal of 12 May 1941, FR Japan, 2:398–425; Tokyo to Washington, 13 May 1941, tr. 13 May 1941, SRDJ 11597, RG 457.

44. Stimson diary, 13 May 1941. Roosevelt saw Secretary Knox and Admiral King at lunch May 13: White House Usher's diary, 13 May 1941, box 320, and president's appointment diary, 13 May 1941, PPF 1-0(1), box 166, FDRL.

45. Japanese consul in Panama to Japanese embassy in Washington, 6 June 1941, SRDJ 12298, RG 457; W. W. Smith to Admiral Kimmel, 3 June 1941, A4-3, box 219, CNO secret, RG 80; Berle diary, 29 May 1941.

46. Stimson diary, 13 May, 18–20 June 1941; British military mission in Washington to British Chiefs of Staff, 7 June 1941, FO 371/26221, A4358/384/45, PRO; director NWPD to chairman General Board, 2 April 1941, A16-1, box 242, CNO secret, RG 80 (reconditioning battleships); Kimmel memo of conversation with FDR, 9 June 1941, A3-2, CNO secret, RG 80.

47. CNO memo for Knox, 7 April 1941, and director NWPD to CNO, 10 April 1941, director NWPD special file #1, box 20, Turner papers, NOA.

48. Stark to Marshall, 22 May 1941, A15-3(10), CNO secret, RG 80; CNO to CINCPAC, 13 May 1941, A16-3, box 90, SPDR, NOA; McNarney to General H. H. Arnold, 7 April 1941, WPD 4402, RG 165; Reynolds, *Anglo-American Alliance*, 229.

49. Forrest C. Pogue, *George C. Marshall: Ordeal and Hope* (New York, 1965), 135; Stimson diary, 14 May 1941.

50. Lauchlin Currie to FDR, 6 May 1941, PSF: Currie, FDRL; Proclamation Nos. 2475, 2476, FR Japan, 2:260–61.

51. Stimson diary, 13 May 1941; German foreign ministry to embassy in Japan, 11, 15, May 1941, #496, #518, DGFP, 12:777, 820; Oshima to Tokyo, 19 May 1941, SRDJ 11815, 11818, RG 457.

52. Stimson diary, 21–22 April, 15–16 May 1941; *New York Herald Tribune,* 16 May 1941; John Hickerson to J. P. Moffat, minister in Canada, 13 May 1941, 711.94/2119A, RG 59.

53. Welles memo of conversation, 23 May 1941, FR 1941, 4:210–12 and fn. 84; FO 371/27908, F4430/86/23 and FO 371/27909, F4570/86/23, PRO; Steinhardt to SecState, 25 May 1941, 704.5561/3, RG 59.

54. FR Japan, 2:427–45.

55. Grew to SecState, 14 May 1941, ibid., 145–46; Heinrichs, *Grew,* 332–33.

56. Barnhart, *Japan Prepares for Total War,* chap. 12; Tsunoda Jun, "The Navy's Role in Southern Strategy," Morley, ed., *Fateful Choice,* chap. 5; Asada Sadao, "The

Japanese Navy and the United States," Borg and Okamoto, eds., *Pearl Harbor as History*, 252–53.

57. Halifax to FO, 2 May 1941, FO 371/26147, A3245/11/45, PRO; Stimson diary, 24 April 1941.

58. Memo by Welles, 14 May 1941, PSF: France, FDRL (Pétain); 740.0011 EW/ 10929, 10980, 10993, 11173, 11212, 11293, RG 59; *New York Times*, 15 May 1941.

59. Wasson (Dakar) to SecState, 21 May 1941, 740.0011 EW/11206, RG 59; FDR to Churchill, 1 May 1941, R-38x, Kimball, ed., *Churchill-Roosevelt Correspondence*, 1:179.

60. FDR memo for Hull and Welles, 14 May 1941, 740.0011 EW/10909, RG 59; SecState to Tangier (for Murphy), 16 May 1941, ibid./11035A; Wasson (Dakar) to SecState, 21 May 1941, ibid./11206; SecState to Leahy, 15 May 1941, FR 1941, 2:171; *New York Times*, 15, 21, 22 May 1941; *New York Herald Tribune*, 18, 20 May 1941.

61. Casablanca to SecState, 19 May 1941 and Algiers to SecState, 21 May 1941 (both from Murphy), 740.0011 EW/11135, 11199, RG 59.

62. MacVeagh to FDR, 8 March 1941, PSF: Greece, FDRL; Maj. Gen. I. S. O. Playfair, *The Mediterranean and the Middle East* (5 vols.; London, 1956), 2:132–51; military attaché London, report of 24 May 1941, 740.0011 EW/11595, RG 59 ("most severe"); military attaché Cairo, report of 26 May 1941, ibid. (*Formidable*).

63. Stimson diary, 24, 27 May 1941; Long diary, 4 June 1941.

64. "Extract from a Letter Written by a Naval Officer to his Wife in England" (n.a., n.d.), PSF: subject file: Coordinator of Information, 1941, FDRL; Roskill, *War at Sea*, 1:chap. 19.

65. J. R. Beardahl memo, 27 May 1941, PSF: Navy: J. R. Beardahl, FDRL (*Modoc*); deck logs of U.S.S. *New York, Texas,* and *Wasp*, RG 24; Churchill to First Lord of the Admiralty and First Sea Lord, 28 May 1941, Prime Minister's records, PREM 3/ 191–3, PRO; OPNAV to naval operating bases at Bermuda, Argentia, et al., 28 May 1941, box 1, CINCLANT message files, NHOB, FRS.

66. FDR to Churchill, 1 May 1941, R-38x, Churchill to FDR, 3 May 1941, C-84x, FDR to Churchill, 10 May 1941, R-39x, Kimball ed., *Churchill-Roosevelt Correspondence*, 1:179–85; North Whitehead minute, 18 April 1941, FO 371/26220, A2782/ 384/45, PRO.

67. Churchill to FDR, 24 April 1941, C-81x, ibid., 173; Welles memo of conversation with Halifax, 17 May 1941, PSF: Cordell Hull: State, FDRL; Langer and Gleason, *Undeclared War*, 369; Stetson Conn and Byron Fairchild, *The Western Hemisphere: The Framework of Hemisphere Defense*, (Washington, 1960), 117–21.

68. Item #5, exec. #4, box 20, OPD, RG 165; Stark to FDR, 22 May 1941, WPD 2789, ibid.; Morgenthau presidential diary, 22 May 1941, FDRL; CINCLANT to CNO, 23 May 1941, "CINCLANT (through May 1941)" box, SOPD, NOA (warships); item #8, exec. #4, box 20, OPD, RG 165 (transports).

69. Stimson to FDR, 24 May 1941, PPF 1820, FDRL.

70. Stimson diary, 27 May 1941; Berle diary, 29 May 1941; Stark to FDR regarding Capt. Forrest Sherman memo, 19 May 1941, enclosing Isaiah Bowman to FDR, 19 May 1941, PSF: Navy, FDRL.

71. Radio Address Announcing the Proclamation of an Unlimited National Emergency, #45, Rosenman, ed., *Public Papers and Addresses of FDR, 1941*, 10:181–94.

72. *New York Times*, 28 May 1941; Sherwood, *Roosevelt and Hopkins*, 298; polls of 14 April (interviewing 3/21–26/41) and 27 June 1941 (interviewing 6/9–14/41), Gallup, *Gallup Poll*, 1:274, 286.

73. Polls of 23 April (interviewing 4/10–15/41), 21 May (interviewing 5/8–12/41), 4 June (interviewing 5/22–27/41), 15 June 1941 (interviewing 6/9–14/41), ibid., 275–84.

74. American naval attaché Lisbon to OPNAV, 26 May 1941, PSF: Cordell Hull: State, FDRL; Conn and Fairchild, *Framework of Hemisphere Defense*, 122; Stetson Conn, Rose C. Engleman, and Byron Fairchild, *Guarding the United States and Its Outposts* (Washington, 1964), 459–68.

75. Miles to COS, 7 April 1941, WPD 4402, RG 165; CNO to chief, Bureau of Ships, 27 May 1941, box 61, Ship Movements Division general correspondence, 1920–42, RG 38, NA (winter clothing); commander Support Force to CINCLANT, 8 April 1941, and reply, 16 April 1941, A3-1 Org., box 153, RG 313, FRS; Marc Milner, *North Atlantic Run: The Royal Canadian Navy and the Battle of the Convoys* (Annapolis, 1985), 41; "Report of Reconnaisance of Iceland by *Niblack*," Commander D. J. Ryan to CNO, 2 May 1941, EF22-1, box 267, CNO secret, RG 80; "Reminiscences of Vice Admiral Roland J. Smoot," oral history transcript, NOA.

76. H. P. Hill and F. Sherman to director NWPD, 6 Feb. 1941, and director NWPD to director ONI and chief, Bureau of Aeronautics, 28 Dec. 1940, box 50, SPDR, NOA; William Paul Deary, "'Short of War': Events and Decisions Culminating in the United States Naval Escort of British and Allied Convoys in the Atlantic and in the Undeclared Naval War with Germany, 1939–1941" (M.A. thesis, George Washington University, 1970), 77. The Deary thesis has been of great assistance on the Iceland question.

77. FDR to Churchill, 11 April 1941, R-36x, and Churchill to FDR, 23 May 1941, C-90x, Kimball ed., *Roosevelt-Churchill Correspondence*, 1:166, 193–95; minutes of Admiralty conference, 13 June 1941, COMNAVFOREUR records, series 2, NOA (St. John's basing); Conn, Engleman, and Fairchild, *Guarding the U.S.*, 106, fn. 17.

78. Roskill, *War at Sea*, 1:446. According to the American military attaché in Cairo, the battleship *Barham* in addition to the *Warspite* and *Valiant* was damaged (report of 5 June 1941, 740.0011 EW/11902, RG 59). Churchill described the fleet as "crippled" (Winant to SecState, 2 June 1941, ibid./11553).

79. C. S. Daniel, Admiralty director of plans, "Proposed Amendments to ABC-1," 21 May 1941, Ghormley correspondence, series 2, COMNAVFOREUR records, NOA; SPENAVO London to OPNAV, 24 May 1941, box 122, SPDR, NOA.

80. Stark to SPENAVO, 28 May 1941, ibid.; CNO to Knox, 10 June 1941, director WPD folder, special file #1, box 20, Turner papers, NOA.

81. Stimson diary, 10 May 1941; FDR to Churchill, 29 May 1941, R-44x, Kimball ed., *Churchill-Roosevelt Correspondence*, 1:199–200; Halifax to FO, 29 May 1941, FO 371/26148, A4071/11/45, PRO.

82. Berle diary, 1, 13 Feb. 1941; Morison, *Battle of the Atlantic*, 58–63.

83. Knox and Stimson to FDR, 22 April 1941 and FDR reply, 30 April 1941, PSF: Greenland, FDRL (Scoresby Sound); Berle diary, 26 May 1941; 740.0011 EW/9376, 10676, 11101, 11322, 11595, 12001, 12172, 12358; Capt. Schuirmann to State Dept., 22 April 1941, MID 2657-B-816/1-3, RG 165; Morgenthau presidential diary, 4 June 1941.

84. Halifax to FO, 29 May, FO 371/26148, A4071/11/45., PRO.

85. Churchill to FDR, 29 May 1941, C-93x, Kimball, ed., *Churchill-Roosevelt Correspondence*, 1:201; appointment diaries, 3, 4 June 1941, box 166, PPF 1-0(1), FDRL; Stimson diary, 3–6 June, 1941; minutes of Joint Army-Navy Board meeting, 13 June

1941, box 1921, U.S. Army Joint Board papers, entry 284, RG 165; Conn and Fair-child, *Framework of Hemisphere Defense*, 121-24.

86. Hull to FDR, 12 May 1941 and enclosed documents #5 and #5a (April 1941), PSF:safe:Germany, FDRL; documents #7 and #8, "Late April 1941" and "End of April 1941," Bonsal file, box 258, Long papers.

87. Hinsley, *British Intelligence*, 1:465-73; John Gilbert Winant, *Letter from Grosvenor Square* (Boston, 1947), 194-95.

88. 740.0011 EW/10471, 11175, 11229, 11278, 11283, 11356, 11466, 11526, 11563, 11614, 11645, 11691, 11879, 11902, RG 59; MID 2074-151/41, RG 165; John Colville, *The Fringes of Power: 10 Downing Street Diaries. 1939-1955* (New York, 1985), 396; Churchill to FDR, 28 May 1941, C-87x, Kimball, ed., *Churchill-Roosevelt Correspondence*, 1:187-88; Berle diary, 5 June 1941; SRDJ 11308, 11693, 11843, 12026, RG 457.

89. Kirk to SecState, 31 May 1941, 740.0011 EW/11544, RG 59; ibid. 11258, 11363, 11610, 11748; FDR to Churchill, 28 May 1941, R-43x, Kimball ed., *Churchill-Roosevelt Coorespondence*, 1:197; SecState to Winant, 27 May 1941, 740.0011 EW/11354A, RG 59.

90. Sherwood, *Roosevelt and Hopkins*, 295.

Chapter 4. June: The Russian Factor

1. Alan Clark, *Barbarossa; The Russian-German Conflict, 1941-1945* (New York, 1965), 12-13; Leach, *German Strategy Against Russia*, 168, 192.

2. Tokyo to Nanking et al., 3 June 1941, tr. 6 June 1941, SRDJ 12029, RG 457; (Ribbentrop-Oshima conversation, 3 June) Berlin to Tokyo, 4 June 1941, tr. 6 June 1941, SRDJ 12036, ibid.

3. Berlin to Tokyo, 4 June 1941, tr. 11 June 1941, SRDJ 12127, ibid. See also Berlin to Tokyo, June 14, 1941, tr. 16 June 1941, SRDJ 12235, ibid.

4. Chargé Johnson to SecState, 11 June 1941, FR 1941, 1:168-69; Hinsley, *British Intelligence*, 1:478.

5. (Examples of slowness of reports sent by pouch) 740.0011 EW/12256, 761.62/999, RG 59; Steinhardt to SecState, 12 June 1941, FR 1941, 1:754-57; Steinhardt to SecState, 19 June 1941, 740.0011 EW/12221, RG 59; Morris to SecState, 8, 21 June 1941, ibid./11763, 12296; Sterling to SecState, 7, 9 June 1941, ibid./11786, 11827; Gunther to SecState, 7 June 1941, ibid./11781; (rumors of German-Soviet deal) ibid. /11769, 12058 and 761.62/956, RG 59; (Vatican) Phillips to SecState, 16 June 1941, 740.0011 EW/12100, RG 59; SecState to Schoenfeld (Helsinki), 10 June 1941, ibid./ 11721 and Tokyo to Berlin, 14 June 1941, SRDJ 12234, RG 457.

6. Hailifax to FO, June 9, 10, FO 371/29482, N2707/78/38 and N2735/78/38, PRO; Berle diary, 19 June 1941; Stimson diary, 17 June 1941.

7. SecState to Steinhardt, 15 June 1941, aide mémoire, 16 June 1941, and Acheson memo of conversation, 16 June 1941, FR 1941, 1:761-64.

8. Steinhardt to SecState, 17 June 1941, FR 1941, 1:764-66. See also Steinhardt to Loy Henderson, 20 Oct. 1940, and Henderson to Steinhardt, 13 Dec. 1940, box 1, Loy Henderson papers, LC.

9. SecState to Winant, 14 June 1941, and Welles memo of conversation with Hal-ifax, 15 June 1941, FR 1941, 1:757-61.

10. American draft proposal, 31 May 1941, FR Japan, 2:446-54.

11. On the discussions of June 1-17: ibid., 454-83.

12. Memoranda of Conversations, 2, 6 June 1941, ibid., 454, 466, oral statement of 6 June 1941, ibid., 467–68.

13. Matsuoka to Berlin, 24 May 1941, tr. 26 May 1941, #534, U.S. Department of Defense, *The "Magic" Background of Pearl Harbor* (8 parts; Washington, 1978), 2A:271; Hamilton memo, 18 June 1941, 711.94/2162 13/14, RG 59; SecState to Grew, 6 June 1941, ibid./2150A; Grew to SecState, 6 June 1941, FR 1941, 4:254. An example of press speculation on the talks: *New York Times*, 6 June 1941.

14. Tokyo to Vichy, 16 June 1941, tr. 17 June 1941, #794, *"Magic" Background*, 2A:411; Tokyo to Vichy, 17 June 1941, tr. 19 June 1941, #796, ibid., 412.

15. Grew to SecState, 9 June 1941, FR 1941, 5:174; Grew to SecState, 10 June 1941, ibid., 4:264–65.

16. Hamilton and Adams memos, 23, 25 June 1941, FR 1941, 4:276–80.

17. Memo of conversation, oral statement and draft proposal, 21 June 1941, FR Japan 1931–41, 2:483–92.

18. Clark, *Barbarossa*, chap. 3.

19. Curzio Malaparte, *The Volga Rises in Europe* (London, 1957), 102, as quoted in Clark, *Barbarossa*, 134–35.

20. Martin Van Creveld, *Supplying War; Logistics from Wallenstein to Patton* (London, 1977), 150–51.

21. Grew Diary, 22 June 1941, Joseph C. Grew Papers, Harvard University, Cambridge; Stimson to FDR, 23 June 1941, PSF:War Department:Henry Stimson, FDRL; letter from Polish ambassador in Washington, 22 June 1941, FO 371/29485, N3283/78/38, PRO; Leahy to SecState, 22, 23, June 1941, 740.0011 EW/12304, 12400, RG 59.

22. FDR to Leahy, 26 June 1941, PSF:France, FDRL; Halifax to FO, 7 July 1941, FO 371/29486, N3540/78/38, PRO.

23. Morris to SecState, 25 June 1941, 740.0011 EW/12458, RG 59; military attaché London, report of 28 June 1941, ibid./13771; military attaché Moscow, report of 30 June 1941, ibid.; Steinhardt to SecState, 26 June 1941, ibid./12615; Stimson to FDR, 23 June 1941, PSF:War Department:Stimson, FDRL; 30 June 1941 conference, box 885, secretary of war conferences, conferences 1938–42, entry 31, army-chief of staff secretariat (cited as COS secretariat conferences), RG 165.

24. 23 June 1941 conference, ibid.; Stimson diary, 2 July 1941.

25. Steinhardt to SecState, 2, 3, 7, 8, 10, 16, 22, July 1941, 740.0011 EW/12741, 12790, 12864, 12907, 12990, 13000, 13232, 13354, RG 59; Steinhardt to SecState, 1 July 1941, 124.61/187, RG 59; Welles to Steinhardt, 17 July 1941, 740.0011 EW/13317A, RG 59; military attaché Moscow, report of 19 July 1941, ibid./13771.

26. Morris to SecState, 30 June, 12 July 1941, ibid./12649, 13078; Harrison to SecState 10, 23 July 1941, ibid./12975, 13420; Leahy to SecState, 14 July 1941, ibid./13151.

27. Memo for General McNarney, 5 July 1941, on meeting in War Cabinet office, #190, minutes of U.S.-British liaison conferences, 1941, series 2, COMNAVFOREUR files, NOA; Moscow military mission to Joint Intelligence Committee (JIC), 17 July 1941, FO 371/29487, N3959/78/38, PRO; Victor Mallet to Sir Orme Sargent, 13 July 1941, FO 371/26522, C8489/19/18, PRO; Reginald Leeper, "Political Aspects of a German Defeat by Russia," 7 July 1941, FO 371/29486, N3718/78/38, PRO; military attaché London, report of 15 July 1941, 740.0011 EW/13771, RG 59.

28. Berle Diary, 15, 16, 23 July 1941.

29. *New York Times*, 21, 24, July 1941.

30. Acting SecState to Steinhardt, 23 June 1941, FR 1941, 1:767-68.

31. Acting SecState to Steinhardt, 28 June 1941, ibid. 773; Henderson memo of conversation with Oumansky and others, 2 July 1941, ibid., 784-85.

32. Welles memo of conversation with Halifax, 10 July 1941, ibid., 788-89; Winant to SecState, 9 July 1941, 740.0011 EW/12943, RG 59.

33. George C. Herring, Jr., *Aid to Russia, 1941-1946: Strategy, Diplomacy and Origins of the Cold War* (New York, 1973), 11; Leighton and Coakley, *Global Logistics and Strategy*, 126-27. Russian supply problems: FR 1941, 1:769-802.

34. Berle Diary, 19 June, 8-11 July 1941 with memoranda to FDR, 8, 9 July 1941.

35. Steinhardt to SecState, 9 July 1941, FR 1941, 1:179-80; Winant to SecState, July 9, 1941, 740.0011 EW/12943, RG 59; Loy Henderson memo of conversation with Polish ambassador Jan Ciechanowski, 30 July 1941, 860C.01/589, RG 59 (Poles seek American intervention); Berle memo to FDR, 8 July 1941, PSF: Great Britain: Winston Churchill, FDRL (national committees in USSR); FR 1941, 1:236-43.

36. FDR to Churchill, 14 July 1941, R-50x, Kimball, ed., *Churchill-Roosevelt Correspondence*, 1:221-22; Berle diary, 8 July 1941.

37. Oliver Harvey diary, 22 July 1941, John Harvey, ed., *The War Diaries of Oliver Harvey* (London, 1978), 22.

38. Sherwood, *Roosevelt and Hopkins*, 308.

39. Winant to SecState, 30 July 1941, FR 1941, 1:243-45; draft telegram, SecState to Winant for Biddle, 5 Aug. 1941, ibid., 247-48; Winant to SecState, 30 July, 1941, 740.0011 EW/13548, RG 59; Anthony Eden, *The Memoirs of Anthony Eden, Earl of Avon: The Reckoning* (Boston, 1962), 316.

40. July 1941 charts, briefing chart file, NOA; "Patrol Reports of Task Forces 2 and 3," 26 April-30 August 1941, O. M. Read memo for Turner, 30 Sept. 1941, box 82, SPDR, NOA; Ghormley to Pound, 22 May 22-30 July 1941, ADM 205/9, PRO.

41. Deck log of U.S.S. *Texas*, 11-30 June 1941, RG 24, NA; U-203 to commander U-boats, 20 June 1941, SRGN 1264, German navy, U-boat messages, RG 457, NA.

42. Commander U-boats to all boats, 21 June 1941, SRGN 1281, ibid; also SRGN 1061, 1210, 1212, 1268, 1273, 1278, ibid.; *Fuehrer Naval Conferences*, 3: 9 July 1941.

43. Deck log of U.S.S. *Yorktown*, 4 June 1941, RG 24; Churchill to FDR, 23 May 1941, C-90x, Kimball, ed., *Churchill-Roosevelt Correspondence*, 1:193; Roskill, *War at Sea*, 1:542 and map opposite.

44. Hinsley, *British Intelligence*, 345-46.

45. FDR to Hull and Welles, 11 June 1941, PSF: Cordell Hull: State Department, FDRL.

46. Welles memo of conversation, 28 June 1941, FR 1941, 2:783; Gerow memo for adjutant general, 5 July 1941, WPD 4493, RG 165; Gerow diary, 19 June 1941, exec. #10, item 2, box 49, OPD executive files, RG 165; Conn, Engelman, and Fairchild, *Guarding the U.S.*, 479-85.

47. Morison, *Battle of the Atlantic*, 76.

48. Perkins (Copenhagen) to SecState, 10 July 1941, 740.0011 EW/13036, RG 59; memo for COS, 12 July 1941, box 889, COS secretariat conferences, RG 165; OPNAV to ALUSNA, 12 July 1941, box 1, CINCLANT World War II message files, NHOB, FRS; Stimson Diary, 12 July 1941; Morgenthau presidential diary, 8 July 1941 (FDR thrilled).

49. Task Force 16 OPLAN (Operations Plan) 1-41, 22 July 1941, A4-3 Ships and Aircraft Movements, box 108, CINCLANT GAF, RG 313 (warships to Iceland); military attaché London, report of 18 April 1941, 740.0011 EW/10345, RG 59 and

naval attaché Vichy, report of 2 May 1941, ibid. /12137 (bombings at Brest); ibid. /12043A, 12473, 12727A (U-boat bases); Cole (Murphy) to SecState, 7 June 1941, ibid./11737, 11738 (Vichy policy); Langer, *Vichy Gamble*, 157–60.

50. Kittredge, "British-American Naval Cooperation," 540–41; Stark memo, 1 July 1941, Iceland dispatches and signed orders, box 50, SPDR, NOA. The president saw Stark 25 June (appointment diaries, box 166, PPF:1-0(1), FDRL).

51. "Abstract of History of Atlantic Convoys as Communicated by Commander Rowbotham, July 13, 1942," "Convoys" folder, box 11, Morison Papers, NOA; memo on North Atlantic Convoy routes, 14 Dec. 1941, box 116, SPDR, NOA; Marc Milner, *North Atlantic Run*, chap. 2; Historical Section, Admiralty, *Naval Staff History, Second World War: Defeat of the Enemy Attack on Shipping: A Study of Policy and Operations* (London, 1957), 33, 71; Morison, *Battle of the Atlantic*, chap. 5; Roskill, *War at Sea*, 1:453–67.

52. Special naval observer London to OPNAV, 13 June 1941, box 122, SPDR, NOA.

53. On these historical tensions in the U.S. Navy: Dean C. Allard to author, 16 July 1985; Allard, "Anglo-American Differences During World War I," *Military Affairs* (April 1980), 44:75–81.

54. CINCLANT to CNO, 2 July 1941, A14-1 (jacket 2), box 108, CINCLANT GAF, RG 313. Also CINCLANT to CNO, 18 June 1941, A7-3(1), box 153, ibid.

55. President's appointment diary, 3 June 1941, PPF 1-0(1), box 166, FDRL; Robert William Love, Jr., "Ernest Joseph King," Love, ed., *The Chiefs of Naval Operations* (Annapolis, 1980), 138; *Time*, 2 June 1941 ("storm within him").

56. CNO to CINCLANT, 16 July 1941, box 82, SPDR, NOA; Stimson diary, 24 June 1941; Halifax to FO, 25 June 1941, FO 371/26221, A4901/384/45, PRO.

57. CNO to special naval observer London, 20 June 1941, box 122, SPDR, NOA; minutes of 2 July 1941 meeting, box 1921, U.S. Army Joint Board Papers, RG 165.

58. Stark to Capt. Charles M. Cooke, 31 July 1941, PHA, 16:2175 (Stark's advice to FDR); Western Hemisphere Defense Plan Three, microfilm SPD-19, WPL 50 and 51 and related correspondence, NOA.

59. CNO to CINCLANT, 22 May 1941, A3-1/DD, box 3, CNO confidential, RG 80 and citations in fn. 26, chap. 2.

60. Stark to FDR, 9 July 1941, "Iceland" folder, box 4, PSF:Safe, FDRL.

61. Appointment diaries, PPF 1-0(1), box 166, and White House usher's diary, box 320, FDR papers, FDRL; CINCLANT to CNO, 13 July 1941, microfilm SPD-19, NOA.

62. (Plan Four) PHA, 5:2294–5; Admiral Charles Little to Admiral Sir Dudley Pound, 15 July 1941, ADM 205/9, PRO.

63. CNO to CINCLANT, 17 July 1941, microfilm SPD-19, NOA. U-boat locations: ALUSNA to OPNAV, 13 June 1941, file #5, COMNAVFOREUR records; ALUSNA to OPNAV, April–June 1941, microfilm reel 2586, "Convoy, In" series, OPNAV message files, RG 38; OPNAV to CINCLANT, June–July 1941, Box 25, CINCLANT World War II message files, NHOB, FRS.

64. On convoy planning and problems in July: microfilm SPD-19, NOA; memorandum of conference in CNO office, 22 July 1941, "Conferences" folder (no record group), NOA; Under Secretary of External Affairs to Rear Adm. P. W. Nelles, 30 June 1941, file 1550-157/1, Directorate of History, National Defense Headquarters, Ottawa, Canada; Commander W.G.D. Lund, "The Royal Canadian Navy's Quest for

Autonomy in the Northwest Atlantic: 1941-1943," *Naval War College Review*, 32 (May-June, 1980), 75-77; Milner, *North Atlantic Run*, 58-61.

65. Emory Land, chairman of U.S. Maritime Commission to Knox, 22 July 1941, WPD 4493, box 285, RG 165; Stark to Land, 25 July 1941, "Great Britain, Pre-War Aid to," folder, box 156, group 24, Hopkins papers; correspondence in SPD-19, NOA; Ghormley to Pound, 30 July 1941 (Ghormley apparently had not been informed by 30 July that the agreement had been rejected); memo of conference in CNO office, 22 July 1941, "Conferences" folder, NOA; CNO to CINCLANT, 29 July 1941, box 82, SPDR, NOA.

66. Admiralty Historical Section, *Naval Staff History*, 1A:71 (U-boat handicaps); Hinsley, *British Intelligence*, 2:163-73 (ULTRA advantage); *Fuehrer Naval Conferences*, 2: 22 May 1941 and also 9 and 25 July, ibid. ("greatly hampered"); Jürgen Rohwer, *The Critical Convoy Battles of March 1943: The Battle of HX 229/SC 122* (Annapolis, 1977), 23-24 (U-boat shift); W.A.B. Douglas and Jürgen Rohwer, "The Most Thankless Task Revisited: Convoys, Escorts, and Radio Intelligence in the Western Atlantic, 1941-1943," James A. Boutilier, ed., *The RCN in Retrospect* (Vancouver, 1982), 192 ("almost impossible"); Roskill, *War at Sea* 1: chap. 21 and Appendix R, 618 (tonnage lost); "Daily Summary of Naval Events," June-Sept. 1941, #129, COMNAVFOREUR records and CNO intelligence reports on convoys, 12 July-5 Sept. 1941, A8-2, box 156, CINCLANT GAF, RG 313 (no ships lost).

67. 30 July, 9 Aug. 1941 charts, daily briefing charts, NOA; Commander Task Force 1 to commander Task Group 1.2, 21 July 1941, box 1, "CINCLANT June-September 1941" box, SOPD, NOA; Commander Task Force 4 to U.S.S. *Lansdale* and *Hughes*, 5 Aug. 1941, box 1, CINCLANT World War II message files, NHOB, FRS.

68. "Latest Returns on Princeton Ballot," PSF:Public Opinion, FDRL; Tokyo to Vichy, 22 June 1941, tr. 23 June 1941, SRDJ 12426 and Tokyo to Berlin, 2 July 1941, SRDJ 12722, RG 457; Dallek, *Roosevelt and American Foreign Policy*, 276-78.

Chapter 5. July: The Containment of Japan

1. On Japanese policy deliberations 22 June-2 July 1941: Hosoya, "Japanese-Soviet Neutrality Pact," Morley, ed., *Fateful Choice*, 94-104; Asada, "Japanese Navy and the United States," Borg and Okamoto, eds., *Pearl Harbor as History*, 252-55; Nobutaka Ike, tr. and ed., *Japan's Decision for War: Records of the 1941 Policy Conferences* (Stanford, 1967), 56-90; Michael Barnhart, *Japan Prepares for Total War*, chap. 11.

2. FDR to Ickes, 1 July 1941, as quoted in Langer and Gleason, *Undeclared War*, 646.

3. Official appreciations of Japanese intentions: R. E. Schuirmann memo for Welles, 9 July 1941, FR 1941, 4:298-99; Max Schmidt (Far Eastern Division) memo, 12 July 1941, 740.0011 EW/13905, RG 59; Hamilton, Adams, Langdon, and Schmidt memos, 23-25 June, 1941, FR 1941, 4:276-80, 981-85; Turner to CNO, 11 July 1941, and CNO to Admiral Thomas C. Hart, 3 July 1941, director NWPD Special File #1, box 20, Turner Papers, NOA; Turner to Knox, 26 June 1941, A1-2/EF37, box 219, CNO secret, RG 80; Australian legation in Washington to Canberra, 24 June 1941, FO 371/29484, N3047/78/38, PRO; OPNAV to CINCAF, CINCPAC, CINCLANT, 3 July 1941, PHA, 14:1396.

4. Tokyo (Matsuoka) to Berlin, 2 July 1941, tr. 3 July 1941, #725–726, *"Magic" Background*, 2A:373; Winant to SecState, 4 July 1941, 740.0011 EW/12770, RG 59; military attaché London, report of 5 July 1941, 740.0011 PW/384, ibid.; Eden memo, "Japanese Intentions in Indochina," 6 July 1941, War Cabinet WP (41) 154, FO 371/27763, F5953/9/61, PRO. On 4 July the British Foreign Office instructed its embassy in Moscow to inform the Soviet government that it had "sure information" that the Japanese had decided "only to watch developments in Eastern Siberia" for the time being (FO 371/29486, N3669/48/38, PRO). On 4 July Winant informed Washington of what appears to have been the contents of Tokyo's 2 July message (740.0011 EW/12770). Presumably he would not have bothered if the British were still depending on American decrypts. So it seems reasonable to conclude that they were themselves decrypting Japanese diplomatic traffic by this time and had independent access to the 2 July intercept.

5. R. E. Schuirmann to Welles, 9 July 1941, FR 1941, 4:298–99; Ghormley to Pound, 4 July 1941, ADM 205/9, PRO; Welles to Grew, 4 July 1941, FR 1941, 4:994.

6. Navy Department to naval attaché, Tokyo, 3 July 1941, 761.94/1365, RG 59; A. H. McCollum to director, ONI, 2 July 1941, PHA 15:1852; Brig. Gen. Leonard T. Gerow diary, 3 July 1941, exec. #10, item #2, box 49, OPD, RG 165; Gauss to SecState, 4 July 1941, 740.0011 EW/12815, RG 59.

7. "Reminiscences of Rear Admiral Arthur N. McCollum," U.S. Naval Institute, Annapolis, 1973, 1:310–16, NOA; Admiral Alan G. Kirk oral history transcript, Columbia University Oral History Collection; "Reminiscences of Rear Admiral Walter C. W. Ansel," U.S. Naval Institute, Annapolis, 1972, p. 88, NOA.

8. Turner to Stark, 11 July 1941, director NWPD special file #1, box 20, Turner papers, NOA; Welles to Winant, 7 July 1941, 740.0011 EW/12771, RG 59.

9. 740.0011 EW/13269, 13297, 13500–13502, 13629, RG 59; Grew to SecState, 29 July 1941 and SecState to Grew, 1 Aug. 1941, ibid./13517.

10. #801, #812–824, #834–872, *"Magic" Background*, 2A:414, 419–29, 435–56.

11. Tokyo to Singapore, 17 July 1941, #822, and Canton to Tokyo, 14 July 1941, #835, *"Magic" Background*, 2A:428, 436; Stimson diary, 29 July 1941; assistant naval attaché Shanghai, report of 19 July 1941, 740.0011 PW/357, RG 59; Wohlstetter, *Pearl Harbor*, 98–131.

12. #100, #318, #354–57, #365–71, #377–79, #382, #384 ("worse to worst"), #400–404, #410–11, #420, #464, *"Magic" Background*, 2A:54–232 passim; *New York Times*, 4, 5 July 1941; minutes of meeting, 12 July 1941, U.S. Joint Army-Navy Board, U.S. Army Joint Board papers, box 1921, entry 284, RG 165; Welles memos of conversations with Halifax, 3, 10 July 1941, FR 1941, 4:289–90, 300–303; Morgenthau presidential diary, 2 July 1941; OPNAV to CINCAF, CINCPAC, 3 July 1941, PHA, 14:1397.

13. Grew to SecState, 17 July 1941, FR 1941, 4:1007.

14. Lu, *From Marco Polo Bridge*, 174–84.

15. Acting SecState to Grew, 30 June 1941, FR 1941, 4:990; Acting SecState to Grew, 9 July 1941, 740.0011 EW 1939/12731, RG 59.

16. Turner to CNO, 21 July 1941, FR Japan, 2:517.

17. Hamilton memo, 17 July 1941, FR 1941, 4:323–24; #144–49, *"Magic" Background*, 2A:79–82.

18. Grew to SecState, 18, 23 July 1941, FR 1941, 4:328–29, 337–38.

19. Tokyo to Berlin, 19 July 1941, tr. 21 July, #593, *"Magic" Background*, 2A:304.

20. Welles memo, 23 July 1941, FR Japan, 2:525–26.

21. Welles memo, 24 July 1941, ibid., 529; Washington to Tokyo, 24 July 1941, #171, "Magic" Background, 2A:97.

22. SRDJ 12752, 12856 ("concerted air and submarine defense"), 12986, 13045, 13082, 13150, 13240, 13251, 13365, 13681 ("cunning dragon"), 13817, 6 June-2 Aug. 1941, RG 457; Tokyo to Nanking et al., 29 May 1941, tr. 3 June, SRH 018, Collection of Japanese Diplomatic Messages, July 1938-January 1942, Department of the Army Intelligence Files, RG 457.

23. "American-Dutch-British Conversations, Singapore, April 1941 Report," PHA, 15:1551-84; Stark and Marshall to special navy and army observers, London, 3 July 1941, PHA 15:1677-79; Capt. W. E. Purnell, report of conversations with Dutch naval authorities at Batavia, 10-14 Jan. 1941, ABDA-ANZAC correspondence, 1941-42, box 117, SPDR, NOA; CINCAF to OPNAV, 3 March 1941, Atlantic dispatches, box 122, ibid.; Hart to Stark, 31 July 1941, director NWPD special file #1, box 20, Turner papers, NOA; OPNAV to naval attaché London, 13 May 1941, series I, COMNAVFOREUR records, NOA; OPNAV to CINCAF, 6 March 1941, OPNAV message file, microreel 2893, RG 38, NA (cypher machine).

24. Morison, Rising Sun, 158-60; Gwyer, part 1, in Butler, Grand Strategy, 3:267-68; Arthur J. Marder, Old Friends, New Enemies: The Royal Navy and the Imperial Japanese Navy: Strategic Illusions, 1936-1941 (Oxford, 1981), 219-21.

25. CNO to CINCLANT, 26 July 1941, box 82, SPDR, NOA; British Naval Detachment in Washington to Admiralty, 17 July 1941, FO 371/26621, A5657/384/45, PRO.

26. Gwyer, part 1, in Butler, Grand Strategy, 3:274-80; S. W. Kirby, Singapore: The Chain of Disaster (London, 1971), 106-13.

27. Memo by A. Cadogan, n.d., PREM 3/156-1, PRO; War Cabinet Defense Committee meeting, 1 Aug. 1941, CAB 69/8, PRO; memo by Lord Ismay, "A Further Southward Move by Japan," n.d., CAB 120/20, PRO; FO 371/27978, F8633 and F8634/1299/23, PRO.

28. Winant to SecState, 1 Aug. 1941, and draft reply, 740.0011 PW/371, RG 59.

29. Bruce, Australian High Commissioner, to Eden, 15 July 1941, FO 371/27764, F6733/9/61, PRO; Halifax to FO, 6 Aug. 1941, FO 371/27974, F7443/1299/23, PRO; Welles memo of conversation with Halifax, 4 Aug. 1941, 740.0011 PW/401, RG 59.

30. "Military Aspects of the Situation That Would Result from the Retention by the U.S. of a Military (Including Naval) Commitment to the Philippines," n.d., WPD 3389-29, RG 165. On the reinforcement of the Philippines: Pogue, Marshall: Ordeal and Hope, 176-83; Louis Morton, The Fall of the Philippines (Washington, 1953), chap. 2; Mark Skinner Watson, The War Department: Chief of Staff: Prewar Plans and Preparations (Washington, 1950), 417-39.

31. J. L. McCrea to Stark, 5 Feb. 1941, A2-A14/EG52, CNO Secret, RG 80, NA.

32. Turner to Capt. A. W. Clarke, 7 June 1941, ABDA-ANZAC correspondence, box 117, SPDR, NOA; comments by British Chiefs of Staff on telegraphic summary of April 1941 report, #8, American-Dutch-British conference at Singapore, April 1941, Series II, COMNAVFOREUR records, NOA.

33. Gerow memo for COS, 30 July 1941 (not sent), WPD 4561-1, RG 165.

34. Visayan project: The Adjutant General (TAG) to Chief of Ordnance, 16 April 1941, WPD 3251, RG 165, NA; Stimson to FDR, 29 Mar. 1941, PSF: War Department, FDRL; MacArthur to Marshall, 1 Feb. 1941, OCS 20891/88, papers of the Office of Chief of Staff, RG 165, NA.

35. Charles F. Romanus and Riley Sunderland, *Stilwell's Mission to China* (Washington, 1953), 17–29; Arthur N. Young, *China and the Helping Hand, 1937–1945* (Cambridge, MA, 1963), 116–53, 187–92; Michael Schaller, *The U.S. Crusade in China, 1938–1945* (New York, 1979), 56–58, 74–82.

36. Morgenthau presidential diary, 10 July 1941; FDR to Welles, 29 July 1941, FR 1941, 5:532; Guy Wint memo, 15 July 1941, FO371/27847, F7694/4366/61, PRO.

37. Welles to Hopkins, 7 July 1941, FR 1941, 5:670–71.

38. Anderson, *Standard-Vacuum Oil*, 158–68; Jonathan G. Utley, "Upstairs, Downstairs at Foggy Bottom: Oil Exports and Japan, 1940–41," *Prologue: The Journal of the National Archives* (Spring 1976), 8:20; H. W. Moseley to L. H. Price, 21 June 1941, and J. C. Green to Dean Acheson, 19 July 1941, 811.20 (D) Regulations/3066, 3844 1/2, RG 59; J. J. O'Connell memo for Morgenthau, 3 July 1941, Morgenthau diary, 3 July 1941 (East Coast gasoline shortage).

39. Morgenthau diary, 8 July 1941; G. S. Walden to Hornbeck, 10 July 1941, 894.24/1559, RG 59.

40. Princeton Public Opinion Research Project, June 3, 1941, PPF 1820, FDRL; letters and postcards from Americans in July 1941, 894.24, RG 59; Morgenthau diary, 15 July 1941.

41. Ibid., 8 July 1941; Anderson, *Standard-Vacuum Oil*, 168–71; Hamilton memo, 22 July 1941, FR 1941, 4:834; Stark to Hull, 22 July 1941 and enclosures, ibid., 835–40.

42. Halifax to FO, 8 July 1941, FO 371/27763, F5959/9/61, PRO.

43. Halifax to FO, 15 July 1941, FO 371/27763, F6273/9/61, PRO; Morgenthau to FDR with excerpt enclosed from *Foreign Relations of U.S.*, 24 July 1940, OF 176, FDRL.

44. D. W. Bell memo of cabinet meeting 24 July 1941, E. H. Foley, Jr., to Bell, 24 July 1941, and "Memorandum of Policy To Be Carried Out in Administering the Freezing Control Order for Japan and China," 25 July 1941, Morgenthau diary, 24, 25 July 1941.

45. PRO:FO 371/27763, F6273/9/61 and F6473/9/61; FO 371/27908, F86/86/23.

46. FO 371, 27972–27975, F6472–F7664/1299/23, PRO.

47. "The Economic Vulnerability of Japan in Petroleum," prepared for the Office of Administrator of Export Control by the Interdepartmental Committee on Petroleum, April 1941, box 10, OSS records, RG 226.

48. Berle diary, 23 July 1941.

49. Soviet Embassy Information Bulletin, 5 Aug. 1941, 740.0011 EW/13900, RG 59. On war developments in late July: Clark, *Barbarossa*, chaps. 4–7.

50. Van Creveld, *Supplying War*, 142–80; Leach, *German Strategy*, chap. 8.

51. Clark, *Barbarossa*, 81.

52. *New York Times*, 21 July–31 July 1941; *Washington Post*, 14 July–1 Aug. 1941.

53. Acting SecState to Bern, 30 July 1941, 740.0011 EW/13606B, RG 59.

54. Steinhardt to SecState, 29 July 1941, military attaché Rome, report of 24 July 1941, Leahy to SecState, 1 Aug. 1941, ibid., /13519, 14790, 13606.

55. Berle diary, 31 July 1941; Leach, *Hitler's Strategy*, 205.

56. Stimson diary, 28, 30 July 1941.

57. Morgenthau presidential diary, 4 Aug. 1941; Davies memo, 31 July 1941, box 69, Joseph E. Davies papers, LC; John Morton Blum, *From the Morgenthau Diaries: Years of Urgency, 1938–1941* (Boston, 1965), 263.

58. Welles memo of conversation with Oumansky, 24 July 1941, FR 1941, 1:795-97; Alexander Schnee memo of meeting 28 July 1941, ibid., 799-802. On aid to Russia in late July: Herring, *Aid to Russia*, 11-14; Blum, *Years of Urgency*, 263-65.

59. Morgenthau as quoted in Blum, ibid., 265; Stimson diary, 1 Aug. 1941.

60. Steinhardt to SecState, 1 Aug. 1941 (two telegrams), FR 1941, 1:814-15; FDR to Coy, 2 Aug. 1941, Roosevelt, *FDR Letters*, 2:1195-96.

61. FDR to Stimson, 27 Aug. 1941 and report on munitions to Russia, 25 Aug. 1941, book 6, Hopkins papers, FDRL; Oumansky to Welles, 29 July 1941, FR 1941, 1:798; Alexander Schnee memo of meeting 28 July, ibid., 799-802; Stimson to Oumansky, 4 Aug. 1941, 337F, box 162, Army Air Force central decimal files, RG 18, NA.

62. These figures were known by July 21: see Halifax to FO, 21 July 1941, FO371/27972, F6599/1299/23, PRO. On Japanese forces in Manchuria: message from Hawaii, 29 July 1941 (possibly from an intercepted message), 740.0011 EW/14838, RG 59.

63. Green to Acheson, 19 July 1941, 811.20(D)Regulations/3884 1/2, RG 59; George Luthringer memo, 30 July 1941, FR 1941, 4:844-46.

64. Memo for Secretary's files, 30 July 1941, Morgenthau diary, ("happiest solution"); Welles to Collectors of Customs, 1 Aug. 1941, 811.20(D) Regulations/3912A, RG 59; Halifax to FO, 2 Aug. 1941, FO 371/27974, F7213/1299/23, PRO.

65. Acting SecState to Grew, 4 July 1941, FR 1941, 4:994-95; Welles memo of conversation, 10 July 1941, ibid., 301.

66. Memo by Hamilton, 31 July 1941, 740.0011 EW/1587, RG 59; memo by Grew, 26 July 1941, FR Japan, 2:532-34; Roosevelt to Churchill, 26 July 1941, #R-52x, Kimball, ed., *Churchill-Roosevelt Correspondence*, 1:225.

67. SecState to Grew, 5 Aug. 1941, 740.0011 PW/417A, RG 59.

68. This interpretation differs from that of Anderson (*Standard-Vacuum Oil*, 177-78) and Utley ("Upstairs, Downstairs," *Prologue*, 8:24-28), who argue that Roosevelt's intent is to be found in the Cabinet decision of July 24 to ship some oil, that the delay in taking action on exchange applications was technical, at the outset anyway, and that Acheson and Foreign Funds Control converted the delay into a stall while the president was away at Argentia. These are valuable studies of the bureaucratic machinery of oil restriction, but on the point of the president's knowledge and intent I disagree.

The key document on this score is the minutes of the Interdepartmental Policy Committee on Foreign Funds Control meeting 29 July ("Memorandum for the Secretary's Files," 30 July 1941, Morgenthau diary, 426:19) at which Acheson said that he had seen Welles who felt that "for the next week or so the happiest solution" would be "to take no action on Japanese applications." Acheson repeated this statement without the time factor in his memoirs (Dean Acheson, *Present at the Creation: My Years in the State Department* (New York, 1969), 26). In fact the time frame Acheson had in mind was probably two weeks. This was the initial trial period when no applications would be approved which had been suggested by Green (memo for Acheson, 19 July 1941, 811.20(D) Regulations/3884 1/2, RG 59) and Luthringer (memo for Acheson, 30 July 1941, FR 1941, 4:844-45). Luthringer attached a note to the memo saying that it was an attempt "to embody the suggestions which you [Acheson] made following the meeting of the Interdepartmental Policy Committee yesterday evening [29 July, the day Acheson saw Welles]." Two weeks from 29 July would be 12 Aug., the day the conference in fact concluded and shortly before Welles returned to Washington by air.

Other document collections examined show withholding of licenses for technical reasons, but are not incompatible with the thesis offered here: box 513, Foreign Funds Control files, general correspondence, Japan, Department of Justice Alien Property Accession 61A109, RG 131 (in custody of Treasury Department, Washington); central files, office of administrator of Export Control, entry 97, RG 169, FRS.

Given the close association of Welles and Roosevelt, the fact that Welles was currently Acting Secretary of State, and the vital importance of the issue, it seems inconceivable that Welles did not secure the president's approval for this course of action, or inaction. The technical need for delay meshed with the policy need for holding up delivery of oil at least until Roosevelt could review the situation with Churchill.

Furthermore, it is difficult to believe that Dean Acheson would pursue a course of action which he believed to be contrary to the wishes of the president. Acheson's career in government had begun dismally in 1933 when he was appointed Under Secretary of the Treasury by Roosevelt and then abruptly dismissed for refusing to sign an order making the devaluation of the dollar legal. That experience, interrupting for eight years his high ambitions for public service, made a lasting impression on him, according to his biographer (David S. McLellan, *Dean Acheson: The State Department Years* (New York, 1976), 25–29). He was not happy with that performance, he reminisced years later in retirement. He had not had enough consideration for the problems of the president. Right or not, an assistant to the president could get into "terrible problems" by "allowing things to get to a point where trouble occurs." He must be "very alert and watchful" to consider the president's position and interests "twice as much as your own" (as quoted in McLellan, *Acheson*, 28). Acheson now had a second chance, this time as assistant secretary of state. It seems very doubtful that he would have jeopardized that chance by again acting against what he took to be the wishes of the president.

69. As quoted in Watson, *Chief of Staff*, 438–39.

70. On air reinforcement of the Philippines: Craven and Cate, *Army Air Forces in World War II*, 1:175–78, 600–605; DeWitt S. Copp, *Forged in Fire: Strategy and Decisions in the Air War over Europe, 1940–1945* (Garden City, N.Y., 1982), 142–50; Daniel F. Harrington, "A Careless Hope: American Air Power and Japan, 1941," *Pacific Historical Review* (May 1979), 48:217–38; Michael S. Sherry, *The Rise of American Air Power: The Creation of Armageddon* (New Haven, 1987), 100–115.

71. Arnold to COS, 5 Dec. 1940, "Expected Production of Aircraft up to June 1941," box 40, General of the Army H. H. Arnold papers, LC; "Special Air Corps Report, Fiscal Year 1941," box 1, Stimson safe file, RG 107; Stimson to Representative Carl Vinson, 24 July 1941, box 2, ibid.

72. Arnold to Lovett, 8 Jan. 1941, box 1, ibid.

73. Stimson diary, 10 July 1941; conference 29 July 1941, box 889, notes on conferences, Army-COS Secretariat, 1941–42, COS files, entry 12, RG 165; Sir Archibald Sinclair to Hopkins, 27 July 1941, "Aircraft Allocations" folder, box 38, Arnold papers; Brig. Gen. Ralph Royce to Arnold, 7 June 1941, "Bombers" folder, box 41, Arnold papers; military attaché London, report of 15 May 1941, 740.0011 EW/ 11293, RG 59.

74. Arnold memo for COS, March 1941, "Hopkins Data on British Needs" folder, box 43, Arnold papers; Arnold to Lovett, May 8, 1941, box 41, ibid.

75. George Strong, assistant COS to COS, 2 March 1940, WPD 4192, box 230, RG 165.

76. Military attaché Cairo, report of 29 June 1941, 740.0011 EW/13771, RG 59. On Crete, the Philippines, and air power, see also: Archer M. R. Allen, office of U.S. Naval Observer in Singapore, to CNO, 5 Aug. 1941, WPD 4192, box 230, RG 165; (n.a.) "The Employment of Aviation in Naval Warfare: Staff Presentation," Naval War College records, SPDR, NA; "The Airborne Invasion of Crete," WPD 4402-100, RG 165.

77. "Development of Air Base Facilities on Mid-Pacific Islands," 686 Hawaii to Philippines-15, box 153, Arnold papers; Craven and Cate, *Army Air Forces in World War II*, 1:178.

78. Carl Spaatz to Stark, 5 Aug. 1941, A4-3/EF 13–45, box 220, RG 80; memorandum on air routes to the Philippines, 27 July 1941, Intelligence Division, Office of Chief of Air Corps, 686 Hawaii-Philippines-64, box 153, Arnold papers.

79. Conference of 28 July 1941, "Secretary of War Conferences" folder, box 885, COS secretariat, RG 165.

Chapter 6. Aug.–Sept.: Crossing the Threshold

1. Theodore A. Wilson, *The First Summit: Roosevelt and Churchill at Placentia Bay, 1941* (Boston, 1969), 5–7.

2. Steinhardt to SecState, 2 Aug. 1941, 740.0011 EW/13642, RG 59; Steinhardt to SecState 5 Aug. 1941, FR 1941, 1:634–35, radioed to president 6 Aug. as 740.0011 EW/13649C, RG 59.

3. Morris to SecState, 2, 6, 7 Aug. 1941, 740.0011 EW/13626, 13745, 13781, RG 59, radioed to president 4, 7, 8 Aug. 1941 as ibid./13649A, D, E; Joint Intelligence Sub-Committee, "German Intentions up to the End of 1941," minutes of War Cabinet meeting, 8 Aug. 1941, FO 371/26523, C9529/19/18, PRO. The American Berlin embassy's report of 6 Aug. was conveyed to the British, but probably not in time for the 8 Aug. paper (British delegation in Washington to Admiralty, 8 Aug. 1941, FO 371/29489, N4456/78/38, PRO).

4. Arnold, longhand notes of the Argentia Conference, box 181, Arnold papers; Arnold, *Global Mission*, 249–50; record of discussion among Marshall, Dill, and Brigadier Dykes, 11 Aug. 1941, PREM 3/485/5, PRO.

5. Arnold, *Global Mission*, 230; Hopkins memos of conferences with Stalin, 30, 31 July 1941, FR 1941, 1:802–14.

6. Hopkins memo of conference with Stalin, 31 July 1941, ibid., 805–14; Arnold longhand notes of Argentia conference, box 181, Arnold papers.

7. WPD 4402-89, RG 165.

8. Hopkins memo of conversation with Molotov, 31 July 1941, FR 1941, 4:1013–14.

9. Welles memo of conversation with Cadogan, 9 Aug. 1941, FR 1941, 1:351–52.

10. Wilson, *First Summit*, chap. 9; Atlantic Charter drafts, 740.0011 EW/14593, RG 59; Welles memos of conversations at Argentia, 10, 11 Aug. 1941, FR 1941, 1:354–67; Joint Statement by Roosevelt and Churchill, 14 Aug. 1941, ibid., 367–69.

11. Minutes of War Cabinet meeting, 8 Aug. 1941, CAB 69/2, Clement Attlee to Churchill, 9 Aug. 1941, PREM 3/485/1, and Prime Minister to Australian Prime Minister Robert Menzies, 16 Aug. 1941, FO 371/27847, F7882/4366/61, PRO; Welles memo, 30 July 1941, FR 1941, 5:240–41 (Thailand). On the question of a war warning: memos by Welles, 9, 11 Aug. 1941, FR 1941, 1:346–49, 357–60; extract from

record of meeting between Prime Minister and President Roosevelt, 11 Aug. 1941, FO 371/27909, F7995/86/23, PRO; Reynolds, *Creation of the Anglo-American Alliance,* 238–39; Wilson, *First Summit,* 88–93, 163–66.

12. "Draft Considered in Discussions with President Roosevelt at Placentia," 10 Aug. 1941, PREM 3/156-1, PRO.

13. Welles memo of conversation with Wakasugi, 4 Aug. 1941, FR Japan, 2:543; Welles memo of conversation with Cadogan, 9 Aug. 1941, FR 1941, 1:347.

14. Arnold longhand notes of Argentia conference, box 181, Arnold papers.

15. Churchill to FO, 11 Aug. 1941, FO 371/27847, F7882/4366/61, PRO.

16. Oral statement and Japanese proposal handed by Nomura to Hull, 6 Aug. 1941, FR Japan, 2:548–50.

17. Churchill to FO, 11 Aug. 1941, PREM 3/156-1, PRO; minute by Ashley Clarke, 20 Aug. 1941, FO 371/27909, F7985/86/23, PRO.

18. Welles memo of conversation, 11 Aug. 1941, FR 1941, 1:358.

19. Arnold longhand notes of Argentia conference, box 181, Arnold papers; FO memo, 15 Aug. 1941, FO 371/27847, F7882/4366/61, Churchill memo, 20 Aug. 1941, PREM 3/485/7, and Churchill to Attlee, 12 Aug. 1941, and to Eden, 15 Aug. 1941, PREM 3/485/1, PRO.

20. Memo (n.a.), 6 Aug. 1941, Atlantic Charter meeting folder #1, box 2, PSF:safe, FDRL; First Sea Lord to First Lord of Admiralty, 11 Aug. 1941, PREM 3/485/1, PRO; notes by Col. Charles W. Bundy, 16 Aug. 1941, of Churchill talk, 9 Aug. 1941, WPD 4402, RG 165; Arnold longhand notes of Argentia conference, box 181, Arnold papers; Sherwood, *Roosevelt and Hopkins,* 311 and facing map; Arnold, *Global Mission,* 249–50.

21. Kittredge, "U.S.-British Naval Cooperation," 575; Hopkins memo of conversation with Stalin, 30 July 1941, FR 1941, 1:804; Roskill, *War at Sea,* 1:488–89, 492.

22. Stimson diary, 19 Aug. 1941; Welles memo of conversation, 11 Aug. 1941, FR 1941, 1:356–57.

23. Leahy to SecState, 26, 29 July 1941 and Cole (Murphy) to SecState, 2 Aug. 1941, FR 1941, 2:402–7; Langer, *Vichy Gamble,* 183–88.

24. Conn, Engelman, and Fairchild, *Guarding the U.S.,* 484–87.

25. Bundy memo, 20 Aug. 1941, of conferences 11–12 Aug. 1941, WPD 4402, RG 165; Stimson diary, 19 Aug. 1941; Welles memo of conversation 11 Aug. 1941, FR 1941, 1:356; Kittredge, "U.S.-British Naval Cooperation," 569.

26. Memo of conversation between Stark and Pound, 11 Aug. 1941, PREM 3/485/5, PRO; CNO to CINCLANT, 26 Aug. 1941, box 82, SPDR, NOA.

27. Churchill, *Grand Alliance,* 446.

28. CNO to SPENAVO London, 28 Aug. 1941, box 82, SPDR, NOA; director NWPD to CNO, 13 Aug. 1941, ibid.; Argentia report, 22 Aug. 1941, minutes of Admiralty conferences, series 2, COMNAVFOREUR records, NOA; Danckwerts memo of conversation with Turner, 19 Aug. 1941, CAB 122/577, PRO; Admiralty to British mission in Washington, 23 Aug. 1941, FO 371/26722, A6715/384/45, PRO; Kittredge "U.S.-British Naval Cooperation," 572.

29. Bureau of Ships memo, 9 Aug. 1941, A4-3/BB, CNO confidential, RG 80, NA; O. M. Hustvedt memo, 11 Sept. 1941, BB 55/58-2, box 307, ibid.; Norman Friedman, *Battleships: An Illustrated Design History* (Annapolis, 1985), 274–75.

30. *Harvey Diary,* 31, 39; Kittredge, "U.S.-British Naval Cooperation," 581.

31. Admiralty to British mission in Washington, 23 Aug. 1941, CAB 122/575, PRO; Kittredge, "U.S.-British Naval Cooperation," 570–71.

32. Dallek, *Roosevelt and American Foreign Policy,* 276-78.

33. *Time,* 7 July-15 Sept. 1941.

34. Draft communication to Japanese ambassador and attached memos, FR 1941, 4:370-76.

35. Memo of conversation, 8 Aug. 1941, FR Japan, 2:550-51; Tokyo to Washington, 7 Aug. 1941, #12, *"Magic" Background,* 3A:8-9; Tokyo to Washington, 9 Aug. 1941, #21, #22, ibid., 14.

36. Hull memo, 16 Aug. 1941, FR Japan, 2:553-54.

37. Halifax to FO, 18 Aug. 1941, FO 371/27909, F7985/86/23.

38. Hull memo, 17 Aug. 1941, and statements handed by Roosevelt to Nomura, 17 Aug. 1941, FR Japan, 2:554-59.

39. Washington to Tokyo, 17 Aug. 1941, #40, #42, *"Magic" Background,* 3A:26, 27.

40. Washington to Tokyo, 18 Aug. 1941, #44, ibid., 3A:28; statement handed to Nomura, 17 Aug. 1941, FR Japan, 2:559.

41. Halifax to FO, 18 Aug. 1941, FO 371/27909, F7985/86/23.

42. *New York Times,* 25 Aug. 1941; Grew to SecState, 27 Aug. 1941, 740.0011 EW/14403, RG 59 (Japanese reaction).

43. *New York Times,* 25 Aug. 1941.

44. Churchill to Hopkins, 29 Aug. 1941, 740.0011 EW/14536 2/4, RG 59; Sterndale Bennett memo, 20 Aug. 1941, FO 371/27976, F8031/1299/23; Hopkins as quoted in Reynolds, *Anglo-American Alliance,* 215.

45. CINCLANT to senior officer present, Argentia, box 25, CINCLANT message files, NHOB, FRS. This account of the U.S. Atlantic Fleet's assumption of escort duty is based on Heinrichs, "Roosevelt's Intervention," *Diplomatic History* (Fall 1986), 10:330-32.

46. Daily briefing charts, 1941, NOA. On the Operational Intelligence Center: Patrick Beesly, *Very Special Intelligence: The Story of the Admiralty's Operational Intelligence Centre, 1939-1945* (New York, 1978).

47. Sources cited in fn. 26, chap. 2 above as well as: escort orders, vol. 1, operational planning materials, Support Force box, SOPD, NOA; "Convoy, In" file, reel 2586, navy message files, RG 38; Aug. and Sept. messages, box 1, CINCLANT message files, NHOB, FRS; Predicted List of Ship Locations, 24 Sept. 1941, A4-3(1)#3, Schedules of Employment, COMDESLANT GAF, RG 313, FRS; U.S. Atlantic Fleet Task Forces, 10 Sept. 1941, A4-3/FF13, CNO Secret, RG 80; CINCLANT to CNO, 26 Aug. 1941, A4-1/PC, CNO confidential, RG 80.

48. Director of Fleet Training to CNO, 19 Sept. 1941, A5-A5/1, CNO confidential, RG 80; Commander Task Unit 4.1.3 to Commander Task Force 4, 26 Nov. 1941, A4-3/FF13-9, CNO secret, ibid.; COMDESRON 27 to Commander Support Force, 29 Aug. 1941, box 25, CINCLANT message files, NHOB, FRS; COMDESRON 27 to CINCLANT, 9 Sept. 1941, ibid.; COMDESLANT to CNO (director of Fleet Training), 6 Aug. 1941, box 3280, COMDESLANT GAF, RG 313, FRS; A. S. Carpender to CNO (director of Fleet Training), 27 Dec. 1941, A5-1(2), box 3278, ibid.; COMDESRON 11 to CNO, 31 Oct., and CINCLANT to CNO, 21 Aug. 1941, A5-1(5), box 3297, ibid.

49. Daily briefing charts, 1941, NOA; Hinsley, *British Intelligence,* 173-74; Roskill, *War at Sea,* 1:467; J. Rohwer and G. Hummelchen, *Chronology of the War at Sea, 1939-1945,* tr. Derek Masters (2 vols.; London, 1972), 1:130; Douglas and Rohwer, "'Most

Thankless Task'," Boutilier, ed., *The RCN in Retrospect*, 197; Rohwer, *Critical Convoy Battles*, 24.

50. Oberleutnant Georg-Werner Fraatz to Commander Submarines, 5, 11 Sept. 1941, SRGN 2720, 2832, box 4, German navy U-boat messages, RG 457; Abbazia, *Mr. Roosevelt's Navy*, chap. 20; daily briefing charts, 3–11 Sept. 1941, NOA; Milner, *North Atlantic Run*, chap. 3; Douglas and Rohwer, "'Most Thankless Task'," Boutelier, ed., *The RCN in Retrospect*, 193–207.

51. *New York Times*, 6 Sept. 1941; Commander Task Force 15 to COMDESDIV 4, 4 Sept. 1941, box 1, CINCLANT message files, NHOB, FRS.

52. CINCLANT to Senior Officer Present Afloat (SOPA), Iceland, 12 Sept. 1941, box 1, CINCLANT message files, NHOB, FRS; CINCLANT to SOPA Iceland, 6 Sept. 1941, ibid.; CINCLANT to OPNAV, 7 Sept. 1941, ibid.; OPNAV to CIN-CLANT, 14 Sept. 1941, ibid.; CINCLANT to holders of Operations Plan 7–41, 22 Sept. 1941, A4-3/FF13 (Sept. 1941), CNO Secret, RG 80.

53. 11 Sept. 1941 speech drafts, Berle diary, Sept. 1941; *New York Times*, 8 Sept. 1941; Sherwood, *Roosevelt and Hopkins*, 370–72.

54. State Department official text of 11 Sept. 1941 speech in Berle diary, Sept. 1941; *New York Times*, 12, 16, 17, 18 Sept. 1941; Stimson diary, 30 Sept. 1941; Gallup, *Gallup Poll*, 1:299.

55. As quoted in Reynolds, *Anglo-American Alliance*, 169.

56. North Atlantic daily briefing charts, 27–30 Aug. 1941, NOA; notes on conferences, Aug. 1941, box 889, Army-COS secretariat files, 1941–42, RG 165; Jürgen Rohwer to author, 2 April, 24 June 1987.

57. CNO to distribution list, 13 Sept. 1941, SPDR, microfilm SPD-19, NOA; FDR to Stimson and Knox, 28 Aug. 1941, WPD 4493-9, RG 165.

58. Admiralty to British naval delegation, Washington, 17 Sept. 1941, SPDR, microfilm SPD-19, NOA; Playfair, *Mediterranean and Middle East*, 2:274.

59. Ghormley to Pound, 19 Sept. 1941, ADM 205/9, PRO. The movement of ships to Argentia and Hvalfjordur: messages of 18–27 Sept. 1941, box 1, CINCLANT message files, NHOB, FRS; Atlantic Fleet Weekly Operational Sheet, 20 Sept. 1941, A4-3/FF13, CNO confidential, RG 80; CNO to CINCLANT, 5 Sept. 1941, A4-3/BB55-56, ibid.; Little to Pound, 26 Sept. 1941, ADM 205/9, PRO.

60. Commander Task Force 7.5 to CINCLANT, 27 Sept. 1941, box 1, CIN-CLANT message files, NHOB, FRS; Capt. F. W. Pennoyer, Jr., report, 10 Oct. 1941, of meeting aboard *King George V*, A14-1/Convoy, box 108, CINCLANT GAF, RG 313, FRS.

61. Churchill to FDR, 1 Sept. 1941, C-113x, Kimball ed., *Churchill-Roosevelt Correspondence*, 1:235–36; Gwyer, *Grand Strategy*, 3 (part 1):173–75, 183–91, 197–203, 206–11.

62. Clark, *Barbarossa*, chap. 7; Erickson, *Road to Stalingrad*, chap. 7; Leach, *Barbarossa*, chap. 9.

63. Steinhardt to SecState, 17, 19, 22, 23 Aug. and 3 Sept. 1941, 740.0011 EW/14025, 14127, 14226, 14276, 14651, RG 59; Harrison (Switzerland) to SecState, 22 Aug. 1941, ibid./14248; military attaché London, report of 2 Sept. 1941, ibid./14964; #2693, box 14, OSS records, RG 226; Hinsley, *British Intelligence*, 72.

64. Erickson, *Road to Stalingrad*, 211; Winant to SecState, 5 Sept. 1941, 740.0011 EW/14752 1/6, RG 59.

65. Churchill to FDR, 5 Sept. 1941, C-114x, Kimball ed., *Churchill-Roosevelt Correspondence*, 1:238; Biddle to SecState, 10 Aug. 1941, 740.0011 EW/14427, RG 59.

66. Churchill to Stalin, 4 Sept. 1941, *Grand Alliance*, 458–60.

67. FDR to Churchill, 5 Sept. 1941, R-55x, Kimball, ed., *Churchill-Roosevelt Correspondence*, 1:237; Morison, *Battle of the Atlantic*, 111.

68. Press conference of 19 Aug. 1941, #762, *Presidential Press Conferences*, 18:91; FDR to Stimson, 30 Aug. 1941, FR 1941, 1:826.

69. Leighton and Coakley, *Global Logistics*, 94; "Special Air Corps Report, FY 1941," box 1, RG 107.

70. Record of meeting of Churchill and COS committee with Hopkins, Harriman, et al., 24 July 1941, miscellaneous papers (1), box 122, SPDR; Kirk to SecState, 18 Sept. 1941, 740.0011 EW/15218, RG 59; FDR to Stimson, 13 Sept. 1941, WPD 4402, RG 165.

71. FDR to Churchill, 8 Sept. 1941, R-56x, draft, not sent, and editorial note, Kimball, ed., *Roosevelt-Churchill Correspondence*, 1:239–40.

72. Leighton and Coakley, *Global Logistics*, 104.

73. Ibid., 135–36, 602; Morgenthau to FDR, 14 Aug. 1941, and enclosure, PSF: Treasury (charts folder), FDRL; Stimson diary, 14 Aug. 1941; Stimson to FDR, 29 Aug. 1941, PSF: War Department: Stimson, FDRL; Stimson to FDR, 23 Sept. 1941, ibid.

74. Exec. #4, item 6, box 20, OPD, RG 165; Leighton and Coakley, *Global Logistics*, 99–101.

75. Raymond H. Dawson, *The Decision To Aid Russia, 1941: Foreign Policy and Domestic Politics* (Chapel Hill, 1959), chaps. 8,10; FR 1941, 1:841–51.

76. "Information used by COS at conference with President, 22 Sept. 1941," box 885, COS secretariat, RG 165; exec. #4, item 8, box 20, OPD, ibid.; Stimson diary, 22–25 Sept. 1941; Leighton and Coakley, *Global Logistics*, 139–40; military attaché London, report of 15 Sept. 1941, 740.0011 EW/15528, RG 59.

77. FDR to Stimson, 18 Sept. 1941, box 15, RG 107; Lovett to Stimson, 12 Sept. 1941, box 1, ibid.; Leighton and Coakley, *Global Logistics*, 101; Craven and Cate, *Army Air Forces in World War II*, 1:145–50, 178.

78. Maj. Gen. Carl Spaatz to Maj. Gen. G. H. Brett, 26 Aug. 1941, 381.E War Plans, box 206, office of the Air Adjutant General general correspondence, 1939–42, entry 301, U.S. Army Air Forces records, RG 18, NA; Stimson diary, 25 Aug. 1941; Lovett to Stimson, 22 July 1941, box 1, RG 107; Martin Caidin, *Flying Forts* (New York, 1968), chap. 8.

79. Robert W. Morse to R. K. Turner, 25 Aug. 1941, box 82, SPDR, NOA; Craven and Cate, *Army Air Forces in World War II*, 1:178–79.

80. "Information Used by COS at Conference with President, 22 Sept. 1941," box 885, COS secretariat files, RG 165; W. T. Scobey memo of meeting in COS office, 20 Sept. 1941, exec. #4, item 8, box 20, OPD, ibid.; Churchill to Stalin, 28 Aug. 1941, CAB 120/681, PRO; Stimson diary, 12, 16 Sept. 1941.

81. Memo on B-17 bombing radii, n.a., n.d. {10 Oct. 1941}, box 1, RG 2, MacArthur papers (I am indebted to Daniel Harrington for providing me this memo, which probably deals with the B-17C, from his own researches and files). See also Tab K, WPD 4510, RG 165, which gives a combat radius of 750 miles from northern Luzon, reaching as far as Okinawa. According to authorities on the subject (Gordon Swanborough and Peter M. Barnes, *United States Aircraft Since 1908* (London, 1971), 96), the B-17E had a range of 2,000 miles (combat radius of 1,000) with a bomb load of 4,000 pounds. A full bomb load was 4,800. Kyushu is approximately 1,000 miles from Luzon, Tokyo another 500 miles farther. According to Harrington (letter to

author, 9 June 1987), a note in box 7 of the papers of General Carl Spaatz gives an 890-mile radius with a 4,200-pound payload. This was probably the B-17E. Stimson diary, 16 Sept. 1941.

82. Col. E. L. Naiden memo, 12 Sept. 1941, telephone conversations, Sept.–Dec. 1941, box 185, Arnold papers; Spaatz memo for COS, 12 Sept. 1941, 320.1 Phil., box 88, ibid.; Adjutant General to CG Philippines Dept., 12 Aug. 1941, 320.1 Phil., box 88, ibid.; Gerow to Chief of Air Corps., 18 Aug. 1941, 452.1 Phil., box 129, ibid.; Stimson to FDR, 22 Sept. 1941, in Stimson diary, 23 Sept. 1941; Gerow memo for COS, 14 Aug. 1941, WPD 3251, RG 165; Marshall to MacArthur, 5 Sept. 1941, Larry Bland et al., eds., *The Papers of George Catlett Marshall* (2 vols.; Baltimore, 1986), 2:599 (infantry reinforcement).

83. On the stalling tactics: Utley, "Upstairs, Downstairs," 24–28; Anderson, *Socony-Vacuum Oil Company*, 177–89.

84. Sir R. Campbell to FO, 27 Sept. 1941, FO 371/27982, F9976/1299/23, PRO.

85. Acheson to Welles, 16 Aug. 1941, FR 1941, 4:858–60.

86. FDR appointment diaries, box 166, PPF 1-0(1), FDRL.

87. Memo by Herbert Gaston, 20 Aug. 1941, Morgenthau diary, 22 Aug. 1941; Campbell to FO, 27 Sept. 1941, FO 371/27982, F9976/1299/23, PRO.

88. Campbell to FO, 21 Aug. 1941, FO 371/27977, F8303/1299/23, PRO; Nomura to Tokyo, 19, 20 Sept., 31 Oct. 1941, SRDJ 15041, 15087, 16272, RG 457; Edward G. Miller, Jr., to Acheson, 5 Sept. 1941, FR 1941, 4:869–70; Nomura to Hull, 3 Oct. 1941, ibid., 892; 840.51 Frozen Credits/3714-3805, RG 59; "Japan-Oil Shipments" folder, box 513, RG 131, U.S. Treasury; memo by B. Bernstein, 29 Oct. 1941, ibid. ("gathering oysters").

89. Acheson memo, 1 Aug. 1941, FR Japan, 1:271; Acheson to Hull, 22 Sept. 1941, 4:881–84; SecState to Grew, 27 Sept. 1941, ibid., 890–91.

90. Alger Hiss and Acheson memos, 26, 27 Sept. 1941, ibid. 886–88; FO 371/27982, F9976 and F9794 and F9966/1299/23, PRO; FO 371/27980, F9322 and F9324/1299/23, PRO.

Chapter 7. Oct.–Nov.: Race Against Time

1. Hosoya, "Japanese-Soviet Neutrality Pact," Morley, ed., *Fateful Choice*, 104–14; Erickson, *Road to Stalingrad*, 237–38.

2. F. C. Jones, *Japan's New Order in East Asia: Its Rise and Fall, 1937–45* (London, 1954), 279.

3. On Japan's decision of 6 Sept. for a diplomatic solution or war, with a time limit: Barnhart, *Japan Prepares for Total War*, chap. 13.

4. Robert J. C. Butow, *Tojo and the Coming of the War* (Princeton, 1961), 245 (from figure of speech by Satō Kenryō).

5. *"Magic" Background*, #285–301, #325, #332, #340, #350, #1033–35, 6 Aug.–3 Oct. 1941, 3A:164–70, 178, 182, 184, 187, 523–24.

6. Butow, *Tojo*, 223, 225.

7. On the Japanese navy's position regarding a decision for war: Barnhart, *Japan Prepares for Total War*, chap. 13; Asada, "Japanese Navy and the U.S.," 254–58; Stephen E. Pelz, *Race to Pearl Harbor: The Failure of the Second London Naval Conference and the Onset of World War II* (Cambridge, MA, 1974), 220–24.

8. Oka, *Konoe*.

9. Ibid., 146-47.

10. Hull memos, 23, 27, 28 Aug., 3 Sept. 1941, and attached documents, Ballantine memos, 28 Aug., 1, 4 Sept. 1941, FR Japan, 2:565-96; Washington to Tokyo 23, 28, 29 Aug., 3 Sept. #65, #89, #90, #91, #92, #118, "Magic" Background, 3A: 39-40, 52-54, 67-68.

11. #77, #96, #97, #98, #99, #100, #104, ibid., 45, 57-60. The name of the correspondent, described in the printed version only as "a reporter for the New York Herald Tribune" (Washington to Tokyo, 28 Aug. 1941, #96, ibid., 57), is given in the original intercept as Fleischer (SRDJ 14489, RG 457, NA). Also: FR 1941, 4:395-96, 421-22; Langer and Gleason, Undeclared War, 703.

12. FR Japan, 2:568-70, 581-82.

13. Washington to Tokyo, 4 Sept. 1941, #129, "Magic" Background, 3A:73.

14. Grew memo, 6 Sept. 1941, FR Japan, 2:604-6; Heinrichs, Grew, 346.

15. Grew to SecState, 18 Aug., 29 Sept. 1941, FR Japan, 2:565, 645-50; comment by Grew, 5 Sept. 1941, ibid., 601-3; Grew to SecState, 30 Aug., 29 Sept. 1941, FR 1941, 4:416-18, 483-89; Grew to FDR, 29 Sept. 1941, ibid., 468-69; Heinrichs, Grew, 339-47.

16. Ibid., 348-50.

17. FR Japan, 2:595-661. The key Japanese proposal is the draft of 6 Sept. 1941, ibid., 608, and the American response is Hull memo and enclosure, 2 Oct. 1941, ibid., 654-61. On "propinquity": proposed instructions to Nomura handed by Toyoda to Grew, 13 Sept. 1941, ibid., 623-24.

18. Stimson diary, 6 Oct. 1941.

19. Japanese draft proposal, 6 Sept. 1941, FR Japan, 2:608; Hull memo and enclosure, 2 Oct. 1941, ibid., 660.

20. Ibid.; FDR to Churchill, 15 Oct. 1941, R-63x, Kimball, ed. Churchill-Roosevelt Correspondence, 1:250. Roosevelt's words were: "The Jap situation is definitely worse and I think they are headed North—however in spite of this you and I have two months of respite in the Far East." Editor Kimball takes this to mean that Roosevelt anticipated two months beyond 15 October before a crisis occurred. Roosevelt's language is open to that interpretation but surely he was writing retrospectively. It was just two months since he had told Churchill that he hoped to gain thirty to sixty days by continuing talks with the Japanese. Further, no evidence has been found that would indicate any particular period of respite from a northward advance.

21. Clark, Barbarossa, 147. On the German offensive against Moscow: ibid., chaps. 8, 9; Erickson, Road to Stalingrad, 212-51.

22. New York Times, 16 Oct. 1941.

23. Ibid.; Lt. Gen. Fritz Bayerlein as quoted in Clark, Barbarossa, 160.

24. Stimson diary, 29 Sept. 1941; military attaché London, report of 1 Oct. 1941, 740.0011 EW/15656, RG 59; Schoenfeld to SecState, 6 Oct. 1941, ibid./15643; New York Times, 4 Oct. 1941; Hinsley, British Intelligence, 2:73.

25. Military attaché London, reports of 6, 8 (with G-2 comment), 12, 13, 15 Oct. 1941, 740.0011 EW/15939, 16155, RG 59; Churchill to director of Military Intelligence, 24 Oct. 1941, CAB 120/681, PRO; Stimson diary, 10 Oct. 1941; Berle diary, 10 Oct. 1941.

26. Hull memo, 3 Oct. 1941, 740.0011 EW/15650, RG 59.

27. Steinhardt to SecState, 28 Oct. 1941, ibid./16213, 16074; Leahy to SecState, 12, 16 Oct. 1941, ibid./15773, 15876.

28. Erickson, *Road to Stalingrad*, 238–39; Chalmers Johnson, *An Instance of Treason: Ozaki Hotsumi and the Sorge Spy Ring* (Stanford, 1964), 158.

29. 740.0011 EW/13930, 14566, 14589, 14770, 14775, 15626, RG 59.

30. Sherman Miles memo for Marshall, 17 Oct. 1941, PHA, 14:1359.

31. Gauss to SecState, 740.0011 EW/15886, RG 59.

32. Naval attaché report, Chungking, 4 Oct. 1941, #4655, box 21, RG 226; Hull memo, 29 Oct. 1941, 740.0011 EW/16293, RG 59; 17 Oct. 1941 conference, notes on conferences, box 889, Army-COS secretariat, 1941–1942, RG 165.

33. Miles to Marshall, 21 Oct. 1941, #2177, box 12, RG 226; CNO memo, 16 Oct. 1941, PHA, 14:1327; R. A. Boone to Turner, 25 Sept. 1941, director NWPD special file #1, box 20, Turner papers, NOA; Admiral Alan G. Kirk transcript, 1962, Columbia University Oral History Collection, p. 182; Wohlstetter, *Pearl Harbor*, 131–66.

34. Halifax to FO, 11 Oct. 1941, FO 371/27910, F10330/86/23, PRO; FDR to Churchill, 15 Oct. 1941, R-63x, Kimball, ed. *Churchill-Roosevelt Correspondence*, 1:250.

35. Reed (Hanoi) to SecState, 3 Oct. 1941, 740.0011 PW/551, RG 59; Grew to SecState, 10 Oct. 1941, ibid./559, 560; military attaché Chungking, reports of 21, 23 Oct. 1941, 740.0011 EW/16336, RG 59; Hull to Grew, 16 Oct. 1941, ibid./15889; Stimson diary, 16 Oct. 1941. Stimson seems to have meant the drawing of lines when he wrote: "[W]e face the delicate question of the diplomatic fencing [original word "touching"] to be done so as to be sure that Japan was [sic] put in the wrong and made the first bad move—overt move."

36. Military attaché London, reports of 20, 21 Oct. 1941, 740.0011 EW/16336, RG 59; R. A. Boone memo, 25 Sept. 1941, director NWPD special file #1, box 20, Turner papers, NOA.

37. #352, #751, #356, "Magic" Background, 3A:188, 372, 189–90.

38. Biddle to SecState, 10 Aug. 1941, 740.0011 EW/14427, RG 59.

39. Halifax to FO, 10 Oct. 1941, FO 371/27910, F10639/86/23, PRO.

40. FO to Sir Stafford Cripps, 2 Nov. 1941, FO 371/27987, F11727/1299/23, PRO.

41. Winant to SecState, 22 Oct. 1941, 740.0011 EW/16039, RG 59; Hull memo, 29 Oct. 1941, ibid./16293.

42. Richard Law minute, FO 371/27984, F10456/1299/23, PRO; Harvey, *Diary*, 40.

43. Ashley Clarke minute, 17 Sept. 1941, FO 371/27910, F9321/86/23, PRO; Clarke minute, 6 Oct. 1941, FO 371/27910, F10329/86/23, PRO; Sterndale Bennett minute, 1 Oct. 1941, FO 371/27883, F10117/12/23, PRO.

44. Stimson diary, 6 Oct. 1941; Col. Hayes A. Kroner to Marshall, 2 Oct. 1941, PHA, 14:1357–58.

45. WPD strategic estimate, Oct. 1941, WPD 4510, RG 165.

46. Transcript of telephone conversation between Marshall and Lt. Cmdr. W. R. Smedberg III (aide to Stark), 25 Sept. 1941, OPNAV telephone records, 1941–1942, NOA; Watson, *Chief of Staff*, 443.

47. Stimson diary, 23 Sept., 16, 20 Oct. 1941; Stimson to FDR, 22 Sept., 14 Oct. 1941, in Stimson diary; Harold Balfour memo, n.d., box 156, Hopkins papers, FDRL; FDR to Stimson 18 Sept., 14 Oct., 1941, box 15, RG 107.

48. A delivery schedule extending to October 1942 was in place as late as 3 Oct. The decision for an accelerated schedule was taken by 21 Oct., when details were sent to MacArthur. The 16 Oct. meeting was the only one the president had with all his principal military advisers between 3 and 21 Oct. Marshall to MacArthur, 3 Oct. 1941, Philippines folder, box 11, RG 107; Stimson diary, 16 Oct. 1941; presi-

dent's appointment diaries, box 166, PPF 1-0(1), FDRL; Adams to MacArthur, 21 Oct. 1941 and chief of air staff to commanding general, air force Combat Command, 22 Oct. 1941, 452.1 Phil., box 129, Arnold papers. A full-strength heavy bombardment group consisted of 68 planes ("U.S. Production Requirements, September 1941" [Victory Program], 145.81-23, frame 1495, microfilm roll A1370, U.S. Air Force Historical Archives, Bolling Air Force Base, Washington, D.C.).

49. Arnold to MacArthur, 14 Oct. 1941, box 1, RG 2, General of the Army Douglas MacArthur papers, MacArthur Memorial Library, Norfolk, VA.; Edward Curtis, secretary of air staff, to Adjutant General, 20 Oct. 1941, box 88, Arnold papers; Gerow to General Moore, deputy chief of staff, 8 Oct. 1941, WPD 4561-3, RG 165.

50. CNO to CINCPAC, 27 Oct. 1941, A3-1/SS, CNO Secret, RG 80; Clay Blair, Jr., *Silent Victory: The U.S. Submarine War Against Japan* (Philadelphia, 1975), 33–35, 54–62.

51. Marshall-Smedberg phone transcript, 25 Sept. 1941, OPNAV phone records, NOA; "Strategic Concept of the Philippines," Gerow to Stimson, 8 Oct. 1941, Philippines folder, box 11, RG 107; Stimson to FDR, 21 Oct. 1941, in Stimson diary, 21 Oct. 1941; Halifax to FO, 13 Oct. 1941, FO 371/27986, F11299/1299/23, PRO; CINCAF to OPNAV, 2 Nov. 1941, box 117, SPDR, NOA.

52. Arnold to MacArthur, 14 Oct. 1941, box 1, RG 2, MacArthur papers; Arnold to COS, 20 Sept. 1941, 686 Haw.-Phil.21, box 153, Arnold papers; Stimson to Hull, 16 Oct. 1941, "Philippines" folder, box 43, ibid.; WPD 4571-1, RG 165.

53. "Strategic Concept of the Philippines," Gerow to Stimson, 8 Oct. 1941, "Philippines" folder, box 11, RG 107 (also in WPD 4510-60, RG 165); Arnold to MacArthur, 14 Oct. 1941, box 1, RG 2, MacArthur papers.

54. Stimson diary, 12 Sept., 7, 21, 28 Oct. 1941, Stimson to FDR, 21 Oct., in Stimson diary, 21 Oct 1941.

55. Marshall-Smedberg phone transcript, 25 Sept. 1941, OPNAV phone records, NOA.

56. Ibid.; Watson, *Chief of Staff*, 442–44; Wohlstetter, *Pearl Harbor*, 138–40, especially fns #135–37; F. J. Haley to W. M. McLintic, 19 Nov. 1941, 633 Phil., box 1117, RG 18; L. R. Whitten to Chief of Facilities Section, Office of Chief of Air Corps, 1 Oct. 1941, 463.7, ibid.; Stimson diary, 7, 9 Oct. 1941; conference in General Marshall's office, 3 Nov. 1941, misc. conferences folder, box 886, Army-COS Secretariat, RG 165; Brig. Gen. Frank D. Lackland to Commanding General, Air Force Combat Command, 28 Oct. 1941, 370.5 Phil.26, box 108, Arnold papers; transcripts of phone conversations between Col. Vanaman and General Emmons, 16 Oct. 1941, "Telephone Conversations, Sept.–Dec. 1941" folder, box 185, Arnold papers; Arnold to COS, 4 Nov. 1941, "Flight of B-17's to Philippines" folder, box 41, Arnold papers.

57. Minutes of War Cabinet Defense Committee meeting, 1 Aug. 1941, CAB 69/8, PRO; Churchill to Pound, 25 Aug. 1941, ADM 205/10, PRO; Eden to Churchill, 12 Sept. 1941, FO 371/27891, F9615/1299/23, PRO. On the genesis of the Eastern fleet: Marder, *Old Friends, New Enemies*, chap. 8.

58. Eden as quoted in Marder, ibid., 224; Harvey, *Diary*, 53.

59. Churchill to R. G. Menzies, 10 Oct. 1941, PREM 3/663-3, PRO; SPENAVO London to OPNAV, 26 Oct. 1941, Pacific-Far East U.S. Joint Staff correspondence #2, box 117, SPDR, NOA; Admiralty to British delegation in Washington, 5 Nov. 1941, ibid.; Danckwerts to U.S. Secretary for Collaboration, 6 Oct. 1941 (schedule of the *Indomitable*), U.S.-British Far East correspondence, reel 6, "Strategic Planning in

the Navy: Its Evolution and Execution, 1891-1945," Scholarly Resources microfilm publication.

60. Churchill to FDR, 2 Nov. 1941, C-125x, Kimball, ed., *Churchill-Roosevelt Correspondence,* 1:265.

61. Admiralty to British delegation in Washington, 5 Nov. 1941, box 117, SPDR, NOA; OPNAV to SPENAVO London, 6 Nov. 1941, ibid.; Cdr. L. R. McDowell to Joint Secretaries of British Joint Staff Mission, Washington, 11 Nov. 1941, WPD 4402, RG 165. On 27 Oct. 1941 Admiral Turner circulated a memorandum by an RAF officer on the virtues of Luzon as an offensive base ("Notes on the Defense Problems of Luzon," report of Group Captain Dorvall, Turner to all naval districts, CINCLANT, CINCPAC, EA-EF, box 102, SPDR, NOA).

62. Admiral Thomas Hart oral history transcript, Columbia University Oral History Collection, New York; Stark to Hart, 7 Nov. 1941, ABDA-ANZAC correspondence, 1941-42, box 117, SPDR, NOA; Ghormley to Pound, 7 Nov. 1941, ADM 205/9, PRO.

63. American objections to ADB plans are set forth in: Maj. Gen. J. E. Cheney and Rear Adm. R. E. Ghormley to COS Committee, 6 Aug. 1941, #8, American-Dutch-British conferences, Singapore, April-Nov. 1941, series 2, COMNAVFO-REUR records, NOA.

64. Harrington, "Careless Hope," *Pacific Historical Review,* (May 1979), 48:217; Marder, *Old Friends, New Enemies,* 213; Sherry, *Rise of American Air Power,* 100-115.

65. Butow, *Tojo,* 314; ibid., 294-327; Barnhart, *Japan Prepares for Total War,* 254-62.

66. Butow, *Tojo,* 296.

67. Memoranda of conversations, 15, 17 Nov. 1941, FR Japan, 2:732-33, 740-41. Conversations of 7-18 Nov. 1941: ibid., 706-50.

68. Memoranda of conversations, 12, 18, Nov. 1941, ibid., 725, 748-49.

69. As quoted in Clark, *Barbarossa,* 167. Erickson, *Road to Stalingrad,* 249-57.

70. 740.0011 EW/16270A, 16336, 16219, 16498, 16585, 16539, 16631, RG 59.

71. Grew to SecState, 7 Nov. 1941, FR 1941, 4:1024-25.

72. Browne (Saigon) to SecState, 29 Oct., 3 Nov., 1941, Reed (Hanoi) to SecState, 3 Nov. 1941, FR 1941, 5:329, 330, 332-33; Hull to Browne and Reed, 30 Oct. 1941, 740.0011 PW/597A, 597B, RG 59; Reed to SecState, 24 Oct., 3, 8 Nov. 1941, ibid./ 582, 606, 612; Browne to SecState, 20 Nov. 1941, ibid./634; naval attaché Tokyo, report of 3 Nov. 1941, 740.0011 EW/16631, RG 59.

73. Ibid.; American communications intelligence reports, 12, 18 Nov. 1941, #90, #139, *"Magic" Background,* 4A:45, 74-75; *New York Times,* 14 Nov. 1941.

74. *New York Times,* 2, 6 Nov. 1941; *Japan Times and Advertiser,* 25 Oct. 1941, as quoted in Grew diary, 25 Oct. 1941.

75. Grew to SecState, 3 Nov. 1941, FR Japan, 2:701-4; Grew diary, 3 Nov. 1941.

76. Tokyo to Washington, 2, 4 Nov. 1941, #20, #22, #23, *"Magic" Background,* 4A:11-13.

77. Langer and Gleason, *Undeclared War,* 839-48.

78. Ibid., 845; 740.0011 EW/16438, 16631 and 740.0011 PW/622, RG 59.

79. FDR to Churchill, 7 Nov. 1941, R-66x, Kimball, ed., *Churchill-Roosevelt Correspondence,* 1:267; memo, "Far Eastern Theater," 1 Nov. 1941, WPD 4510, RG 165.

80. Ibid.; Ingersoll statement to Joint Army-Navy Board, 3 Nov. 1941, exec. #4, item 8, "Far East" folder, OPD, RG 165.

81. Langer and Gleason, *Undeclared War*, 845; minutes of meeting 3 Nov. 1941, box 1921, U.S. Army Joint Board papers, entry 284, RG 165.

82. Ibid.; C. W. Bundy memo, 1 Nov. 1941, WPD 4510, RG 165; memos for Stimson, n.a., n.d., "Philippines" folder, box 43, Arnold papers; MacArthur to Marshall, 28 Oct. 1941, WPD 4477, RG 165.

83. Tokyo to Washington, 5 Nov. 1941, tr. same date, #44, *"Magic" Background*, 4A:22.

84. Gerow to Arnold, 8 Nov. 1941, 370.5 Phil. 26, box 108, Arnold papers; Grew to SecState, 17 Nov. 1941, FR Japan, 2:743–44; *New York Times*, 6, 11, Nov. 1941.

85. Stimson diary, 23 Oct. 1941; Ghormley to Pound, 14 Nov. 1941, A16-3, CNO secret, RG 80; King to Stark, 5 Nov. 1941, director NWPD folder, special file #1, box 20, Turner papers.

86. OPNAV to Admiralty, 9 Oct. 1941, reel 2590, OPNAV messages: convoy, out, RG 38; 16 Nov. 1941 chart, navy briefing charts, NOA; Jürgen Rohwer to author, 2 April 1987; Abbazia, *Mr. Roosevelt's Navy*, chaps. 23, 25.

87. Roskill, *War at Sea*, 1:473–75.

88. Little to Pound, 6 Nov. 1941, ADM 205/9, PRO.

89. Roskill, *War at Sea*, 1:532–34; Marder, *Old Friends, New Enemies*, 229–30.

90. Langer and Gleason, *Undeclared War*, 860; Hull memo, 10 Nov. 1941, FR Japan, 2:718; Washington to Tokyo, 10 Nov. 1941, #79, *"Magic" Background*, 4A:39.

91. Tokyo to Washington, 4 Nov. 1941, #29, *"Magic" Background*, 4A:16.

92. Washington to Tokyo, 18 Nov., and Tokyo to Washington, 14 Nov. 1941, #146, #150, ibid., 80, 82; Washington to Tokyo, 18 Nov. 1941, tr. 21 Nov. 1941, SRDJ 16780, RG 457.

93. Hull memo of conversation, 18 Nov. 1941, FR Japan, 2:750; proposal handed to Hull by Nomura, 20 Nov. 1941, ibid., 755–66; Tokyo to Washington, 19 Nov. 1941, tr. 20 Nov. 1941, SRDJ 16733, 16735, 16736, 16739, RG 457.

94. Hamilton to Hull, 18 Nov. 1941, 711.94/2540 17/35, RG 59; Langer and Gleason, *Undeclared War*, 871–81.

95. As Langer and Gleason (ibid., 872) argue, 17 Nov. 1941 is the more likely date of this outline than "probably ... shortly after November 20" as the State Department noted (FR 1941, 4:626, fn. 52). Roosevelt would undoubtedly have included the Nomura-Kurusu proposal in his outline if he had written it after 18 Nov.

96. 22 Nov. 1941 draft *modus vivendi* with outline comprehensive agreement and revised 24 Nov. draft, ibid., 635–40, 642–46.

97. Halifax to FO, 22 Nov. 1941, FO 371/27912, 12654/86/23, PRO; Washington (Campbell) to FO, 18 Nov. 1941, FO 371/27917, F12475/86/23, PRO; Hull memo of conversation, 22 Nov. 1941, FR 1941, 4:640; Reynolds, *Creation of the Anglo-American Alliance*, 243.

98. FO to Craigie, 8, 24, 26 Nov. 1941, FO 371/27911, F11672/86/23, and /27912, F12544/86/23, PRO; Churchill to prime ministers of Canada, Australia, New Zealand, 23, 24 Nov. 1941, FO 371/27912, F12654/86/23, PRO; minute by W. G. Hayter, 27 Nov. 1941, FO 371/27914, F14304/86/23, PRO; Harvey, *Diary*, 24, 26 Nov. 1941, 65–66; Hull memo of conversation, 25 Nov. 1941, and Halifax to Hull, 25 Nov. 1941, FR 1941, 4:654–57; *New York Times*, 23 Nov. 1941 (*Prince of Wales*); Reynolds, *Creation of the Anglo-American Alliance*, 242–44. On continuing withholding of British 1941 intelligence documents on Japan: Rear Adm. Edwin T. Layton with Capt. Roger Pineau and John Costello, *"And I Was There": Pearl Harbor and Midway—Breaking the Secrets* (New York, 1985), 534, fn. 5.

99. Lattimore to Currie, and Hull memo of conversation, 25 Nov. 1941, FR 1941, 4:652-54; Soong to Stimson, 25 Nov. 1941, "Unfiled Papers" folder, box 14, Stimson safe file, RG 107.

100. Halifax to FO, 25 Nov. 1941, FO 371/27912, F12765/86/23, PRO; Hull memos of conversations, 24, 25 Nov. 1941, FR 1941, 4:646-47, 655-57; FDR to Churchill, 24 Nov. 1941, R-69x, and Churchill to FDR, 26 Nov. 1941, C-133x, Kimball, ed., *Churchill-Roosevelt Correspondence*, 1:275-78; *New York Times*, 23 Nov. 1941 ("alphabetical lute"); Reynolds, *Creation of the Anglo-American Alliance*, 245.

101. Tokyo to Washington, 22 Nov. 1941, tr. 24 Nov. 1941, SRDJ 16849, RG 457; SRDJ 16850, 16852, ibid.; Tokyo to Washington, 22, 24 Nov. 1941, #162, #163, *"Magic" Background*, 4A:89.

102. 740.0011 PW/645-647, 667; Col. Hayes A. Kroner to COS, 25 Nov. 1941, exec. #8, book A, box 40, OPD, RG 165; Navy Department to Department of State, 22 Nov. 1941, FR 1941, 5:344-45; OPNAV to CINCPAC, CINCAF, 21 Nov. 1941, #160, *"Magic" Background*, 4A:87.

103. OPNAV to CINCAF, CINCPAC, 27 Nov. 1941, #210, *"Magic" Background*, 4A:117; "Japanese Navy—Organization of Fleets," 28 Nov. 1941, #211, ibid., 117; Navy Department to Department of State, 22 Nov. 1941, FR 1941, 4:633; Stimson to FDR, 26 Nov. 1941, OCS 18136/125, box 11, Chief of Staff files, entry 12, RG 165; "Japanese Troop Movement," n.d. (about 26 Nov. 1941), "Far East (Before Dec. 7, 1941)" folder, box 4, RG 107; Wohlstetter, *Pearl Harbor*, 243.

104. Carl Spaatz to COS, 13 Nov. 1941, and memo (n.a., n.d.) "Philippines" folder, box 43, Arnold papers; memos for Crawford and Gerow, 26 Nov., 1 Dec. 1941, exec. #8, book A, box 40, OPD, RG 165; "Reinforcement of the Philippines," memo for Stimson, 28 Nov. 1941, WPD 4561-7, RG 165; Stark to FDR, 27 Nov. 1941, OCS 18136/125, box 11, COS files, RG 165; "Data Concerning Far Eastern Situation," 1 Dec. 1941, frame 1781, microfilm reel A1370, USAF archives, Bolling AFB.

105. *New York Times*, 21-25 Nov. 1941; Morgenthau presidential diary, 26 Nov. 1941.

106. Clark, *Barbarossa*, 172-79; Erickson, *Road to Stalingrad*, 257-65.

107. Ibid., 262; *New York Times*, 21-25 Nov. 1941; Morgenthau presidential diary, 26 Nov. 1941.

108. Gerow to Hull, 21 Nov. 1941, exec. #8, book A, box 40, OPD, RG 165.

Epilogue. Japan Attacks

1. Telegrams from consuls in Saigon and Hanoi, 25 Nov.-1 Dec. 1941, 740.0011 Pacific War/645-64, RG 59; "Japanese Troop Movements," n.d., notes in Stimson's handwriting, "Far East (Before Dec. 7, 1941)" folder, box 4, RG 107.

2. Gordon W. Prange, *At Dawn We Slept: The Untold Story of Pearl Harbor* (New York, 1981), 439-40; Butow, *Tojo*, 349.

3. "Daily Information Summary, December 1, 1941," "Far Eastern Situation" folder, box 47, SPDR, NOA.

4. 740.0011 Pacific War/659, 666-67, RG 59; Prange, *At Dawn We Slept*, 447-48.

5. Langer and Gleason, *Undeclared War*, 899, 911.

6. Halifax to FO, 1 Dec. 1941, FO 371/27913, F13114/86/23, and 4 Dec. 1941, FO 371/27914, F13219/86/23, PRO; Stimson diary, 28 Nov. 1941; Reynolds, *Anglo-American Alliance*, 246; S. Woodburn Kirby, *The War Against Japan: Volume 1, The Loss of*

Singapore (London, 1957), 173–75; James Leutze, *A Different Kind of Victory: A Biography of Admiral Thomas C. Hart* (Annapolis, 1981), 224–26.

7. The message is in FDR to Hull, 6 Dec. 1941, FR 1941, 4:723–25.

8. Thurston (Kuibyshev) to SecState, 1 Dec. 1941, 740.0011 EW/16992, RG 59.

9. Layton et al., *"And I Was There,"* 287. On the coming of war: Morison, *Rising Sun*, chaps. 5–6; H. P. Willmott, *Empires in the Balance: Japanese and Allied Pacific Strategies to April 1942* (Annapolis, 1982), chap. 5; Stanley L. Falk, *Seventy Days to Singapore* (New York, 1975); Prange, *At Dawn We Slept*, chaps. 59ff.

10. Herwig, *Politics of Frustration*, 235–36; Roskill, *War at Sea*, 1: 614 (Appendix Q).

Bibliography

Unpublished Sources

(Note: Those sources extensively used and centrally important to this study are marked with an asterisk*)

MANUSCRIPT COLLECTIONS

At the Franklin D. Roosevelt Library, Hyde Park, New York: Franklin D. Roosevelt papers (President's Secretary's File*, Official File, President's Personal File, White House Usher's diary); Adolf A. Berle Jr. diary (microfilm)*; Harry Hopkins papers; Henry J. Morgenthau Jr. presidential diary and diary.

At the Library of Congress, Washington: Henry H. Arnold papers*, Joseph E. Davies papers, Loy Henderson papers, Cordell Hull papers, Ernest J. King papers, Breckinridge Long papers, Laurence A. Steinhardt papers.

Oral history transcripts at Columbia University Oral History Collection, New York: Walter S. Anderson, Thomas C. Hart, Alan G. Kirk. Oral history transcripts at U.S. Navy Operational Archives, Navy Yard, Washington: Walter C. W. Ansel, Arthur N. McCollum, Roland J. Smoot.

Other collections: Joseph C. Grew papers, Harvard University Library, Cambridge, MA; Henry L. Stimson diary (microfilm)*, Yale University Library, New Haven. At U.S. Navy Operational Archives, Navy Yard, Washington: Paul R. Heineman papers, Richmond Kelly Turner papers*.

U.S. NAVY RECORDS

At U.S. Navy Operational Archives, Navy Yard, Washington: Briefing Chart file, July–December 1941*; Commander U.S. Naval

Forces in Europe records*; "Conferences" folder; Microfilm SPD-19 (WPL 50 and 51 and Related Correspondence); Strategic Plans Division records*; Strategical and Operational Planning Documents file; "Strategical Planning in the Navy: Its Evolution and Execution, 1891-1945" (microfilm document collection, Scholarly Resources, Wilmington, DE); Office of the Chief of Naval Operations telephone transcripts file, 1941-1942*; Samuel Eliot Morison office files, 1911-1969; Tenth Fleet files; World War II Command files.

At National Archives, Washington: Ships' Deck Logs, Record Group 24; Ship Movements Division general correspondence, 1920-1942, and Office of Chief of Naval Operations message files, Record Group 38; Chief of Naval Operations secret and confidential records, 1940-1941, Record Group 80.

Other collections: Commander-in-Chief Atlantic Fleet World War II message files, 1941-1945, U.S. Naval History Operating Branch, Federal Record Center, Suitland, MD*; Commander Destroyers Atlantic Fleet and Commander-in-Chief Atlantic Fleet general administrative files, Record Group 313, Federal Record Center, Suitland, MD*; Historical Section, Office of Commander-in-Chief Atlantic Fleet, "U.S. Naval Administration in World War II: Commander-in-Chief Atlantic Fleet," microfiche, U.S. Navy Historical Center, Navy Yard, Washington.

MILITARY RECORDS

Records of the War Department General and Special Staffs, 1920-1941, Record Group 165, National Archives, Washington: Army-Chief of Staff Secretariat records*; Chief of Staff general correspondence, Military Intelligence Division files*, Operations Division executive files*, War Plans Division numerical files*, Army Joint Army-Navy Board records.

Other collections: Army Air Forces central decimal files, 1939-1942, Record Group 18, National Archives, Washington; Army Intelligence Project decimal file (Germany), 1941-1945, Record Group 319, Federal Record Center, Suitland, MD; Military Intelligence Division regional files, Record Group 165, Federal Record Center, Suitland MD; Secretary of War (Henry L. Stimson) Safe File, 1940-1945, Record Group 107, National Archives, Washington*; U.S. Air Force Historical Archives (microfilm), Bolling Air Force Base, Washington, DC.

AMERICAN AND FOREIGN GOVERNMENT RECORDS

United States: Department of State Decimal File, Record Group 59, National Archives, Washington*; Office of Strategic Services records, Record Group 226, National Archives, Washington; Foreign Funds Control general correspondence, Alien Property records, Record Group 131, Treasury Department; Office of Administrator of Export Control records, Record Group 169, Federal Record Center, Suitland, MD.

Great Britain: Public Record Office, Kew: Foreign Office (FO 371)*, Admiralty*, Cabinet office, Prime Minister's office records. Germany: German navy U-boat messages (SRGN), Record Group 457, National Archives, Washington.

Japan: translations of Japanese diplomatic messages (SRDJ)*, and collection of Japanese diplomatic messages, July 1938–January 1942 (SRH), Record Group 457, National Archives, Washington. (Note: This unpublished MAGIC file (SRDJ) is more satisfactory than the published version (U.S. Department of Defense, *The "Magic" Background of Pearl Harbor*) because some documents are missing from the latter, others are incomplete, and the organization of documents is awkward.)

Published Sources

SELECTED BOOKS AND ARTICLES

Abbazia, Patrick. *Mr. Roosevelt's Navy: The Private War of the U.S. Atlantic Fleet, 1939–1942*. Annapolis, 1975.

Acheson, Dean. *Present at the Creation: My Years in the State Department*. New York, 1969.

Addington, Larry H. *The Blitzkrieg Era and the German General Staff, 1865–1941*. New Brunswick, 1971.

Allard, Dean. "Anglo-American Differences During World War II." *Military Affairs* (April 1980), 44:75–81.

Anderson, Jr., Irvine H. *The Standard-Vacuum Oil Company and United States East Asian Policy, 1933–1941*. Princeton, 1975.

Arnold, H. H. *Global Mission*. New York, 1949.

Barnhart, Michael A. *Japan Prepares for Total War: The Search for Economic Security, 1919–1941*. Ithaca, 1987.

Beesly, Patrick. *Very Special Intelligence: The Story of the Admiralty's Operational Intelligence Centre, 1939–1945*. New York, 1978.

Blair, Jr., Clay. *Silent Victory: The U.S. Submarine War Against Japan*. Philadelphia, 1975.

Borg, Dorothy, and Shumpei Okamoto, eds. *Pearl Harbor as History: Japanese-American Relations, 1931–1941.* New York, 1973.

Borg, Dorothy. *The United States and the Far Eastern Crisis of 1933–1938: From the Manchurian Incident Through the Initial Stage of the Sino-Japanese War.* Cambridge, MA, 1964.

Burdick, Charles B. *Germany's Military Strategy and Spain in World War II.* Syracuse, 1968.

Burns, James MacGregor, *Roosevelt: The Soldier of Freedom.* New York, 1970.

Burns, Richard Dean, and Edward M. Bennett, eds. *Diplomats in Crisis: United States-Chinese-Japanese Relations, 1919–1941.* Santa Barbara, 1974.

Butow, Robert J. C. *Tojo and the Coming of the War.* Princeton, 1961.

————. *The John Doe Associates: Backdoor Diplomacy for Peace, 1941.* Stanford, 1974.

————. "The Hull-Nomura Conversations: A Fundamental Misconception." *American Historical Review* (July 1960), 65:822–36.

Calder, Angus. *The People's War: Britain, 1939–1945.* New York, 1969.

Churchill, Winston. *The Grand Alliance.* Boston, 1950.

Clark, Alan. *Barbarossa: The Russian-German Conflict, 1941–1945.* New York, 1965.

Cole, Wayne S. *Roosevelt and the Isolationists, 1932–45.* Lincoln, NE, 1983.

Collier, Basil. *Defense of the United Kingdom.* London, 1957.

Complete Presidential Press Conferences of Franklin Delano Roosevelt. 25 vols. in 12. New York, 1972.

Conn, Stetson, and Byron Fairchild. *The Western Hemisphere: The Framework of Hemisphere Defense.* Washington, 1960.

Conn, Stetson, Rose C. Engleman, and Byron Fairchild. *The Western Hemisphere: Guarding the United States and Its Outposts.* Washington, 1964.

Copp, DeWitt S. *Forged in Fire: Strategy and Decisions in the Air War Over Europe, 1940–1945.* Garden City, NY, 1982.

Craven, Wesley Frank, and James Lea Cate. *The Army Air Forces in World War II.* 7 vols. Chicago, 1948–58.

Crowley, James B. *Japan's Quest for Autonomy: National Security and Foreign Policy, 1930–1938.* Princeton, 1966.

————. "Japan's Military Foreign Policies." In James William Morley, ed. *Japan's Foreign Policy, 1868–1941: A Research Guide.* New York, 1974.

Dallek, Robert. *Franklin D. Roosevelt and American Foreign Policy, 1932–1945.* New York, 1979.

Dawson, Raymond H. *The Decision to Aid Russia, 1941: Foreign Policy and Domestic Politics.* Chapel Hill, 1959.

Deary, William Paul. "'Short of War': Events and Decisions Culminating in the United States Naval Escort of British and Allied Convoys in the Atlantic and in the Undeclared Naval War with Germany, 1939-1941." M.A. thesis, George Washington University, 1970.

Divine, Robert A. *Roosevelt and World War II.* Baltimore, 1969.

Douglas, W.A.B., and Jürgen Rohwer. "'The Most Thankless Task' Revisited: Convoys, Escorts, and Radio Intelligence in the Western Atlantic, 1941-1943." In James A. Boutilier, ed., *The RCN in Retrospect.* Vancouver, British Columbia, 1982.

Eden, Anthony. *The Memoirs of Anthony Eden, Earl of Avon: The Reckoning.* Boston, 1962.

Fahey, James C. *The Ships and Aircraft of the United States Fleet: Victory Edition.* New York, 1945.

Falk, Stanley L. *Seventy Days to Singapore.* New York, 1975.

Feis, Herbert. *The Road to Pearl Harbor.* New York, 1964.

Freidel, Frank. *Franklin D. Roosevelt: Launching the New Deal.* Boston, 1973.

Friedlander, Saul. *Prelude to Downfall: Hitler and the United States.* New York, 1967.

Gallup, George H. *The Gallup Poll: Public Opinion, 1935–1971.* 3 vols. New York, 1972.

Grew, Joseph C. *Turbulent Era: A Diplomatic Record of Forty Years, 1904–1945.* Walter Johnson, ed. 2 vols. Boston, 1952.

Gwyer, J.M.A., and J.R.M. Butler. *Grand Strategy.* Vol. 3: *June 1941–August 1942.* London, 1964.

Hancock, W. K., and M. M. Gowing. *British War Economy.* London, 1949.

Harrington, Daniel F. "A Careless Hope: American Air Power and Japan, 1941." *Pacific Historical Review* (May 1979), 48:217–38.

Harris, Ruth R. "The 'Magic' Leak of 1941 and Japanese-American Relations." *Pacific Historical Review* (Feb. 1981), 50:76–95.

Harvey, John, ed. *The War Diaries of Oliver Harvey.* London, 1978.

Henrichs, Waldo. "President Franklin D. Roosevelt's Intervention in the Battle of the Atlantic, 1941." *Diplomatic History* (Fall 1986), 10:311–32.

————. *American Ambassador: Joseph C. Grew and the Development of the United States Diplomatic Tradition.* Boston, 1966.

Herring, George C. *Aid to Russia, 1941–1946: Strategy, Diplomacy and Origins of the Cold War.* New York, 1973.

Herwarth, Hans von, with Frederick Starr. *Against Two Evils.* New York, 1981.

Herwig, Holger. *Politics of Frustration: The United States in German Naval Planning, 1889–1941.* Boston, 1976.

Hinsley, F. H. *British Intelligence in the Second World War: Its Influence on Strategy and Operations.* 3 vols. New York, 1979–84.

Hull, Cordell. *The Memoirs of Cordell Hull.* 2 vols. New York, 1948.

Ickes, Harold. *The Secret Diary of Harold L. Ickes: The Lowering Clouds, 1939–1941.* New York, 1954.

Iriye, Akira. *Across the Pacific: An Inner History of American-East Asian Relations.* New York, 1967.

————. *The Origins of the Second World War in Asia and the Pacific.* New York, 1987.

Israel, Fred L., ed. *The War Diary of Breckinridge Long: Selections from the Years 1939–1944.* Lincoln, NE, 1966.

Johnson, Chalmers. *An Instance of Treason: Ozaki Hotsumi and the Sorge Spy Ring.* Stanford, 1964.

Jones, F. C. *Japan's New Order in East Asia: Its Rise and Fall, 1937–1945.* London, 1954.

Kimball, Warren F., ed. *Churchill and Roosevelt: The Complete Correspondence.* 3 vols. Princeton, 1984.

Kirby, S. Woodburn. *The War Against Japan: Volume 1, The Loss of Singapore.* London, 1957.

————. *Singapore: The Chain of Disaster.* London, 1971.

Kittredge, Captain Tracy B. "United States-British Naval Cooperation, 1940–1945." Microfilm NRS II-226. U.S. Naval Historical Center, Washington.

Langer, William L. *Our Vichy Gamble.* Hamden, CT. 1965.

Langer, William L., and S. Everett Gleason. *The Challenge to Isolation: The World Crisis of 1937–1941 and American Foreign Policy*. New York, 1952.

———. *The Undeclared War, 1940–1941*. New York, 1953.

Layton, Rear Admiral Edwin T., with Captain Roger Pineau and John Costello. *"And I Was There": Pearl Harbor and Midway—Breaking the Secrets*. New York, 1985.

Leach, Barry. *German Strategy Against Russia, 1939–1941*. Oxford, 1973.

Leighton, Richard M., and Robert W. Coakley. *The War Department: Global Logistics and Strategy 1940–1943*. Washington, 1955.

Leutze, James. *A Different Kind of Victory: A Biography of Admiral Thomas C. Hart*. Annapolis, 1981.

———. *Bargaining for Supremacy: Anglo-American Naval Collaboration, 1937–1941*. Chapel Hill, 1977.

Love, Jr., Robert William. "Ernest Joseph King". In Love, ed. *The Chiefs of Naval Operations*. Annapolis, 1980.

Lu, David J. *From Marco Polo Bridge to Pearl Harbor: Japan's Entry Into World War II*. Washington, 1961.

Lund, Commander W.G.D. "The Royal Canadian Navy's Quest for Autonomy in the Northwest Atlantic: 1941–1943," *Naval War College Review* (May–June 1980), 32: 73–92.

Marder, Arthur J. *Old Friends, New Enemies: The Royal Navy and the Imperial Japanese Navy: Strategic Illusions, 1936–1941*. Oxford, 1981.

Matloff, Maurice, and Edwin M. Snell. *The War Department: Strategic Planning for Coalition Warfare, 1941–1942*. Washington, 1953.

May, Ernest R., ed. *Knowing One's Enemies: Intelligence Assessments Before the Two World Wars*. Princeton, 1984.

May, Ernest R., and James C. Thompson, Jr., eds. *American-East Asian Relations: A Survey*. Cambridge, MA, 1972.

McLellan, David S. *Dean Acheson: The State Department Years*. New York, 1976.

Milner, Marc. *North Atlantic Run: The Royal Canadian Navy and the Battle of the Convoys*. Annapolis, 1985.

Morison, Samuel Eliot. *The Rising Sun in the Pacific. 1931–April 1942*. Boston, 1948.

———. *The Battle of the Atlantic, September 1939–May 1943*. Boston, 1947.

Morley, James William, ed. *Japan's Road to the Pacific War: The Fateful Choice, Japan's Advance into Southeast Asia, 1939–1941. Selected Translations from Taiheiyō sensō e no michi: Kaisen gaikō shi*. New York, 1980.

Morton, Louis. *The War in the Pacific: The Fall of the Philippines*. Washington, 1953.

Nobutaka, Ike, tr. and ed. *Japan's Decision for War: Records of the 1941 Policy Conferences*. Stanford, 1967.

Office of Naval Information. *Fuehrer Conferences on Matters Dealing with the German Navy, 1941*. 2 vols. Washington, 1947.

Oka, Yoshitake. *Konoe Fumimaro: A Political Biography*. Tr. Shumpei Okamoto and Patricia Murray. Tokyo, 1983.

Pelz, Stephen E. *Race to Pearl Harbor: The Failure of the Second London Naval Conference and the Onset of World War II*. Cambridge, MA, 1974.

Perkins, Frances. *The Roosevelt I Knew*. New York, 1946.

Playfair, Major General I.S.O. *The Mediterranean and the Middle East*. 5 vols. London, 1956.

Pogue, Forrest C. *George C. Marshall: Ordeal and Hope*. New York, 1965.

Prange, Gordon W. *At Dawn We Slept: The Untold Story of Pearl Harbor.* New York, 1981.

Reynolds, David. *The Creation of the Anglo-American Alliance 1937–41: A Study in Competitive Cooperation.* Chapel Hill, 1981.

Rohwer, J., and G. Hummelchen. *Chronology of the War at Sea, 1939–1945.* Tr. Derek Masters. 2 vols. London, 1972.

Rohwer, Jürgen. *Critical Convoy Battles of March 1943: The Battle of HX 229/SC 122.* Annapolis, 1977.

Romanus, Charles F., and Riley Sunderland. *Stilwell's Mission to China.* Washington, 1953.

Roosevelt, Elliot, ed. *F.D.R.: His Personal Letters, 1928–1945.* 2 vols. New York, 1947–50.

Roskill, Captain S. W. *The War at Sea, 1939–1945.* 3 vols. London, 1954–61.

Schaller, Michael. *The U.S. Crusade in China, 1938–1945.* New York, 1979.

Schroeder, Paul W. *The Axis Alliance and Japanese-American Relations, 1941.* Ithaca, 1958.

Sherry, Michael S. *The Rise of American Air Power: The Creation of Armageddon.* New Haven, 1987.

U.S., Congress. *Hearings Before the Joint Committee on the Investigation of the Pearl Harbor Attack.* 79th Cong., 1st sess., 1946. 39 parts. Washington.

U.S. Department of Defense, *The "Magic" Background of Pearl Harbor.* 8 vols. Washington, 1978.

U.S., Department of State. *Foreign Relations of the United States: Japan, 1931–1941.* 2 vols. Washington, 1943.

————, *Foreign Relations of the United States, 1941.* 7 vols. Washington, 1956–63.

————, *Documents on German Foreign Policy, 1918–1945.* Washington, 1962. Series D.

Utley, Jonathan G. "Upstairs, Downstairs at Foggy Bottom: Oil Exports and Japan, 1940–41." *Prologue: The Journal of the National Archives* (Spring 1976), 8: 17–28.

————. *Going to War with Japan, 1937–1941.* Knoxville, TE, 1985.

Van Creveld, Martin. *Hitler's Strategy: The Balkan Clue, 1940–1941.* London, 1973.

————. *Supplying War: Logistics from Wallenstein to Patton.* London, 1977.

Watson, Mark Skinner. *The War Department: Chief of Staff: Prewar Plans and Preparations.* Washington, 1950.

Weinberg, Gerhard L. *The Foreign Policy of Hitler's Germany: Diplomatic Revolution in Europe, 1933–36.* Chicago, 1970.

————. *The Foreign Policy of Hitler's Germany: Starting World War II, 1937–39.* Chicago, 1980.

Welles, Sumner. *Time for Decision.* New York, 1944.

Whaley, Barton. *Codeword BARBAROSSA.* Cambridge, MA, 1973.

Willmott, H. P. *Empires in the Balance: Japanese and Allied Pacific Strategies to April 1942.* Annapolis, 1982.

Wilson, Theodore A. *The First Summit: Roosevelt and Churchill at Placentia Bay, 1941.* Boston, 1969.

Winant, John Gilbert. *Letter From Grosvenor Square.* Boston, 1947.

Wohlstetter, Roberta. *Pearl Harbor: Warning and Decision.* Stanford, 1962.

Young, Arthur N. *China and the Helping Hand, 1937–1945.* Cambridge, MA, 1963.

Index

ABC-1 plan, 39, 40, 51, 68, 82, 85, 112, 113, 115, 157, 158, 205, 228n13. *See also* Atlantic, Battle of the; Royal Navy; U.S. Navy
ABCD powers, 132, 182, 192, 199, 200, 210–11. *See also* American-British-Dutch collaboration
Acheson, Dean, 70, 141, 177–78, 246–47n68
ADB-1 plan, 127–28, 198. *See also* American-British-Dutch collaboration
Adams, Walter, 99
Admiral Scheer, 29–30
Admiralty (Britain), 29, 112, 115, 159, 164, 169, 197, 198, 206
Aircraft production, 175–76. *See also* B-17 bombers; B-24 bombers
Aleutian Islands, 182, 218
Alsop, Joseph, 28
American-British-Canadian plan. *See* ABC-1
American-British-Dutch collaboration, 120, 130, 135, 153, 195, 217; and China, 126, 127, 183. *See also* ABCD powers
American-Soviet relations. *See* Soviet-American relations
American Standard-Vacuum Oil Company, 35, 133
Anderson, Irvine H., Jr., 246n68
Ankara embassy (U.S.), 25
Appeasement, 9, 98, 104, 154, 214
Argentia, 114, 165, 166, 169
Argentia Conference. *See* Atlantic Conference
Arkansas, 40, 66, 108
Arnold, Henry H., 143, 144, 148, 195
Asiatic Fleet (U.S.), 38, 194, 198, 212
Atlantic, Battle of the: beginnings, 9–10, 27–28; British advantage in, 116; effect

of German-Soviet war on, 102; and Japanese situation, 126, 204, 205; named, 30; and Rainbow 3, 228n13; Roosevelt commitment to, 48, 84, 159; status of, 110, 164, 166, 205–6; U.S. intervention in, 40, 42, 46, 82, 117, 126, 145, 161, 185; and U.S.-British relations, 108; westward extension of, 112. *See also* Atlantic Fleet; Royal Navy; U-boats; ULTRA
Atlantic Charter, 151–52, 158
Atlantic Conference, 116, 135, 141, 144–46, 148–61, 177, 180, 246n68
Atlantic Fleet (U.S.): development of, 31, 40–41, 66–67, 128; destroyers, 43, 113–14, 165–66, 169; and escort of convoy, 87, 113–14, 164; expansion of operations, 108–9, 116, 165–69; Iceland defense, 88, 110–11; intelligence, 164; Roosevelt's interest in, 17–18, 88; and Royal Navy 168–69; strength of, 45, 68, 83. *See also* Atlantic, Battle of the; Escort of convoy; Royal Navy; U.S. Navy
Attlee, Clement, 197
Augusta, 122, 146, 148, 156
Australia, 152. *See also* ABCD powers; British Commonwealth
Austria, 3, 5, 7
Axis alliance, 5, 6, 7, 9. *See also* German-Japanese relations; Japanese-American relations
Azores, 26, 46, 64, 67, 78, 82, 84, 85, 88, 157

B-17 bombers, 75, 87, 127, 132, 142–43, 144, 148, 154, 159, 173, 175–76, 179, 193, 194, 197, 204, 219, 252–53n81
B-24 bombers, 143, 193, 194, 195